DEVELOPING A THINKING SKILLS PROGRAM

Barry K. Beyer
George Mason University

Allyn and Bacon, Inc.
Boston London Sydney Toronto

Library of Congress Cataloging-in-Publication Data

Beyer, Barry K., 1931–
  Developing a thinking skills program.

  Bibliography: p.
  Includes index.
  1. Thought and thinking–Study and teaching–United States. 2. Curriculum planning–United States. 3. Cognition in children. I. Title.
LB1590.3.B48   1988   370.15′7   87-26920
ISBN 0-205-11133-5

Printed in the United States of America
10 9 8 7 6 5 4 3 2   91 90 89 88

for KURT and EDITH BEYER

as all good parents, the best educators of all—
with love and admiration

and for

BECKY and JIMMY
their newest great-grandchildren,
as all newborn, educators too . . .
with love and affection!

Contents

Foreword

Schools all over the United States, and indeed the world, are beginning to plan seriously for teaching thinking. No curriculum development effort could be more exciting or productive. Clearly, a well-developed and executed thinking skills program promises to improve the capabilities of students to engage in the intellectual activities central to schooling and to effective citizenship in general. In addition, an emphasis on teaching thinking skills can unify an entire staff, as well as provide stimulus for their professional growth.

Most educators have always intended to teach their students to think. In one sense, education and thinking are inseparable. Nevertheless, many students are not very good at the abstract, formal reasoning needed for school success. Despite recent educational reforms, today's high-school students score lower on scholastic aptitude tests than their counterparts of two decades earlier. The majority do poorly on National Assessment of Education Progress exercises requiring application and understanding, including relatively simple writing tasks.[1]

Many teachers, administrators, parents, and employers do not need national statistics to know about this problem; they see evidence daily that students have not developed their intellectual potential and do not

[1] National Assessment of Educational Progress, *The Writing Report Card* (Princeton, N.J.: Educational Testing Service, 1986).

make full use of the mental capabilities they possess. As Theodore Sizer observed after visiting high schools for a national report on secondary education, too many students are "intellectually docile."[2]

Some responses, however well-intended, have probably just made things worse. Regardless of what was sought by proponents of the "back to basics" movement of the late 1970s and early 80s, the result in many schools has been an emphasis on teaching academic skills apart from their meaningful use. Although in some cases standardized test scores went up as they were supposed to, students did not necessarily become better educated, in the sense of being prepared to contribute to society and to live satisfying lives.

Recognizing that educated people must be able to solve problems, make decisions, and learn on their own, educators have recently shown renewed interest in teaching thinking skills. In part, the impetus has come from a growing awareness that our information-rich technological society requires a higher level of literacy than was necessary in an economy dominated by agriculture and manufacturing. This theme has been sounded in several national reports, including the influential statement by the National Commission on Excellence in Education,[3] which cited data from the National Assessment of Education Progress, international comparisons, and other sources to support its call for higher standards.

Another reason for educators' interest in teaching thinking is a growing body of research-generated knowledge about cognitive processes. Some of this knowledge has been incorporated in published programs specifically designed to improve students' intellectual functioning. The available evaluation data, although sketchy, suggests that these programs have been moderately successful.[4] The very existence of such programs leads educators to address the issues they raise.

One way of responding to this situation and to the calls for improvement is to promote conventional views about what teaching thinking is. Those not fully informed may have the impression that the only changes needed are in instruction, and that those changes, though perhaps neglected in practice, are fairly well established. Some would say teachers

---

[2] Theodore Sizer, *Horace's Compromise: The Dilemma of the American High School* (Boston: Houghton Mifflin, 1984), p. 53.

[3] National Commission on Excellence in Education, *A Nation at Risk* (Washington, D.C.: U.S. Government Printing Office, 1983).

[4] Raymond S. Nickerson, David N. Perkins, and Edward F. Smith, *The Teaching of Thinking* (Hillsdale, N.J.: Lawrence Erlbaum Associates, 1985); and Robert Sternberg and Bhana Kastoor, "Synthesis of Research on the Effectiveness of Intellectual Skills Programs: Snake-Oil Remedies or Miracle Cures?" *Educational Leadership* 44 (October 1986):60–67.

need to ask better questions, perhaps guided by Bloom's taxonomy.[5] They would urge teachers to make class activities more interesting and relevant, and to permit students to make choices and plan projects. Others, believing that the key to better thinking is higher expectations, would prescribe more challenging academic tasks and more intensive teacher-led discussion.

Whereas all these reforms undoubtedly have merit, they do not reflect the essence of current efforts to improve students' thinking, which is to identify the cognitive skills students are believed to need in order to process information, and then to take steps to ensure that students acquire them. That takes planning and coordination.

A thinking skills program must be coordinated because (1) students do not necessarily become better thinkers as a result of learning subject matter; (2) thinking skills are applicable to many subjects, so teachers need to know what other teachers are doing to develop them; (3) no teacher can teach all the skills students need in only a year or in just one subject; (4) without a plan, some teachers will teach only the skills they happen to know about, while others will teach none at all; and (5) thinking abilities develop gradually over time. Consequently, it is important that thinking skills be introduced appropriately and reinforced periodically across a number of grade levels and in a variety of subject areas.

These are familiar program concerns. Any important school outcome must be planned for with sequenced, articulated instructional and assessment activities. What makes this especially difficult insofar as thinking skills are concerned is that, for such a program to be effective, the entire faculty must be involved. The multitude of curricular and instructional options available can be confusing, not only because no teacher or group of teachers could undertake them all, but because we lack much of the research data needed to make sound decisions. Finally, the content proposed to be taught—descriptions of mental processes, attitudes, heuristics of various sorts—are relatively unfamiliar to many educators.

Barry Beyer has examined the research on skill learning and developed a thorough but practical procedure for planning a thinking skills program. In this book, he offers informed commentary on the many issues involved, based on his work with schools as well as his own research and development efforts. He also goes further, however, by providing procedures for engaging in the planning process and sample

---

[5] Benjamin S. Bloom et al., *Taxonomy of Educational Objectives: Handbook I—The Cognitive Domain* (New York: Longman, 1956).

components of model thinking skills materials and program elements. For example, when he advises that the description of each skill includes steps, rules, and so on, he provides sample descriptions for the skills on his own recommended list as well as for other commonly taught thinking skills.

Curriculum leaders convinced of the need for more conscious attention to student thinking, but unsure of how to achieve it, will find *Developing a Thinking Skills Program* a valuable guide as they undertake this fascinating challenge.

RON BRANDT, EXECUTIVE EDITOR
Association for Supervision and Curriculum Development

Preface

This book is for educators charged with developing or revising programs to teach thinking skills. It is for classroom teachers and curriculum supervisors, instructional materials developers and department heads, building principals and other administrators, test makers, teacher trainers, staff developers—and for anyone else seeking ideas or assistance in carrying out such a charge.

The pages that follow are designed to guide you through the major steps of producing and implementing a thinking skills program in a way that will ensure that the final product will have some reasonable chance of significantly improving student thinking. The ideas apply to program development efforts at all levels of schooling, from a single course, subject area, or grade level to an individual school building or entire school system. By incorporating these ideas into any effort to revise or develop a thinking skills program, you can avoid the pitfalls and overcome the obstacles that seem all too often to undermine or completely sidetrack many program development efforts of this kind.

It has become quite apparent over the past several years that developing or improving thinking skills programs at all levels of education have become tasks of high priority for many individual educators as well as entire school faculties and school systems. For a variety of reasons, colleges, both private and public, and schools, both elementary and secondary, have become aware of the need for teaching thinking skills.

Some have already begun to develop such programs. In some cases, their efforts seem to be producing significant results. Yet others, although interested in "doing something" along this line, seem hesitant to start, often for lack of direction, or of an understanding of the nature of the task, or of inadequate command of the development process. So, while this book has benefited from the experiences of many of the former, perhaps by sharing some of their experiences, it can contribute to the future successes of the latter.

Efforts to develop thinking skills programs certainly do not lack for justification. I believe that of all things our schools teach, few are as important to us individually and collectively as skillful thinking. Systematic, explicit instruction in thinking benefits students and teachers, as well as society as a whole. Teaching thinking is quite probably the single most important activity in which our schools can today engage.

Serious teaching of thinking benefits students in at least four ways. First, it helps students to become more effective, skillful thinkers. Second, it can improve student achievement in academic and other school subjects. Third, it can help students develop more positive self-concepts and thus attain even higher levels of achievement, out-of school as well as in school. Fourth, the teaching of thinking can help students develop those habits and abilities of thinking that are required for effective citizenship in our increasingly complex, changing world. Therefore, the teaching of thinking offers students survival and success now and in the future. Their survival—and success—are society's survival and success.

Systematic classroom instruction in thinking also benefits teachers. The improved thinking to which such teaching leads helps students achieve other substantive, academic goals of classroom teaching, goals that are dear to our professional hearts. Student use of the skills taught as thinking skills raises the level of discourse in classrooms beyond the tedium of drill and practice and rote memorization. Thoughtful student performance in classrooms can lead to the kinds of intellectual engagement, interplay of ideas, and quests for meaning that serve as hallmarks of real learning and teaching and that make teaching as rewarding and satisfying as any other profession. In sum, the successful teaching of thinking can enrich the act of teaching and the minds of teachers as much as it can enrich the minds of the students who benefit from it.

Development of skillful thinking benefits society as well as individuals. The ability of individuals to tackle successfully the issues and problems—or, to put it a more positive way, to meet the challenges and take advantage of the opportunities—presented to us in our world of today and tomorrow depends considerably on their abilities to think skillfully. We all benefit—individuals, neighborhoods, nations, and humanity as a whole, both those living and those yet to be born—from the exercise of such thinking. Educational programs designed to develop abilities and dispositions to think skillfully have impact far beyond S.A.T. scores or year-end averages, far beyond the walls of the local school or even the work place. No other educational endeavor is as important in this day and age as is the effort to devise and implement programs to improve and develop the ability of our young people to think skillfully and effectively.

My position regarding the teaching of thinking and the importance of having or developing thinking skills programs in every school ought thus to be clear right from the start. Thirty years of classroom experience and research in education have led me to believe every school system and college or university should have a comprehensive program that teaches thinking skills systematically and directly to all students throughout the curriculum. Every public or private school system ought to be able to guarantee to the public that those who leave, even at the end of the tenth grade, can execute to an acceptable degree of proficiency the cognitive operations required for skillful thinking. Colleges and universities should build systematically on these skills and habits in their curricula. Teaching thinking is a responsibility of all educating institutions, and doing so directly is by far the most effective and efficient way to carry out this responsibility.

My companion volume to this book, *Practical Strategies for the Teaching of Thinking*, describes in detail specific strategies for providing continuing, direct classroom instruction in thinking and the skills, dispositions, and knowledge of which it is comprised.* But use of such strategies, or any other strategies for that matter, cannot have much lasting impact if they are restricted to isolated classrooms, school buildings, or single courses. To be most effective, the teaching of thinking in any school at any level must be part of a multigrade, broadly based systematic instructional program that aims explicitly at developing student proficiency in selected thinking skills and strategies. Unfortunately, few such programs seem to exist. Developing these programs is—or ought to be—a matter of some urgency and importance. The ideas presented here will hopefully facilitate efforts to this end.

The contents of this book are as much a result of experience and observation as of theory and research. In working with almost 100 schools in the United States and Canada over the past few years, I have had the opportunity to meet with educators involved in thinking skills program development efforts, to see their work at first hand, and even to contribute to it. In many instances, their handling of "real life" program development provided me numerous insights into ways such efforts might be most productive. I have added these insights from prac-

---

* Barry K. Beyer, *Practical Strategies for the Teaching of Thinking* (Boston: Allyn and Bacon, Inc., 1987).

tice to the theory and research gleaned from the literature on thinking and on program development.

The ideas presented here are as practical as possible, always tempered with the realities of classrooms and school bureaucracies. These pages probably raise more questions than provide answers, but hopefully these questions are at least those that need to be considered in developing any worthwhile thinking skills program. They include those most likely to be encountered by any educator engaged in this task, especially:

What should we teach?

Why?

Where?

How?

How will we know if we are successful?

What must we do to produce a program that will carry out our design?

Although there may be no single correct way to develop a useful thinking skills program, there certainly are some ways that work better than others—better in the sense that if followed they will produce viable programs that have a real chance of significantly improving student thinking. The suggestions, guidelines, and examples presented here are offered as options and idea generators for those who are serious about this task. The recommendations represent only one synthesis of these suggestions and options.

Developing a thinking skills program at any level in any school setting is a unique educational endeavor. It is especially unique because it is an exercise in thinking. In fact, developing an educational program is one professional activity that requires those involved actually to engage in the very thing they are attempting to develop for instruction to others. Producing a thinking skills program requires of program developers critical as well as creative thinking; recall as well as analysis, synthesis, and evaluation; information processing as well as decision making. Consequently, this effort is an education in itself. It benefits both developers and those who use the final program—teachers, students, and parents. We all benefit in many ways, and that is what makes undertaking this task worth the effort. It is an opportunity to be welcomed by all who are interested in the developing of human potential and the well-being of society in general.

ACKNOWLEDGMENTS

I have relied on many sources to produce the ideas presented in this book. These include the efforts of program developers and faculty committees in a number of schools throughout the United States and Canada. I wish to acknowledge the insights that they shared with me or helped generate. I especially wish to thank the social studies faculty of the Greenwich, Connecticut, senior high school, and their coordinator Michael Batchellor. I am also grateful to the faculty program development committees of the D.C. Everest Area Schools in Schofield, Wisconsin; Lynnhaven Junior High School in Virginia Beach, Virginia; the Amphitheater Public Schools in Tuscon, Arizona; and the Kirkland (Missouri) Public Schools, the DesMoines (Iowa) Public Schools, and the Mt. Lebanon (Pittsburgh, Pennsylvania) Public Schools. My continuing work with these educators has introduced me to the practicalities of program development that are reflected in the pages that follow. I thank them for assisting in working out some of the ideas presented here.

In addition, I wish to thank the hundreds of educators with whom I have worked in workshops and training sessions over the past several years. This includes the experienced and novice teachers in my thinking skills classes at George Mason University who certainly have taught me as much as I have tried to teach them about teaching thinking. I also appreciate the insights shared by those teachers with whom I have worked at the invitation of the Education Service Center of Region XIII in Austin, Texas, and of Seattle Pacific University, and with teachers and supervisors in Monroe and Lee Counties, Florida, the Highline Public Schools in Seattle, the Poudre (Colorado) Public Schools, and the Network for Educational Development in St. Louis.

I wish also to thank a number of individuals who have helped in one way or another to develop ideas presented here. Ron Brandt and Gordon Cawelti of A.S.C.D. have given me numerous opportunities to meet and share ideas with educators from all over the country, and for these opportunities I am most thankful. Barbara Presseissen of Research for Better Schools, Inc., Jay McTighe of the Maryland State Department of Education, Ben Sauers of Shady Side Academy in Pittsburgh, Pennsylvania, Bill Lampheres of the Poudre School District in Fort Collins, Colorado, and Peter Kneedeer of the California State Department of Education have provided valuable advice, assistance, and helpful criticism. Editors of the *NASSP Bulletin, Educational Leadership, Phi Delta Kappan,* and *Social Education* have graciously published articles of mine that presented early forms of some of the ideas included here. For the opportunities they provided me to circulate these ideas and to receive helpful feedback from colleagues throughout the country, I am most grateful.

Hiram Howard and Susanne Canavan, formerly of Allyn and Bacon, have done much to expedite the publication of this book and its companion volume, and for their hard work I am truly grateful. Working with staff development specialist Jim Bellanca has been an education in itself—a good one! To all these individuals, a hearty thanks.

Last, but by no means least, I wish to acknowledge the heroic efforts of the two individuals who typed the manuscript for this book. My wife, Judy, has typed a substantial portion of it in addition to attending to all her other chores and activities. For her tireless efforts on behalf of this endeavor, I salute her and thank her publicly. Sue Woodfine, of George Mason University, has worked overtime and doubletime to prepare the rest of this manuscript. For her persistent processing of my nearly indecipherable scribbling, I am most appreciative. I could not have produced this work without the hard work of these two wonderful people, their patience, and their constructive assistance. A sincere thanks to them both.

BARRY K. BEYER
Fairfax, Virginia

1

Defining the Task

Developing a thinking skills program is both a challenge and an opportunity. The challenge lies in the fact that there are few comprehensive or up-to-date program models to build on or adopt. Thinking, as a learning goal in classrooms and school curricula, is rather nebulous and ill-defined, at best. Developing a thinking skills program is also an opportunity because, when done well, a program designed to teaching thinking skills benefits faculty and students immensely in their out-of-school lives as well as in their school work. It is precisely the opportunity that this task presents that makes accepting the challenge so worthwhile. There is probably no more significant educational program development effort in which a school faculty can engage than developing a practical, comprehensive thinking skills program for their students.

BASIC INGREDIENTS OF A THINKING SKILLS PROGRAM

Most schools are already committed to teaching students to think, or at least to think better than they generally seem to do. It would be an unusual school system that could not endorse the following statement as a major curriculum goal: *Our graduates should be able to make well-reasoned decisions, solve problems skillfully, and make carefully thought-out*

1

judgments about the worth, accuracy, and value of information, ideas, claims, and propositions. Being able to engage effectively in skillful thinking implied by this statement is precisely the learning aim of any worthwhile thinking skills program.

Achieving such a goal is another matter, however. Learning to think is not the incidental outcome of classroom study directed at information telling, or memorizing, or the study of diverse subjects. Nor is it the result of simply responding to teacher or textbook questions. Being willing and able to engage in skillful, effective thinking requires, instead, purposeful learning of how to execute the procedures used in decision making, problem solving, and other major thinking tasks. In turn, learning these skills requires explicit attention to the more basic thinking operations of critical thinking, information processing, and reasoning. If learning to think is really important, then a school must work directly, continuously, and systematically to accomplish it. A well-constructed, effectively executed, and well-supported thinking skills program provides the vehicle for doing so.

What would such a program look like? Although it could come in many variations, it should consist at the very least of continuing, direct instruction in a range of specific thinking skills and strategies—as well as in the attitudes or dispositions that support these operations—across all grade levels from kindergarten onward. Some of the skills and strategies that constitute the program might be introduced in stand-alone, nonacademic courses; others would be presented in regular, academic subject matter courses. However, in all instances, instruction in these skills and strategies would also be carefully integrated into regular academic courses. The attitudes and dispositions supportive of these skills and strategies would be reinforced in every course students take, as well as in the general atmosphere of each school building and classroom. A thinking skills program, although clearly distinguishable as an entity in itself, should also be an integral part of a school's entire curriculum.

The specific thinking operations and dispositions to be included in a thinking skills program may vary according to the reasoned judgments of a school district. At the minimum, however, any worthwhile thinking skills program should include continuing instruction from introduction to transfer and independent student application of a number of key cognitive operations of various levels of complexity. These should include major thinking strategies such as problem solving and decision making, as well as more basic thinking skills such as evaluation, synthesis, various forms of analysis and relationship making, and reasoning. Selected specific critical thinking operations, such as identifying unstated assumptions, author's frame of reference, bias, inconsistencies in a line of reasoning, and fallacies in logic ought to be included also.

This program should also include instruction in metacognition and in the dispositions that support and guide skillful thinking. Metacognitive operations such as planning, monitoring, and assessing various thinking operations should be practiced and, in the upper grades, taught directly. Dispositions or attitudes that support and drive thinking should be reinforced throughout all classes at all grade levels. These dispositions should include those that typify effective thinking behavior. Among these are the dispositions to persist in resolving a problem, to look at a problem from a variety of points of view, to use credible resources, to seek and give evidence and reasons, and to base judgments on the quality of evidence and reasoning rather than on whim or dogma.

Such a program consists of several other major elements. Certainly what is to be learned by way of thinking constitutes its "content" core. But the instruction and activities by which this content is translated into learning either make or break any thinking skills program. A program as the one just described would limit the number of thinking operations to be introduced each year and would stagger their introduction over a number of subject areas and grade levels. It would provide repeated and continuous instruction in these operations throughout a curriculum. Such a program would also emphasize the development of basic thinking dispositions early in the primary grades, and thereafter reinforce them consistently in every classroom, in every facet of the school, and at all grade levels. The specific teaching and testing strategies employed would be what research suggests are most effective in developing proficiency in the operations being taught.

The curriculum documentation describing, organizing, and supporting instruction constitutes a second element of any effective thinking skills program. At the minimum, this documentation should include:

1. A scope and sequence, showing subject areas and grade levels where each skill or strategy is to be introduced, given guided practice, transferred, and applied independently by the students
2. Subject area scope and sequences for each subject, indicating by grade level where the particular skills and strategies to be taught in that subject will be introduced, given guided practice, transferred, and applied independently by students
3. Lists of specific thinking skills or strategies keyed to those places in the text(s) or other major instructional materials used in each subject at each grade level where opportunities exist for introducing and continued "teaching" of the thinking operations to be learned
4. Detailed descriptions of the major skills and strategies that comprise the program

To be most useful to teachers and supervisors, such documentation should also include two other types of material:

5. Model lesson plans illustrating the different types of strategies teachers can use at various stages of skill teaching
6. Model unit and semester test formats and test items for assessing proficiency in the thinking operations to be learned in various skills and/or subject matter courses

These six kinds of documents provide the support and the direction required for executing an effective thinking skills curriculum. Moreover, these documents also provide the kind of assistance and guidance needed by teachers and supervisors unfamiliar with either the thinking operations and dispositions to be taught and/or effective procedures for teaching them. Such documents can thus provide both curriculum direction and actual instructional guidance. Their availability is indispensable for the effective translation of any thinking skills program into classroom teaching and student learning.

To be effective, a thinking skills program also requires support for instruction and learning, as well as assessment for program improvement and program policy making. Staff development and training, continued coaching, and teacher support are all necessary to ensure that program procedures and content are turned into instruction that maintains the integrity of the program. Continuing assessment of student achievement and classroom instruction at classroom and school-wide levels are also essential in order to accommodate program policies to the realities of classroom instruction, and to ensure the attainment of program goals. The nature of instruction and the support provided for that instruction are as much a part of any skills program as are its scope and sequence and its curriculum guides. Thinking skills programs, just as any worthwhile educational program, consist of more than spiral-bound documents or fine-sounding statements of intent.

DEVELOPING A THINKING SKILLS PROGRAM

Developing or revising a thinking skills program like that just described, at whatever level, is a task not to be lightly undertaken. At best, such an effort takes time. It requires both sustained effort and leadership, and probably some amount of staff development as well. It almost certainly will also require some changes in classroom teaching, supervision, and testing, as well as in what is taught in a school. Noting this is not intended to discourage a school from undertaking such a development effort. Rather, it is simply to point out that the nature of the task and the effort required to bring it to successful fruition should be neither under-estimated nor kept hidden from those involved. Developing a thinking skills program is a significant task, but it is also envigorating and stimu-lating. The major result, improved student learning, is of considerable benefit to all involved—teachers as well as students, society as a whole as well as parents and school.

How would school officials know whether or not it is worth the effort to revise an existing thinking skills program or develop a new one? One way is to examine the scores of their students on those parts of the state or district reading or competency tests that purport to assess profi-ciency in higher-order thinking operations to determine if their students were performing at levels acceptable to them and to the community. They could also conduct a "wants" assessment of teachers and parents to see if there were any significant local desires to improve student proficiencies in thinking. They could refer to national studies and re-ports on the state of student learning for analysis of student thinking deficiencies and for recommendations. They could also conduct an in-ventory of what is currently being done in their schools and classrooms to teach thinking to determine the extent it corresponds to what research suggests ought to be done to teach thinking most effectively. Or they could do all four. By comparing where the students and teachers are to a system's expressed goals and standards—where they ought to be—decision makers will be able to judge what needs to be done, if anything, by way of developing or revising a thinking skills program.

There are many different procedures that can be used to conduct a wants/needs analysis appropriate to this task. Thinking skills assess-ment is often built into the reading and various competency tests al-ready in common use in school districts. Special thinking skills tests are also available for this purpose.* Instruments for assessing current think-ing skill teaching policies and procedures in a school are more difficult to locate, however. Consequently, Table 1.1 presents one survey instru-ment that may prove useful for this purpose. The items on this checklist solicit information about teaching, teacher supervision, and assessment practices, as well as about those elements typically associated with edu-cational program documentation itself. This instrument can be used to collect information on teaching thinking on a single grade level or in a single subject area, as well as in an entire school building or school district.

Use of this checklist can actually serve two purposes. It can provide information useful in deciding precisely what needs to be done by way of program development, staff development, assessment, and teacher

---

* See Chapter 11 for a list and description of some of these instruments.

Table 1.1 A Thinking Skills Checklist

	Yes	In Progress	No
1. Does your school system have:			
1.1 A list of major thinking skills to be taught throughout the system?	____	____	____
1.2 Agreement among all subject areas that these skills should be taught throughout the system?	____	____	____
1.3 A K–12 curriculum document that clearly delimits which thinking skills are to be taught at each grade level in each subject area?	____	____	____
1.4 A K–12 curriculum document that presents thinking skills to be taught in a developmental sequence based on the cognitive development of learners, nature of the target skills, and subject matter needs?	____	____	____
1.5 A thinking skills curriculum that provides for continuing instruction in these thinking skills across many grade levels and subjects?	____	____	____
1.6 Detailed descriptions of the operating procedures, rules, and distinguishing criteria of each major thinking skill/strategy to be taught?	____	____	____
1.7 Appropriate thinking skill descriptions in the immediate possession of every teacher and administrator?	____	____	____
1.8 Provisions for instruction in each skill with a variety of media, in a variety of settings, and for a variety of goals?	____	____	____
1.9 A classroom and school climate supportive of thinking?	____	____	____
2. Do your teachers:			
2.1 Use a common terminology and instructional language to describe the thinking skills they are required to teach?	____	____	____
2.2 Provide instruction in thinking skills when these skills are needed to accomplish subject-matter learning goals?	____	____	____
2.3 Understand the major components of the thinking skills they are teaching?	____	____	____

Table 1.1 (*Continued*)

	Yes	In Progress	No
2.4 Provide continuing instruction in each thinking skill through stages of introduction, guided practice, application, transfer, guided practice, and use?	___	___	___
2.5 Introduce thinking skills as explicitly as possible by explaining and modeling each skill and having students apply the skill with their guidance?	___	___	___
2.6 Provide frequent, guided practice in each skill with appropriate instructive feedback?	___	___	___
2.7 Show students how to transfer thinking skills to new settings, media?	___	___	___
2.8 Require students to reflect on and discuss how they make each skill operational?	___	___	___
2.9 Test on their own unit tests the thinking skills they are responsible for teaching?	___	___	___
3. Do your provisions for evaluating the learning of thinking skills include the:			
3.1 Continuous assessment of student proficiency in the skills taught?	___	___	___
3.2 Use of instruments that measure student performance on skills taught in the program?	___	___	___
3.3 Use of instruments that are valid measures of thinking skill competency?	___	___	___
3.4 Use of instruments that provide the maximum data for diagnostic/monitoring purposes?	___	___	___
4. Do your supervisors and instructional leaders:			
4.1 Understand the nature of the thinking skills to be taught and how to teach and measure them?	___	___	___
4.2 Provide in-service instruction in the nature of the thinking skills to be taught and in different ways to teach these skills?	___	___	___
4.3 Help teachers in different subject areas and grade levels share methods for teaching thinking skills?	___	___	___

Table 1.1 *(Continued)*

	Yes	In Progress	No
4.4 Use classroom observation instruments keyed to the attributes of effective skill teaching?	___	___	___
4.5 Provide coaching for teachers learning how to teach thinking skills?	___	___	___
4.6 Provide instructional materials appropriate to teaching and learning thinking skills?	___	___	___
4.7 Ensure that teachers follow the thinking skills curriculum?	___	___	___
4.8 Ensure the continuing revision of the thinking skills curriculum, instructional strategies, and instructional materials as appropriate?	___	___	___

support to improve the teaching of thinking in the areas to which it is applied. It also alerts those who are asked to complete it to those features of the teaching of thinking that could or ought to exist if this teaching is to be most productive. Use of this thinking skills checklist can be a very useful first step in any effort to revise or develop a thinking skills curriculum.

Regardless of exactly how a thinking skills program development effort is organized, to be most successful its assumptions should be clear. The first premise concerns students. All students think. And all of them can think better. Teaching thinking must be for *all* students, and not restricted to those of one ability or grade level in one or two subject areas. Second, teaching thinking ought not to be considered as an end in itself. Students need to develop the skills that constitute thinking to achieve more substantive, larger goals. The ultimate goals of learning thinking, or any other kinds of skills for that matter, are to understand better the subjects being studied; to be able to function independently as thinking, contributing citizens in the world; and to deal constructively with personal issues and concerns. Teaching thinking is a legitimate teaching and learning objective in all courses in a school's curriculum. Learning the skills that constitute thinking ought to be an explicit, public goal of learning in every course, as well as a publicly affirmed part of a school's mission.

For best results, any effort to develop a thinking skills program should proceed through a number of stages. Table 1.2 outlines the major tasks that might constitute a reasonably full-fledged effort to develop a district or school-wide program for the teaching of thinking skills. Placement of these tasks by years is rather arbitrary, of course, but the sequence of activities reflects the practicalities of successful program development. Moreover, any effort to produce a complete, locally developed program is likely to take anywhere from three to five years or so. Obviously, efforts built around incorporating already existing commercially developed programs may take less time.

Any effort at educational program or curriculum development—regardless of its content—must attend, of course, to the politics of such development. This includes securing the support and commitment to the program to be developed of those affected by the program, especially those who can provide the resources needed to develop it, those who will be ultimately responsible for executing it, and those who will have to live with its results! This means administrators, teachers, and the community as a whole. Efforts to secure and maintain this support and commitment must commence early in the effort and continue throughout the process.

Experienced program and curriculum developers are quite familiar with techniques and strategies for building program support and commitment. They know that involvement in the process, job assessments, judicious use of building level as well as individual classroom test scores, inducements of various kinds, and rational analysis of educational goals and conditions can all be used to accomplish these goals. They also know that support and commitment are not ends in themselves but rather means to an end—in this case to the development and implementation of effective educational programs. Consequently, in building support and commitment they never lose sight of the fact that the focus of the overall effort needs to be on the substance of the program being developed.

Developing a thinking skills program may not be as familiar to many as will be building program support and commitment. Consequently, the pages that follow focus primarily on what seems to be required to develop the content of the program to be developed, especially the skills, knowledge, and dispositions to be taught, the instructional approaches to be used, and the assessment and support systems to be employed. Here we will assume familiarity with the politics of successful program development and focus instead on how to develop a thinking skills program that has promise of making a real difference in any educational setting.

Initially, attention needs to be given to information gathering, program assessment, and developing teacher and parent awareness of the local situation, of what is going on elsewhere regarding efforts to improve the teaching of thinking, of options available given the results of a

Table 1.2 A Three-Year Plan for Developing a Thinking Skills Program

First Year	Second Year	Third Year
Collecting Information	*Planning and Development (cont't)*	*Training*

1. Survey, study and discuss
  • what the experts say
  • appropriate research
  • available programs
  • what key schools are doing
  • what is being done in the district
	3. Prepare initial
	  • scope and sequences
	  • skill descriptions
	  • sample lesson plans
	  • model skills tests
		1. Training of teachers and administrators
		  • demonstrations
		  • discussions
		  • practice/feedback
		  • coaching

2. Identify
  • components of potential program to be adopted or developed
  • skills that could be taught
  • strategies that could be used
	4. Pilot prototypes of lesson strategies, materials, tests
	
	5. Revise and develop
	  • scope and sequence
	  • skill descriptions
	  • model lesson plans
	  • model skills tests
		2. Trial-teaching and practice
		  • with support
		  • with coaching
		
		3. Additional training as needed

3. Experiment with, try out
  • different programs
  • different teaching strategies
	Preparation for Training
	1. Selection of training teams
	  • planning/revising lessons
		Classroom Introduction
		1. Transfer to classrooms
		  • with coaching
		  • integrate into courses

4. Plan development effort
   - task analysis
   - time lines
   - resources needed
   - constraints

Planning and Development

1. Identify and describe
   - curriculum structure to be employed
   - skills/strategies to be taught
   - teaching strategies to be used
   - assessment procedures to be used
2. Sequence skills to be taught
   - across grade levels
   - across subject areas
   - within subjects

   - providing feedback for development
   - experimenting with program components
2. Training trainer teams
   - demonstrating
   - observing/discussing
   - practice/coaching
3. Planning training program
4. Scheduling teachers to facilitate coaching

2. Revising program components
   - using feedback from teachers
   - modifying program

Institutionalizing

1. Systematic teaching of program
2. Continued training
3. Monitoring and formative feedback
4. Continued revision
5. Planning for program assessment (to be conducted after program has been implemented at least 3 years)

local wants/needs assessment, and of available resources and other constraints or dictates. Program development can then build on the results of these predesign efforts. At this stage, attention should focus on construction of a thinking skills scope and sequence and related instructional supports, as well as the development and classroom tryout of prototype lessons and activities designed to carry out the program. Finally, the program must be introduced into the school's classrooms, a stage that requires attention to training teachers to teach and assess thinking skills, and to providing the support, coaching, and revision needed to ensure successful execution of the program.

Although a variety of vehicles can be employed to carry out this effort, a committee of teachers, supervisors, administrators, and perhaps even parent representatives may prove most useful for this purpose. Such a committee may originally consist of a limited number of volunteers—a number of influential teachers and administrators among them. As its work progresses, additional individuals can join. As the committee gets into the task of developing guides and other materials or specifications for materials, a great deal of help and talent is needed. Over a period of a year, such a committee in one school system grew from its original twelve members to include thirty-one additional volunteers! As a result of several awareness workshops and a newsletter circulated periodically to the entire faculty reporting the work of the committee and inviting ideas and contribution of teacher-developed thinking skill lesson plans and materials, faculty actually demanded to join the committee and were invited to do so! The more who participate in the planning and developing of a thinking skills program development effort, the easier it is later to implement the program finally adopted or developed.

To initiate a development effort, teachers and administrators involved should read and discuss as much as they can about thinking skills and the teaching of thinking. These activities are especially important when attempting to define or describe the thinking operations selected for instruction. Too often educators attempt to tackle curriculum tasks without appropriate preparation, and consequently merely institutionalize what is currently being done locally. Reading, attendance at professional conferences, awareness workshops, use of teacher training audio and video tapes, study of appropriate research, and even participation in a special course or seminar are useful devices for helping committee members to develop the background for a productive development effort.

Throughout the planning and development effort, those engaged in this task must keep other faculty and parents informed of what they are doing. This can be accomplished through periodic newsletters, awareness workshops conducted by outside experts or local educators, demonstrations of potential program components, presentations at faculty meetings, reports on conferences attended, drop-in video or reading discussions, circulation and discussion of important articles and teacher-made lessons, and so on.

Table 1.3 outlines the key tasks that must be undertaken to produce and institutionalize an effective thinking skills program where none (or only a relatively ineffective or fragmented one) exists. Carrying out these tasks requires answers to at least the questions listed after each task, as well as other questions recommended by experience or by local conditions. Executing these tasks may well be the agenda for any local program development in thinking skills.

Table 1.3 Key Tasks in Developing a Thinking Skills Program

Tasks	Key Questions to Be Answered
1. Setting goals and building a rationale	1.1 What are the goals?
	1.2 What evidence is there that students are not now accomplishing them?
	1.3 What can be done to close the gap?
	1.4 Why is this worth doing?
2. Defining thinking, its key components, and their interrelationships	2.1 What are the key components of thinking upon which the program is to be based?
	2.2 How do they relate to each other?
3. Structuring the program	3.1 What will the final program structure look like? • commercial or local? • special thinking courses? • integrated into content? • a combination?
	3.2 Who is it for? Where?
	3.3 What can be done temporarily to improve student thinking while a complete program is developed?
4. Selecting the skills and strategies to be included in the program	4.1 Which skills *could* be taught?
	4.2 At the end of the major school-leaving grades, which

Table 1.3 (*Continued*)

Tasks	Key Questions to be Answered
	thinking skills/strategies *should* students have mastered?
	4.3 What skills must students know in order to engage successfully in the target skills and strategies?
	4.4 Which skills *will* be taught?
	4.5 Why?
5. Defining in detail the attributes of these skills and strategies	5.1 What are the critical attributes of the thinking skills and strategies chosen for teaching?
	5.2 How do these attributes differ for each skill or strategy at its different levels of complexity?
6. Sequencing and organizing thinking skills and strategies	6.1 How are the various skills and strategies selected for teaching interrelated?
	6.2 In what ways do the attributes or dimensions of these operations change with experience in applying them?
	6.3 In which subjects/courses will these skills and strategies be introduced and taught? Reinforced/transferred?
	6.4 What in these subjects/ courses will be shortened/ eliminated to make room for teaching specific thinking operations?
7. Selecting appropriate teaching strategies	7.1 What teaching strategies can be best used to ensure student learning of the thinking skills and strategies?
	7.2 Where in each course will each skill be "taught"?
	7.3 What adjustments will be made for exceptional students?

Table 1.3 (*Continued*)

Tasks	Key Questions to be Answered
	7.4 What kinds of classroom testing can teachers use to assess student thinking?
8. Providing the training, materials, and environment needed to implement the program	8.1 What environment is most conducive to teaching/learning thinking skills and strategies?
	8.2 What kinds of instructional materials are most helpful in the teaching of thinking?
	8.3 What kinds of staff development will be needed so teachers can execute the program as intended?
9. Providing the support and assessment needed to ensure continuation of the program	9.1 What kinds of support are needed to keep the program going as intended?
	9.2 How will it be provided?
	9.3 What kinds of assessment can be used for formative purposes?
	9.4 How will teachers/district know if the instruction is successful—if the program goals are being achieved?
10. Continuously revising the program	10.1 What will need to be revised?
	10.2 What procedures can be used for this purpose?
	10.3 What can be done to refine the program?

The goals selected for a thinking skills program are especially important because they largely shape the entire development effort. Such goals may be simply to improve student achievement on local or state thinking skills competency examinations, or on major examinations like the Scholastic Aptitude Test. Or, the goals might be to develop a given level or proficiency in those thinking operations that will be required for effective citizenship in the twenty-first century. Other goals may also be developed. Whatever the goals selected, they will help identify the kinds of skills to be taught in the program, the students for whom the program is intended, and the key features of the program to be developed.

Figure 1.1 presents a worksheet that a planning committee or faculty can use to identify and articulate goals for a thinking skills program. The questions on this worksheet can also help refine these initial goal statements into more precisely worded statements that can then serve as guides to subsequent program development, instruction, and assessment.

A decision to build a program based on skills already presumed to be taught in a subject, school, or district can launch a development effort on a positive note, and at the same time educate the developers about thinking. Such skills can be identified in a variety of ways. Lists of these skills can be compared, collated, shortened, revised, and modified as the skills are resequenced, gaps are filled, and the skills are described in enough detail to facilitate classroom teaching and testing. It is important for both teachers and administrators to engage in these skill-defining tasks in order to develop commitment to and ownership of the evolving program, and to understand better the skills to be included in the program.

In carrying out these and other tasks involved in improving or developing a thinking skills program, program planners, supervisors, and teachers should "think small" and proceed slowly. Initially, only a limited number of thinking skills should be selected for instruction as part of a school or district-wide thinking program. As teachers become experienced in teaching these operations, new skills can be added and other modifications can be made. However, teachers should obviously not be limited to teaching only those thinking skills included in the overall thinking skills program. What such a program should, in effect, indicate is that the school asssumes responsibility for developing a high degree of student proficiency in the selected skills by the time students leave school. Teachers would be expected to teach these skills to the levels of proficiency indicated in the program. However, they may—and should—teach other thinking skills, especially those closely related to their subject areas, as they have seen fit to do in the past. A school-wide thinking skills program should be viewed as a core of skills, but not the only skills to be taught.

IMPLEMENTING A THINKING SKILLS PROGRAM

In conducting any program development effort, educators should be sure to employ the basic principles and procedures of program development and implementation as defined by specialists such as David W. Pratt.[1] The tasks identified in Table 1.3 do not incorporate all these

1. What do you hope to accomplish by revising or developing a thinking program?

2. Why is this goal (or these goals) worth achieving?

3. Define your goal(s) in operational/performance terms. What will students know or be able to do or feel as a result of your program that they don't/can't now?

   a.

   b.

   c.

   d.

   e.

4. What would be acceptable as evidence that the above (item #3) have been accomplished?

Figure 1.1 Setting Your Program Goals

principles but specify only those tasks of special relevance to developing thinking skills programs. Other tasks may have to be added or modified to meet local conditions, as well as to conform to exemplary practice in program development. What is important and what needs to be emphasized is that planning is the key to the successful development of any locally produced thinking skills program. Even though such planning precedes the actual development and final implementation of the program, the latter must always be kept in mind by the planners and developers. Planning a program development effort without acknowledging and accommodating what will be required for its implementation will result in little more than an exercise in frustration.

In undertaking development of any thinking skills program, developers must pay particularly close attention to the changes the program is likely to bring about and to how these changes may shape the program's implementation. Any newly developed thinking skills program, especially one based on current research and theory, is quite likely to be an innovation of some magnitude in most school systems. Such a program is almost certain to demand or bring about some change in classrooms, as well as in curriculum, teaching, and testing. If such a program is to be implemented as intended, it should incorporate features designed to help teachers and others adjust to and make these changes.

Research on educational change in the past indicates that those educational changes or innovations best received by teachers and most likely to be implemented as designed possessed five major features:

1. Relative advantage
2. Compatability
3. Simplicity
4. Trialability
5. Observability[2]

The implications of this research for developing and implementing a thinking skills program seem quite apparent: to be successfully carried out in a school and in its classrooms, a program to teaching thinking skills must exhibit these same features.

To be implemented as designed, a new thinking skills program must clearly demonstrate to teachers and to students its superiority over the way thinking has currently been taught, especially in terms of the time and effort required, and in ultimate learning. Any proposed curriculum or teaching change must be compatible with the abilities and inclinations of those who will use it, as well as with the context of the institution and curriculum in which it is to be used. Otherwise, provisions must be made to adjust these abilities and the teaching context to accommodate the features of the new program. It must also not be so complex as to be impossible or too difficult to understand or manage. In addition, to be accepted and successfully implemented, such a program should be capable of being observed by teachers without their committing themselves irrevocably to it. Teachers must be able to try it out in private or with their colleagues without threat of evaluation or punishment should they not "get the hang of it" for some time. Finally, the proposed program should produce results that teachers, students, and parents can perceive and understand with relative ease. Any newly developed thinking skills program must exhibit these features if it is to be successfully implemented.

In "selling" a proposed thinking skills program to teachers, parents, and others, program developers must show how it will produce better results with relatively little additional resources, time, or effort beyond those now expended by teachers involved. The shortcomings of the conventional teaching of thinking skills are readily acknowledged by most informed educators. For example, few teachers are truly satisfied with the thinking performances of their students. Most are convinced that their students can think better than they now do, and they, the teachers, can do things to improve student thinking. Diagnostic tests may provide convincing data to support such feelings. Local research projects can readily identify the enhanced learning of subject matter for students receiving explicit instruction in thinking skills in subject matter courses. Provision of the necessary support and training can minimize time and effort required of teachers to implement new teaching and testing strategies.

To demonstrate compatibility, developers can identify where a school's present program of studies already calls for the teaching of thinking operations akin to those included in a proposed new thinking skills program. By limiting the number of skills to be systematically taught, and by relating these skills to the subject areas of the teachers who are to teach them, further compatibility can also be demonstrated. Efforts to tie the new thinking skills to be taught closely to already accepted subject matter objectives can also help achieve this goal. Thus, for instance, starting model lesson plans for teaching a skill with a content objective that can be accomplished in the course of the skill lesson may alert teachers to the value of such lessons.

Implementing any new program obviously involves more teacher time and work—things most teachers are willing to give if they are provided with appropriate support and reasonable payoffs. Providing the training and support needed to minimize such time and work, as well as to facilitate program implementation can speak to this situation. This includes providing development and training *on school time*, time to observe and try out the innovation in nonthreatening situations, and appropriate support for classroom teaching strategies, test preparation, and developing knowledge of the skills to be taught. Keeping a new program and what is required to execute it relatively simply can also enhance its chances of success. By acknowledging these features of effective educational change, developers of thinking skills programs can produce programs with a good chance of succeeding.

GETTING ON WITH DEVELOPING A THINKING SKILLS PROGRAM

The chapters that follow present options, principles, and procedures for carrying out the tasks enumerated above. The suggestions and information presented may be readily applied to single grades or subjects, to individual school buildings or system-wide subject areas, and to school districts as a whole. Chapter 2 outlines a rationale for giving concerted attention to teaching thinking and suggests essential features of an effective thinking skills program. Chapter 3 defines the nature of thinking and some of its constituent skills, as well as presents a model of functional thinking that relates these skills to each other and to thinking as a whole. Various options for organizing a thinking skills program are explored in Chapter 4, as are criteria for choosing from existing programs, should program developers so desire. Appendix A supplements Chapter 4, with descriptions of selected existing thinking skills programs.

Chapters 5, 6, 7, and 8 then examine in some detail the key tasks involved in devising a thinking skills program from scratch, including selecting thinking skills and strategies to teach, describing them in enough detail so teachers can teach them thoroughly, and organizing these thinking operations to ensure their effective learning. Chapters 6 and 7 provide procedural descriptions of numerous thinking skills (with additional, more complete descriptions presented in Appendix B), and Chapter 7 provides additional descriptions of major thinking skills. Chapter 8 describes selected thinking strategies at various levels of complexity, and presents a K–12 scope and sequence for teaching thinking.

But the task does not end here. A scope and sequence will be only as effective as the instructional delivery system by which it is translated into classroom learning. Thus, Chapter 9 outlines the kinds of instruction that must be provided to teach thinking skills and strategies most effectively. It also describes procedures for incorporating thinking skills lessons into any subject matter course.

The remaining chapters focus on the implementation and maintenance of the thinking skills program resulting from the completion of the preceding steps in the process. Chapter 10 explores the kinds of staff development and training required to implement a program, employing the teaching strategies described in the preceding chapter. Chapter 11 describes the types of coaching, teacher and student support, and assessment and revision required to keep a newly installed program in operation. The Appendices noted above and a selected list of references on thinking and thinking skills conclude these pages. Study of the chapters and materials herein can help program developers generate and implement a thinking skills program with some assurance of success if they do a reasonably good job at each task along the way.

SUMMARY

The most effective teaching and learning of thinking does not simply happen on its own. Few teachers have studied or have much training in various major thinking operations, or in cognition, skill learning, and skill teaching. Yet over the past several decades, research has unearthed a great deal about all these areas. By developing improved programs for the teaching of thinking that incorporate the findings of this research, educators can close the gap between what is known about thinking and how to teach it. Such efforts can involve all faculty in a school and cut across all subject areas and grade levels, thus uniting an entire faculty in a common effort. Beneficiaries will include the faculty as well as the students. Aspiring to excellence in education can allow us to do no less.

ENDNOTES

1. David W. Pratt, *Curriculum Design and Development* (New York: Harcourt, Brace, Jovanovich, 1983).

2. Warren G. Bennis, Kenneth D. Benne, Robert Chin, and Kenneth E. Corey, *The Planning of Change*, 3rd ed. (New York: Holt, Rinehart and Winston, 1976); Ernest R. House, *The Politics of Educational Innovation* (Berkeley, Calif.: McCutchan Publishing, 1974); Edgar F. Huse and Thomas G. Cummings, *Organization Development and Change*, 3rd ed. (St. Paul, Wis.: West Publishing, 1985).

2

Teaching
Thinking Skills—
A Rationale

Why should a school system or district have a comprehensive, explicit thinking skills program? If its teachers already teach thinking, why should they alter what they are doing? If changes should be made, what could or should they be? What are the essential features of a worthwhile thinking skills program? Answering these questions helps to articulate goals appropriate to the effective teaching—and improved learning—of skillful thinking. Devising a rationale for an effort to achieve these goals thus serves as a useful way to initiate developing a program for skillful thinking. This chapter addresses this task.

IMPROVING THINKING: WHY?

The development of skillful thinking has been an explicit, if sometimes ill-defined, goal of formal schooling in America for at least a century.[1] Yet our schools have never quite been able to achieve this goal to the satisfaction of all.[2] Indeed, the gap between our aspirations and accomplishments in the development of student thinking seems to be widening rather than closing. Schools need now, as never before, to make serious, sustained efforts at program development to arrest this trend and close this gap.

Why is it so important now to develop school-wide instructional programs to improve student thinking? There are four major reasons. First, it has become quite evident that an embarrassingly large proportion of our high school graduates and college students cannot think as well as they might. Second, conditions of life today and in the foreseeable future demand a citizenry skilled at making thoughtful decisions. Third, the response to complaints of student deficiencies in thinking contained in reports of national commissions, by respected professional educators, and by state officials has demonstrated a growing public concern about these deficiencies. Fourth, recent research findings in teaching, skill learning, and cognitive science have alerted us to the inappropriateness of the methods presently used to teach thinking, and have provided new insights into much of what is required to remedy this deficiency. A brief explanation of each of these four factors underscores the importance of developing and implementing effective educational programs to improve student thinking.

Evidence that too many of our youth lack proficiency in higher-order thinking comes from many sources. Business leaders lament the low level of problem-solving skills in our school graduates.[3] College instructors decry the inability of undergraduates to engage in analytical thinking.[4] National test results back up these complaints. These test results indicate that many of our seventeen-year-olds simply cannot engage in the more complex thinking operations of information processing and analysis. For example, National Assessment of Educational Progress test results suggest that anywhere from 38 to 85 percent of our students cannot engage in complex thinking, and that the proportion continues to grow.[5] It seems clear that too many of our school graduates simply cannot engage in higher-order thinking operations as well as educators and others believe they should.

When juxtaposed against the demands of living in today's world and in the world of the twenty-first century, this situation is simply unacceptable. The existence of conditions essential to human survival— such as the spread of nuclear weapons, the existence of racism, and diminishing natural resources, to name but a few—require citizens who can engage effectively in thinking about ways to deal with them.[6] What former president of Johns Hopkins University, Milton Eisenhower, noted years ago is even more pressing today:

> As never before in our history we now need citizens who can reason objectively, critically and creatively within a moral framework; we need, in other words, a new breed of Americans who will devote as much time and energy

to being *wise,* democratic citizens as they do to being good physicians, engineers or businessmen.[7]

The rapidly accelerating information explosion going on about us makes attention to improving the thinking of young people and others even more imperative. In 1970 the amount of information available to us was doubling every 10 years. In 1985 it was doubling every 5½ years. With 6,000 to 7,000 new scientific articles being published every day, world wide, it is estimated that the information available to us by 1991 will be doubling every 20 months. It has now become virtually impossible for any individual to rely on his or her storehouse of information alone to resolve problems. Consequently, it seems imperative that schools must redouble their efforts, as Harvard's Patricia Cross has written, to develop the "cognitive skills that serve as the basic tools of lifelong learning."[8] Given the volume and almost transient nature of information around us, the long-range value of proficiency in thinking takes on special significance, as noted by psychologist Robert Sternberg:

> Bodies of knowledge are important, of course, but they often become outdated. Thinking skills never become outdated. To the contrary, they enable us to acquire knowledge and to reason with it, regardless of the time or place or the kinds of knowledge to which they're applied. So in my opinion, teaching thinking skills is not only a tall order but the first order of business for a school.[9]

Recognizing the importance of thinking and the deficiencies exhibited by our youth in thinking, many influential groups of noneducators as well as educators have in recent years called for increased attention to the teaching of thinking in our schools. In 1983 the President's National Commission on Excellence in Education, in its report *A Nation at Risk,* deplored the inability of many of our students to engage in higher-level thinking, and called for immediate efforts to improve its teaching in our schools.[10] This call followed hard on the heels of a report by the Education Commission of the States, which called for more attention to a wide range of thinking operations in our schools—from creative to analytical thinking. It was followed almost immediately by a similar report of a Task Force on Education for Economic Growth, which called upon schools to do more to develop student "thinking tools" and higher-order skills such as problem solving and analysis.[11] The College Board issued a call for more attention to developing student reasoning,[12] and a National Science Board commission urged that developing student "capacities for problem solving and critical thinking in all areas of learning" become a fundamental goal of our schools,[13] a call later echoed by the National Alliance of Black Educators.[14] Virtually every major professional teaching organization, including those of social studies, English, biology, and mathematics educators, has added its voice to the general public concern about improving the learning and teaching of thinking in our nation's schools.[15]

Simultaneously with these reports, studies of our nation's schools by professional organizations and respected educators have reinforced the need for more attention to thinking in our schools. A survey of education professionals conducted in 1983 by the Association for Supervision and Curriculum Development, for example, found that over 82 percent of those queried listed improved teaching of thinking skills as a top priority for educational planning for the 1980s.[16] Ernest Boyer, president of the Carnegie Foundation for the Advancement of Teaching, called upon schools to develop student abilities to "think critically" in his much publicized report on American high schools.[17] As a result of an intensive study of schools throughout the country, John I. Goodlad, dean of UCLA's School of Education, appealed in *A Place Called School* for more attention to developing thinking,[18] as did Brown University's Theodore Sizer in his study for the National Association of Secondary School Principals and the National Association of Independent Schools.[19] This was reiterated by Mortimer Adler in *The Paideia Proposal*.[20]

More than rhetoric has been involved, of course. Driven, or at least encouraged, by reports and demands such as those noted above, increasing numbers of state and local education agencies have recently taken action to institutionalize more direct attention to student thinking. Vermont's requirement that its schools teach reasoning predated these reports and studies.[21] However, education departments in states such as California responded to them by requiring the teaching of critical thinking in their public schools and state colleges. In fact, California has gone so far as to develop a state-wide test to ensure that its thinking skills requirement is carried out.[22] Additional state education agencies—Connecticut, Michigan, North Carolina, New Jersey, and New York, to name but a few—also initiated or planned major efforts to see to it that schools attend to this important area of instruction.

These national reports, the testimony of respected professionals, and the mandates of state education agencies have reinforced efforts already underway to improve student thinking.[23] They also have forcefully called the attention of the public and of the entire education community to the continued need for attending to this concern. The actions of a growing number of state agencies in developing state-wide curricula and testing mandates has, in fact, made attention to the teaching of thinking imperative for teacher as well as student survival!

We know more today than ever before about cognition, effective teaching, and the teaching and learning of skills—not all there is to know, certainly, but enough to enable us to teach thinking skills immeasurably better than we could even a decade ago. Research on the brain and in the fields of artificial intelligence, knowledge engineering, information processing, cognition, skill learning, and effective teaching have not only demystified thinking to a large extent, but have also provided useful insights on how to teach the operations of which it consists.[24] No longer can thinking be considered something magic, something that just mysteriously happens. No longer can we conceive of the mind as a muscle. And no longer can we rely on teaching techniques that approach improving thinking as simply another form of muscle building.

Although we know thinking is a natural function, the research of individuals such as Benjamin Bloom, Lois Broder, Reuven Feurestein, and Arthur Whimbey have demonstrated that much of good thinking is not natural.[25] As David Perkins has pointed out:

> . . . Everyday thinking, like ordinary walking, is a natural performance we all pick up. But good thinking, like running the 100 yard dash or rock climbing, is a *technical* performance, full of artifice. In a number of ways good thinking goes against the natural grain. People tend not to consider the other side of a case, look beyond the first decent solution that presents itself, or ponder the problem before rushing to candidate solutions, for example.[26]

In fact, there is considerable evidence to indicate that most individuals do not, on their own, develop much proficiency in the more complex thinking operations and processes, such as critical thinking or problem solving.[27] Because skillful thinking is neither as natural nor as common as we would like, and because it is not likely to develop automatically or incidentally, we need to intervene in formal educating settings to help students improve their abilities of how to engage in this important process.

All these elements—especially the concerns about the state of student thinking stimulated and articulated by prominent and influential political, professional, and business groups and the recent availability of new insights about the nature of thinking and of skill learning—converge today to make improving student thinking not only timely and desirable but also possible. What remains to be done, then, is to develop and institute educational programs that will actually enable us to achieve the educational goals in thinking development that have been sought for so long.

But what exactly should be done? Are state or school district competency tests the solution? Are state or district curriculum mandates the answer? Is exhortation by professional groups or well-meaning citizens the solution? No. None of these actions address directly the crux of the thinking skills problem in our schools. The most effective—and one is tempted to add, *the only*—way to improve student proficiencies in thinking is to alter what goes on in the way thinking is treated and taught in the curricula and classrooms of our schools.

FACTORS INHIBITING THE LEARNING OF THINKING

For years, educators have sincerely attempted to teach thinking. Why, then, aren't the graduates of our schools as proficient in thinking as many observers believe they should be? Poor student achievement in thinking has been attributed to just about everything from atomic fall-out, to changing student demographics, to video games and television.[28] However, given what we have learned from research over the past several decades, it seems apparent that the major reason for the lack of student proficiency in thinking lies in *what* schools attempt to teach about thinking and *how* they go about doing it. In general, what most schools have been doing by way of teaching thinking actually *inhibits* rather than facilitates effective thinking skill learning. To put it even more directly, conventional approaches to teaching thinking simply have not done the job. Identifying those things now done in most schools that inhibit student learning of thinking is the first step toward improving student proficiency in this important process.

Teaching thinking in our schools today is characterized by at least five major conditions that often get in the way of improving student thinking. First, in spite of the best of intentions, the instructional methods used by most teachers to teach thinking do not really help students learn this process as well as they might. Second, testing procedures used by many teachers and school systems fail to reinforce, and in some cases to provide appropriate support for, teaching and learning the operations that constitute thinking. Next, school curricula suffer from severe skill overload. Fourth, educators in general have reached little consensus on exactly which thinking operations are most worth teaching. And finally, most teachers, test makers, materials developers, and curriculum builders have not defined as precisely as is required for effective instruction the essential features of those thinking operations they have selected for teaching. Becoming aware of how these five practices and conditions inhibit the teaching and learning of thinking can help us identify what specifically can be done to develop programs that will enhance rather than restrict the abilities of our students to engage in thinking.

Inappropriate Teaching Methods

Although many teachers sincerely believe they teach thinking in their classrooms, much, if not most, of what they usually do to this end consists only of *making* students think. Research suggests there is little if any explicit instruction in thinking in most classrooms.[29] Instead of providing instruction in *how* to engage in thinking, teachers generally put students into situations where they must engage in thinking to whatever degree they can. This approach assumes that simply by forcing students to think, however well the students understand how they are doing it, they will learn to think better. This is a fallacious assumption.[30] By honoring it in practice, teachers actually inhibit rather than promote the development of student proficiency in thinking.

What most teachers customarily do to "teach" thinking or its constituent operations is, in fact, not instructional at all. In spite of research findings and admonitions of experts to the contrary, many teachers assume that by focusing exclusively on content they are in fact teaching the operations or skills students need to process that content.[31] Frequently, these teachers simply exhort their students to "think" or "think again" or even "think harder," and assume that by so doing they are actually teaching thinking. Others ask students a series of carefully sequenced questions that move from recall to information processing and applying, assuming that somehow in the struggle to answer such questions students actually learn how to think.[32] Many teachers use textbooks and other materials that do the same thing. Indeed, having students write out answers to end-of-chapter "Questions for Further Thought" appears to be a common method used by teachers seeking to teach thinking. Other teachers, making the same assumption, assign puzzles or dittoed worksheets of the fill-in-the blank or multiple-choice variety, review the correct answers, and go on to the next worksheet. Some teachers give students rules to follow in thinking, such as "work as quickly as you can" or "use all the information given," in spite of the fact that research has shown that many such rules, including these two, are quite dysfunctional.[33] Still others engage the students in inquiry or discovery learning, hoping that by engaging in these processes students will learn the operations of which they consist. Teachers who rely almost exclusively on these methods often believe they are doing all that can be done to teach thinking.

Emphasis on content processing and/or use of exhortation, questions, worksheets, and other similar techniques do not by themselves help many students improve their thinking. These practices do not constitute *teaching*. They may encourage thinking, stimulate it, and provoke it, but they do not teach it. Such practices, instead, are what reading specialist Ann Brown calls "blind training."[34] At best, they provide practice only. At worst, they test. Neither practice nor testing is enough to achieve proficiency in thinking. What these techniques really do is put students in the position of having to use, as best they can, a skill or skills they may not know how to use, with failure and frustration a common result. Such practices inhibit rather than carry forward the learning of thinking because they fail to provide actual instruction. Educators and instructional materials authors who persist in using such practices as the core of techniques for "teaching" thinking simply delude themselves and others into believing they are engaging in teaching thinking when, in fact, they are not.

Inadequate Skills Testing

As unlikely as it may seem, the testing of thinking as usually carried out also inhibits the effective teaching and learning of thinking. This is, true of standardized, commercially made tests and teacher-made tests as well.

The nature of many standardized thinking tests and the ways they are sometimes used by educators often create problems for teaching and learning thinking. For example, many tests measure only discrete cognitive operations in isolation from one another, ignoring, by and large, student abilities to engage in a sequence of such operations. Some twenty years ago, educator Harold Berlack pointed out the dangers of assuming that measures of isolated skill performance could be interpreted as adequate measures of basic thinking processes such as problem solving.[35] Yet test makers continue to offer tests that measure almost exclusively student performance on individual thinking operations.

In addition, professional test developers rarely share with teachers whatever thinking descriptions or models they use (if, indeed, they use any) as the basis for designing their test items or for identifying the behaviors they seek as indicative of thinking. In the absence of such information, teachers proceed on their merry ways, trying to teach prescribed thinking operations as best they know them, whereas the tests often seem to be going in other directions. Without congruence between thinking as it is tested and thinking as it is taught, both are often little more than hit-or-miss affairs insofar as producing quality teaching.

These problems are exacerbated by the uses to which standardized thinking tests are often put. Items designed to measure competence in a particular thinking operation, once they become public, frequently come to be viewed by teachers as prototypes for materials they can use to help their students learn the operation. Some so-called teaching of thinking consequently consists largely of providing students practice in answering old test questions, a procedure that may well focus student learning on question-answering techniques rather than on learning the specific cognitive operations which are the presumed goals of such activities.

Moreover, it is not uncommon for reliance on standardized thinking tests to lull school officials into believing student scores on these instruments are the only valid measures of such learning and teaching. Many school officials trap themselves into believing that their diagnostic or minimum competency or criterion-referenced tests measure the student competencies they are intended to measure, when in reality they may not be doing so at all.

Teacher-testing policies also inhibit the effective teaching of thinking. For one thing, most teachers rarely test the thinking operations they teach. A study some years ago of teacher-made tests in science and history indicated that only 8 percent of the test items assessed thinking skills above the level of recall.[36] There is little evidence to suggest that the sample of tests in this study was atypical. Given the tendency for students to study only what they believe will be tested, and the fact that few if any teacher-made test items measure any thinking operation above the level of recall, it is not surprising that teacher test procedures communicate to students that thinking skills are not worth attending to in the classroom. Consequently, there is little student need to attend to whatever skills might be a teacher's intended focus of instruction. Instead, subject matter learning carries the day.

Skill Overload

A third feature of conventional schooling that actually inhibits student learning of thinking skills is skill overload—attempting to teach too many skills in too short a time. This customarily takes the form of rapid-fire bombardment of students with immense numbers of skills over the course of a year. It manifests itself in three related ways.

First, there are the sheer numbers of skills selected for instruction. It is not unusual to find science, language arts, and social studies programs and texts claiming to provide instruction in dozens of thinking skills in a single, one-year course. For example, in addition to offering instruction in almost three dozen geography, study, and research skills, one social studies text also claims to teach seventeen different thinking skills—from "conveying personal opinions" to "creating novel solutions"—all in 180 days! One local school district curriculum guide even lists 232 skills to be taught in one grade level alone! Two years later, this same curriculum calls for the teaching of 370 skills.[37]

Seeking to cover large numbers of thinking skills in a relatively short time, most curricula and texts provide students with little more than one recognizable encounter with each skill. Such an encounter is often referred to in teaching instructions or statements of objectives as an "exposure." There is, of course, the implicit hope that such an exposure might result in the target skill being "caught" by students in epidemic proportions! But faith in such happy accidents is no substitute for purposeful teaching. Students do not and should not be expected to master even a single skill when they are subjected to one-time, scatter-gun experiences with dozens of vaguely defined skills over the course of a few months or so. Emphasis on quantity actually inhibits the quality of skill learning in our schools.

Thinking skill overload also manifests itself by the absence in most school systems and in many textbooks of any developmental or other type of overall sequential skill curricula. Many curricula and texts, especially at the secondary level, seem to have been developed in almost complete isolation from each other. Thinking skills introduced in one grade level are all too often never reinforced or practiced in subsequent grade levels. Thinking skills introduced in one content area are rarely deliberately transferred to or reinforced in other content areas, even at the same grade level. One newly proposed state-sponsored skill sequence in social studies, for instance, introduces the skill of problem identification in the third grade, mentions it again only in the sixth grade, and ignores it thereafter.[38] Unfortunately, such a skills program is not atypical, either at a state or local level. The sheer quantity of skills mandated for instruction and the frequent absence of coherent, sequential skill programs inhibit effective skill teaching. These practices make it virtually impossible for teachers to relate their skill teaching to what has been done with skills in previous grades, or to provide a basis for skills to be dealt with in detail in later grades, or do much more than cover as quickly as possible all the skills assigned for instruction.

Diversity of Skills

The catalog of what is taught as thinking skills seems to be almost endless. Some schools teach skills they describe as logical analysis, skills such as syllogistic reasoning, detecting logical contradictions, deductive logic, sequential synthesis, and inferencing.[39] Others focus on a hierarchy of cognitive skills, often derived from the work of educator Benjamin Bloom and his colleagues.[40] Some school systems teach inquiry, whereas others emphasize problem solving, decision making, or conceptualizing. Schools teach taxonomies as well as grab-bags of discrete skills, mnemonics as well as creative thinking, and Socratic reasoning as well as reflective thinking. Some schools even teach their own sets of thinking skills—skills one school system lists as clarifying issues, giving one's opinion, explaining, predicting, generalizing, and concluding. Publishers also offer a wide variety of thinking skills for instruction, including one set of such skills consisting of "qualification, . . . structure analysis, operation analysis and seeing analogies."[41]

There simply is little widespread agreement among educators—whether classroom teachers, materials developers, or curriculum builders—about the major thinking skills upon which schools should focus. Consequently, many schools or texts attempt to cover all the thinking skills that they know exist. Sometimes each publisher and teacher seems to have his or her own favorites. Either or both situations makes thinking skill learning virtually impossible for many students; in many cases, a confusion in terminology only further confuses learners.

Confusion Over Skill Meanings

Unfortunately, little has occurred in the last fifteen years to remedy what Hilda Taba once referred to as the "haziness about what is meant by thinking."[42] Educators today still exhibit considerable diversity and fuzziness in what they select to teach as thinking skills in our schools.

All too often, we find thinking skills so ill-defined that meaningful teaching, learning, and assessing are virtually impossible. At times, the same word is used to denote different skills. For example, whereas one prominent social studies text defines a conclusion as a generalization, a science text used at about the same grade level defines concluding as explaining similarities and differences, and yet a third text describes a conclusion simply as "a summary."[43]

Sometimes different labels are used erroneously to denote one particular skill. For instance, many educators customarily equate problem solving with critical thinking, or equate reflective thinking with either or both of these, in spite of the fact that each consists of a very unique set of subskills used in a specific order to accomplish very different tasks. What reading teachers often describe as "critical reading" skills, social studies teachers usually refer to as "critical thinking" and English teachers sometimes designate "literary analysis."[44] And the term *inquiry*, in practice, has come to mean just about anything it is stipulated to mean.

Nor is it uncommon to find thinking skills defined inaccurately. One well-intentioned school system, for example, has produced a skills continuum that defines the skill of "inquiry" as "to remember previously gained material," and then gives as its operational definitions to "differentiate between facts and opinions" and to "locate factual information on a time line to answer specific questions."[45] To equate inquiry with recall is simply erroneous. To equate the processes involved in distinguishing fact from opinion with those involved in matching events with dates and centuries is inaccurate, to say the least!

This confusion over skill meanings reflects a vagueness about the essential attributes of specific thinking skills. Skills are often considered to be essentially "doing" things, but researchers have discovered that they have important knowledge and affective dimensions as well.[46] Attempting to teach students a skill in ignorance of all its essential attributes usually leads to less than a desirable level of performance. Where such "haziness" about skills exists, it is no wonder that students "taught" these skills do poorly on standardized skills tests and become befuddled when moving from one classroom, text, teacher, or school to another. Clearing up the ambiguities regarding what thinking skills mean is an important prerequisite to improving student proficiencies in thinking in our schools.

These five features of conventional approaches to thinking are closely interrelated. Most teachers don't teach or test thinking skills effectively, not because they don't want to or don't believe these are worthwhile. The great number of skills that they feel constrained by texts and curriculum guides to cover simply precludes, in their minds, much continuing attention to or in-depth testing of any single skill. The great variety of thinking skills that could be taught, and the general indecision over which thinking skills all students should master, reinforce this tendency. Also reinforcing this direction is the failure to understand that skill teaching differs from information teaching; whereas a piece of information, a fact, or a generalization is usually taught once, teaching a thinking skill requires more than a single lesson. Confusion or lack of knowledge about the nature of skills and effective skill instruction prevent teachers and program developers from understanding exactly how best to go about incorporating instruction in these skills in any program beyond the most superficial levels.

Although the practices and conditions cited here are very real obstacles to effective thinking skill teaching and learning, they are but symptomatic of an even more fundamental reason for less than desired student thinking proficiencies. The fact that these practices and conditions persist is simply evidence of the classic and everwidening gap that exists between classroom teaching and research findings related to content, teaching, and learning.[47] Nowhere does this gap seem wider than in the area of instruction in thinking. As noted earlier, research and experience over the past several decades have generated a wealth of information and insight about effective ways to organize instruction in thinking that have yet to be put into practice. Communicating this information and these insights to educators, and suggesting ways to translate them into effective programs and instruction, can help close this gap. And by doing so, educators will greatly improve the teaching—and the learning—of thinking skills in our schools. The suggestions for improving student thinking that follow here seek to accomplish precisely this goal.

IMPROVING STUDENT PROFICIENCIES IN THINKING

If the preceding diagnosis is accurate, we can markedly improve the abilities of our youth to engage in productive and skillful thinking by addressing directly those classroom and curriculum practices that undermine development of those abilities. First, we must teach thinking and its constituent cognitive skills directly rather than indirectly, as is conventionally done. Second, we must develop a clearer and more accurate understanding of the thinking operations we attempt to teach. Third, we must make the teaching and learning of thinking an explicit part of the entire school curriculum, throughout all major subject areas and across all grade levels.

Direct Teaching of Thinking

For too long classroom teachers and other educators have hidden the teaching of thinking skills in the study of subject matter. For too long teachers have substituted exhortation and challenge for instruction. To improve the quality of student thinking as much as we can, we must turn to teaching directly the skills and strategies that constitute thinking. Such teaching has three dimensions: it makes thinking skills and strategies the subject of instruction, the substance to be learned; it focuses explicitly on the attributes of the skills and strategies being taught; and it employs techniques of direct instruction.

Many experts in the teaching of thinking agree that to be most effective the teaching of thinking should focus on the specific operations that constitute thinking. That is, the substance of lessons designed to teach thinking must be the specific operations in which we engage when thinking. At present, much conventional teaching of thinking seems to assume thinking is an intuitive, mysterious phenomenon that, when properly triggered, just happens. If this were so, then encouraging, stimulating, fostering, challenging, and initiating it would be sufficient to do the job of improving it. But thinking is not something that just happens. Thinking consists of a multitude of discrete cognitive operations that can be identified and addressed directly. By providing explicit attention to these operations, as Professors David Perkins, Robert Sternberg, and Jane Stallings, among others, point out, teachers can dramatically improve student proficiency in thinking in general.[48] Psychologist R. E. Snow made this point perhaps most clearly when he wrote in 1982:

> Attempts to train abilities must go well beyond simply manipulating practice and feedback . . . ; they must provide substantial training in the component processes and skills involved in task performance and they must also train directly the superordinant and control strategies involved in guidance. . . .[49]

Furthermore, in the teaching and learning of thinking, especially in its initial stages, student and teacher must focus on the specific skill or strategy being developed rather than on content.[50] Although subject matter may be used as a vehicle for learning a thinking operation, attention must be directed to the operation rather than to the subject matter. Deliberate, conscious attention to skill learning rather than unconscious exercise of skills is required to improve one's thinking most effectively.

Finally, to teach skillful thinking, the instructional techniques employed must go beyond practice and exercise. Direct instruction is required. According to researcher Walter Doyle, direct instruction consists primarily of:

1. Carefully structured academic tasks
2. Explicit instruction in how to accomplish them

3. Systematic guidance through a series of practices to mastery
4. Numerous opportunities for directed practice
5. Appropriate assessment[51]

Note that the goal of such teaching is not memorization or imitation of any given thinking skill model. Rather, it is the use of skill models or descriptions as springboards for generating, articulating, and internalizing the students' own conceptions of these operations. It is neither prescriptive nor limiting, but it is instructive. It goes far beyond fostering, stimulating, encouraging, or even forcing students to think. Instead, it shows and explains to students exactly what is involved in executing any thinking skill or strategy, and how to do it by providing instruction, modeling, feedback, and considerable guided practice. Providing such direct instruction is the classroom key to the improvement of student thinking.

Understanding the Skills to Be Taught

Much conventional teaching of thinking is based on a lack of knowledge or on outdated knowledge about the nature of thinking. This is not surprising. Few educators have undertaken formal study of thinking or cognition. Few schools provide the kinds of staff development required to keep their faculties abreast of new research in these fields. But student thinking abilities will be improved only when those attempting to improve them understand fully what it is they are trying to improve.

Thinking occurs in different forms, for different purposes, in different arenas. Moreover, thinking itself consists of a wide variety of cognitive operations. Each of these operations consist of specific rules, procedures, and certain kinds of knowledge.[52] Proficiency in a skilled task, as Benjamin Bloom notes, requires an understanding of these components of the task: "The ability to understand instruction may be defined as the ability of the learner to understand the nature of the task . . . and the procedures he is to follow. . . ."[53] Educators who attempt to teach or assess thinking must know the key attributes of the skills and strategies they seek to teach. Any program to improve student thinking must focus on the nature of the operations that constitute thinking, both in carrying out such teaching and in assessing what is learned as a result.

Teaching Thinking Throughout the Curriculum

If students are to develop to the fullest extent possible their abilities to think, instruction in thinking must pervade the entire school curriculum.[54] The teaching of thinking must be an essential part of all major subjects across the grade levels for three reasons: One has to do with the students, themselves; another has to do with the nature of thinking; and the third is derived from the role of thinking in the subject matter learning on which most schools focus.

Teaching thinking across the curriculum speaks directly to student survival, in classrooms as well as in life in general. Teachers of every subject continuously ask questions, give tests, and require tasks that make students use whatever thinking skills they possess to come up with content answers, and then the students are graded on the correctness of their answers. If teachers persist in doing this without showing or teaching those students who cannot come up with the desired responses how to do so better, they put the students in a no-win situation. It seems contrary to good teaching and effective learning to conduct classes that make students perform thinking tasks without showing them how to engage in these tasks.

Teaching students how to be more skilled at thinking can help them develop greater self-confidence and self-esteem, both of which seem to be crucial prerequisites for leading self-fulfilling and contributing lives. Because they do not know how to think as well as they could, too many youngsters feel they are victims of their own thinking or lack of it. They feel they are controlled by their minds rather than being in control. Direct teaching of thinking raises to a level of consciousness student awareness of how they think and of how to engage in thinking effectively; such teaching can give students a sense of control over their own thinking and thus over their own lives. Awareness of this control contributes to a positive self-concept, a developing sense of self-assurance and confidence that sharply enhances not only school achievement but also success in out-of-school endeavors.[55] Descartes's "I think, therefore I am" aptly describes this interrelationship of effective thinking, self-confidence, and self-concept. The teaching of thinking can contribute significantly to a student's positive sense of self.

Additionally, the teaching of thinking in certain subject matter has important humane benefits. Teaching thinking skills in subjects such as philosophy, English, social studies, or history, for example, humanizes learning, as Matthew Lipman and others so eloquently point out.[56] Teaching thinking skills in isolation of such subjects may communicate a mechanistic view of thinking skills and strategies, and thus produce mere skill technicians, devoid of the affective components related to such skills and their uses. However, teaching thinking skills in more humanistic-oriented subjects can provide a sense of the values implicit in the interplay and contexts in which these skills find daily use. The teaching of thinking across the curriculum can contribute significantly to the quality of student lives, as students, as citizens, and as human beings.

The nature of thinking itself also calls for the teaching of thinking throughout the curriculum. Thinking skills simply cannot be taught or learned to any degree of proficiency in one or two attempts. No matter where skills are introduced—at what grade level or in what context—to be mastered they require repeated, frequent practice with instructional guidance over extended periods of time.[57] Skills grow and develop as they are adapted to and used in different contexts. This growth requires continued instructional attention to skills in as many settings as possible where these skills can be useful and over an extended period of time. It is doubtful that any complex functional thinking skill can be mastered or maintained by instruction limited to a year or two and to contexts that are free of subject matter. This means especially concerted attention to teaching these skills in the variety of subject matter courses that constitute at least the core of most school curricula.

Moreover, one cannot assume that, having been introduced to thinking skills in one setting or subject, students will automatically transfer these skills into other settings or subjects. On the contrary, there is every indication that such transfer does not readily occur.[58] Thinking skills are very much tied to and informed by the contexts in which they are first introduced. And they are, to some degree, modified by each new type of content, data, or media with which they are used.[59] To use them successfully in new settings or with new data, students need continued guidance and instruction. For maximum learning of thinking skills, these skills must actually be taught and practiced with teacher guidance in a variety of subject matter courses over the years, whether or not they are introduced in contexts that are free of subject matter.

In this same vein, there is some evidence to indicate that students need to be at the stage of formal abstract reasoning to apply successfully complex reasoning, problem solving, and critical thinking skills in contexts different from those in which these skills are introduced. Although almost two thirds of our students do not achieve this level, even by the time they leave high school, many are moving in this direction.[60] In order to reach these students, and to help them achieve some degree of proficiency in these skills, they need attention throughout their secondary school years and, in many instances, beyond. Because at this level virtually all courses are subject matter courses, thinking skills ought to be taught in subject matter courses at the secondary as well as in the elementary grades.

Teaching thinking throughout a curriculum has practical value for learning in all subjects. If there is one place in school where students need to think, it is in the subjects they study. Not only is thinking required to learn the information, concepts, and generalizations taught in most subjects, but it is also required to apply the knowledge thus gained in out-of-classroom settings. Morever, thinking skills are informed and, to some degree, shaped by various kinds of subject matter in which they are employed. Subject matter serves as a vehicle for the learning of thinking, just as thinking serves as a vehicle to learn about the subjects taught. Neither subject matter nor thinking skill learning can be accomplished in a vacuum. Interestingly, research indicates that when skills like thinking skills are taught in subject matter courses, students learn more about the subject matter, as measured on end-of-course content examinations, than when such skill teaching is not part of such courses.[61] And learning subject matter is, after all, one very important goal of schooling.

Not only does teaching thinking in subject matter contexts lead to greater learning of subject matter, it also leads to greater motivation to learn such skills. Research suggests that students are more highly motivated to learn a skill when it is introduced and practiced at a time when it is needed to achieve a subject matter-related goal.[62] Assigned to make inferences from a mass of disorganized data, students are much more ready to attend to instruction in how to categorize data to make more meaningful inferences than they would be in a course or unit designed simply to practice categorizing for the sake of categorizing. Learning a skill to achieve subject matter goals provides a functional purpose for skill learning, and provides for the kind of attention and commitment crucial to such learning.

TOWARD THE TEACHING OF THINKING

The importance of "doing something" to improve student proficiency in thinking cannot be denied; neither can the fact that conventional thinking skills programs do not seem to do the job as well as they should. The widespread existence of those factors listed above as major obstacles to the effective teaching and learning of thinking simply limit the usefulness of even these conventional approaches. If we, as educators, are to improve the abilities of students to think, we must develop and implement coherent, continuing educational programs that speak directly to this goal. These programs should provide for the direct teaching of thinking skills and strategies throughout a school's curriculum.

ENDNOTES

1. John Dewey, *How We Think* (Boston: D.C. Heath, 1910); Henry Johnson, *Teaching of History*, rev. ed. (New York: The Macmillan Company, 1940), p. 62; Rolla M. Tyron, "The Social Sciences as School Subjects," *Report of the Commission on the Social Studies of the American Historical Association*, Part XI (New York:

Scribner's, 1935), pp. 76–100; *The Study of History in the Schools* (New York: American Historical Association, 1899); National Commission on Excellence in Education, *A Nation at Risk* (Washington, D.C.: U.S. Government Printing Office, 1983); Walter B. Kolesnik, *Mental Discipline in Modern Education* (Madison: University of Wisconsin Press, 1958), pp. 11–12.

2. Howard Anderson, ed., *Teaching Critical Thinking In Social Studies, 13th Yearbook* (Washington, D.C.: National Council for the Social Studies, 1942), p. v; Catherine Cornbleth and Willard Korth, "If Remembering, Understanding and Reasoning Are Important . . . ," *Social Education 45*, 3 (April 1981): 276, 278–279; Bryce B. Hudgins, *Learning and Thinking* (Itasca, Ill.: F. E. Peacock, 1977), pp. 146–147; John Goodlad, "A Study of Schooling: Some Findings and Hypotheses," *Phi Delta Kappan 64*, 7 (March 1983): 465–470.

3. Research and Policy Committee, *Investing In Our Children* (New York: Committee on Economic Development, 1985); Task Force on Education for Economic Growth, *Action for Excellence* (Denver: Education Commission of the States, 1983), pp. 16, 38; "Future Directions in Social Studies Discussed," *The Council Developer* (Washington, D.C.: National Council for the Social Studies) 25 (September 1983): 1.

4. Gene Maeroff, "Teaching to Think: A New Emphasis in Schools and Colleges," *New York Time Magazine*, January 9, 1983, pp. 1, 37; Raymond Starr, "Teaching Study Skills in History Courses," *The History Teacher 16*, 4 (August 1983): 489–504; Marshall M. True and Mark A. Stoler, "Teaching the U.S. History Survey Course: A Staff and Skills Approach," *The History Teacher 16*, 1 (November 1982): 19, 21.

5. *Reading, Thinking and Writing: Results from the 1979–80 National Assessment of Reading and Literature* (Denver: National Assessment of Educational Progress, 1981); Ina V. S. Mullis, "What Do NAEP Results Tell Us About Students' Higher Order Thinking Abilities?" Unpublished paper, delivered at the ASCD Wingspread Conference on Teaching Thinking Skills, May 17–19, 1984; *Secondary School Reading: What Research Reveals for the Classroom* (Urbana, Ill.: National Council of Teachers of English, 1982).

6. Neil Postman, "Critical Thinking in the Electronic Era," *National Forum 65*, 1 (Winter 1985): 4–8, 17; Edward M. Glaser, "Educating for Responsible Citizenship in a Democracy," *National Forum 65*, 1 (Winter 1985): 24–27.

7. Milton Eisenhower, "Ike's Brother Delivers Talk," *Columbus Dispatch*, June 9, 1968. (italics mine)

8. K. Patricia Cross, "The Rising Tide of School Reform Reports," *Phi Delta Kappan 66*, 3 (November 1984): 172.

9. Nelson Quimby and Robert J. Sternberg, "On Testing and Teaching Intelligence: A Conversation with Robert Sternberg," *Educational Leadership 43*, 2 (October 1985): 53.

10. *A Nation at Risk*, pp. 9, 25.

11. *The Information Society: Are High School Students Ready?* (Denver: Education Commission of the States, 1982), p. 12; Task Force on Education for Economic Growth, *Action for Excellence*, pp. 16, 39.

12. *Academic Preparation for College: What Students Need to Know and Be Able to Do* (New York: College Entrance Examination Board, 1983), pp. 9–10.

13. National Science Board Commission on Precollege-Education in Mathematics, Science and Technology, *Educating Americans for the 21st Century* (Washington, D.C.: National Science Foundation, 1983), p. 9.

14. Karen Farkas, "Black Educators Seek Afro-American Perspectives, Academic Rigor," *Education Week*, November 28, 1984, p. 8.

15. *An Agenda for Action*, (Reston, Va.: National Council of Teachers of Mathematics, 1980); *Essentials of English* (Urbana, Ill.: National Council of Teachers of English, 1982); "In Search of a Scope and Sequence for Social Studies," *Social Education 48*, 4 (April 1984): 253; National Science Board Commission.

16. "Thinking Skills Achievement Ranked High in ASCD," *ASCD Update* (June 1983): 2–3.

17. Ernest Boyer, *High School: A Report on Secondary Education in America* (New York: Harper and Row, 1983).

18. John I. Goodlad, *A Place Called School: Prospects for the Future* (New York: McGraw-Hill, 1983).

19. Theodore Sizer, *Horace's Compromise: The American High School* (Boston: Houghton Mifflin, 1984).

20. Mortimer Adler, *The Paideia Proposal* (New York: Macmillan, 1982), p. 9.

21. Thomas Toch, "That Noble and Most Sovereign Reason . . . States, School Districts Display Growing Interest in The Teaching of Thinking Skills," *Education Week* (June 9, 1982): 7, 16; Vermont Department of Education, *Basic Competencies: Reasoning* (Montpelier, Vt.: State Department of Education, 1979).

22. *Assessment of the Critical Thinking Skills In History Social Science* (Sacramento: California State Department of Education, 1985).

23. Toch, "That Noble and Most Sovereign Reason."

24. Jack Lochhead and John Clement, eds., *Cognitive Process Instruction: Research on Teaching Thinking Skills* (Philadelphia: The Franklin Institute Press, 1979); Judith W. Segal, Susan F. Chipman, and Robert Glaser, eds., *Thinking and Learning Skills*, Vol. 1 (Hillsdale, N.J.: Lawrence Erlbaum Associates, 1985); Walter Doyle, "Academic Work," *Review of Educational Research 53*, 2 (Summer 1983): 159–199.

25. Benjamin Bloom and Lois Broder, *Problem Solving Processes of College Students* (Chicago: University of Chicago Press, 1950); Reuven Feuerstein, *Instrumental Enrichment: An Invervention Program for Cognitive Modifiability* (Baltimore: University Park Press, 1980), pp. 71–103; Arthur Whimbey and Linda Shaw Whimbey, *Intelligence Can Be Taught* (New York: E. P. Dutton, 1975).

26. David N. Perkins, "Thinking Frames: An Integrative Perspective on Teaching Cognitive Skills." Unpublished paper, delivered at ASCD Conference on Approaches to Teaching Thinking, Alexandria, Va., August 6, 1985, p. 1.

27. David H. Russell, *Children's Thinking* (Boston: Ginn and Company, 1956), p. 287; Edward M. Glaser, *An Experiment in the Development of Critical Thinking* (New York: Bureau of Publications, Teachers' College, Columbia University, 1941), p. 69; Anderson, *Teaching Critical Thinking In Social Studies*, p. vii.

28. Ernest J. Sternglass and Steven Bell, "Fallout and SAT Scores: Evidence for Cognitive Damage During Early Infancy," *Phi Delta Kappan 64*, 8 (April 1983): 539–545; Maeroff, "Teaching to Think."

29. Goodlad, *A Place Called School*; Catherine Cornbleth and Willard Korth, "In Search of Academic Instruction," *Educational Researcher 9*, 5 (May 1980): 1–9; Cornbleth and Korth, "If Remembering . . . ," pp. 276, 278–279.

30. Edward deBono, *Teaching Thinking* (London: Maurice Temple Smith, 1976), p. 104; Cornbleth and Korth, "If Remembering . . . ,"; Goodlad, *A Place Called School*.

31. Hilda Taba, "The Teaching of Thinking," *Elementary English* 42 (May 1965): 534; James P. Shaver, "Educational Research and Instruction for Critical Thinking," *Social Education 26*, 1 (January 1962): 14, 16; Anderson, *Teaching Critical Thinking In Social Studies*; Glaser, *An Experiment in the Development of Critical Thinking*.

32. R. T. Dillon, "The Multi-Disciplinary Study of Questioning," *Journal of Educational Psychology 74*, 2 (April 1982): 147–165; R. T. Dillon, "To Question and Not to Question During Discussion," *Journal of Teacher Education 32*, 5 (September/October 1981): 51–55 and *32*, 6 (November/December 1981): 15–20; David R. McNamara, "Teaching Skill: The Question of Questioning," *Educational Research 23*, 2 (February 1981): 104–109; Meredith D. Gall, "The Use of Questions in Teaching," *Review of Educational Research 40*, 5 (December 1970): 707–721; Philip H. Winne, "Experiments Relating Teachers' Use of Higher Cognitive Questions to Student Achievement," *Review of Educational Research 49*, 1 (Winter 1979): 13–49; Doris L. Redfield and Elaine Weldman Rousseau, "A Meta-Analysis of Experimental Research on Teacher Questioning Behavior," *Review of Educational Research 51*, 2 (Summer 1981): 237–245.

33. Robert J. Sternberg, "Teaching Intellectual Skills: Looking for Smarts in all the Wrong Places." Unpublished paper, delivered at ASCD Wingspread Conference on Teaching Thinking Skills, May 17–19, 1984, pp. 7–10.

34. Ann L. Brown, Joseph C. Campione, and Jeanne D. Day, "Learning to Learn: On Training Students to Learn from Texts," *Educational Researcher*, 10 (February 1981): 15.

35. Harold Berlack, "New Curricula and the Measurement of Thinking," *Educational Forum 30*, 3 (March 1966): 305, 309.

36. Richard W. Burns, "Objectives and Content Validity of Tests," *Educational Technology* (December 15, 1968): 17–18; Goodlad, *A Place Called School*.

37. Barry K. Beyer, "Improving Thinking Skills—Defining the Problem," *Phi Delta Kappan 65*, 7 (March 1984): 486–490.

38. Ibid.

39. See the Philosophy for Children program, described by Matthew Lipman, "The Cultivation of Reasoning Through Philosophy," *Educational Leadership 42*, 1 (September 1984): 51–56.

40. Benjamin Bloom, et al., *Taxonomy of Educational Objectives—Handbook I: Cognitive Domain* (New York: Longmans, 1956).

41. Beyer, "Improving Thinking . . . ."

42. Hilda Taba, "Implementing Thinking as an Objective in Social Studies," in Jean Fair and Fannie R. Shaftel, eds., *Effective Thinking in the Social Studies* (Washington, D.C.: National Council for the Social Studies, 1967), p. 26.

43. Beyer, "Improving Thinking . . . ."

44. Barry K. Beyer, "Critical Thinking: What is It?" *Social Education 49*, 4 (April 1985): 270–271.

45. Beyer, "Improving Thinking . . . ."

46. Perkins, "Thinking Frames"; Barry K. Beyer, "What's In A Skill? Defining The Skills We Teach," *Social Science Record 21*, 2 (Fall 1984): 19–23.

47. Elliot Eisner, "Can Research Inform Educational Practice?" *Educational Leadership 65*, 7 (March 1984): 447–452.

48. Brown et al., "Learning to Learn," pp. 16–18; Robert J. Sternberg, "How Can We Teach Intelligence?" *Educational Leadership 42*, 1 (September 1984): 38–48; Carl Bereiter, "How to Keep Thinking Skills from Going the Way of All Frills," *Educational Leadership 42*, 1 (September 1984): 76; Arthur Whimbey, "The Key to Higher Order Thinking Is Precise Processing," *Educational Leadership 42*, 1 (September 1984): 66–70; Perkins, "Thinking Frames," pp. 5–6.

49. Quoted in Norman Frederiksen, "Implications of Cognitive Theory for Instruction in Problem Solving," *Review of Educational Research 54*, 3 (Fall 1984): 382.

50. Ibid; Perkins, "Thinking Frames," pp. 1–15.

51. Doyle, "Academic Work," p. 173; Jane Stallings, "Effective Strategies for Teaching Basic Skills," in Daisy G. Wallace, ed., *Developing Basic Skills Programs in Secondary Schools* (Alexandria, Va.: Association for Supervision and Curriculum Development, 1983), pp. 1–19.

52. See, for example, Perkins, "Thinking Frames"; Beyer, "What's In A Skill?"

53. Benjamin Bloom, "Mastery Learning," in James H. Block, ed., *Mastery Learning: Theory and Practice* (New York: Holt, Rinehart and Winston, 1971), p. 52.

54. Jerry Stonewater and Barbara B. Stonewater, "Teaching Problem Solving: Implications from Cognitive Development Research," *AAHE Bulletin 36*, 6 (February 1984): 7–10; *Items for an Agenda: Educational Research and the Report on Excellence* (Washington, D.C.: American Educational Research Association, 1985), p. 20; John McPeck, *Critical Thinking and Education* (New York: St. Martin's Press, 1981), pp. 132–150; Raymond S. Nickerson, "Kinds of Thinking Taught in Current Programs," *Social Education 42*, 1 (September 1984): 27.

55. William W. Purkey, *Self-concept and School Achievement* (Englewood Cliffs, N.J.: Prentice-Hall, 1970); Jerome Bruner, *The Process of Education* (Cambridge, Mass.: Harvard University Press, 1960), pp. 64–66.

56. Matthew Lipman, "Philosophy for Children and Critical Thinking," *National Forum 65*, 1 (Winter 1985): 20.

57. Michael I. Posner and Steven W. Keele, "Skill Learning," in Robert M. W. Travers, ed., *Second Handbook of Research on Teaching* (Chicago: Rand McNally College Publishing, 1973), pp. 805–831.

58. Ibid.; Hudgins, *Learning and Thinking*, pp. 142–172.

59. Nickerson, "Kinds of Thinking Taught in Current Programs"; McPeck, *Critical Thinking and Education.*

60. Stonewater and Stonewater, "Teaching Problem Solving," p. 7.

61. Thomas H. Estes, "Reading In The Social Studies—A Review of Research Since 1950," in James Laffery, ed., *Reading in the Content Areas* (Newark, Del.: International Reading Association, 1972), pp. 178–183.

62. Carl Bereiter, "Elementary School: Necessity or Convenience?" *Elementary School Journal 73*, 8 (May 1973): 435–446.

3

Defining Thinking and Thinking Skills*

On first impression, thinking seems to be rather amorphous. Many individuals seem content to leave it at that, believing that since they seem to engage in thinking all the time anyway they already must know what there is to know about it, even if their understanding of it is at a rather intuitive and impressionistic level. But a deeper and more conscious understanding of thinking is necessary to teach it to others. In the teaching of thinking, the subject (or content) to be taught and learned is thinking. Anyone who seeks to develop a program designed to teach thinking—whether a district-wide curriculum or textbook, a textbook series, or another type of instructional program—must know as precisely and in as much detail as possible what it is about thinking that is to be taught, and presumably learned, in this program.

Understanding the nature of thinking and those components of it that can serve as goals of instruction is thus a prerequisite to building

---

* A similar but more detailed version of this chapter may be found in the companion volume to this book, *Practical Strategies for the Teaching of Thinking* (Boston: Allyn and Bacon, 1987).

45

any potentially effective thinking program. Such an understanding can develop by examining three things: the general nature of thinking and its key components, the interrelationships of the various functions that thinking serves, and the various kinds of mental processes or procedures by which thinking is operationalized. This chapter presents a brief analysis of these three topics in order to establish a baseline understanding of thinking. This understanding, when shared with others engaged in program development and teaching, can then serve as a springboard for development of a viable educational program in skillful thinking.

THE NATURE OF THINKING

Thinking, Hannah Arendt once wrote, is "the quest for meaning."[1] But just what is the nature of this quest? John Dewey clarified it a bit by defining thinking as "that operation in which present facts suggest other facts (or truths) in such a way as to induce belief in the latter upon the ground or warrant of the former."[2] To be even more precise, thinking is the mental manipulation of sensory input and recalled perceptions to formulate thoughts, reason about, or judge.

The synonyms assigned to the verb *to think* suggest the many facets or dimensions of thinking. For instance, we use the verb *to think* to mean *to decide,* as in "I think (I have decided that) I'll buy this book." We use the verb *to think* to mean *to recall,* as in "I think the phone number is 373–2391." We use the verb *to think* to mean *to believe,* as in "I think this is true." Indeed, the verb *to think* is also synonomous with *ponder, invent, weigh, imagine, anticipate, predict,* and *form in the mind.* Thinking involves and serves a multitude of functions. It is a complex phenomenon, indeed.

Components of Thinking

As complex as it may appear, however, thinking is neither mystery nor magic. Research over the past several decades has revealed a great deal about the mind and how it works to make meaning. It appears that thinking has at least three major components: a number of mental operations, certain kinds of knowledge, and certain attitudes. Any act of thinking engages elements of all three of these components. Figure 3.1 outlines a conception of thinking that identifies these components. An explanation of this concept follows.

Most experts agree that thinking consists of some type of mental activity. This activity can be described in terms of operations that the mind seems to perform when thinking. These operations seem to be of two general types: cognitive and metacognitive. The former consists of

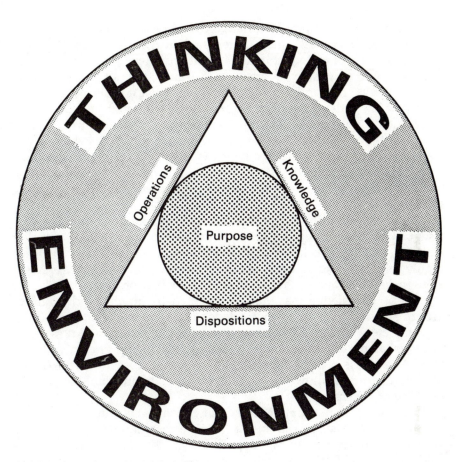

Figure 3.1 A Concept of Thinking

those operations used to generate or find meaning. These operations include a variety of complex strategies, such as decision making and problem solving, as well as more discrete, less complex skills, such as the processing skills of analyzing and synthesizing, reasoning, and critical thinking (e.g., distinguishing statements of fact from value claims).

The second type of operation, metacognition, consists of those operations by which we direct and control these meaning-making strategies and skills. Metacognition has often been described as thinking about thinking.[3] In part, it consists of those operations involved in directing one's efforts to find or make meaning, especially the major operations of planning, monitoring, and assessing one's thinking. Any act of thinking involves a combination of operations designed to produce meaning (cognitive operations) and to direct how that meaning is produced (metacognitive operations).

There is an important knowledge component of thinking, as well. This component consists, first, of general heuristics—rules of thumb—for how to execute various thinking operations. Heuristics are principles or rules, based on past experiences, that usually, but not always, lead to desired results. In learning to be a good teacher, for example, one heuristic that has proven important is that during the first year in a classroom one "should not smile until Thanksgiving nor laugh until Christmas." In terms of thinking, a valuable heuristic is "Look before you leap," meaning to consider all factors before drawing conclusions. Knowledge of such heuristics shapes how one goes about thinking almost as much as does skill in executing the operations that constitute thinking.

Another dimension of the knowledge component of thinking consists of knowing something about the nature of knowledge itself. For instance, this includes knowing that what we believe in as knowledge is highly selective, fragmentary, and interpretive. Moreover, such knowledge includes knowing that what one individual or group believes or accepts as knowledge may not be accepted by another individual or group. Furthermore, as new knowledge is developed, it often modifies or completely replaces what was previously accepted as knowledge. Thus, what passes as "knowledge" is ever-changing and most tentative.[4] Awareness of these aspects of knowledge shapes how we go about thinking, as well as how we treat the products of our thinking and the thinking of others.

Knowledge of the subject area about which one is thinking—usually referred to as *domain-specific knowledge*—is a third important part of the knowledge component of thinking. This includes knowing various reliable sources of data in a particular subject or discipline, any special heuristics for handling this domain-specific data, and specific analytical concepts useful for generating, organizing, and making sense of knowledge in specific fields.[5] Not surprisingly, those individuals most successful at thinking in a given field or subject are those who know the most and most deeply about that field or subject.[6] The assertion that "Discovery favors the well-prepared mind" underscores precisely this relationship between thinking and knowledge.[7] Certainly, the ways individuals go about thinking are very much shaped and informed by their knowledge or lack of knowledge of the subject matter being used or thought about. Yet, it should be noted, knowledge of subject matter is itself no substitute for knowledge of and proficiency in the operations employed in thinking. On the contrary, knowledge of subject matter as well as proficiency in thinking are *both* essential ingredients of skillful thinking.

Executing the operations and applying the knowledge that constitute thinking are hard work. To apply these operations and knowledge effectively requires certain attitudes, or dispositions, as educator Robert

Ennis calls them.[8] These dispositions, habitual inclinations of individuals to behave in a certain way, constitute a third component of thinking. They support skillful thinking, guide it, and, in effect, drive it. According to Ennis, researcher David Krathwohl, and others, the more significant of these include the dispositions to:

Dispositions

- Seek a clear statement of a problem or question
- Question the assumptions on which problems or theses are based
- Deliberately examine a variety of viewpoints
- Use credible sources
- Seek and give reasons and evidence in support of a claim
- Be open-minded
- Willingly change a position or judgment when evidence and reasons so warrant
- Judge in terms of situations, issues, purposes, and consequences rather than in terms of fixed, dogmatic precepts or emotional, wistful thinking
- Suspend judgment when appropriate/sufficient supportive evidence and reasoning are lacking
- Persist in carrying out a thinking task
- Be objective
- Be slow to believe; exhibit a healthy skepticism
- Seek a number of alternatives after an apparently acceptable alternative has been proposed
- Secure as much information as possible before making a judgment[9]

In short, effective thinking involves a willingness, indeed a desire, to engage in thinking, a determination to stay at it until the goal has been achieved, and an awareness—almost a faith—that, by skillful use of one's mind, one can achieve the established goal. An effective thinker is as much characterized by attitudes or dispositions such as these as he or she is knowledgeable about thinking and skilled at executing the various operations of which thinking consists. Figure 3.2 summarizes the major attributes of these key components of thinking.

These three components of thinking—operations, knowledge, and dispositions—are closely interrelated. Each builds out of and contributes to the others. The more knowledgeable one is about a subject and about various heuristics related to it, the better able one is to use general thinking operations to their maximum effect. What one understands about the nature of knowledge informs and supports attitudes of skepticism, caution, and care in processing information, generating thinking, and accepting the products of thinking. A disposition toward skepticism, a desire for evidence and reasoning, and a willingness to stick to a

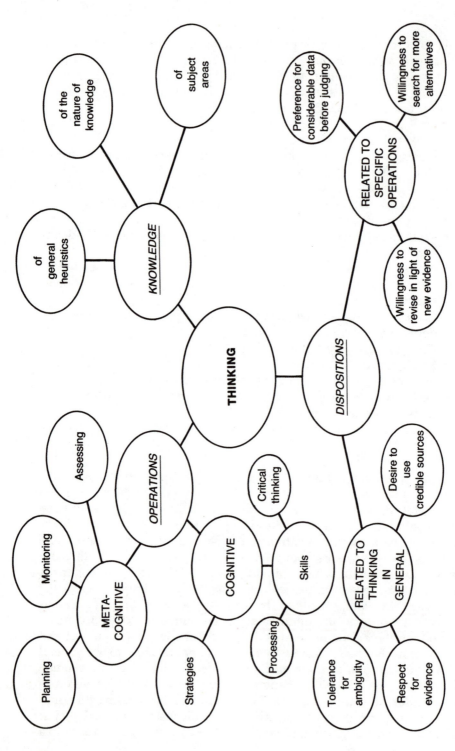

Figure 3.2 Key Components of Thinking

thinking task all drive thinking, shaping the operations selected for use, and the knowledge applied in the process. In any thinking act, these operations, knowledge, and dispositions are so intertwined they are often impossible to separate one from one another.

Factors That Shape Thinking

At least two important variables directly influence how these components of thinking engage to produce meaning. One variable—the context or environment in which thinking occurs—is external to the individual doing the thinking. The other variable—the purpose for thinking—is very much a part of the individual, however, and exerts an internal, idiosyncratic influence on thinking.

The environment in which thinking occurs has considerable influence on how the three components of thinking engage to produce results.[10] This environment has three important dimensions. One of these is *time*. Any thinking act occurs over a period of time, whether it be of a shorter or longer duration. It is affected by this duration, or amount of time, devoted to it as much as by the data processed and the incidents occuring in the environment as thinking occurs. Moreover, the tempo or degree of intensity of thinking varies. At some times thinking may be intense and very active, at others thinking may be more reflective, almost dormant, as thoughts and data mingle in seemingly unconscious ways.

The *arena* in which thinking occurs is a second part of any thinking environment. Thinking that occurs in the course of a dialogue requires use of knowledge, cognitive operations, and attitudes that in some instances differ considerably from those involved in solitary, reflective settings. Participating in an argument where the purpose is to persuade others that a given position is the "best" position requires use of somewhat different cognitive operations, attitudes, and knowledge than does participating in an argument or discussion whose final goal is uncovering the "truth." A classroom that values independent thinking, risk taking, and an objective search for knowledge reinforces and develops quite a different kind of thinking than does a classroom that emphasizes essentially "lesson hearing" or content "covering."

A third part of any thinking environment is the *subject* or topic being thought about and the data or subject matter being used.[11] This substantive content of thinking informs and shapes how one thinks about it. Thinking, in history, for example, is shaped by the discipline of history, the kinds of causal questions typically asked by historians, and the kinds of connections or relationships that typify inquiry in that discipline. Specific thinking operations employed in history may differ somewhat in construct from these same operations when performed with linguistic mathematical data, or in a literary environment. Environments shape thinking. As environments change, so too does how we think.

Thinking is also shaped very much by the purpose of the individual doing the thinking. Thinking is, generally, purposeful in the sense that individuals think to achieve some goal. Usually the purpose is to resolve some discordant situation, or to close a perceived gap between what is and what is desired. Whatever it is, however, one's purpose for engaging in thinking guides the selection and use of the thinking operations employed, the knowledge used, and the dispositions drawn on to energize and direct that thinking. This aspect of thinking is very much at the center of any thinking act.

Of course, it is important here to acknowledge several other features of thinking. One is the developmental nature of thinking. That is, the structures and contexts of any thinking operation and of thinking as a whole become more sophisticated and complex as individuals grow and develop physically and as they accumulate experiences.[12] Furthermore, thinking occurs in different modalities; individuals think in figurative, symbolic, verbal, quantitative, and spatial modalities and, as educator Barbara Presseisen notes, thinking is to some extent carried on differently in each modality.[13] These variables also affect thinking and alter it as individuals grow and develop.

In sum, thinking consists of certain dispositions, knowledge, and operations. These elements give it both character and substance. They are, in effect, the gears of thinking. As they mesh, thinking occurs. The stage of development of the individual doing the thinking, the environment(s) in which the thinking is carried on, the purposes for which it is engaged, and the modalities in which it is employed shape the direction, quality, and precision of thinking. These facets of thinking all interact to produce the results of thinking. Understanding thinking involves understanding the nature and interrelationships of its various components and the internal and external variables that influence it.

A MODEL OF FUNCTIONAL THINKING

As significant as are the major components of thinking in understanding thinking, it is important to remember that thinking is a *process*.[14] It is only when these components engage with the variables noted earlier that thinking occurs. However, for purposes of teaching, we can single out the major components of thinking—operations, knowledge, and dispositions—for special attention. By focusing especially on the thinking operations in terms of the functions they serve in thinking, we can intervene to improve thinking. By providing direct instruction in how to execute these various thinking operations, teachers can sharply improve student abilities to engage in all kinds of thinking. And since the knowledge and dispositions associated with thinking come into play as these operations are executed, attention to thinking operations also enhances the knowledge and disposition components of thinking as well. Thus, focusing on the major functions of thinking and the interrelationships of the key thinking operations that are used to carry out these functions can serve as a basis for a viable instructional program to improve thinking.

As noted earlier, thinking involves two kinds of operations: cognitive and metacognitive. These two types of mental operations differ in the levels at which they are performed, the objects on which they act, and the procedures of which they consist. This two-level conception of thinking operations can be illustrated by focusing on the major operations that constitute each of these levels of thinking. Imagine these operations as a series of concentric circles or rings, as in Figure 3.3. The

Figure 3.3 A Model of Functional Thinking Operations

cognitive or meaning-making operations that constitute thinking make up the central core. The metacognitive, or thought-directing, functions make up the outer ring that wraps around and is superordinate to the inner core of operations used to produce meaning. A further explanation of this concept will clarify the interrelationships of these operations and their functions in thinking.

Cognitive Functions and Operations

The goal of cognition is meaning-making. When any individual thinks, it is for the purpose of producing a specific meaning—a solution to a problem, a new truth, a clearer understanding, a judgment, and so on. To produce such meanings, thinking employs both complex general strategies and more specific, subordinate thinking skills of which these strategies consist. A thinking strategy is an overall plan, such as decision making or problem solving, to produce a thinking product. A thinking skill is a mental operation such as recall or analysis or inductive reasoning, used in conjunction with other similar operations to execute a thinking strategy.

For example, in making a decision or engaging in any other major thinking strategies, an individual takes in and processes all kinds of information, perceptions, and impressions. He or she records input gathered by the senses of sight, smell, touch, and so on, and recalls from memory related data, impressions, and previously constructed thoughts. As this input becomes available, it is manipulated and processed in a number of ways. Individuals reason with and about it, inductively and deductively, analogically and sometimes even metaphorically. They take it apart by analyzing it. They rearrange it creatively to discover or make connections, patterns, and relationships within and among the input and emerging thoughts about it. And they examine it critically to judge the accuracy, worth, and reliability of the input, as well as of the patterns, meanings, and connections perceived or invented. Any purposeful act of thinking, such as to resolve a problem, to make a choice, or to invent or elaborate a concept, involves all of these kinds of thinking operations.

Thus, one might liken the operations that constitute meaning-making—cognition—to a sort of gyroscope. The major thinking strategies constitute a stationary outer rim, keyed to the prescribed strategic goal to be accomplished. The operations on the inner rings of the model—recording and recalling, reasoning and processing, and critical and creative thinking—engage in a variety of combinations, just as the various planes of a gyroscope spin simultaneously as the device proceeds in a specific direction toward the thinking goal. The result is some meaning or truth that did not exist before.

Metacognitive Functions and Operations

Making meaning involves more than simply applying the strategies and skills of cognition to some type of input. It also involves metacognition.[15] Metacognition operates at a level superordinate to that of meaning-making, hence its position in Figure 3.3 as an outer ring of operations. Metacognitive operations are applied to the strategies and skills used to produce meaning rather than directly to data or experience. Metacognitive thinking seeks to control these meaning-making operations—to guide, correct, adjust and, in a word, to direct the selection, sequencing, and execution of the cognitive operations by which one seeks to make meaning. In effect, metacognitive thinking requires individuals to stand outside of their own heads and to be aware of how they are going about their own thinking so they can better accomplish what it is they are trying to accomplish.

Thus, when engaging in decision making, for example, an expert plans in advance what kinds of thinking operations must be undertaken, and monitors how he or she is carrying out these operations as thinking progresses. Alert to obstacles in the way of successful completion of the process, this expert can "shift" cognitive gears to perhaps seek additional or more credible sources to overcome these obstacles, or can redirect his or her thinking to otherwise overcome them. As the process unfolds, the individual continuously assesses the extent to which he or she is approaching the goal, so appropriate operations can be brought into play even if they were omitted from the initial plan. Thinking about one's thinking is a difficult kind of thinking in which to engage, but employing it is one characteristic of individuals who are rated as superior in thinking.[16]

Thinking to make or find meaning differs considerably from metacognition, thinking about how one is engaged in that meaning-making. The former seeks to produce a product; the latter seeks to direct the cognitive operations being employed to produce that product. The former acts directly on data, experience, thoughts, and perceptions; the latter acts on the cognitive operations that generate and manipulate these phenomenon. Mastery of the former is what educators customarily focus on in teaching thinking; mastery of both kinds of thinking, however, is what distinguishes effective and efficient thinkers from novices.

The labels used to describe the thinking operations discussed above do not by any means adequately describe what goes on in one's head when trying to make meaning. Each of the major thinking operations noted in the inner circles of Figure 3.3, for example, consists of several (sometimes many) subordinate and interrelated operations. And each of these operations consists of a procedure or series of steps driven by some rule(s) or principle(s), and informed by specific criteria or knowledge. The operations that constitute thinking consist of much more than can be described by simple, one-word labels or single-sentence definitions. The pages that follow describe some of these major meaning-making or cognitive operations. A description of metacognitive operations then follows. Any educational program designed to improve thinking should attend to both cognitive and metacognitive operations as its instructional core.

COGNITIVE STRATEGIES AND SKILLS

Over the years, cognitive psychologists, educators, and others have identified literally scores of cognitive operations that are employed to make sense out of experience. Some are rather discrete, simple procedures, hereinafter referred to as *skills*. Others are more complex, complicated processes, referred to hereafter as *strategies*. Figure 3.4 lists some of these skills and strategies that seem to cut across a variety of subject areas and disciplines, and which are often included in inventories of thinking operations for teaching. These operations are arranged in three levels, based on their complexity, inclusivity, and functional interrelationships, and are related directly to the model of functional thinking presented earlier.

Thinking Strategies

The operations designated in Figure 3.4 as Level I operations are extremely complex strategies for thinking. Three of these strategies—problem solving, decision making, and conceptualizing—are listed here and described briefly in terms of the major steps or procedures by which they are operationalized. Similarly complex operations, such as comprehension, may also appropriately be considered as thinking strategies.

Four features distinguish thinking strategies from other kinds of thinking operations. First, these strategies are major functions of purposeful thinking, as noted in Figure 3.3. Moreover, each strategy consists of a number of subordinate operations, and each of these subordinate operations itself consists of even more refined and precise subordinate operations. Third, individuals proceed through these strategies generally in the sequence represented by the steps listed here (in Figure 3.4), but not always. In some instances, the various operations are repeated, or the strategy itself is recursive, until one arrives at a final product. Finally, each of these strategies and its subordinate operations utilizes in varying combinations the other thinking skills listed in Figure 3.4. In effect, the strategies of problem solving, decision making, and conceptualizing all serve as structures or frameworks in which individ-

I. THINKING STRATEGIES

Problem Solving

1. Recognize a problem
2. Represent the problem
3. Devise/choose solution plan
4. Execute the plan
5. Evaluate the solution

Decision Making

1. Define the goal
2. Identify alternatives
3. Analyze alternatives
4. Rank alternatives
5. Judge highest-ranked alternatives
6. Choose "best" alternative

Conceptualizing

1. Identify examples
2. Identify common attributes
3. Classify attributes
4. Interrelate categories of attributes
5. Identify additional examples/nonexamples
6. Modify concept attributes/ structure

II. CRITICAL THINKING SKILLS

1. Distinguishing between verifiable facts and value claims
2. Distinguishing relevant from irrelevant information, claims, or reasons
3. Determining the factual accuracy of a statement
4. Determining the credibility of a source
5. Identifying ambiguous claims or arguments
6. Identifying unstated assumptions
7. Detecting bias
8. Identifying logical fallacies
9. Recognizing logical inconsistencies in a line of reasoning
10. Determining the strength of an argument or claim

III. MICRO-THINKING SKILLS

1. Recall
2. Translation
3. Interpretation
4. Extrapolation
5. Application
6. Analysis (compare, contrast, classify, seriate, etc.)
7. Synthesis
8. Evaluation

Reasoning

inductive
deductive
analogical

Figure 3.4 Major Cognitive Operations

uals apply a number of more precise skills in order to produce a meaningful product, such as a solution, a decision, a concept, or an understanding.

Many different descriptions of problem solving exist.[17] The generalized strategy outlined in Figure 3.4 represents a model often used in
mathematics or science, whereas somewhat different models are used in
the social sciences and other disciplines.* Regardless of how problem
solving is conceptualized, most specialists seem to agree that it involves
proceeding through a number of steps—from problem finding and clarifying to identifying a solution and checking it—each of which consists of
many subordinate procedures. Properly executed, this thinking strategy
is a complex plan for resolving problems and situations where there are
solutions that can be objectively determined as correct or preferable to
any other solution.

Decision making, another major thinking strategy, is often considered to be identical to problem solving. Indeed, some experts combine
the two into one extended procedure and treat all problems as essentially situations requiring decisions about solutions.[18] Other experts see
decision making as a process that differs considerably from problem
solving. In their view, decision making, unlike problem solving, involves (1) choosing from a number of acceptable alternatives when there
is generally no accepted, best, or correct alternative; (2) simultaneous
evaluation of alternatives rather than serial testing; (3) use of nonexperi-
mental, qualitative, and quantitative criteria in analyzing various alternatives; and (4) repeated reference to values in applying these criteria.[19]
Whereas to some, decision making may seem very much like problem
solving, to others it is a distinct type of thinking process. Here, it is
treated as a distinct strategy.

Like other major thinking strategies, decision making is extremely
complex, consisting of a number of operations each of which embodies
additional subordinate operations. The description of decision making
outlined in Figure 3.4 clearly distinguishes this strategy from a general
problem-solving strategy. Probably the most significant feature of this
strategy is the making, analyzing, and evaluating of choices, and then
the reevaluation of a selected number of highly ranked options before
making a final choice.

The decision-making model presented in Figure 3.4 is but one conceptualization of this strategy. As Joe B. Hurst and his colleagues have
pointed out, it has been conceptualized in other ways, too.[20] The point
to remember here, however, is that in its most refined form, decision
making can be extremely complex and involve a host of rather precise
cognitive operations at each step of the way.

---

* Detailed descriptions of selected thinking skills and strategies may be found in
Chapters 6, 7, and 8.

Conceptualizing is a third major thinking strategy. Individuals engage in conceptualizing when they generalize from specifics to invent concepts or models. Like problem solving and decision making, conceptualizing is a lengthy and complex process, consisting of many operations and subordinate operations. The breakdown of key steps in conceptualizing in Figure 3.4 enumerates some of the most important of these operations.

Essentially, conceptualizing involves identifying the key or critical attributes of several members of a class or category of phenomena, and then, by continued application of these attributes to additional specific examples of the phenomena, building a generalized mental image that articulates the common features of the examples and their interrelationships.[21] Individuals build a concept of "pet" from examples of domesticated birds, cats, dogs, horses, and so on. They build a concept of analytical thinking from examining repeated examples, often self-generated, of how it seems to operate. Through this or similar processes, individuals build mental models that enable them to make sense out of the increasingly voluminous and disparate experiences and data that constitute life.[22]

Micro-Thinking Skills

These Level III cognitive skills are of two types: basic information processing operations and reasoning operations. The information processing operations are derived from Benjamin Bloom and his colleagues' analysis of cognitive educational objectives.[23] The reasoning operations are those traditionally taught in logic and philosophy.[24]

Bloom and his colleagues, it may be recalled, identified only six key operations, combining translation, interpretation, and extrapolation as comprehension. However, for purposes of clarity and efficient teaching, these three operations are recognized here as important enough to stand individually. Bloom and his colleagues furthermore conceptualized all these operations as a taxonomy in which each operation included all those antecedent to it; thus, when one analyzes data, one engages in recall, translation, interpretation, extrapolation, and application, as well as in those specific procedures that constitute analysis.

These skills are relatively simple and straightforward, as are the others at this level of thinking. The skill of analysis, for example, comes in many forms, including comparing, contrasting, classifying, and identifying all kinds of relationships and patterns. However, analysis, in essence, involves a relatively uncomplicated procedure. Operationalizing this skill involves:

- Determining the purpose of the analysis
- Recalling or identifying the clues or criteria needed to achieve the purpose

- Searching data piece-by-piece to find evidence of these clues or criteria
- Determining the pattern among this evidence or these clues
- Stating the results of the analysis

Other information processing skills are at about this same level of complexity. None are as complex as the major thinking strategies. Each micro-thinking skill consists of only a limited number of steps, procedures, and rules.

Reasoning is the lubricant by which the various processing operations of interpretation, analysis, synthesis, and evaluation are operationalized and executed. By reasoning inductively from many specifics, one can infer broader meaning such as generalizations, principles, and the like. By reasoning deductively, one can move from general principles to specifics. Most syllogisms, for example, involve deductive reasoning, as, for instance:

- Only students in trouble get called to the office.
- A student, Ronnie, was just called to the office.
- Ronnie is in trouble!

The process involved in such reasoning is used in many critical thinking operations and other higher-level skills to move us from accepted truths to new ones.

The micro-thinking operations listed in Figure 3.4 are actually the building blocks that constitute those operations described as Level I strategies. Each of them is used repeatedly at different steps in every thinking strategy. Analysis, for example, is used in identifying a problem, again in generating hypothetical answers or solution plans, and in processing data as these hypotheses are tested and plans applied. This also applies to the other micro-thinking skills. They serve as building blocks to flesh out the structures that thinking strategies establish.

Critical Thinking

Critical thinking is one of the most abused terms in our thinking skills vocabulary.* Generally, critical thinking means whatever its users stipu-

---

* Ideally, the term *critical thinking* will some day be replaced by a more precise term, such as *evaluative thinking*. Critical thinking has unfortunate, negative connotations. It implies harsh criticism, fault finding, or negative judgments. Use of this term to describe important skills of evaluation used in everyday acts of thinking evokes needless confusion, suspicion, and at times even hostility. Referring to these specific skills as *evaluative thinking* can eliminate this negative

late it to mean. In some circles, the term *critical thinking* is used to mean all thinking operations, from decision making, to analysis of part-whole relationships, to recall. In other circles, it means the skills drawn from Bloom's taxonomy. Actually, critical thinking is none of these. According to experts in critical thinking, this type of thinking consists essentially of judging the authenticity, worth, or accuracy of something.[25] That something may be a piece of information, a claim or assertion, or a source of data. It is essentially what Dewey described as:

> . . . active persistent and careful consideration of any belief or supposed form of knowledge in the light of the grounds that support it and the further conclusions to which it tends.[26]

Contrary to assumptions that critical thinking is, of necessity, negative or carping, when this type of thinking is properly employed, it is objective and free of substantive bias. As educator Catherine Cornbleth writes, this means two things:

> First, critical thinking is not inherently negative. Skepticism is not synonomous with negativism. It means questioning what might otherwise be taken for granted or summarily rejected. Critical thinking can lead to affirmation on firmer grounds as well as to debunking and modification or rejection of ideas. Critical thinking thus has both conservative and liberating potential. Second, the skepticism that characterizes critical thinking is not frivolous. It does not mean automatically questioning anything and everything.[27]

In sum, critical thinking is essentially evaluative in nature. It involves precise, persistent, and objective analysis of any claim, source, or belief to judge its accuracy, validity, or worth.

Unlike problem solving, decision making, or other Level I operations previously described, critical thinking is not a strategy. It does not consist of a sequence of operations and subordinate procedures through which one proceeds in generally sequential fashion. Instead, critical thinking is a collection of specific operations that may be used singly or in any combination or in any order.[28] Figure 3.4 lists ten of these critical thinking operations, those most often referred to in the literature of science, language arts, and social studies instruction. They are listed not as a taxonomy but rather are arranged from the simple to the more complex. An individual may engage in one or more of these, in any

---

reaction and describe even more accurately the operations to which it refers. However, to avoid adding to an already confusing labyrinth of ill-defined terminology and concepts regarding thinking skills, the term *critical thinking* will be used throughout these pages to describe what experts today generally mean by this label.

order, and have engaged in critical thinking. For instance, one can search for bias, distinguish statements of fact from value judgments, and identify logical fallacies without engaging in any other of the operations listed in Figure 3.4, and have engaged in critical thinking.

Each critical thinking operation, furthermore, involves both analysis and evaluation. That is, each of these operations involves, first, taking data apart to find evidence related to certain criteria and, then, judging the extent to which what has been found meets the criteria implied by the skill. In trying to determine if a paragraph is relevant to a given claim, for example, one first takes the paragraph apart sentence-by-sentence and judges the extent to which each sentence and then the overall paragraph pertains to the claim. Consequently, critical thinking operations are more complex than the micro-thinking skills listed as Level III skills, but less complex than the Level I thinking strategies.

However, like the Level III micro-thinking skills, the operations that constitute critical thinking are used at various points in each of the major thinking strategies listed in Level I. Thus, for example, the skill of distinguishing statements of fact from value claims is performed in the course of recognizing a problem, as well as in executing a solution strategy such as the strategy of testing hypotheses. This same skill is also used in identifying decision opportunities and in evaluating alternatives as one engages in decision making. Critical thinking operations are thus somewhere between major thinking strategies and micro-thinking skills in complexity, function, and inclusivity, and hence are listed here as Level II skills.

Probably the most all-inclusive act of critical thinking is that of argumentation—argument making and argument analyzing. An argument, in critical thinking terms, is an assertion or claim accompanied by a line of reasoning that supports this claim and that denies any alternative claims. Most of the critical thinking skills listed in Figure 3.4 are used in producing and judging such arguments.[29] Either of these processes constitute a useful framework for teaching and practicing the other skills of critical thinking.

It should be noted that not all operations commonly assumed to be useful in critical thinking are, in fact, useful. For example, although some specialists include separating facts from opinions as such a skill, many do not.[30] There will probably always be some disagreement about which operations are important critical thinking operations.* However,

---

* The skill of distinguishing facts from opinions is particularly troublesome. Successful execution of this skill depends on one's definition of a "fact." Is a fact a true statement? Is a fact something that has been proven? Is a fact something that is capable of being proven, now or some time in the future, true or false? A *verified* fact implies something that has already been proven true or correct. A

the single most important criterion for delineating a thinking operation as a critical thinking skill must remain the criterion that, as educator Isidor Starr once wrote, the skill seeks to "differentiate truth from falsehood, fact from fiction."[31] The operations presented in Figure 3.4 as components of critical thinking fit this criterion exactly.

Unlike micro-skills, critical thinking is also distinguished by a large and unique number of dispositions that inform and drive it. Educators Dorothy McClure Fraser and Edith West noted that individuals adept at critical thinking exhibit: (1) an *alertness* to the need to evaluate information, assertions, and sources; (2) a *willingness* to test opinions; and (3) a *desire* to consider all viewpoints.[32] Philosopher Richard Paul calls the attitudes that constitute critical thinking "passions," and he includes among them:

- A passion for clarity, accuracy, and fair-mindedness
- A fervor for getting to the bottom of things
- A compelling drive to seek out evidence
- An intense aversion to contradiction, sloppy thinking, inconsistent application of standards
- A devotion to truth as against self-interest
- A [willingness] to question what is passionately believed and socially sanctioned
- A [willingness] to conquer the fear of abandoning a long and deeply held belief[33]

A critical thinker approaches information, assertions, and experi-

---

verifiable fact suggests something capable of being submitted to impartial testing so it can be proven true or false. Unless it is perfectly clear to students what a fact is, attempting to classify statements like the following can lead to more heat than light:

The earth is flat.

This statement is not a fact in one sense of the term because it has been proven false; yet it can be considered a statement of fact that can be submitted to impartial testing, which can prove it true or false. This is not a verified fact but a verifiable factual statement.

In this instance, testing of this particular skill poses a special problem. Test makers rarely define the criteria implicit in this skill as they test it. And the only way to decide which definition of fact is used by a particular test assessing facts and opinions is to check the answers to fact/opinion questions to identify the nature of the answers deemed correct. Only tests that match the definitions used in teaching this skill should be used. Teachers must be sure that definitions of fact or statement of fact are clear to the students, and that there is congruence between the way the skill is taught in class and the way it is tested.

ence with a healthy skepticism about what is *really* true, accurate, or real, as well as with a desire to search through all kinds of evidence and engage in considerable analysis to determine that "truth." As philosopher John McPeck writes, critical thinking involves not only knowing "when to question something and what sorts of questions to ask" but an inclination to do so.[34] Critical thinking, in its most refined state, is a frame of mind, set of attitudes and dispositions, as well as a number of cognitive operations.

Creative Thinking

Although no skills specifically labeled as creative thinking are shown in Figure 3.4, a word about creative thinking should be added here.* Figure 3.3 suggests that creative thinking is related to critical thinking, as indeed appears to be the case. Perhaps philosopher Michael Scriven has described this relationship most accurately in noting:

> Critical skills go hand in hand with creative ones; creativity is not just a matter of being different from other people, its a matter of having a different idea that works as well or better than previous ideas. . . . [O]riginality . . . means novelty and validity.[35]

Clearly, however, creative and critical thinking are not the same thing. Whereas creative thinking is divergent, critical thinking is convergent; whereas creative thinking seeks to generate something new, critical thinking seeks to assess worth or validity in something that exists; whereas creative thinking is carried on often by violating accepted principles, critical thinking is carried on by applying accepted principles. Although creative and critical thinking may very well be different sides of the same coin, they are not identical.

On the other hand, creative thinking, like critical thinking, is distinguished by a number of unique dispositions. In fact, as Alan J. McCormack and David Perkins note, creative thinking is largely a state of mind.[36] It seems to be primarily guided—indeed, driven—by a desire to seek the original. It values mobility, it revels in exploration, it feeds on

---

* The term *creative thinking*, although posing less of a communication problem than that of *critical thinking*, also deserves to be replaced by one less tinged with unfortunate connotations. Over the years, creative thinking has come to be tied essentially to the fine arts and to literary enterprise, in spite of the fact that *creative thinking*—the invention of new patterns, relationships, combinations, or products—occurs in all disciplines and subject areas in the forms of synthesizing and inductive reasoning. Consequently, a more descriptive and less restrictive label such as *generative thinking* might be a more appropriate descriptor of this type of thinking.

flexibility, and it honors diversity. As Perkins notes, creative thinking attends to purpose as much or more than to results, works at the edge of one's competence, and is driven by intrinsic motivation to be original.[37] Creative thinking may well be more the application of these dispositions and motives in the course of executing major thinking strategies like problem solving than it is any particular set of unique thinking skills.

Some experts, in fact, consider creative thinking to be closely related to problem solving. For them, creative thinking is problem solving applied to creative ends.[38] Cognitive psychologist John R. Hayes, for example, asserts, "A creative solution is a problem solving act, and, in particular, it is the solution of an ill-defined problem."[39] Hayes points out that the key cognitive operations in creative thinking—problem finding, idea generating, and planning—are all part of problem solving. Furthermore, the more specific operations that constitute these key operations appear to be largely what Benjamin Bloom and his colleagues labeled *synthesis*. One may invent a rather creative hypothesis out of an in-depth analysis of a problem; one may develop an original solution to a problem; one may invent an argument by combining reasoning and evidence in a new way; one may invent alternatives or, as philosopher Michael Scriven notes, reason from old truths to new truths.[40] All of these are the products of synthesis making. Although many educators have devised numerous heuristics or conditions for stimulating creativity, none seem to have identified clearly any cognitive skills that can be said to be exclusively creative, other than the skill of synthesis making.[41]

In thinking for virtually any purpose—to resolve a problem or make a decision or conceptualize—one engages in creative as well as critical thinking over and over again. One invents new combinations and critically evaluates them. One also employs reasoning in both creative and critical thinking. And all of these operations are performed in executing problem solving and other major cognitive strategies. Table 3.1 illustrates this interaction of skills and strategies in terms of how selected critical and micro-thinking skills are used in a general problem-solving strategy. In this example, for instance, the skill of distinguishing the relevant from irrelevant is used in recognizing a problem, as well as in representing a problem and executing a solution strategy. Inductive and deductive reasoning are used in every step of this strategy. Synthesizing produces a problem statement, a solution strategy, and a conclusion. These same skills are also used at various stages in decision making and conceptualizing. Various critical and micro-thinking skills are used over and over again in various combinations to execute different thinking strategies.

The intermixing of these various kinds of thinking in any specific thinking act merely attests to the complexity of thinking. Yet these thinking strategies and skills can be identified as discrete operations.

Table 3.1 Role of Selected Thinking Skills in a Problem-Solving Strategy

Strategy / *Problem Solving*	Skills Used / *Critical Thinking*	*Micro-Thinking*
Recognize a Problem	Distinguish relevant from irrelevant Distinguish facts from value claims Identify bias Identify ambiguous/equivocal claims Identify logical fallacies	Recall Interpret Extrapolate Analyze—compare, contrast, classify Identify parts of a pattern/whole Reason inductively, deductively
Represent a Problem	Distinguish relevant from irrelevant Recognize components of an argument Identify unstated assumptions Recognize logical inconsistencies in a line of reasoning	Recall Analyze Extrapolate/predict Synthesize Reason inductively, deductively, analogically
Plan/Choose a Solution Strategy	Determine credibility of a source Identify bias Identify unstated assumptions Distinguish relevant/irrelevant	Recall Extrapolate Reason inductively, deductively Reason by analogy Evaluate Synthesize

Execute the Solution Strategy	
Distinguish relevant/irrelevant	Recall
Distinguish fact/value claim	Interpret
Determine credibility of a source	Extrapolate
Determine factual accuracy of a statement	Apply
Recognize logical inconsistencies	Analyze
	Synthesize
	Reason inductively, deductively
Evaluate the Solution and Strategy	
Recognize bias	Analyze—compare, contrast
Recognize unstated assumptions	Evaluate
Recognize ambiguous claims	Reason inductively, deductively
Recognize logical inconsistencies in a line of reasoning	
Determine the strength of a claim	

Thus it is possible to attend to them individually, to intervene, and to provide instruction in each of them that will enable the entire process of thinking to work better whenever it engages. An effective program in the teaching of thinking makes explicit provision for such instruction throughout a number of grades and subjects in specific skills and strategies that constitute thinking.

METACOGNITIVE STRATEGIES AND SKILLS

Skillful thinking involves thinking about how one thinks as well as thinking to make meaning. The mental operations by which individuals control the cognitive skills and strategies they use to make meaning is referred to by experts as *metacognition*. A number of educators and researchers consider metacognition as the highest, most sophisticated form of thinking.[42] Many, in fact, conceive of it as the executive function of the mind, that operation by which individuals manage and direct how they go about using their minds.[43]

Metacognition can be described as an overall general strategy or plan for thinking that employs very specific procedures or skills to carry out that plan. As a strategy, metacognition consists essentially of three major operations: planning, monitoring/directing, and assessing a thinking task. Furthermore, each of these three operations consists of a number of subordinate procedures by which that operation is carried out. Figure 3.5 outlines one model of this process.

Components of Metacognition

Although metacognition, as described here, may appear to be rather sequential, in practice it is not strictly linear but recursive. In executing any cognitive skill or strategy, an effective thinker customarily starts by planning how she or he will go about doing it and then continuously refers to that plan in carrying out the operation. Then, in executing the plan, he or she assesses the extent to which the plan is working, and may revise the plan and even perform unplanned operations as a result of this continuing assessment.[44]

Planning is perhaps the most important facet of metacognition. Before jumping into a thinking task, skillful thinkers plan just how they are going to carry it out. Such anticipatory thinking or predicting not only makes the actual execution of the thinking operations involved easier, but is more likely than undirected thinking to achieve the desired goal and to produce a product of quality. Three major tasks are usually involved in such planning: setting a clear goal, laying out a strategy or plan for achieving that goal, and anticipating potential roadblocks to successful execution of the plan.

I. PLANNING

> Stating a goal
> Selecting operations to perform
> Sequencing operations
> Identifying potential obstacles/errors
> Identifying ways to recover from obstacles/errors
> Predicting results desired and/or anticipated

II. MONITORING

> Keeping the goal in mind
> Keeping one's place in a sequence
> Knowing when a subgoal has been achieved
> Deciding when to go on to the next operation
> Selecting next appropriate operation
> Spotting errors or obstacles
> Knowing how to recover from errors, overcome obstacles

III. ASSESSING

> Assessing goal achievement
> Judging accuracy and adequacy of the results
> Evaluating appropriateness of procedures used
> Assessing handling of obstacles/errors
> Judging efficiency of the plan and its execution

Figure 3.5 Key Operations in Metacognition

After stating and clarifying the goal to be accomplished, an individual selects the most appropriate thinking operations to perform—whether to identify the type of data needed, search for common characteristics in that data, or whatever—and then arranges these operations in a sequence that gives promise of accomplishing that goal. This operation also usually involves attempts to identify any obstacles that may arise, such as the absence of some data that may be needed, or errors that could be made, and seeks to plan immediately how to overcome such obstacles or correct or avoid any anticipated errors. These acts require recalling past experience with the particular operations chosen or data to be used, and predicting on the basis of similar past experiences. Finally, by predicting the desired and anticipated results of the task to be undertaken, the individual can keep a focus on the goal in executing the thinking plan just devised.

As the individual then executes the thinking plan, he or she consciously checks or monitors what is going on mentally to ensure executing the task as planned, to avoid skipping or using incorrectly any steps or rules, and to see if the operations being used are producing the desired results. As educator Arthur L. Costa notes, monitoring thinking involves both looking backward to the plan and looking ahead to anticipate appropriate future moves.[45] It also involves attending very carefully to what is going on at the moment. Juggling all three types of operations requires considerable mental effort and skill, and it involves the ability to deal with different levels of abstractions.

Monitoring and directing any act of thinking consists of keeping one's place in a sequence of planned operations and applying criteria of effectiveness and accuracy to each procedure used. These operations help to assess when a subgoal has been achieved and provide a basis for deciding when it is appropriate to move on to the next procedure in carrying out the thinking strategy. This involves recalling what has occurred thus far. It also involves assessing the reasonableness and accuracy of the results obtained as of the moment. And it involves comparing the current status of the act with similar efforts performed in the past and with the results anticipated in the earlier planning of the process.

Metacognitive thinking requires that the individual continuously keeps the goal in mind—a forward-looking task—so as to anticipate what is likely to or should happen next. Hence, one must not only recall the sequence of planned operations remaining to be used, but remain alert to possible obstacles and errors likely to be encountered down the line, as well as what to do at the moment to minimize the likelihood that problems will crop up or what to be ready to do if they do occur. This means the individual must be receptive to various types of feedback and must know the kinds of information needed from it. In essence, monitoring a thinking act consists of being conscious of what one is doing, where it fits in a planned sequence of steps, and what ought to occur next even as one is actually engaged in the thinking act itself, and then making mental moves to move the process forward to fruition.

A third major step in metacognition consists of assessing both the process employed to achieve the goal and the product produced by this process. During and at the conclusion of a thinking task, an individual engaging in metacognition assesses the entire operation. This involves attending to three things: the quality of the product, the quality of the procedures used to generate the product, and the way in which any obstacles were handled. The individual assesses the reasonableness and accuracy of the substantive product generated by the thinking skill or strategy in which he or she has been engaged (e.g., the solution, the decision, the classification scheme) to determine the extent to which the goal was achieved. The process itself and the operations of which it consisted are also evaluated to determine the extent to which they proved useful and efficient in achieving the desired goal and any subgoals along the way. As part of this process, one also reflects on the obstacles or errors encountered to determine how well they were anticipated and handled, as well as whether they could have been avoided altogether or handled differently. Finally, an overall judgment is usually made about the efficiency of the overall plan. Modifications are made in it for future use on similar occasions before storing the entire experience in long-term memory.

The Nature of Metacognition

This description of metacognition represents a rather idealized conception of what happens in one's mind when engaging in thinking most effectively and efficiently. It is not something that young students or novices customarily do or do well. Because thinking about thinking involves engaging in abstract processing or other rather abstract processes, it appears to be tied closely to the development of an individual's stage of formal abstract thinking, which in many instances does not mature until after students leave high school.[46] As surprisingly as it may seem, for example, while 68 percent of high school freshmen are at the concrete operational stage of cognitive development, about 66 percent of our students are at this same stage upon graduation from high school three years later, even though more of them are making significant movement in this direction by that time.[47] Thus, learning how to engage in metacognition comes slowly for even may older students.

Metacognition is also linked closely to the dispositions, knowledge, and cognitive operations that constitute thinking. The effort and attention that generate thinking are applied essentially through metacognitive operations. Thus, key dispositions such as the willingness to engage in thinking, a disposition to stay at it until the goal has been achieved, and an insistence on evidence and reasoning to justify conclusions and assertions directly support and drive metacognitive activity. The dispositions described earlier in this chapter seem, in fact, to be integral to successful metacognition.

THINKING AND THINKING SKILLS

Thinking operations can be conceptualized in a number of ways. One such conceptualization, a model of functional thinking, was presented in Figure 3.3. Beyond its major functions, thinking consists of many discrete operations and strategies, some quite complex, and others less so. Some of these operations are so general as to cut across and undergird various types of thinking; others are very precise and primarily related to specific cognitive tasks. Figure 3.4 identified some of the more important of these strategies and skills. Most of these operations are used in different combinations with each other in order to achieve different purposes.

Thinking and thinking skills, it should be remembered, are not synonymous. We need to distinguish clearly between them. *Thinking* is a holistic process by which we mentally manipulate sensory input and recalled data to formulate thoughts, reason about, or judge. It involves perception, prior experience, conscious manipulation, incubation, and intuition, as well as the application of certain operations, knowledge, and dispositions. Through this complex and only partially understood phenomenon, we give meaning to experience.

Thinking skills and strategies, on the other hand, are very specific operations we deliberately perform on or with data in order to accomplish our thinking goals—operations like identifying a problem, finding unstated assumptions, or assessing the strength of an argument. Like any other skill performance, thinking is a combination of many variables, but greater in sum than all of these variables combined. Just as tennis consists of many specific skills (serving, making drop shots, lobbing, and volleying), thinking also consists of specific skills, the mastery of each of which contributes to the effective performance of the entire process. Just as playing tennis requires the integration of specific skills with an overall strategy in a given context for a purpose, so too does thinking require the integration of specific skills with an overall strategy in a given context for a purpose. Deliberate, continuing, explicit attention to these specific skills can improve proficiency in the complete performance of thinking. Developing an educational program to improve student thinking consists of selecting these skills and arranging the education and training required to accomplish this goal. The remaining chapters address this task.

ENDNOTES

1. Hannah Arendt, "Thinking II," *The New Yorker* (November 28, 1977), p. 121.

2. John Dewey, *How We Think* (Boston: D.C. Heath, 1910), pp. 8–9.

3. Ann L. Brown, Joseph C. Campione, and Jeanne D. Day, "Learning to Learn: On Training Students to Learn from Texts," *Educational Researcher 10*, 2 (February 1981): 14–21; Arthur L. Costa, "Mediating the Metacognitive," *Educational Leadership 42*, 3 (November 1984): 57–62.

4. Barry K. Beyer, *Teaching Thinking in Social Studies* (rev. ed.) (Columbus, Ohio: Charles E. Merrill, 1979), pp. 22–26

5. Walter Doyle, "Academic Work," *Review of Educational Research 53*, 2 (Summer 1983): 163–173.

6. John McPeck, *Critical Thinking and Education* (New York: St. Martin's Press, 1981); Raymond S. Nickerson, "Kinds of Thinking Taught in Current Programs," *Educational Leadership 42*, 1 (September 1984): 35–36.

7. Jerome Bruner, *The Process of Education* (Cambridge, Mass.: Harvard University Press, 1960), pp. 181–185.

8. Robert Ennis, "A Logical Basis for Measuring Critical Thinking Skills,"

Educational Leadership 43, 2 (October 1985): 46; Robert Ennis, "Rational Thinking and Educational Practice," in Jonas F. Soltis, ed., *Philosophy and Education: 80th Yearbook of the National Society for the Study of Education, Part I* (Chicago: National Society for the Study of Education, 1981).

9. Ibid.; David R. Krathwohl, et al., *Taxonomy of Educational Objectives— Handbook II: Affective Domain* (New York: Longmans, 1964), pp. 181–185; Arthur L. Costa, "Thinking: How Do We Know Students Are Getting Better At It?" *Roeper Review* (April 1984): 197–198.

10. Herbert A. Simon, "Information-processing Theory of Human Problem Solving," in W. K. Estes, ed., *Handbook of Learning and Cognitive Process, Vol. 5: Human Information Processing* (Hillsdale, N.J.: Lawrence Erlbaum Associates, 1978), pp. 271–295.

11. Doyle, "Academic Work," pp. 159–199.

12. Irving E. Sigel, "A Constructionist Perspective for Teaching Thinking," *Educational Leadership 42*, 3 (November 1984): 18–21; Irving Sigel and R. R. Cocking, *Cognitive Development from Childhood to Adolescence* (New York: Holt, Rinehart & Winston, 1977).

13. Barbara Z. Presseisen, *Thinking Skills Throughout the Curriculum: A Conceptual Design* (Philadelphia: Research for Better Schools, 1985).

14. See, for example, Robert J. Sternberg, *Beyond I.Q.: A Triarchic Theory of Human Intelligence* (New York: Cambridge University Press, 1985); John Anderson, *The Architecture of Cognition* (Cambridge, Mass.: Harvard University Press, 1983); Richard W. Burns and Gary D. Brooks, "Processes, Problem Solving and Curriculum Reform," *Educational Technology 10* (May 1970): 10–13.

15. John H. Flavell, "Metacognitive Aspects of Problem Solving," in Lauren B. Resnick, ed., *The Nature of Intelligence* (Hillsdale, N.J.: Lawrence Erlbaum Associates, 1976), pp. 231–235; Brown, Campione, and Day, "Learning to Learn," pp. 14–21.

16. Benjamin Bloom and Lois Broder, *Problem Solving Processes of College Students* (Chicago: University of Chicago Press, 1950).

17. Norman Federiksen, "Implications of Cognitive Theory for Instruction in Problem Solving," *Review of Educational Research 54*, 3 (Fall 1984): 363–407.

18. Charles E. Wales and Anne Nardi, *Successful Decision-Making* (Morgantown: West Virginia University Center for Guided Design, 1984).

19. Charles H. Kepner and Benjamin B. Trego, *The New Rational Manager* (Princeton, N.J.: Princeton Research Press, 1981).

20. Joe B. Hurst, et al., "The Decision Making Process," *Theory and Research in Social Education 11*, 3 (Fall 1983): 17–43.

21. Peter H. Martorella, *Concept Learning: Designs for Instruction* (Scranton, Pa.: Intext Educational Publishers, 1982); David Merrill and Robert D. Tennyson, *Teaching Concepts: An Instructional Design Guide* (Englewood Cliffs, N.J.: Education Technology Publications, 1977).

22. Beyer, *Teaching Thinking in Social Studies*, pp. 184–190.

23. Benjamin Bloom, et al., *Taxonomy of Educational Objectives—Handbook I: The Cognitive Domain* (New York: Longmans, 1956).

24. See, for example, Michael Scriven, *Reasoning* (New York: McGraw-Hill, 1976); W. H. Werkmeister, *An Introduction to Critical Thinking—A Beginner's Text in Logic* (Lincoln, Neb.: Johnsen Publishing, 1957).

25. Robert Ennis, "A Concept of Critical Thinking," *Harvard Educational Review 32*, 1 (Winter 1962): 81–111; McPeck, *Critical Thinking and Education.*

26. Dewey, *How We Think*, p. 9.

27. Catherine Cornbleth, "Critical Thinking and Cognitive Process," in William B. Stanley, ed., *Review of Research in Social Studies Education 1976–1983,* Bulletin #75 (Washington, D.C.: National Council for the Social Studies, 1985), p. 14.

28. For an elaboration of this point, see Barry K. Beyer, "Critical Thinking: What Is It?" *Social Education 49*, 4 (April 1985): 270–276.

29. Steven Toulmin, Richard Rieke, and Allan Janik, *An Introduction to Reasoning* (2d ed.) (New York: Macmillan, 1984).

30. Jean Fair, "Skills in Thinking," in Dana Kurfman, ed., *Developing Decision-Making Skills: 47th Yearbook* (Washington, D.C.: National Council for the Social Studies, 1977), pp. 38–39.

31. Isidor Starr, "The Nature of Critical Thinking and its Application in Social Studies," in Helen McCracken Carpenter, ed., *Skill Development in Social Studies: 33rd Yearbook* (Washington, D.C.: National Council for the Social Studies, 1963), p. 36.

32. Dorothy McClure Fraser and Edith West, *Social Studies in Secondary Schools* (New York: Ronald Press, 1961), p. 222.

33. Richard Paul, "Dialogical Thinking: Critical Thought Essential to the Acquisition of Rational Knowledge and Passions," in Joan Baron and Robert Sternberg, eds., *Teaching Thinking Skills: Theory and Practice* (New York: W. H. Freeman, 1987), pp. 127–148.

34. McPeck, *Critical Thinking and Education*, pp. 7, 9, 152.

35. Scriven, *Reasoning*, p. 37.

36. Alan J. McCormack, "Teaching Inventiveness," *Childhood Education* (March/April 1984): 249–255; David Perkins, "Learning by Design," *Educational Leadership 42*, 1 (September 1984): 18–25.

37. Perkins, "Learning by Design."

38. See, for example, Sidney Parnes, *Creative Problem Solving* (Buffalo, N.Y.: D.O.K. Publishers, 1978); A. F. Osborne, *Applied Imagination* (New York: Scribner's, 1963).

39. John R. Hayes, *The Complete Problem Solver* (Philadelphia: The Franklin Institute Press, 1981), p. 125.

40. Scriven, *Reasoning*, p. 57.

41. See, for example, the summary of research in Bryce Hudgins, *Learning and Thinking* (Itasca, Ill.: F. E. Peacock, 1977), pp. 256–294.

42. Sternberg, *Beyond I.Q.*; Robert J. Sternberg, "How Can We Teach Intelligence?" *Educational Leadership 42*, 1 (September 1984): 38–50; Raymond S. Nickerson, David N. Perkins, Edward E. Smith, *The Teaching of Thinking* (Hillsdale, N.J.: Lawrence Erlbaum Associates, 1985), pp. 100–109.

43. Brown, Campione, and Day, "Learning to Learn," pp. 14–21; Judith W. Segal and Susan F. Chipman, "Thinking and Learning Skills: The Contributions of NIE," *Educational Leadership 42*, 1 (September 1984): 86.

44. Arthur Whimbey, "Students Can Learn to Be Better Problem Solvers,"

Educational Leadership 37, 7 (April 1980): 560–565; Ann L. Brown, "Knowing When, Where and How to Remember: A Problem of Mega-cognition," in Robert Glaser, ed., *Advances In Instructional Psychology* (Hillsdale, N.J.: Lawrence Erlbaum Associates, 1978).

45. Costa, "Mediating the Metacognitive," pp. 57–62.

46. Ibid., p. 57.

47. H. T. Epstein, "Growth Spurts During Brain Development: Implications for Educational Policy and Practice," in J. F. Chall and A. F. Mirsky, eds., *Education and the Brain* (Chicago: University of Chicago Press, 1987); Martin Brooks, Esther Fusco, and Jacqueline Grennon, "Cognitive Levels Matching," *Educational Leadership 41*, 8 (May 1983): 4–5.

4

Structuring a Thinking Skills Program

In developing a thinking skills program, curriculum developers must make a number of crucial decisions. Of paramount importance, of course, are those relating to the specific thinking skills and strategies that are to form the subject matter of the program and the strategies by which to teach these skills and strategies. However, to a considerable extent these decisions are shaped by and do themselves shape decisions about something even more crucial—the organization or structure of the overall thinking skills program of which they are to be a part.

For good or ill, no single "best" thinking skills program or "best way" to structure a thinking skills program exists, but a variety of promising options do. This chapter outlines some of these options and the factors that ought to be considered in making key decisions about the nature of any multigrade thinking skills program. It concludes by identifying criteria for determining the potential quality of whatever kind of thinking skills program is eventually developed and offered for adoption.

STRUCTURING A THINKING SKILLS CURRICULUM

What are some of the ways in which to structure the teaching of thinking? Basing his work on that of Robert Ennis, philosophy instructor Philip A. Pecorino suggests there are essentially four options.[1] One option is to assume each course in a school's curriculum automatically teaches appropriate thinking skills, and leave it at that. However, such an approach seems to be the conventional approach that is so lacking already. It suffers from at least three weaknesses insofar as teaching thinking skills is concerned. First, content teaching generally takes precedence over skill teaching in such courses at present. Second, there is no locus of responsibility in this arrangement for teaching specific thinking operations. Finally, most teachers seem unaware of how best to teach these skills and strategies. Such conditions make skill learning in this approach largely a hit or miss affair—mostly a "miss."

A second option for structuring a thinking skills program consists of assigning the responsibility of teaching selected thinking skills and strategies to clusters of courses, defined primarily by subjects. In this option, according to Pecorino, science courses might thus concentrate on teaching principles and procedures of inductive reasoning, hypothesis testing, and quantitative analysis. Math courses might focus on teaching deductive reasoning and the symbolic representation of problems, solution plans, and argument forms. Writing might provide a vehicle for argument generation and analysis, as well as for various critical thinking operations such as determining logical consistency, detecting logical fallacies, and determining the credibility of sources. By assigning the skills to be taught to specific subject areas, this option reduces the burden on all teachers. However, it fails to provide for transfer and elaboration of all skills across the variety of subject areas required to generalize skill learning. In addition, this option suffers from all the faults of the first option, cited above.

A third choice consists of having certain thinking skills and strategies taught in a special thinking skills course. This might involve offering instruction in thinking as an elective or as a special course. In this approach, total responsibility for teaching selected thinking skills would fall to the instructors of such "stand alone" courses. However, without follow-up skill instruction, transfer, and elaboration in subsequent subject matter courses, such special thinking skills courses offer little hope of developing the level of student proficiency in thinking that other options offer.

The fourth option provides for the introduction of selected thinking skills and strategies in a special "subject matter-free" course for all students, but with follow-up instruction in these thinking operations provided in subsequent subject matter courses. In this structure, langauge arts courses might thus reinforce thinking skills associated with reading, writing, and speaking; science and math courses could reinforce quantitative analysis, scientific reasoning, and inference-making skills; history and literature courses could reinforce relationship making, explanation, and various analytical skills such as cause/effect and so on; arts and humanities courses could reinforce skills associated with creative thinking. Here, the special, introductory "content-free" thinking skills course that stands by itself is followed by skills transfer and elaboration in subsequent subject matter courses.

Other options may also exist, but these four seem to represent the range open to most thinking skills program developers. Consideration of these options raises a number of questions that all thinking skills program developers must sooner or later address. Of these, three are crucial. Examining each of these reveals some of the important factors that must be taken into account in developing a thinking skills program.

Separate Course or Integrated?

In organizing a thinking skills program, developers must sooner or later decide whether to teach thinking skills in a "content-free" course or courses, or within subject matter courses, or in some combination of the two. Making a decision on this matter requires consideration of the advantages and disadvantages of each of these three options, especially in terms of faculty interests and abilities, available resources, and what research suggests about the most effective ways to learn and teach cognitive skills and strategies.

A special course in thinking skills, whether it be a self-developed course or a commercial program such as *Instrumental Enrichment, Creative Problem Solving, Philosophy for Children, Odyssey,* or a similar program, appears at first glance to have many advantages. The instructional focus can clearly be on thinking operations; academic subject matter will not "get in the way." Time will be available for guided practice in the skills being taught without having to worry about subject matter coverage. If it is to be taught only by a few teachers, the problem of staff development may also be minimized. Finally, a number of thinking skills tests already exist that may make evaluation of student learning and instruction in such courses relatively easy.

However, such an approach also has a number of significant disadvantages. New courses, whatever their apparent value, are hard to fit into existing overcrowded curricula, especially where a curriculum is managed by already defined and tested outcomes that may leave little time or room to attend to new sets of learning objectives, whatever their value. Teachers selected to teach special courses most certainly will need training in the instructional methods and materials to be used or developed, as well as in the nature of the thinking operations to be taught. Moreover, subject matter teachers of students who will take the special course will also have to be trained in the nature of the thinking operations taught there in order to help students transfer these skills and strategies to the subjects they teach.

In fact, this latter point is a major disadvantage of a "subject-matter free" approach. A single course on selected thinking skills will simply not be sufficient to help students develop the understanding and proficiency in the types of thinking that a viable thinking skills program could and ought to develop. Unless provisions are made for continuing, explicit follow-up skill instruction in subsequent subject matter courses, both to help students transfer the skills and to elaborate them, thinking skills and strategies taught in a special course are quite likely to atrophy and disappear. To hope such transfer or elaboration will occur automatically is merely wishful thinking, and flies in the face of learning research as well as experience.[2] Although perhaps an attractive way to approach the teaching of thinking, a single skills course by itself falls far short of what is needed or desirable.

As an alternative, instruction in thinking can also be integrated directly into already existing subject matter courses. In fact, research suggests that instruction in these skills at the time they are needed to achieve subject matter objectives provides better motivation for learning such skills than does skill instruction in "content-free" courses or units.[3] Furthermore, if such instruction is ongoing throughout a course or courses, it provides for better maintenance—retention—of these skills and processes.[4] Research also suggests that students who are taught skills within subject matter courses learn the subject, as well as the skills, better (as measured on end-of-course, subject matter, final exams) than do students who do not receive instruction in these same skills within a subject matter course.[5] The payoff for students, in terms of subject matter and skill learning and retention, seems greater when skills are taught within subject matter courses.

In order for such an approach to be successful, however, it must differ considerably from the conventional approach to skill teaching in subject matter courses. Teaching thinking skills in subject matter courses does not mean simply teaching for subject matter objectives as is normally done, hoping or assuming that students will automatically learn how to engage in thinking skills as they try to use these skills to achieve the subject matter objectives. As educators Edward Glazer, Hilda Taba, and others have repeatedly pointed out, there is little evidence that students learn thinking skills as "a necessary by-product" of the study of any given subject or body of content.[6]

Rather, teaching thinking skills in subject matter courses means using the subject matter of any course as an arena in which to provide instruction in these skills, as well as a vehicle for providing such instruction. It also means using these skills to manipulate and process the subject matter in order to achieve the subject matter learning objectives sought. The teaching and learning of subject matter and thinking skills complement each other in such an approach.

More precisely, the teaching of thinking skills in subject matter requires three things: (1) the content used should be that of the regular, subject matter courses; (2) learning thinking skills should be as explicit and publicly affirmed a goal of teaching and learning in these courses as is subject matter learning; and (3) whenever it is time to use a new or important thinking skill to achieve a subject matter goal (to learn some information, a concept, an understanding, or a generalization), the teacher should take the time to introduce or provide guided practice in the skill or help students transfer the skill. Such teaching focuses clearly on the skill, temporarily subordinating emphasis on subject matter to the skill but without interrupting the flow of subject matter being studied. Once the skill has been executed and discussed, student attention returns to what has been learned about the subject matter as a result of using the skill, and the lesson continues.

Unless the teaching of thinking skills and strategies in subject matter courses is conducted as described above, there is little likelihood that students will learn these skills any better than they do now. Training in appropriate skill teaching strategies, as well as in the nature of the thinking operations to be taught, has to be provided to all those teachers in the subject areas who will be expected to teach the specific thinking skills and strategies selected for instruction. Many subject area teachers are unfamiliar with the attributes of most complex thinking operations, as well as with ways to provide explicit instruction in these skills. Moreover, most teachers do not realize the extent to which teaching a thinking skill differs from teaching content. That is, in teaching a thinking skill one must provide *continuing* instruction in the skill, whereas single items of content can be taught in single lessons. Considerable effort must also be expended in coordinating instruction to ensure proper introduction, guided practice, transfer, and elaboration of these skills across a number of subject areas and grade levels.

Furthermore, most teachers think their subject matter courses already include too much content. Adding skills to what they are to teach will simply overburden their students and them, they commonly assert. A teacher's natural inclination to "cover content" usually thus inhibits adequate attention to thinking skills. Even where some content is removed from such courses to make room for attention to skill learning, teachers still need assistance to minimize content interference in the early stages of skill learning. A common instructional language for the skills being taught will also have to be devised and used in all subject areas. Finally, teachers need assistance in preparing appropriate assessments of skills taught and of their teaching of these skills, both for formative and summative purposes. The task of successfully integrating thinking skill instruction into all subject matter courses seems most ambitious, to say the least. Yet, it can be done.

In the long run, however, perhaps some combination of both separate thinking skills units or courses and skills teaching in subject matter may prove most workable and, in terms of student learning, most effective. One form of this combined approach could start with instruction in creative problem solving, logical thinking, and/or thinking skills heuristics across a number of elementary grades using already existing thinking skills programs. A special thinking skills course could then be offered in the first semester of the first year in middle or junior high school, and again in the first semester of the first year students are in high school. These special middle/junior and senior high school thinking skills courses could build on appropriate previous elementary school instruction, and lead to transfer and elaboration of these skills in selected subject matter courses to follow. Figure 4.1 illustrates such a program structure.

Specifically, existing programs, such as Edward deBono's *CoRT* (Cognitive Research Trust), or Sidney Parnes's *Creative Problem Solving*, or Mastery Learning's *Odyssey*, or Matthew Lipman's *Philosophy for Children*, could be used at appropriate grade levels K–6. A special middle or junior high thinking skills course could introduce and teach to mastery a model of decision-making and selected analytical skills using current events and life-experience data. It could be team taught by all personnel in a building, including administrators, counselors, coaches, nurses,

Thinking Heuristics or Creative Problem Solving or Logical Thinking as (a) Separate Course(s)	Decision-Making Course	Language Arts ——— Math ——— Science ——— Social Studies ——— Others	Critical Thinking Course	Language Arts ——— Math ——— Science ——— Social Studies ——— Others
K	3	6–7	8–9	12

Figure 4.1 A Thinking Skills Program Combining Separate Thinking Skills Courses with Skill Follow-Up in Subject Matter Courses

and so on. Teachers of all subject matter areas in that and the remaining semesters could then teach lessons in these skills in a predetermined sequence that reinforces, translates, and elaborates the operations introduced in the special course.

The special course during the first semester of high school could build on these operations and reinforce them, and then introduce and teach to initial mastery a sophisticated model of problem solving and/or selected critical thinking operations. It could be conducted and organized in the same fashion as its middle/junior high counterpart, with all educators in a building team teaching the initial course and systematically teaching to transfer, elaboration, and independent application in their subjects these and the skills introduced in junior high school.

This option has much to recommend it. It could provide instruction in a sequence of selected thinking skills strategies at increasingly elaborate levels of sophistication in a variety of subject areas after introducing them and providing guided practice in content within the understanding of the students. It would bring together all new students in a building, providing them with a common, integrated learning experience in a subject—thinking—of use in all subsequent subject areas. Teaming teachers would allow them to share talents and expertise, and at the same time break down subject matter barriers and provide a common basis for later instruction. And by having all personnel engage in introducing the common core of skills, this approach would provide the initial training needed by all staff to understand the thinking skills to be taught throughout the school, thus minimizing the need for specially funded follow-up staff development. Such an approach might easily incorporate a sequential skills development curricula in a variety of subjects across a K–12 or 6–12 curriculum, thus meeting the criteria of a most effective thinking skills program.

Commercially Prepared or Locally Developed?

Should a thinking skills program consist of already available, expert, or commercially developed programs, or should it be locally developed? This is another important decision with which curriculum planners must grapple. Again, some combination of these two options may prove quite workable and effective.

A number of important efforts have already been made to close the research–practice gap regarding the teaching of thinking. Over the past several years, researchers and educators have developed a number of programs that may enable schools to teach thinking skills better than ever before. These range from Edward deBono's *CoRT*, Matthew Lipman's *Philosophy for Children*, to Reuven Feuerstein's *Instrumental Enrichment*, Arthur Whimbey's analytical reading program, Innovative Sciences' *Strategic Reasoning*, Mary and Robert Meeker's *Structure of the Intellect*, and Sidney Parnes's *Creative Problem Solving*, to name but a few of the more prominent. Figure 4.2 briefly describes one of these programs, a Venezuelan-sponsored, Cambridge-based project published in the United States in 1986 as the *Odyssey* program. Similar descriptions of twenty of these already-developed thinking skills programs may be found in Appendix A.[7] Examination of these descriptions will reveal the varied types of thinking skills for which teaching programs already have been devised, as well as the wide range of grade levels in which these programs may be used.

Most of these programs build on the results of recent research in cognition, effective teaching, and skill learning. They generally consist of instructional materials, student activities, teacher guides, and in some cases, tests, and they may be used to teach a variety of thinking skills at a variety of grade levels to students of varying abilities, interests, and motivations. Many of these programs have been tried out extensively in classrooms throughout the nation and some have student performance data to back up, at least to some degree, the claims they make.[8] It is possible to adopt or adapt one or several of these programs and incorporate ready-made and tried thinking skills programs directly into a school's existing curricula, should one choose to do so.

Creating a thinking skills program that consists of already developed and tested or commercially available programs is an attractive approach to program development for many reasons. Many schools lack the teacher expertise, knowledge, and resources needed to create viable thinking skills programs on their own. Commercially or expert-developed programs have already made the often tough and time-consuming decisions about what instructional strategies to use and which thinking operations to emphasize. Many also contain expert-developed instructional materials, lesson plans, and student tests. Some even have data attesting to the degrees of success that can be expected from using them. In short, adopting existing programs eliminates the necessity of engaging in often costly program development at the local level. For schools seeking relatively quick results, adopting such programs also cuts the time lag involved in designing, piloting, and institutionalizing a locally developed program.

Commercially or expert-developed thinking skills programs present some drawbacks, however. Without denigrating the high quality of some of these programs, which appear to do an excellent job in so far as they go, their limitations should be clearly understood. Some do not provide for continuous skill teaching over an extended period of years. Many ignore the fact that skills are not learned once and for all in a given period of time, but developed over time and change as they are consciously applied in different contexts and for different purposes. Some

ODYSSEY

GOAL   To enhance the ability of students to perform a wide variety of thinking skills.

INTENDED AUDIENCE   Upper elementary and middle school students. The program originally developed for use in Venezuela as part of that country's Project Intelligence. It is intended for regular heterogeneously grouped classes.

ASSUMPTIONS   Performance of intellectually demanding tasks is influenced by various types of factors.
Some of these are modifiable and can be taught.

SKILLS   Skills include careful observation and classification, deductive and inductive reasoning, the precise use of language, the inferential use of information in memory, hypothesis generation and testing, problem solving, inventiveness and creativity, and decision making.

PROCESS/ MATERIALS   Approach is deliberately eclectic. It combines knowledge from current cognitive research with the methods of direct instruction. Some lessons involve a Socratic inquiry approach, while others are based on a Piagetian-like analysis of cognitive activities. Still others emphasize exploration and discovery. Materials include six teacher manuals and student books:
     Foundations of Reasoning
     Understanding Language
     Verbal Reasoning
     Problem Solving
     Decision Making
     Inventive Thinking
These are intended to be used in the above order.

TIME   Three to five lessons per week. Each lesson about 45 minutes.

DEVELOPER   A team of researchers from Harvard University, Bolt Berarek and Newman Inc., and the Venezuelan Ministry of Education. D. N. Perkins helped to develop a portion of this program (creative thinking) and has popularized the *Inventive Thinking* materials.

AVAILABLE FROM   Mastery Education Corporation
85 Main Street
Watertown, MA 02172

Figure 4.2 Description of a Thinking Skills Program

Developed by Barbara Presseisen, Research for Better Schools, Inc., Philadelphia. Used with permission. (Additional programs are described in Appendix A.)

are so tightly structured that instructors who use them really do not have to be capable of engaging in the skills they teach, which raises the danger of rather mechanistic instruction. Those that consist of lessons to be taught by specially trained teachers in a prescribed time period, may, as Madeline Hunter has pointed out, make it too easy for teachers to teach thinking skills as a once or twice-a-week exercise, and then drop back into their more conventional, routine subject matter teaching.[9] Or these programs may give the erroneous impression that only those teachers who use them are responsible for the teaching of thinking in a school, and that no one else need worry about it.

There are also other limitations in these programs. One is that most of them are free of subject matter. That is, they "teach" the skills on which they focus by using content drawn primarily from the presumed life experiences of the students, usually their out-of-school life experiences, or hypothetical, fantasy-like situations. Few make any consistent attempt to teach these skills in academic subject matter or content of societal import. Thus, they fail to provide for the transfer and elaboration required for effective generalization of these skills and strategies.

Teaching thinking skills in subject matter-free contexts does have at least one important advantage, however, especially when introducing a particular skill. It minimizes subject matter interference and thus keeps the focus on the skill where research indicates it belongs.[10] Unfortunately, however, many subject matter-free programs fail to achieve even this because the personalized content they choose to use has such emotional or personal feelings bound up in it for the students (and sometimes the teachers) that the students get sidetracked into focusing on the subject instead of the skill. No matter in what context thinking skills are introduced or initially taught, they should be taught throughout the curriculum in major subject areas, if students are to generalize these skills to the point where they own them.

Finally, few commercial thinking skills programs set the teaching of specific thinking operations in a context such as problem solving or decision making that gives structure and purpose to the discrete skill operations (like classifying or distinguishing relevant from irrelevant information). Some employ instructional strategies of questionable utility in *teaching* skills, relying as they do primarily on techniques that emphasize practice over instruction. Although a single program might meet the special needs of a particular segment of students at a given grade level, it seems highly improbable that it will suffice as the only thinking skill program for all students in any district.

Combining a number of expert-developed thinking skills programs into a multigrade program may be worth considering, however. Judicious integration of some of these programs can, to a considerable degree, do much to offset their inherent limitations. A case can be made for a number of possible combinations. As shown in Figure 4.3, these pro-

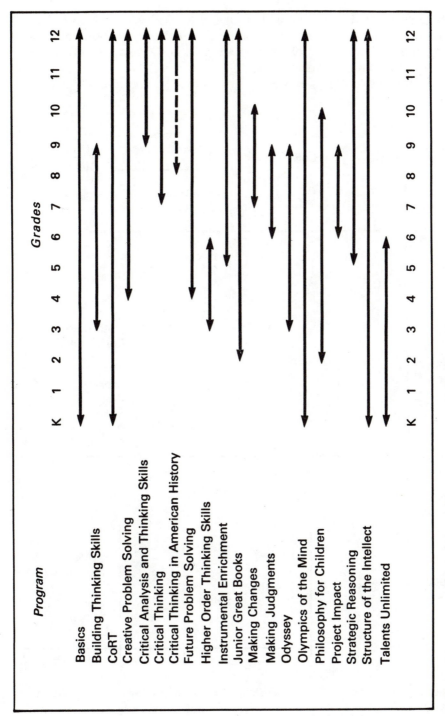

Figure 4.3 Grade Level Uses of Selected Thinking Skills Programs

grams seem applicable to a wide range of grade levels and, to a lesser extent, to several subject areas. Some optional combinations of these programs will illustrate both the possibilities and drawbacks of this approach to program development.

Figure 4.4 outlines three possible ways to organize commercial

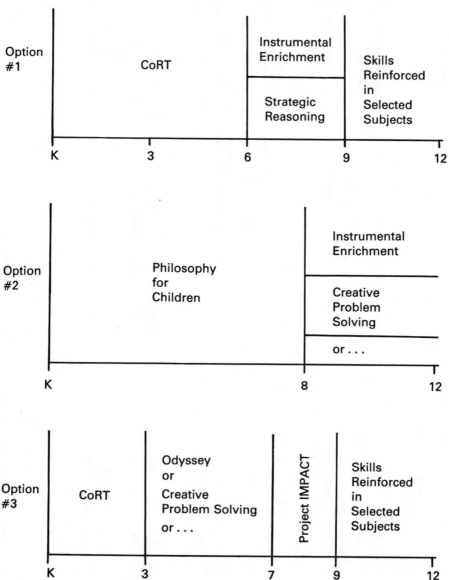

Figure 4.4 Possible Thinking Skills Curricula Consisting of Already-Prepared Programs

thinking skills programs into multigrade programs. As option #1 indicates, a program such as *CoRT* can be taught in its entirety to all students through grade 6; such instruction is relatively light handed, focusing more on heuristics or rules of thumb useful in triggering thinking than on detailed, step-by-step instruction in specific thinking skills. In its later levels, *CoRT* integrates these heuristics into simple decision-making models and processes. *CoRT* is also easily integrated into existing classroom teaching and into any subjects. Its use can contribute much to creating the kind of curriculum and classroom contexts supportive of thinking. Starting in grade 7, a program such as *Instrumental Enrichment* could then be offered to all students to provide a more formal basis for general intellectual development or be offered only for slower students who may benefit most from it. Other students with special needs in this area could be offered *Strategic Reasoning* or another appropriate program. Subsequent subject matter courses can reinforce the skills taught earlier, as desired.

Option #2 suggests the use of *Philosophy for Children*, starting in grades 2 or 3 and continuing to later grades as materials are available and subjects are appropriate. This approach allows for the development of habits and skills of logical thinking as foundations for specific use of reasoning skills through the middle or junior high grades. Thereafter, programs such as *Instrumental Enrichment* or *Creative Problem Solving* may be used for all or for special groups of students, to provide instruction needed for improving general intellectual abilities or abilities to think in various subject matter areas. Follow-up reinforcement of these skills in selected subject matter courses can reinforce such instruction as appropriate. Use of such programs offers students training in a variety of skills useful in many different kinds of thinking.

Finally, option #3 suggests teaching a number of heuristics from the first three or four levels of *CoRT* up to grade 3, followed by use in grades 3–6 or 7 of the *Creative Problem Solving* or *Odyssey* programs, incorporating selected use of the *CoRT* heuristics introduced earlier. Starting in the junior high school, the *Project IMPACT* program can be introduced and taught through the 9th grade for all students, or a special program can be offered for students in special need of more generalized skill training. This option focuses the primary grades on use and encouragement of thinking, rather than on direct instruction in specific skills or strategies, and then integrates the heuristics introduced in those grades into more structured problem-solving strategies. Attention can then be turned to more formal instruction in thinking in a variety of subject matter areas starting in grade 7 in order to refine the general problem-solving model; use of other programs can also be used from here onward, as appropriate.

Programs other than those identified here may be used in such an approach as appropriate, of course. However, exclusive use of these or any already-developed programs still has its limitations. Teachers will need to be trained to teach their respective programs and to understand and reinforce the skills taught in programs their students will take prior to enrolling in their classes. Special efforts will still have to be made to ensure transfer and elaboration of the skills taught in each program in various subjects. Efforts will also have to be made to develop teacher commitment to these programs since teachers will not have been involved in developing them and will be unfamiliar with them.

The alternative to adopting already existing thinking skills programs is to develop a complete program locally from scratch. By doing so, the perceived skill deficiencies of local students can be addressed directly. Such an approach also allows a district or school to build on what it already does by way of teaching these skills. Furthermore, by engaging in the process necessary to develop a local program, teachers can build a degree of commitment and receive on-the-job training useful in implementing the program as designed. On the other hand, such an undertaking is extremely costly in terms of time, financial resources, and effort. In fact, many schools may not have faculty with the training or knowledge about thinking skills or skill teaching required for such an undertaking. Moreover, the time and effort required to produce any worthwhile locally developed program is usually considerable, perhaps three to five years in many instances.

In spite of any drawbacks posed by this approach, many school systems elect to design their own thinking skills programs because for them the commitment and staff development aspects of the effort outweigh the disadvantages, and they can afford the effort. Schools electing to follow this route need to proceed through selecting, defining, and sequencing of thinking skills in order to develop a scope and sequence, and then to decide where and in what types of courses these skills and strategies will be introduced, practiced, and elaborated. This effort should result in the sequential development of thinking skills across a number of subjects and grade levels. Figure 4.5 illustrates one such skill sequence.* Assigning skills to be newly introduced and taught to some degree of initial proficiency in a number of subjects and in clusters of several years allows for "slippage" in teaching. By spreading the responsibility for introducing the skill or strategy, the failure of a single teacher to teach the skill properly will not seriously impair student learning of the skill or undermine the learning of skills to be introduced later. It also allows for learning to a high degree of proficiency in one subject cluster before attempting transfer and elaboration in other, quite differ-

---

* This skill sequence is elaborated in Chapter 8.

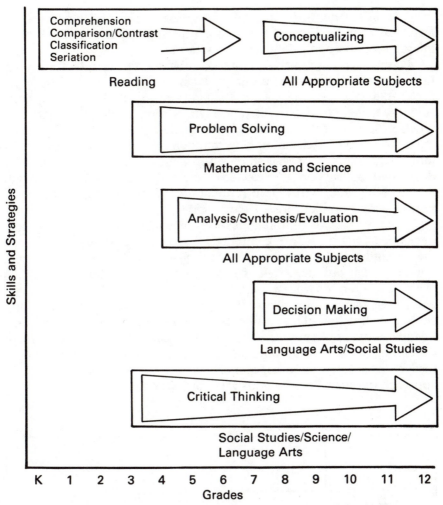

Figure 4.5 A Scope and Sequence for Thinking Skills and Strategies

ent, subjects. Although producing an educational program that carries out such an approach is challenging, it can be a rewarding school-wide endeavor that is intellectually stimulating, involves all faculty regardless of subject areas or grade levels, and develops school-wide commitment to the entire curriculum.

As attractive and useful as each of the preceding approaches may appear, they may for any number of reasons be considered to be wanting or impossible to adopt. Instead, some combination of them may seem more useful and less costly. Thus, elementary grades may use several existing programs but with special locally developed efforts to transfer and elaborate the thinking skills and strategies thus developed into specific matter areas in following grades. Efforts at the secondary level may then be directed at creating a thinking skills program wholly integrated into appropriate subject matter areas.

Figure 4.6 outlines some possible combination programs. It suggests use of an already existing program, such as *Odyssey,* or *Philosophy for Children,* and/or *Creative Problem Solving,* in grades K–6, as appropriate. A locally developed sequence in problem solving, centered in math and science courses, can begin in the intermediate grades. A locally developed sequence in decision making can then commence in the middle or junior high school in social studies and language arts courses. Locally developed instruction in selected critical thinking skills can begin around 9th grade, with the introduction of several of these skills each year in various subject areas as appropriate.

When these two components—commercially produced and locally developed programs—are combined, the resulting program builds on the strengths and minimizes the weaknesses of the various program options earlier outlined. Use of some already developed programs, as explained, often provides a solid, tested foundation for the locally developed skills program to follow. It is the continued teaching of thinking skills and strategies across a number of years and the teaching of these operations in subject matter areas that most local thinking skills program development efforts must address. Most existing skills programs simply neglect these two crucial aspects of teaching for thinking. The sample approach outlined here demonstrates one way this might be done.

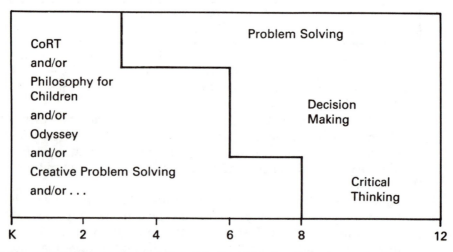

Figure 4.6 Components of Possible Combination Thinking Skills Programs

Short Range as Well as Long Range?

Because the development and implementation of an effective thinking skills program takes a number of years, curriculum planners pursuing this approach may not wish to wait that long before "doing *something*" to address the perceived needs of their students in thinking. For the interim period between planning and implementing a local program, schools may wish to employ temporarily one or more already available thinking skills programs. These programs can then be dropped or incorporated into the locally developed program when that program is judged ready for implementation.

It is unreasonable to expect to build from scratch a locally developed K–12 sequential program for immediate use. Instead, planners may consider the temporary use of one or more already developed programs in a series of self-contained, but repeated, three-year sequences, while development of a local program proceeds more slowly. Each sequence can infuse key thinking skills into subject areas and can be dropped one by one as locally produced components are ready to be implemented. Two possible interim options are presented in Figure 4.7. Option #1 consists of one six-year and two three-year components. *CoRT* or *Odyssey*, for example, can be taught in the elementary grades. Another program such as *Creative Problem Solving*, or *Instrumental Enrichment*, or Whimbey's analytical thinking program can then be offered in grades 7–9 to all students, or to those for whom the programs seem appropriate. At the same time, *CoRT* can be taught to all students in grades 10 through 12. *CoRT* seems very appropriate for use in this way because its in-service and materials costs are minimal, its teaching techniques and the heuristics it teaches can easily be transferred into virtually any subject area, it is readily usable by most teachers, and it is easily adaptable to students of any grade or ability levels. Some other commercial programs are also adaptable to follow-up instruction in any subject area.

Option #2 consists of four components built around *CoRT*, with other programs added as appropriate. Any of these programs can be put in place relatively quickly and conducted independently of the other programs.

With such an interim program in place, local attention can then be given to producing a more permanent thinking skills program for each cluster of grades. At the end of three years' work, each new cluster can be introduced into those classrooms, and the temporary program at each level can be incorporated into it or dropped altogether. This can be done before students who have taken a specific program in earlier grades arrive at a grade level where it would have to be repeated. But the interim training received would provide a useful foundation for the

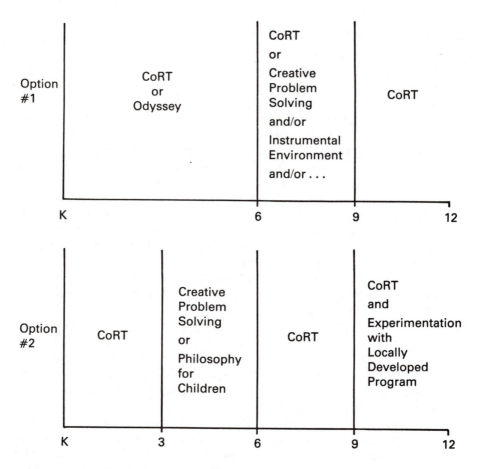

Figure 4.7 Sample Interim Thinking Skills Programs

newly implemented local program, both in terms of student learning and teacher training. Certainly, programs selected even for temporary use at these earlier grade levels ought to be selected with this support and training function in mind, as well as with consideration of the ease of implementing them and their general utility for students.

As the local program's pieces are initially tried out and implemented, teachers can determine the extent to which foundational or prerequisite skills need to be taught at earlier grades, then build them into relevant parts of the new program without drastically revising something already developed. Use of already prepared programs on an interim basis can also fill the gap between a decision to improve thinking skill learning and the availability of a sound, locally developed and tested program.

It is difficult to implement a complete, sequential, or developmental skills program all at once because prerequisite skills will not have been taught to students getting the more advanced or complex skills in the upper levels of the program. Thus, it may be best to implement a thinking skills program in stages. A three-year implementation process proves useful in carrying out this task.

Suppose a school system wanted to introduce selected critical thinking skills at the junior high-school level (grades 7–9), and introduce the micro-thinking skills of analysis, synthesis, and evaluation, and a decision-making strategy at the intermediate level (grades 3–6). The micro-thinking skills provide a basis for critical thinking skills which, in effect, are applications of analysis and evaluation. Decision making provides a framework for thinking within which students can use these micro-thinking skills as well as various critical thinking skills. Knowing this framework and being proficient in these three micro-thinking skills will make learning the critical thinking skills in grades 7–9 much easier.

However, if the complete program were to be implemented all at once, students taking critical thinking for the first several years would be doing so without the benefit of grounding in the skills of analysis, synthesis, and evaluation, and without a sense of the process of decision making to be provided in grades 4–6. This could be remedied, however, if the program were implemented over a three-year period, as illustrated in Figure 4.8. In following this approach, a school system could:

Year #1   Introduce selected critical thinking skills in grade 9; analysis, synthesis, and evaluation in grades 7–8; and a simple decision-making process in grades 5–6.

Year #2   Keep teaching decision making in grades 5 and 6, but also move it down to grades 3 and 4; keep teaching analysis, synthesis, and evaluation in grade 7, eliminate them from grade 8, and move them downward into grades 5 and 6. Keep teaching the selected critical thinking skills in grade 9 and start teaching additional critical thinking skills in grade 8, because in both grades students will now have a background in analysis, synthesis, and evaluation.

Year #3   Institutionalize initial instruction in decision making in grades 3 and 4, and in analysis, synthesis, evaluation *and* decision making in grades 5 and 6. Continue teaching the selected critical thinking skills in grades 8–9 and move them downward to start in grade 7. At this point, students entering grades 7 and 8 will have background in these other skills and operations sufficient to make the study of critical thinking most effective.

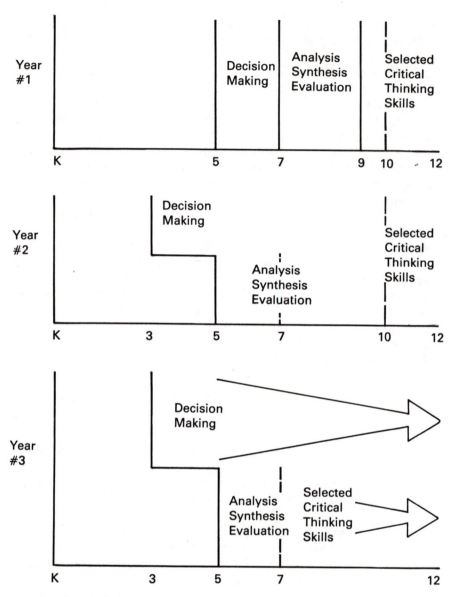

Figure 4.8 Stages in Implementing a Sequential Thinking Skills Program in Selected Grade Levels

A gradual introduction of this sort of any thinking skills program allows time for students to develop prerequisite skills and permits teachers to become familiar with the range of thinking skills students in these grades will be learning. Any range of thinking skills can be introduced using this approach.

CRITERIA FOR ADOPTING A THINKING SKILLS PROGRAM

In planning a school-wide thinking skills program, curriculum leaders and developers must ensure that any program finally developed meets the criteria of effective thinking skill programs. Developers may apply the same criteria of program effectiveness to any thinking skills program, whether it be a commercially developed program, a locally designed program, or some combination of the two. Several experts in thinking skills have suggested criteria useful for this purpose.

Psychologist Robert Sternberg has suggested the following criteria for use in judging the appropriateness and potential for success of thinking skills programs. In his judgment, an acceptable program should:

1. Be based on a psychological theory of thinking that integrates the skills taught
2. Be based on an educational theory that addresses especially transfer and maintenance of the skills taught
3. Provide explicit training in the mental processes used in executing the skills taught and in strategies of executive control
4. Take individual differences into account
5. Motivate students
6. Be sociologically appropriate to the students
7. Explicitly link to subject matter areas and to the students' out-of-school world
8. Have demonstrated empirical success in settings with students like those with whom it is to be used
9. Have a well-tested teacher training component.[11]

Sternberg intended these criteria to apply to commercially prepared or already developed thinking skills programs a school might be considering for adoption. However, with the possible exception of criteria 8 and 9, these criteria prove equally appropriate in judging the value of locally developed thinking skills programs as well. For such locally made programs, data regarding student performance in the program may be lacking initially, as may data about the effectiveness of any teacher training associated with the program. Thus, information related to these two criteria may not be available in the early stages of implementing such a program. However, before any thinking skills program, whether expert-devised or locally developed, is finally institutionalized, these criteria must be addressed. In the interim, a program can be piloted or tried out in order to collect information that will be useful in judging its effectiveness and that of its associated teacher training.

Additional criteria should be added to those listed above in order to ensure a wise decision regarding a thinking skills program. Edward deBono, for example, suggests that any thinking skills program worth adopting should:

10. Be usable by teachers having a wide range of teaching talents (and a wide range of understanding about the skills they are asked to teach)
11. *Not* require extensive teacher training
12. Be "robust" enough to resist damage as it passes from developer(s) through trainers to teachers for classroom implementation, and as it is executed in a variety of classroom settings
13. Employ parallel construction so that if some parts are poorly done or omitted the remainder of the program will be valuable and successful
14. Be enjoyable for both students and teachers
15. Focus on skills that will help learners function better outside of school.[12]

Whereas Sternberg's criteria generally refer to the content of a thinking skills program, deBono's criteria refer to its structure and how it relates to the teachers who will use it. When combined, as here, these fifteen criteria seem most appropriate for making adoption decisions about any thinking skills program for any grade level or subject area. One needs to add to these only the following criteria, for emphasis if nothing else. Whether a thinking skills program is to be adopted from outside or designed locally, it should also:

16. Provide for explicit instruction in and transfer of thinking skills to a variety of subject areas and contexts, as well as to students' out-of-school life
17. Provide explicit attention to and, in upper grades, training in strategies of metacognition and executive control
18. Explicitly integrate specific thinking skills into the functional thinking strategies of problem solving, and decision making at the very least
19. Incorporate continued instruction in thinking skills and strategies over a number of years to elaborate as well as transfer and maintain proficiency in them

Of course, adoption or approval of any thinking skills program, whatever its origin, should occur in the context of the goals sought by the school. Programs that show little promise of achieving the goals already established by a school should not be adopted. As Sternberg cautions, the expectations of educators approving a program ought to be appropriate to the program—they should not expect a program that seeks to accomplish one type of goal or teach one type of thinking to achieve quite different goals or teach quite another approach to thinking. In other words, any useful thinking skills program should:

20. Be congruent with the general educational goals and expectations of the institution or group adopting or approving it.[13]

Figure 4.9 presents a worksheet that can be used to facilitate the evaluation of thinking skills programs proposed for adoption in a subject, school, or school district. The form presented here incorporates many of the evaluative criteria suggested by Sternberg and deBono, but other criteria may be added or substituted, of course. Once data relevant to each criteria have been collected and entered in the appropriate boxes, judgments can then be made on a comparative as well as absolute basis about the merits of each program under consideration.

While thinking skills should be infused in subject matter throughout a curriculum, any thinking skills program as finally developed should have three essential features. It should provide for *direct instruction* in the thinking skills and processes selected for instruction. That is, continuing instruction should be provided in each of the skills/strategies that constitute the program throughout a number of subjects and grade levels. Skill learning should also be *purposeful*. Individual skills should be taught and applied in the context of functional thinking processes; thinking skills should be used to advance learning of subject matter as well as to deal with out-of-school situations; skills should be introduced when they are needed by the students and when they can most benefit from formal instruction in them. Finally, thinking skill instruction should be *developmental:* skills should build on each other. Individual skills should be elaborated as they are used with increasingly sophisticated data for increasingly complex purposes; learning should move from teacher-directed to student motivated and directed.[14]

In addition to the preceding criteria, local school systems may well employ other criteria unique to their own students, goals, or situations. What is important about approving, adopting, or developing any thinking skills program is that the proper questions are asked—and answered sufficiently well—so valid judgments regarding effectiveness, both potential and achieved, can be made. In lieu of carefully thought-out criteria developed locally, the criteria listed here may well serve this purpose.

SUMMARY

In sum, curriculum developers have a number of options to choose from in deciding how to structure a building or district-wide thinking skills curriculum. Such a curriculum may consist of commercially available

Selected Criteria	#1	#2	#3	#4	#5
1. Skills are related to each other?					
2. Accounts for ... maintenance?					
... transfer?					
3. Provides explicit instruction in ... cognitive skills?					
... executive control?					
4. Motivates?					
5. Accommodates individual differences?					
6. Links subject areas to out-of-school life?					
7. Usable by most teachers?					
8. Requires much teacher training?					
9. Provides for back-up instruction?					
10. Provides sufficient instructions for teacher?					

Figure 4.9 Selecting Thinking Programs

programs only, of a locally developed program only, or of some combination of the two. It may consist of subject matter-free skills courses only or thinking skills instruction infused in academic subject matter courses only or some combination of the two. And, initially, it may consist of some interim program where the same skill instruction is provided over a two- or three-year period to students in each level—primary, intermediate, junior and senior high—and then replaced by locally developed or other commercial programs designed or selected specifically for a particular level.

Each approach has its advantages and disadvantages, costs and benefits, in terms of teacher training, installation and monitoring, and student learning. Consideration of these pluses and minuses requires careful attention to and use of a carefully thought-out decision model, perhaps one like that presented in Chapter 7 and Appendix B. In fact, making the decisions about which option to choose or develop requires use of many of the various thinking operations a final thinking skills program is designed to teach, including critical as well as creative thinking, information processing, conceptualizing and decision making. Structuring a thinking skills program for a subject area, at a building level or across an entire district, is in itself a major thinking task.

ENDNOTES

1. Philip A. Pecorino, "Models for Developing Critical Thinking in the Two Year College Curriculum," Unpublished paper delivered at the Christopher Newport College Conference on Critical Thinking, April 12, 1985.

2. David N. Perkins, "Thinking Frames," Unpublished paper delivered at the Connecticut Thinking Skills Conference, March 11, 1985, pp. 14–15; Bryce B. Hudgins, *Learning and Thinking* (Itasca, Ill.: F. E. Peacock, 1977), pp. 142–172; Michael I. Posner and Steven W. Keele, "Skill Learning," in Robert M. W. Travers, ed., *Second Handbook of Research on Teaching* (Chicago: Rand McNally College Publishing Company, 1973), pp. 824–825.

3. Carl Bereiter, "Elementary School: Necessity or Convenience?" *Elementary School Journal* 73 (May 1973): 435–446.

4. Posner and Keele, "Skill Learning," pp. 814–816, 820–825.

5. Thomas H. Estes, "Reading in the Social Studies—A Review of Research Since 1950," in James L. Laffery, ed., *Reading in the Content Areas* (Newark, Del.: International Reading Association, 1972), pp. 178–183.

6. David Russell, *Children's Thinking* (Boston: Ginn and Company, 1956), p. 287; Edward M. Glaser, *An Experiment in the Development of Critical Thinking* (New York: Bureau of Publications, Teachers College, Columbia University, 1941), p. 69; Hilda Taba, "Teaching of Thinking," *Elementary English* 42, 5 (May 1965): 534; Howard Anderson, ed., *Teaching Critical Thinking in Social Studies: 13th Yearbook* (Washington, D.C.: National Council for the Social Studies, 1942), p. vii.

7. Developed by Barbara Presseisen, Research for Better Schools, Inc., Philadelphia, Pa. Used with permission.

8. Paul Chance, *Thinking In the Classroom: A Survey of Programs* (New York: Teachers College Press, 1986); Raymond S. Nickerson, David N. Perkins, and Edward E. Smith, *The Teaching of Thinking* (Hillsdale, N.J.: Lawrence Erlbaum Associates, 1985), pp. 147–309.

9. Madeline Hunter, Keynote Address, Annual Conference of the Association for Supervision and Curriculum Development, Chicago, March 23, 1985.

10. Barak V. Rosenshine, "Teaching Functions in Instructional Programs," *Elementary School Journal 83*, 4 (March 1983): 338–345; Hudgins, *Learning and Thinking*, pp. 142–172; Posner and Keele, "Skill Learning," pp. 824–825.

11. Robert J. Sternberg, "How Can We Teach Intelligence?" *Educational Leadership 42*, 1 (September 1984): 47–48.

12. Edward deBono, "The Direct Teaching of Thinking As a Skill," *Phi Delta Kappan 64*, 10 (June 1983): 705.

13. Sternberg, "How Can We Teach Intelligence?" p. 48.

14. Barry K. Beyer, "Common Sense About Teaching Thinking Skills," *Educational Leadership 41*, 3 (November 1983): 44–49.

5

Selecting Thinking Skills to Teach

Regardless of whether a school's thinking skills program is adopted, invented, or adapted, one of the first tasks in piecing it together consists of identifying those thinking operations—strategies and skills—that are to constitute the content of the program. This task involves answering three important questions: What thinking operations *could* be taught? What thinking operations *should* be taught? What thinking operations *will* be taught? This chapter presents sources from which answers to these questions can be derived, as well as options that may be chosen or developed. Guidelines and procedures that can be followed in making these decisions are also presented.

First, the thinking operations that *could* be taught need to be identified. Most likely the resulting list of possibilities will be a long one, for there is no general agreement as to a common core of operations to be taught. There are literally dozens and dozens of thinking operations that could be legitimately included in such a list, ranging from very complex, all-encompassing processes or strategies like problem solving, to rather discrete, simple skills like classifying. But because it takes considerable time to introduce and teach to an acceptable degree of proficiency any single thinking operation of major significance,* it is quite probable that not all the operations on such a list can be included among those that are to be emphasized in a final program. Choices have to be made.

Choosing which skills *should* receive continuing district or school-wide attention in a thinking skills program is the second step in the selection process. Making this choice requires attention to certain criteria. It also involves one's view of learning and of human development— whether one adheres essentially to developmentalism and constructivism or to some other theory of human growth and learning—as well as reference to some conceptual model of thinking that interrelates these skills. This also requires articulation and consideration of the philosophy of education to which a district or school adheres, the goals of the planned thinking skills program, and the nature of the students that the program is to serve.

Once the thinking operations that *should* be included in a program have been identified, a decision has to be made about those that *will* be taught—those to which the district or school faculty commits itself to having students learn to some high degree of proficiency. Again, time is lacking to treat all the thinking skills and strategies that may be selected as desirable with the instructional attention needed to accomplish this goal. Thus, choices have to be made again, this time about which operations to emphasize on a course, building, or district-wide basis. Making these three kinds of decisions not only launches the effort of developing a thinking skills program, but the process educates the decision-makers about the nature of thinking.

IDENTIFYING THINKING SKILLS THAT *COULD* BE TAUGHT

Before deciding which thinking skills will comprise a thinking skills program, program developers ought to identify as many as possible of the thinking operations that could be included in such a program. Conducting such a broad search is necessary in order to avoid getting locked into a narrowly conceived collection of skills, or becoming restricted by local, conventional perceptions of the nature of thinking and its constituent operations. One way to initiate such an inventory of operations is to identify those already taught, or supposedly taught, throughout one's district. By starting at this point, program developers acknowledge what most teachers believe to be true—that they are already teaching thinking. A program development effort that begins here actually allows a district to build a revised or new program on what already

---

* See Chapter 9.

exists, which can be an essential ingredient of any successful program development effort.[1]

Before undertaking this inventory of what a district currently does or claims to do by way of teaching thinking skills, it may be useful to develop a generic definition of *thinking skills,* acceptable to all involved in this undertaking. Having a shared understanding of exactly what a thinking skill is—or is not—helps to minimize confusion and to keep everyone on relatively the same track in collecting appropriate examples of such skills. Such a process can be initiated by examining a number of dictionary or expert definitions of *thinking* and of *skills* and then preparing a composite definition on which all can agree. Such definitions can be fleshed out by considering a number of examples and nonexamples. Contrasting these examples makes the exact nature of thinking operations clearer than can a simple definition alone. To do this, the following examples might be discussed initially:

IS a thinking operation	*IS NOT a thinking operation*
	Group I
Classifying	Tying one's shoe
Generalizing	Penmanship
Comparing	Hitting a baseball
Making a hypothesis	Balancing a book on one's head
	Group II
Identifying information relevant to a topic	Making note cards
Problem solving	Listening
Making analogies	Observing
	Doing library research

All the items listed under the IS column are examples of thinking operations in terms of the definitions presented by most authorities. The items under the IS NOT column in Group I are clearly not examples of thinking operations. The distinction between Group I IS and IS NOT items clarifies the exact nature of what can be identified as thinking operations.

The items under the IS NOT column in Group II are not in themselves thinking skills even though they may involve a number of thinking operations. Making note cards, for example, certainly involves a number of thinking operations (e.g., distinguishing relevant from irrelevant information), but it is not primarily or exclusively a thinking operation. Here the distinction between thinking skills and other kinds of skills may not be so clear. Discussion of the differences between examples and nonexamples of thinking skills, and grappling with the fine distinctions between thinking operations and other skills that may partially consist of thinking operations, clarifies more precisely than does reference to simple definitions the essential nature of thinking and its constituent operations. Engaging in this defining effort before and during the search for thinking skills that could be included in a local program can make the search and the resulting analysis extremely productive—and educational.

Having agreed on a definition of the kinds of operations to look for, program developers can launch their search for thinking skills that are currently being taught. Information about what is now being done in a district, school, or subject area can be gleaned primarily from four sources: district curriculum guides or courses of study, the texts used in all the subject areas of the district at all grade levels, standardized tests administered to district students, and reports by teachers themselves. Those involved in this task can use a retrieval chart similar to that in Figure 5.1 to list, subject by subject, the skills already taught either at each grade level or at clusters of grade levels. One such chart can be used to record those thinking skills found listed in a district's curriculum guides or programs of study. Another copy of the chart can be used to record, subject by subject, those thinking skills taught in the texts used at each grade level in each subject. Still another copy of the chart can be used to record the thinking skills assessed on standardized tests used at different grade levels by the district. Finally, the chart can be used to record what skills teachers of various subjects report they try to teach in their subjects at each grade level.

Collecting such information at this point proves productive in at least three ways. First, it reveals which thinking skills teachers in the district may already be teaching, or at least be committed to teach. Second, it may reveal those thinking skills common to a number of subject areas and/or grade levels. Third, this procedure may also reveal significant gaps in those skills or sequences of skills, or repetitions in those already scheduled for instruction. In sum, such a procedure not only identifies skills to which there is already some district-wide commitment, but it also reduces the task of selecting skills from one of building a skills curriculum completely from scratch to merely adding a limited number of new ones to fill in the gaps in a skills sequence already in place.

Surveying a district's existing curricula to pinpoint which thinking skills are already listed can also lead to a number of surprises. For example, this effort may point up major thinking strategies and skills that are missing from the curriculum. It may also alert one to a subject area or department that has already identified an impressive catalog of thinking skills and that may well already be doing a good job of deliber-

Subjects	Grades K–3	Grades 4–6	Grades 7–9	Grades 10–12
Science				
Math				
Language Arts				
Social Studies				
Other:				

Figure 5.1 Thinking Skills Presently Taught

ately teaching such skills. In fact, such a discovery may alert program developers to a core of teachers who can be most helpful in revising or modifying a thinking skills curriculum or providing staff development for other faculty.

There are other sources of thinking operations program developers can consult beyond those that may emanate directly from the local district. For instance, some specialists in cognition and in teaching have already identified thinking operations they feel are essential for including in any program to teach thinking. The thinking skills and strategies described in Chapter 3 and listed in Figure 3.4 constitute one such list. Because of their functional utility, these thinking operations could well serve as the core skills and strategies for any school district thinking skills curriculum. On the other hand, educational program developer Barbara Presseisen recommends teaching other kinds of thinking skills, including basic skills such as qualification, classification, and transformations; more complex skills such as problem solving and critical thinking; and the metacognitive operations of monitoring and strategy selection.[2] Robert Marzano, of the Mid-Continent Regional Educational Laboratory, advocates the teaching of learning-to-learn skills such as attending, goal setting, and power thinking; subject area thinking operations such as concept attainment, pattern recognition, and synthesizing; and reasoning skills such as storing in memory, analogical reasoning, extrapolation, problem solving, and invention.[3] The *Tactics* program, distributed by the Association for Supervision and Curriculum Development, incorporates the McREL skills.

Special interest groups and professional education organizations also recommend various thinking operations for instruction. Business and political leaders, for example, have identified thinking skills they feel all secondary school graduates should have mastered in order to be successful in the world of work. Without further elaboration, they usually describe these skills as problem solving and/or critical judgment.[4] Educational and civic organizations have also identified thinking skills they believe will be essential for civic life in the years to come. One of these, the Education Commission of the States, listed in 1982 the following thinking operations among what it believed were "the basics for tomorrow" to be taught in all schools:

- Evaluation and analysis
- Critical thinking
- Problem solving
- Synthesis
- Creativity
- Decision making given incomplete information[5]

A number of instructional programs have also already been developed to teach specific kinds of thinking operations.* Many of these have incorporated the suggestions of experts in thinking or in cognitive research. Examination of these programs can identify many thinking operations that could be considered for inclusion in any thinking skills program. The program *Strategic Reasoning*, for example, seeks to teach what semanticist Albert Upton identified as six basic thinking skills: thing making (conceptualizing), qualification (identifying attributes), classification, structure analysis (parts of an object), operation analysis (steps in a process), and analogy.[6] Reuven Feuerstein's *Instrumental Enrichment*, on the other hand, identifies as key thinking skills such operations as spatial organization, analytic perception, relationship-finding and making, and syllogistic reasoning.[7] Based on the work of Guilford, who identified some 127 mental abilities, psychologists Mary and Robert Meeker have built a program to teach approximately 27 of those deemed especially relevant to academic success, including comprehending numerical progressions, conceptualizing, spatial conservation, evaluating symbolic relations, producing notational transformation, and inferential (and other types of) reasoning.[8]

Other specialists offer different operations as key thinking skills. Some emphasize the operations identified by Benjamin Bloom and his colleagues in their *Taxonomy of Educational Objectives*—recall, comprehension, application, analysis, synthesis, and evaluation.[9] Edward deBono's *CoRT* program seeks to teach heuristics—rules of thumb that trigger certain thinking operations—such as AGO ("aims, goals, and objectives"), CAF ("consider all factors"), and C&S ("consequences and sequels").[10] Still other experts emphasize such operations as making and identifying assumptions, syllogistic reasoning, comparing/contrasting, making analogies, identifying contradictions, inferring, reasoning inductively and deductively, predicting, and distinguishing among premises, conclusions, assumptions, and inferences.[11] Some of the skills included in these programs are linked to specific disciplines or fields of knowledge, such as logic or philosophy, whereas others are thought to be generic, underlying the very basis of intelligence in general.

Finally, there is yet another source that might be consulted in seeking thinking operations for possible inclusion in a program for the teaching of thinking. Developers of such programs might consult the research of specialists Benjamin Bloom, Lois Broder, Reuven Feuerstein, and Arthur and Linda Shaw Whimbey to identify those behaviors that seem to typify individuals who are unsuccessful in thinking and then develop

---

* See Appendix A.

a thinking program designed to alter such behaviors.[12] According to these experts, individuals *not* rated as effective in thinking, generally, among other things:

- Are impulsive, often jumping to conclusions
- Give up quickly, if unsuccessful in solving a problem on first or second try
- Are inflexible in approaching thinking tasks
- Use imprecise language
- Plunge into a thinking task without planning what to do
- Fail to check their work for accuracy
- Are reluctant to secure as much data as possible
- Skip steps in executing a thinking task
- Are unable to engage in a line of reasoning
- Are often incapable of launching a thinking task

Habits, dispositions, and cognitive operations that would counteract these behaviors and attitudes can be readily identified. These more positive operations and dispositions could then become the core of a potentially powerful program for the teaching of thinking.

Program developers and teachers not only have a great number of thinking operations from which to choose, but these operations are of various types as well. Some, like those recommended by Presseisen, Marzano, and others, are rather generic operations, not readily linked to any specific subject area or thinking function but believed to underlie all more specific thinking operations. Other types of operations are like those identified by *Project IMPACT* and the operations listed in Chapter 3 of this book. These are tied very closely to thinking strategies and skills commonly recognized as useful in academic learning, as well as in everyday life. Still other operations, like those presented in the *CoRT* program, are essentially rules of thumb or heuristics rather than cognitive operations. Additional operations, like the reasoning and logical thinking skills identified by Ennis, are closely tied to specific disciplines such as philosophy. Finally, there are behaviors illustrative of skillful thinking—behaviors such as persisting in working a problem. However, these represent not so much specific skills as they do attitudes and habits supportive of such thinking operations. Building an effective thinking skills program involves sorting through these varied kinds of cognitive operations to select those most likely to be meaningful to students and teachers, as well as those operations that are teachable within the constraints of the overall curriculum in which they are to be included.

Developers of a thinking skills program must be as concerned about the knowledge and affective dimensions of thinking as well as the thinking operations to be included in such a program. In making these determinations, they should be especially concerned about the dispositions that support and direct skillful thinking. Reference to the works of David Krathwohl and his colleagues in defining the affective domain of educational objectives, Bloom and Broder's research on thinking behaviors, and Robert Ennis's suggestions on this topic are helpful in identifying those dispositions that should be goals of an entire K–12 thinking program. Descriptions of many of these may be found in Chapter 3. Attention must be given to the affective dimension of thinking at each point in the process of selecting, defining, and sequencing what to include in a program to teach thinking as well as to thinking skills and strategies.

IDENTIFYING THINKING SKILLS THAT *SHOULD* BE TAUGHT

The number of cognitive operations designated as thinking skills of fundamental import seems almost limitless. Making sense of this myriad of skills and selecting those that ought to be taught are major tasks for anyone seeking to improve student thinking.

One way to initiate the process of deciding which specific operations to include in a thinking skills program is to determine which of the thinking operations identified as part of an existing local curriculum seem to be common to a number of grade levels, courses, and subject areas. For example, analysis of some lists of thinking skills reportedly taught already in a subject or district may reveal that a specific skill or number of skills appears in a number of subjects at a particular grade level. Table 5.1 illustrates how four key thinking skills may show up in three different subject areas commonly taught in the secondary grades.[13] Awareness that certain thinking operations such as these appear to be common to a number of subjects at a specific grade level can alert program developers to skills that might well be included in a thinking skills program. Going through the process to locate such common skills may also reveal gaps in the sequencing of skills presently taught.

Teaching the skills that are common to several subjects at a given grade level can both minimize the amount of skill teaching any single teacher will have to do and also offer maximum opportunities for teaching these skills to transfer in a wide variety of contexts. Identifying when and where such overlap occurs can help identify where in a curriculum skills can be introduced and taught to some degree of proficiency with maximum effectiveness.

For instance, Table 5.2 shows the thinking skills one school system's staff compiled in their effort to identify operations that could be taught in their middle schools. Their source was a state list of learning outcomes for major subject areas taught in grades 6–8. Examination of this

Table 5.1 Examples of Higher Order Thinking Skills in Selected Subject Areas

	Science	Social Science	Literature
1. Analyze	Identify the components of process and the features of animate and inanimate objects	Analyze components or elements of an event	Identify components of literary, expository, and persuasive discourse
2. Compare	Compare the properties of objects or events	Compare causes and effects of separate events; compare social, political, economic, cultural, and geographic features	Compare meanings, themes, plots, characters, settings, and reasons
3. Infer	Draw conclusions; make predictions; pose hypotheses, tests, and explanations	Predict, hypothesize, and conclude	Infer characters' motivation; infer cause and effect
4. Evaluate	Evaluate soundness and significance of findings	Evaluate credibility of arguments, decisions, and reports; evaluate significance	Evaluate form, believability, significance, completeness, and clarity

Source: Edys S. Quellmalz, "Needed: Better Methods for Testing Higher-Order Thinking Skills," *Educational Leadership 43:*2 (October 1985): 31. Reprinted with permission of the Association for Supervision and Curriculum Development. Copyright © 1985 by the Association for Supervision and Curriculum Development. All rights reserved.

list of skills reveals several significant things. First, it reveals how new skills or more refined versions of the same skill have been added at successive grades in the same subject area. Whereas the skill of analysis appears only twice at the sixth-grade level in social studies, it appears four times at the eighth-grade level in that subject. In most instances, skills to be taught at each grade level in each subject increase in number or in the types of learning to which they are to be applied as one progresses upward through the grades, at least in these three grades in this curriculum document.

Second, examination of these data shows how the same or similar thinking skills repeat in different subjects at the same and at successive grade levels. Problem solving is listed in sixth grade science, math, and language arts; critical thinking appears in sixth grade language arts, science, and social studies. The skill of analysis, while listed only in social studies at the sixth grade, appears in science, language arts, and social studies in the eighth grade. Critical thinking also appears at several grade levels and in a number of subject areas.

By first identifying all that is now or is supposed to be taught at one grade level or in one subject area, these program developers were thus in a position to identify commonly taught skills. Table 5.2 clearly suggests that both problem solving and critical thinking are at least supposed to be taught at the sixth-grade level in most subjects. These skills and strategies are thus likely candidates for including in any thinking skills program that should be adopted for that grade level throughout their school system. Furthermore, the skill of analysis appears in three subject areas in the seventh grade, in addition to critical thinking and problem solving. Finally, a host of new but common skills appear at the eighth-grade level, including reasoning skills, interpretation, comparing/contrasting, and so on. Those skills that seem to be common to several subject areas are likely to be skills appropriate for teaching across all these areas. Listing and analyzing all the skills identified in curriculum documents, tests, and other similar sources certainly does assist program developers in identifying any sequence or types of thinking skills common across a number of grade levels and subjects. It also makes it easier to distinguish the more useful and important from the less important thinking operations students are asked to perform in school.

However, the list of skills presented in Table 5.2 also points up a serious problem with compiling and working with such skill lists. Many of the terms used to denote these skills are terribly vague. Exactly what is meant by *process skills* (grade 6, science) or *critical thinking* (grade 6, language arts) is quite unclear. Such vagueness is more a curse than a blessing for those charged with implementing curriculum specifications. Although it does allow teachers to make their own choices as to what to teach as process skills or critical thinking, it fails to provide the specific guidance required to make appropriate choices or choices consistent with effective skill learning and assessment. Certainly, more precise specification of the kinds of critical thinking skills to be taught, such as those provided under grade 8, language arts (*forming analogies, testing for fallacies in reasoning*) are much more useful for purposes of program development and teaching.

The words or phrases that designate or label thinking operations often get in the way of communicating exactly what these operations are. It is not uncommon to find educators using different labels to indicate the same cognitive operation, or to be using the same term to mean

Table 5.2 Thinking Outcomes in a State Curriculum Framework

	6th Grade	7th Grade	8th Grade
Social Studies	Analyze relationships (cause and effect, etc.).	Analyze relationships (cause and effect, etc.).	Analyze relationships (cause and effect, etc.).
	Suggest solutions and consequences for identified world problems.	Suggest solutions and consequences for identified world problems.	Suggest solutions and consequences for identified world problems.
	Understand interdependent relationships.	Understand interdependent relationships.	Understand interdependent relationships.
	Utilize appropriate geographic, study, critical thinking and decision making skills.	Utilize appropriate geographic, study, critical thinking and decision making skills.	Utilize appropriate geographic, study, critical thinking and decision making skills.
	Assess the significance of individuals and events of historical periods.	Assess the significance of individuals and events of historical periods.	Assess the significance of individuals and events of historical periods.
	Analyze impact of cultural diversity.	Analyze impact of cultural diversity.	Analyze impact of cultural diversity.
	Compare, infer, evaluate, interpret.	Compare, infer, evaluate, interpret.	Compare, infer, evaluate, interpret.
		Categorize in a variety of ways.	Analyze contributions and impacts of groups on societies and their writings.
			Analyze specified concepts.
Science	Use process skills as tools for investigation.	Use process skills as tools for investigation.	Use process skills as tools for investigation.
	Use process skills in problem solving.	Use process skills in problem solving.	Use process skills in problem solving.
	Apply critical thinking skills to solve problems.	Apply critical thinking skills to solve problems.	Apply critical thinking skills to solve problems.

	Analyze essential life processes. Analyze and interpret principles of genetics and heredity.	Compare and contrast conventional and nuclear forms of energy. Analyze relationship between magnetism and electricity.
Math	Apply problem solving strategies. Interpret maps, tables, graphs, etc.	Apply problem solving strategies. Interpret maps, tables, graphs, etc.	Apply problem solving strategies. Interpret maps, tables, graphs, etc.
Language Arts	Use reading comprehension skills. Demonstrate knowledge of thinking and problem solving. Apply study and test-taking skills. Apply critical thinking skills in communications. Analyze and apply cause - effect - category, etc.	Use reading comprehension skills. Demonstrate knowledge of thinking and problem solving. Apply study and test-taking skills. Apply critical thinking skills in communications. Analyze and apply cause - effect - category, etc. Analyze selected work of various genre for basic elements.	Use reading comprehension skills. Demonstrate knowledge of thinking and problem solving. Apply study and test-taking skills. Apply critical thinking skills in communications. Analyze and apply cause - effect - category, etc. Use appropriate critical thinking and problem solving skills. Relate study of literature to and understanding of self and others. Compare and contrast elements of major literary genre. Identify and apply fundamentals of logic such as forming analogies, testing for fallacies in reasoning, and drawing sound conclusions.

quite different operations. Highly specialized or technical terms, without further definition (terms such as *restructuring* or *encoding skills*) communicate little to nonexperts unfamiliar with the thinking skills field, as, frankly, many teachers and materials developers are. Furthermore, commitment to teaching certain skills closely related to one's subject may lead individuals to insist upon selection of particular subject-specific skills in spite of their limited general utility. Precision of language and clear definitions can reduce, but not wholly eliminate, much of the difficulty inherent in choosing which operations to teach.

The fact that certain thinking skills appear already to be commonly identified with certain subjects and/or grade levels is not necessarily an indicator that these skills should actually be taught in those subjects or at those grade levels at all. There is uneven attention to thinking operations in many subjects and grade levels in most school and textbook programs. Many thinking skills and strategies frequently found in a particular subject may be better taught or at least taught equally well in other subjects. The skill of analyzing to find cause-and-effect relationships is a case in point. Although generally associated with social studies, this skill is usually taught in terms of memorizing and recall rather than analysis; texts and courses assert certain variables were causes or effects of other variables and students are asked simply to commit these assertions to memory. Actual analysis of data to identify cause-and-effect relationships might more effectively be initiated in science courses where students can see such relationships in actual experiments, and where they can be demonstrated in concrete, observable instances. This may be true of other thinking operations as well.

Seeking information about where skills are now taught serves as a useful procedure for launching the process of trying to decide which specific operations should be taught in a multigrade or multisubject thinking skills program, however. By engaging in this process, program developers can begin to develop a sense of which thinking operations are most worth the kind of instructional attention required to develop significant student proficiency in thinking. Engaging in this process also helps articulate criteria useful in making a final decision about which of these skills ought to comprise a thinking skills program.

No widely agreed upon criteria exist for selecting which thinking operations should form the core of any thinking skills program. Yet it is obvious that making such a decision requires that such criteria must be clearly spelled out, defined, and agreed upon prior to making the decision. A number of such criteria have been used by experts to select skills to teach in the programs they have developed. Research in skill acquisition and cognition suggest still others. The following questions embody a number of these criteria. They may be used to decide which thinking skills and strategies should be included in a thinking skills program:

1. Does the skill or strategy have frequent, practical application in the students' everyday, out-of-school life?
2. Does the skill or strategy have frequent, practical application in a number of subject areas?
3. Does the skill or strategy build on or incorporate other skills and/ or strategies, or support or comprise more complex skills and/or strategies?
4. Does the subject matter of a variety of courses lend itself to efficient instruction in and learning of this skill or strategy?

Skills or strategies that receive the most positive responses to each of these questions will be those most appropriate for inclusion in any thinking skills program or curriculum.

The criteria implicit in the preceding questions apply specifically to the thinking operations that form the substance (the content or subject matter) of any thinking skills program. These criteria should be the same, whether applied to existing thinking skills programs such as *CoRT* or *Structure of the Intellect,* or to operations being considered for inclusion in a locally developed program. Additional criteria may be used also. It should be clear, however, that such criteria should at this point apply directly to the operations under consideration—not to teacher knowledge of these operations nor to teacher training, not to evaluation of programs nor to pedagogical implications or strategies, not to evaluation nor to supervision. These latter considerations properly come into play once the specific skills, judged in terms of their inherent value and utility, have been selected for instruction.

In selecting from all those skills that *could* be included in a curriculum those few that *should* be included, program developers also have to make some other, related decisions. Do they want to focus on generic thinking skills (operations that are believed to undergird intelligence in general), or skills related to specific functions of thinking, or heuristics that trigger thinking, or some combination of these? Do they wish to include all skills of a certain type (e.g., all the skills classified as "cognitive reconstruction"), or only a few of what seem to be the most useful of this category of thinking operations? These and other similar issues raised by these questions must be addressed in the process of selecting which thinking operations should be goals of a thinking skills program. However, hard and fast determinations about each of these need not be made before making final skill selections. Rather, final decisions on these issues can evolve as developers grapple with what students ought to learn as well as with what can and should be taught. And decisions made at this point can always be modified. But such decisions, however tentative they may be, must be made in the course of this phase of program building.

SELECTING THINKING SKILLS THAT *WILL* BE TAUGHT

The criteria outlined earlier need to be applied twice in order to select those thinking operations that a district or school finally commits itself to teach to some acceptable level of proficiency. First, these criteria need to be applied to all the thinking operations that could be taught in order to generate a list of those operations that ought to be taught. Almost inevitably the number of thinking operations thus selected will still be more than can be handled well by any faculty, given the various constraints of time, student attendance, subject matter coverage, and time requirements for effective skill teaching. Hence, these criteria will have to be applied again to reduce the number of operations on the "should be taught" list. This should be a manageable number that the faculty can agree *will* most certainly be taught to the point that students can demonstrate acceptable proficiency on any acceptable measure of performance.

Thus, in applying the criteria outlined earlier to the selection of those thinking operations to be taught in the classroom, program developers must be mindful of two major, seemingly contradictory, factors. First, they should select a wide enough variety of operations and processes to represent the various major functions that thinking generally serves. Second, they must, as educator Jerry Brown has cautioned, avoid the temptation to "overstuff the sausage" by selecting too many operations to teach.[14]

The teaching of thinking is not an either–or proposition. It is not enough to teach generic thinking operations as opposed to function-specific operations, or to teach major thinking strategies to the exclusion of the more precise constituent skills. It is not whether to teach critical as opposed to creative thinking, or reasoning skills as opposed to those operations triggered by the heuristics that constitute programs like *CoRT*. Nor is the issue whether to teach problem solving rather than conceptualizing, or decision making rather than critical thinking. The teaching of thinking, to be most beneficial to students, requires appropriate attention to those operations useful in all these major kinds of thinking, if students are to develop to their fullest potentials their capabilities of thinking. It must be remembered, the ultimate goal in the teaching of thinking is not mastery of certain cognitive operations simply as ends in themselves, but rather developing proficiency in the thinking tools requisite for living effective, contributing, and satisfying lives as citizens.

To achieve this goal, educators must avoid substituting quantity for quality. The marks of an effective thinking skills program are not how many skills are supposedly taught, but what skills of major importance are taught and how well they are taught and learned. The number of thinking operations to be included in a district's thinking skills program should be limited, at least in the initial years. The reason for restricting the number is a practical one. It takes considerable time to teach a skill from introduction to some degree of proficiency in a variety of contexts.[15] Such instruction might require from ten to twenty lessons per year for *each* newly introduced skill.* This is a considerable amount of time when one considers introducing even only two or three skills a year: a minimum of twenty or thirty skills lessons a year in each course. In addition, thinking operations introduced in previous grades must be reinforced and perhaps even reviewed each year; some have to be transferred to new contexts or otherwise elaborated. Such lessons require additional time. The higher the grade level, the more such skills require this type of attention. If only two new thinking skills were introduced each year starting in the first grade, a tenth-grade teacher could be reinforcing and elaborating as many as eighteen or twenty previously introduced thinking operations, as well as teaching in detail several new ones—an immense task.

Most teachers feel they don't have anywhere near this much time to devote to teaching thinking skills and still teach the subject matter they feel compelled to teach. Consequently, it may be much more productive to select for continuing instruction a few key thinking processes and key operations used in these processes rather than scores of operations of varying levels of complexity. Devising a curriculum that purports to teach 272 skills at a single grade level, as does at least one school system, or 72 distinct skills as does one sixth-grade social studies text, is simply dysfunctional and terribly misleading to students and the public. The more practical alternative is to devise a program that introduces only two to three new thinking operations each year or two, while also providing for practicing, elaborating, and applying all the other thinking skills and strategies previously introduced. As teachers become more experienced in teaching thinking skills and as time permits, new ones can be added later.

Applying this principle to the thinking skills presented in Table 5.2 could produce a reasonably valid core of thinking operations for instruction in grades 6–8. Certainly, the general strategies of problem solving and decision making are worth teaching at these grade levels—so, too, is the generic skill of analysis and its application for various purposes in the different subject areas. Perhaps analogical reasoning or several critical thinking skills might also be appropriate at these grade levels. However, all of the skills that are common to the grades and subjects on this list cannot be introduced and taught to any reasonable degree of proficiency in these three grades. Some will have to be introduced prior to

---

* See Chapter 9.

WHAT THINKING SKILLS/STRATEGIES SHOULD WE TEACH?

Part I

1. List five to eight thinking skills/strategies you believe ought to be taught.

2. Clarify for another person what you mean by at least two of the skills or strategies on the above list. Give a clear definition and example of each.

3. What thinking skills/strategies did you and your colleagues list in common?

Figure 5.2 A Guide to Selecting Thinking Skills for Teaching

Part II

4. What criteria should be used to select thinking skills/strategies for teaching?

5. Put a check in front of the skills/strategies on your list in item 3 that meet these criteria. List here the skills/strategies you checked.

6. Pick two additional thinking skills/strategies NOT on the above list that you believe should also be taught: List these to the right of those listed in item #5 above.

7. Rank order the skills strategies in item #5 above in the order of their importance according to the above criteria (#1 is most important, etc.) and then list the top five, starting with the most important, below:

Figure 5.2 (continued)

the sixth grade and some held for later grades. Restricting the number of thinking skills to receive emphasis in any grades or subjects is absolutely necessary to ensure effective teaching and learning of those finally selected for introduction.

One procedure for narrowing a long list of thinking skills and strategies into a workable number for purposes of instruction is represented by the list of questions in Figure 5.2. By having a faculty committee respond to each of these questions, it is possible to arrive at a consensus list of thinking operations to serve as a core of a school's thinking skills program.

Limiting the number of thinking operations to be included in a district-wide or subject area thinking skills program does not, of course, mean that these are the only thinking skills that teachers can teach. The thinking skills selected merely become those skills for which all teachers assigned to teach them and the district or school building as a whole accept responsibility for teaching to mastery. Teachers are thus committed to teaching them where and as assigned. Such commitment is essential not only for the students, but also for other teachers. Teachers in succeeding years must be able to count on the fact that skills prerequisite to those they are supposed to introduce have been properly taught and learned. But teachers should also be free to teach any other thinking skills they feel are important. In many instances these will be skills closely related to the subjects they teach. Agreement on a district-wide thinking skills program should in no way restrict the opportunities of teachers to teach thinking skills not included in the overall district program, if they feel it necessary to do so, so long as the agreed-upon program skills and strategies receive priority.

SUMMARY

Deciding what to teach as thinking—what strategies, skills, or other thinking operations—initiates the development of a thinking skills program. This task involves identifying what thinking operations and dispositions could be taught, which of these are worth learning and thus teaching, and of these which will be selected as the core of a subject, school, or district-wide thinking skills program. The importance of successful completion of this task cannot be overstated. It is crucial to the development of any effective thinking skills program and to the training and education of any educators charged with implementing such a program.

ENDNOTES

1. Warren G. Bennis, Kenneth D. Bennis, Robert Chin, and Kenneth E. Corey, *The Planning of Change* (3rd ed.) (New York: Holt, Rinehart and Winston, 1961/1976).

2. Barbara Z. Presseisen, *Thinking Skills Throughout the Curriculum: A Conceptual Design* (Philadelphia: Research for Better Schools, Inc., 1985), pp. 23–47.

3. Robert Marzano and C. L. Hutchins, *Thinking Skills: A Conceptual Framework* (Aurora, Col.: Mid-continent Regional Educational Laboratory, 1985).

4. Research and Policy Committee, *Investing in Our Children* (New York: Committee on Economic Development, 1985).

5. *The Information Society: Are High School Students Ready?* (Denver: Education Commission of the States, 1982).

6. Albert Upton, *A Design for Thinking* (Palo Alto, Calif.: Pacific Books, 1961); John Glade and Howard Citron, "Strategic Reasoning," in Arthur Costa, ed., *Developing Minds: A Resource Book for Teaching Thinking* (Alexandria, Va.: Association for Supervision and Curriculum Development, 1985), pp. 196–202.

7. Reuven Feuerstein, *Instrumental Enrichment: An Intervention Program for Cognitive Modifiability* (Baltimore: University Park Press, 1980).

8. J. P. Guilford, *Way Beyond the I.Q.* (Great Neck, N.Y.: Creative Synergetic Associates, 1977); Mary N. Meeker, "SOI," in Costa, ed., *Developing Minds*, pp. 187–192.

9. Benjamin Bloom et al., *Taxonomy of Educational Objectives—Handbook I: Cognitive Domain* (New York: Longmans, 1956).

• 10. Edward DeBono, *CoRT Thinking* (New York: Pergamon Press, 1973/1983).

11. Matthew Lipman, et al., *Philosophy in the Classroom* (Montclair, N.J.: Institute for the Advancement of Philosophy for Children, 1977).

12. Benjamin Bloom and Lois Broder, *Problem Solving Processes of College Students* (Chicago: University of Chicago Press, 1950); Feuerstein, *Instrumental Enrichment*; Arthur Whimbey and Linda Shaw Whimbey, *Intelligence Can Be Taught* (New York: E. P. Dutton, 1975).

13. Edys S. Quellmalz, "Needed: Better Methods for Testing Higher Order Thinking Skills," *Educational Leadership 43*, 2 (October 1985): 31.

14. Jerry L. Brown, "Defensive Curriculum Development," *Educational Leadership 39*, 3 (November 1981): 108–109.

• 15. Bruce R. Joyce and Beverly Showers, *Power in Staff Development Through Research in Training* (Alexandria, Va.: Association for Supervision and Curriculum Development, 1983).

6

Describing
Thinking Skills

As important as it is, selecting thinking skills and strategies for teaching is only one of several tasks that must be undertaken to have effective thinking skills instruction. Describing each skill thus selected is another, equally important task. Teachers, instructional materials developers, and test makers need to know as much as possible about the skills they seek to teach or assess. Developing and providing clear, detailed descriptions of the attributes or components of every major thinking operation to be taught or assessed are critically important to the effective teaching of thinking.

Thinking skills and strategies cannot be adequately described, at least for purposes of teaching or testing, by a single word, a short phrase, or even a sentence or two. These operations, whatever their levels of complexity, are much more intricate than such simple labels or definitions can communicate. To define as fully as possible a thinking skill or strategy requires identifying the procedures by which we operationalize a skill, the rules or principles that direct its use, and the criteria or other skill-related knowledge that enable us to execute the operation in an expert way. Procedures for producing such descriptions constitute the subject of this chapter.

A CONCEPTUAL MODEL OF A THINKING OPERATION

There is more to a thinking operation than simply doing it. Any thinking operation—whether it be a discrete thinking skill such as recalling or classifying, or a critical thinking skill like detecting bias, or a complex strategy like decision making—can be conceptualized as having a label, a definition, a set of unique, interrelated attributes, and a superordinate and subordinate relationship to other thinking operations. Figure 6.1 outlines such a model. Mastery of a thinking skill or strategy consists of knowing these features of the operation to the point of being able to execute it in a rapid, accurate, expert fashion.

The essence of a thinking skill or strategy is its attributes. These attributes consist, first, of a set of steps or a procedure through which one proceeds while executing the operation, whatever it is. Generally, this procedure is executed in a step-by-step fashion, but in some instances linear sequencing is neither crucial nor apparent. Each thinking operation also consists of a number of rules or principles that direct its efficient and effective execution. Finally, each thinking operation includes certain kinds of skill-related knowledge, such as criteria or standards and evidential clues in the case of many evaluative or critical thinking skills, that informs and guides use of the skill. Although procedures are most important, it should be noted that thinking operations consist also of rules and specific kinds of knowledge used in executing these procedures.

To clarify this concept of any thinking skill or strategy, consider how one engages in the simple skill of using a textbook's index. Although this is not a major thinking skill, it is specific enough to exemplify this concept. Try finding or imagining how to find the page number(s) in a science text where Boyle's Law is explained. As you do this, try to remain aware of what you do and why you do it.

Individuals who execute this skill well indicate that they go through the following procedures:

1. First, they decide to use the index (rather than to thumb through the book or use the table of contents).
2. Then they decide to look under *B* for Boyle's Law.
3. Next, they open the text and flip to the back to locate the index.
4. Upon finding the index, they go straight to the *B* section and then to *Bo* where they skim to find the entry, Boyle's Law.
5. Finding the entry, Boyle's Law, they search under this term to find the specific topic (in this example, its explanation).
6. They identify the page number(s) following this topic entry.

Individuals possess certain knowledge that enables them to engage in

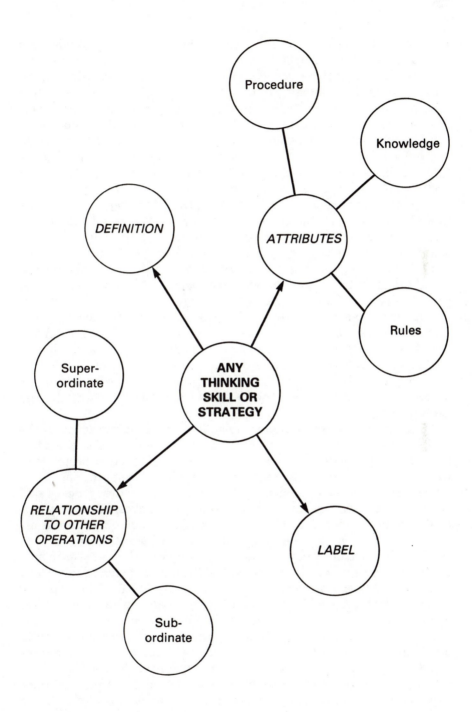

Figure 6.1 A Conceptual Model of a Thinking Operation

this procedure effectively and efficiently. They know, for example, what an index is (a rather detailed alphabetical listing of content items in a publication showing the page(s) on which each item is located). They know an index is customarily found at the back of a text or book and that certain items such as people's names are listed surname first, and events or other items are listed first word first. They know that under each heading they can find related, subordinate headings—sometimes in chronological order, sometimes in alphabetical order, and sometimes in the order presented in the text. And they know the meaning of symbols, such as 114–117, 114, 117, and 114ff.

Those good at using an index also follow certain rules or guidelines in employing this skill procedure. For example, these individuals use this skill when they wish to find text information quickly. They may start by deciding what particular search word they will hunt for. If they can't find that particular term or word, they identify synonyms or associated terms (in the case of this example, perhaps Combined Gas Laws, pressure, or so on) and search for them; they will use the same alternative approach in searching for specific aspects of a topic if they can't find them under the main term they are using. If they cannot find the index, they flip to the table of contents to see if there is an index and where it begins. And they know what to do after they have identified the page numbers they seek. In effect, individuals successful at using a textbook follow these guidelines as if they were rules to guide the way they go about using an index.

Competency in any thinking operation, just as competency in the skill of using a textbook index, consists of: (1) being able to execute a procedure rapidly and accurately, (2) knowing when it is appropriate to use the skill, and (3) being willing to use it when it is appropriate to do so. This behavior is based on an understanding of the three types of skill attributes—procedures, rules, and knowledge—that constitute any particular thinking operation. Figure 6.2 describes in detail the various aspects of each of these three major attributes of any thinking skill or process. The *procedure* that constitutes any thinking skill consists of specific steps, some of which may consist of a number of subordinate steps or components. These steps may be commonly executed in a specific sequence, as illustrated in the example of the skill of using a text index, or in some type of pattern wherein certain steps may be done in the beginning and others later, but where there may be no special order other than that. In addition, most thinking skills operate, or are executed, according to skill-specific guidelines that have the effect almost of *rules* or principles. Three types of rules are especially important: rules governing the conditions when it is appropriate to use a skill (e.g., in the case of using a text index, when one seeks certain information in a hurry); how to initiate use of the skill; and what to do in emergencies (e.g., what to do if one cannot find the index or the item sought).

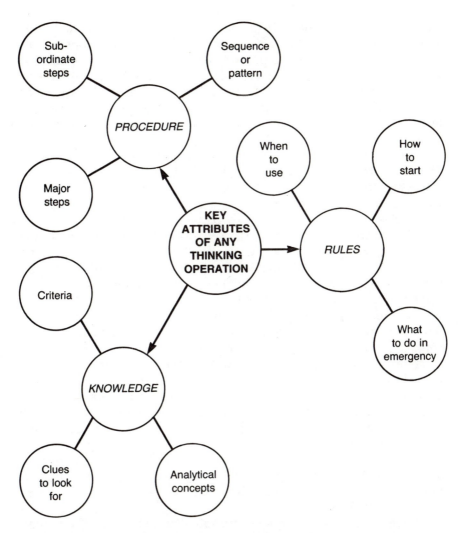

Figure 6.2 Key Attributes of Any Thinking Skill or Strategy

The *knowledge* component of a thinking operation varies according to the type of operation—whether a thinking strategy, a critical thinking skill, or a micro-thinking skill. Many thinking operations are distinguished by certain clues to look for as they are executed. For example, in distinguishing value claims from other types of claims, one searches for the use of superlatives or personal judgments as clues. Other skills are distinguished by certain criteria or standards that must be met in order for specific conditions to exist; for example, educator Robert Ennis asserts that in judging the strength of a conclusion or claim, the following criteria are among those that must be met: the claim or conclusion must explain the evidence and must be consistent with other relevant known facts; competing alternative explanations must be inconsistent with the evidence and other facts; and the proposed claim must appear plausable.[1] Some analytical concepts may also inform a skill. For instance, knowing what a fact is informs the skill or distinguishing between statements of fact and of value claims. In many instances, the knowledge attribute of a skill may be rather subject-specific and may change in terms of application depending on the context or subject with or in which the skill is being applied.

Knowledge and use of this model can help identify the key attributes of any thinking operation and describe it in enough detail to permit teachers to teach it and materials developers or test makers to produce appropriate materials. Figure 6.3, for example, applies this model to the skill of classifying. Teachers who keep in mind a model of any particular thinking operation they are teaching will be able to teach it better than will teachers who have only a fuzzy notion or a one-sentence definition of the same operation. Students who work toward describing a skill in terms of its procedure, rule, and knowledge attributes will come to understand it better than if they treat it as a procedure alone.

For purposes of clarity, the thinking skill model shown in Figure 6.3 omits any reference to affective attributes. Although there is such a component of thinking, this component is tied not so much to any discrete skill as it is to the type of thinking or thinking strategy of which the skill is a part. There is probably no unique affective dimension to the skill of classifying, for example. Rather, the dispositions associated with this skill are the same as those associated with information processing thinking in general. Classifying is an information processing skill; making analogies is a reasoning skill; hypothesizing is a problem-solving skill; and so on. Each of these particular skills is related to the set of dispositions supportive of the kind of thinking that it typifies. Thus, it is not necessary to clarify any specific affective dimension as an attribute of any given thinking skill.

It should be noted that any conceptual model of a thinking operation provides simply a glimpse of that operation at a given point in time. One's understanding of a skill grows and evolves in complexity and degree of sophistication as the operation is used over and over in a variety of contexts for a variety of purposes. A model can help make sense out of information about a thinking operation, but what it reveals should not be considered the last word or the only legitimate description of any particular operation. Instead, a model of any thinking operation should be considered as a device for organizing instruction and as a general target of such instruction, but the exact conceptualization will vary with the data in which it is developed and the degree of expertise of the developer.

Presently, the states of cognitive science and skill teaching are such

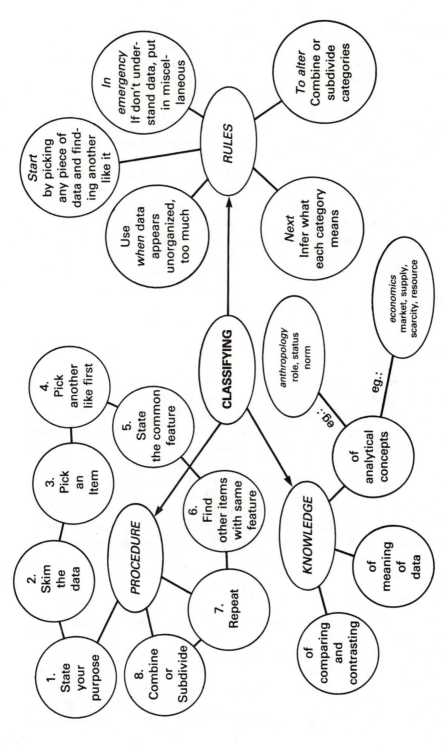

Figure 6.3 Key Attributes of the Skill of Classifying

131

that descriptions of most skills tend to concentrate almost exclusively on their procedures. Although explications of this attribute are certainly crucial for those charged with teaching a given thinking skill or strategy, the absence of descriptive information relative to the other types of attributes (rules and knowledge) makes for an imperfect and often one-sided understanding of a total skill or strategy. Yet descriptions of thinking operations in terms of their procedures alone are better than no descriptions at all. Moreover, focusing attention on the procedures by which a thinking skill or strategy is operationalized proves to be the easiest way to generate more complete descriptions of the other major attributes of that skill or strategy. Such limited descriptions can also be used by teachers to create lessons in which students, through application of the given procedure, can articulate what seem to be the rules and knowledge associated with the procedures. In time, students will generate for themselves and for teachers a more complete understanding of the skill. Both teacher and student knowledge of thinking skills or strategies can increase considerably while such skill procedures are being taught.

IDENTIFYING THE ATTRIBUTES OF THINKING SKILLS

Asserting the importance of detailed descriptions of even the procedural attributes of each thinking operation selected for instruction is one thing; finding such descriptions is quite another. At present, there is no single comprehensive source of such descriptions. But there are at least three kinds of sources educators can turn to in order to find or develop at least partial descriptions of these attributes. These include: (1) the work of theoreticians and researchers reported in the professional literature, (2) individual attempts to do the skill, and (3) student efforts to execute a skill. Each of these kinds of sources can provide descriptions of differing degrees of completeness, utility, and precision; all should be consulted in building descriptions of thinking operations for use in teaching and testing.

Professional Literature

Over the years, researchers have developed a number of techniques for identifying the nature and attributes of various types of cognitive operations. One of these techniques, product or outcome analysis, involves the analysis of a product of someone's thinking to infer what might have been done to produce that product. This technique has been used with writing in trying to reconstruct the processes of generating, organizing, composing, and revising written texts, and with working mathematical problems to reconstruct various mathematical operations and processes.[2] Another related and more refined technique, protocol analysis, consists of having individuals engage in a thinking task (e.g., solving a mathematical problem, making a decision, writing a certain type of statement) and while doing so, reporting aloud what he or she is doing.[3] A record or transcript of the individual's movements and remarks is then analyzed to identify the kinds of cognitive operations he or she is presumed to have made.

For example, the operation of analogy making is a widely tested and sometimes taught thinking skill. This skill is used in making such relationships as:

$$A \quad : \quad B \quad = \quad C \quad : \quad D$$

George Washington is to one as Abraham Lincoln is to _____ ?

(five, ten, fifteen, or twenty)

Psychologist Robert Sternberg reports that studies of protocols of how experts execute operations such as this one indicate the key steps in making analogies are to:

1. Identify/translate the key terms or elements in the first pair of the analogy (A and B).
2. Recall knowledge associated with each of these key terms or elements (A and B).
3. Infer the appropriate relationship between the key elements in the first pair (A and B).
4. Map the inferred relationship onto the key elements of the second pair of the analogy (C and D).
5. Apply the relationship inferred in the first pair (A and B) to the missing element(s) of the second pair (D) in order to complete the analogy.[4]

Other researchers have produced skill descriptions based on similar types of inquiry. Reading specialist Ann L. Brown and her colleagues, for example, identify what they believe to be the key steps in the skill of summarizing as follows:

1. Delete what is
   - trivial
   - redundant
   - irrelevant

2. Substitute the category label for
   - items in a list (such as: cat, dog, pony, bird become *pets*)
   - action items (such as: ran, jumped, rolled around become *played*)
3. Tie together the major ideas by
   - selecting the topic sentence, or
   - inventing one's own topic sentence[5]

The most crucial part of this procedure, Brown points out, is the final step, tying together the main ideas of the item summarized. She and her colleagues estimate, however, that less than 30 percent of tenth graders execute this final step, and only about 50 percent of college seniors do it. Engaging in the steps that precede this step make it easier to do this. Knowing all these steps in the procedure of summarizing can help teachers teach this skill explicitly to students and thus improve students' ability to execute this operation with some degree of proficiency. Descriptions of procedures that appear to constitute other thinking skills have also been reported by other researchers.

Through analysis of dozens of protocols, researchers have been able to generate almost step-by-step descriptions of how individuals of varying degrees of proficiency in particular thinking operations perform these operations. These descriptions appear increasingly in the professional literature, especially in collections of papers delivered at conferences, professional journals, studies in cognition and skill acquisition, and in reports of research in learning.

Theoreticians and specialists in various types of thinking have also inferred procedures and principles used in executing certain thinking operations, especially in the areas of problem solving, decision making, conceptualizing, and logical reasoning. In some cases, they have reported their descriptions of these operations in texts, essays, or articles in professional journals. Philosopher Michael Scriven, for example, has described the procedures for analyzing an argument as follows:

1. Clarify the meaning of the argument and its components.
2. Identify the stated and unstated conclusions.
3. Portray the structure of the argument.
4. Formulate the unstated assumptions.
5. Criticize the premises (given and "missing") and the inferences.
6. Introduce other relevant arguments.
7. Judge the argument in light of operations 1 through 6.[6]

Although a considerable amount of professional literature on thinking skills does exist, it is of uneven quality. However, educators seeking workable and reasonably detailed, if somewhat only partial, descriptions of various thinking operations may find the sources in Figure 6.4 most helpful.

Other types of written materials may also provide some of the major attributes of important thinking operations. Textbook and thinking test items, for example, can be used to infer some elements of thinking skills included in these materials. However, the sources listed here may be most useful, especially for those seeking to identify the key procedural attributes of these operations. Unfortunately, most of these sources devote little attention to rules or principles followed in executing these operations or to the knowledge components of these operations. Nevertheless, curriculum builders and teachers can use these procedural descriptions to initiate instruction in and student application of these operations in order to help students become aware of and learn the principles or rules that also constitute thinking skills.

Individual Attempts to Execute a Skill

Teachers can also identify some of the key attributes of any thinking skill or strategy by analyzing what individuals do as they engage in a task requiring execution of that skill or strategy. Such a task analysis can be done with the aid of a colleague or other individual recognized as having some degree of proficiency at executing the operation in question or by the teacher himself or herself. Either procedure requires a number of cases or tries—one cannot come to understand any thinking operation on the basis of a single try or case. However, analysis of how so-called experts execute a thinking task can contribute significantly to one's awareness and introductory understanding of the major attributes of important thinking operations.

Conducting a task analysis of a thinking operation consists essentially of securing a record of how an individual executes a specific operation. This record may be obtained by interviewing an individual engaged in executing the operation and getting him or her to talk aloud as he or she performs the operation, reporting on what is going on in his or her mind throughout the process. Or, the individual can be video taped as he or she silently executes the task. Either method produces a record that can be later analyzed and compared to similar records of others engaged in the same task. From analyses of many such records, one can at least build a beginning awareness of some key attributes of thinking operations.

Interviewing individuals engaged in a thinking task is often a challenging and exciting intellectual adventure. It not only allows one to watch other minds at work, but what one learns often comes almost as a "discovery." However, in conducting any such task analysis, it is important to remember that the greater the degree of an interviewee's exper-

1. Bloom, Benjamin, et al. *Taxonomy of Educational Objectives — Handbook I: Cognitive Domain*. New York: David McKay, 1956.
   This volume describes the nature of different types of educational objectives presented in the form of a taxonomy of cognitive behaviors moving from recall to comprehension, application, analysis, synthesis, and evaluation.

2. Damer, T. Edward. *Attacking Faulty Reasoning*. Belmont, Calif.: Wadsworth Publishing Company, 1980.
   In this small, college-level book, philosopher Damer describes fifty-eight common logical fallacies, providing for each a definition, several examples, and the way to attack it.

3. Ennis, Robert H. "A Concept of Critical Thinking." *Harvard Educational Review* 32:1 (Winter 1962), pp 81 – 111.
   This classic analysis of critical thinking includes the identification of key critical thinking skills and a general description of various attributes of these operations.

4. Frederiksen, Norman. "Implications of Cognitive Theory for Instruction in Problem Solving." *Review of Educational Research* 54:3 (Fall 1984), pp 363 – 407.
   In this summary of research studies into the nature of problem solving, Educational Testing Service psychologist Frederiksen analyzes various models of the process and how it is used with ill-defined as well as with clearly defined problems. He also explains a number of key implications for teaching problem solving.

5. Friedman, Michael and Steven Rowls. *Teaching Reading and Thinking Skills*. New York: Longman, 1980.
   On pages 169 – 211 the authors describe some of the characteristics of different thinking skills including categorizing, fact/opinion, relevant/irrelevant, deductive reasoning, inductive reasoning, predicting, and conceptualizing.

6. Hayes, John R. *The Complete Problem Solver*. Philadelphia: Franklin Institute Press, 1981.
   This text in general problem solving for college students includes sections on problem representation, memory and ways to use it, learning strategies, decision making, and creativity and invention. This is best read after Polya's work (below).

7. Hurst, Joe B., et al. "The Decision-Making Process." *Theory and Research In Social Education* 11:3 (Fall 1983), pp. 17 – 43.
   Although less complete than Frederiksen's analysis of research on problem solving, Hurst's survey of studies and articles on decision making provides a useful insight into various models and components of this major thinking process.

8. Kepner, Charles H., and Benjamin B. Tregoe. *The New Rational Manager*. Princeton, N.J.: Princeton Research Press, 1981.
   One of the clearest and most detailed explications of a decision making process available, this large work presents a step-by-step description of decision making from problem analysis to decision analysis. It can provide a basis for teaching this process throughout a curriculum.

9. Nickerson, Raymond S. *Reflections on Reasoning*. Hillsdale, N.J.: Lawrence Erlbaum Associates, Publishers, 1986.
   This exploration of reasoning explains in detail the nature of beliefs, assertions, arguments, and stratagems and then briefly describes twenty-one common reasoning fallacies. It concludes with ten basic rules for rational thinking.

10. Polya, Gyorgy. *How to Solve It*, 2d ed. Princeton: Princeton University Press, 1957, 1973.
    This classic explication of problem solving presents basic principles and procedures for problem solving with examples illustrating each major step.

11. Raths, Louis, et al. *Teaching for Thinking: Theories, Strategies, and Activities*, 2d ed. New York: Teachers' College Press, 1986.
    This is a new edition of a classic title. Chapter 1 provides general descriptions of such skills as summarizing, observing, classifying, interpretating, criticizing, looking for assumptions, imagining, hypothesizing, applying, decision making, and designing. Following that are chapters on ways for students to practice each in elementary and secondary grades.

12. Scriven, Michael. *Reasoning*. New York: McGraw-Hill, 1976.
    One of many good college texts on reasoning, Scriven's book describes and explains briefly the nature of reasoning and explains in detail key steps in analyzing an argument.

13. Toulmin, Steven, Richard Rieke, and Allan Janik. *An Introduction to Reasoning*, 2d ed. New York: Macmillan, 1984.
    An extremely clear introduction to argumentation, this text explains the structure of arguments and then how to determine the soundness and strength of arguments and how to identify common fallacies in argumentation. The authors then discuss applications of argumentation in different fields including science, the arts, and ethics. Examples, applications, and visual diagrams enhance understanding of the principles explained.

14. Wales, Charles E., Anne H. Nardi, and Robert A. Stager, *Professional Decision Making*. (Morgantown, W. Va.: Center for Guided Design, West Virginia University, 1986).
    This manual is a revision and elaboration of Wales and Nardi's 1984 Successful Decision-Making. It presents a detailed step-by-step explanation, analysis, and application of a 12-step decision-making process that is structured in four major operations and three modes of thinking.

15. Weddle, Perry. *Argument—A Guide to Critical Thinking*. New York: McGraw-Hill, 1978.
    In this guide, the author explains the nature of argument, selected fallacies, and the use of language in argumentation. He then examines the role of authority, generality, comparison, and cause. Numerous examples and applications are provided.

16. Whimbey, Arthur, and Jack Lochhead. *Problem Solving and Comprehension*, 3d ed. Philadelphia: Franklin Institute Press, 1982.
    This small book illustrates errors in reasoning and then provides instruction in problem solving, verbal reasoning, analogy making, analyzing of trends and patterns, and solving word problems; it is replete with examples, explanations, and opportunities for application.

Figure 6.4 Sources of Thinking Skills Descriptions

tise in the thinking operation being examined, or the greater one's expertise in the subject in which the operation is to be applied, the less likely it will be that the interviewee will be able to explain in the abstract exactly how the skill or strategy in question is executed. This is because experts seem to have "forgotten" how to do a skill; they simply do it automatically whenever it is appropriate to do so. As Polanyi once noted, experts often know more than they can tell.[7] Thus, to assist interviewees in recalling or articulating exactly how they execute a particular operation, it is usually advisable to engage the interviewee in executing the operation in order to illustrate how it is done.

For example, suppose we wished to identify the various components of the critical thinking skill of finding unstated assumptions. We could prepare an interview like that in Figure 6.5. This interview starts

---

Finding Unstated Assumptions

1. *Definitions*

    1.1 assume: to take for granted

    1.2 assumption: a statement accepted or supposed to be true without proof or demonstration

    in logic, a minor premise

    that which has to be true, if what is given is to be accepted as true

    1.3 unstated assumption: that which has to be true—but which is *un*written or *un*spoken—if what actually is given or stated is to be accepted.

2. *Examples: What must be true, if the answer to the following is to be accepted as correct?*

    2.1 If a person purchased two apples for a total of 10 cents, how much is each?

    ANSWER: 5¢ each.

    2.2 If this answer is correct, then we must *assume* that even though it is not so stated, the apples are equal in price. That the prices of all apples are equal is an *un*stated assumption. We should note that it could be possible that the cost of the first apple is 6¢ and each additional apple 4¢.

3. *Problem: Find two assumptions the author of the following passage makes but does not actually state about the European colonization of Africa:*

    . . . until the very recent penetration by Europe, the greater part of Africa was without the wheel, was without the plough and transport animals; without writing and so without history. Mentally and physically the African was helpless before a European intru-

---

sion all the more speedy and overwhelming because it came at a time when science had given Europe such tremendous material power.

M. Perham, "The British Problem in Africa," *Foreign Affairs* 30 (1951): 152

4. *Problem:* Find two assumptions the author of the following passage makes but does not actually state about the Bantu.

The school must equip the Bantu to meet the demands which the economic life of South Africa will impose on him. There is no place for him in the European community above the level of certain forms of labour. Within his own community, however, all doors are open. Until now he has been subject to a school system which drew him away from his own community and misled him by showing him the green pastures of European society in which he is not allowed to graze. . . . What is the use of teaching a Bantu child mathematics when it cannot use it in practice? That is absurd. Education is not, after all, something that hangs in the air. Education must train and teach people in accordance with their opportunities in life. It is therefore necessary that native education should be controlled in such a way that it should be in accordance with the policy of the State.

Hendrik Voerward, Minister of Bantu Development, Republic of South Africa, from *Last Grave at Dimbaza.*

Figure 6.5 A Sample Thinking Skill Interview Activity

with dictionary definitions of the skill to be investigated, provides an example with an explanation, and then asks the respondent to engage in the skill twice. By having a colleague or friend who is recognized as quite good in executing this task complete this activity and then discuss it with us, we might be able to identify *how* at least one person executes this skill, what rules he or she seems to follow in doing so, and what it is that he or she knows that makes it possible to execute the task. The more individuals we can get to complete this task and share with us how they did it and why they did it as they did, the closer we can come to uncovering some of the key attributes of this or any thinking operation.

We can conduct this task analysis in any of several ways. We could sit with a respondent who works through the written activity and reports aloud every few seconds what he or she is thinking and doing, while we write down his or her comments as nearly verbatim as possible (and/or record comments on a tape recorder for later analysis). By analyzing the resulting transcript (protocol), we can infer some of the key attributes of the skill. By conducting many such interviews and analyzing the protocols of each, we can begin to develop an understanding of key attributes of this skill.

Rather than require a respondent to talk aloud, we could video tape him or her silently doing the activity as directed therein, focusing the camera on his or her hands and face. After completing the activity, we can then have the respondent review the tape to explain what he or she was thinking as each move was made. The explanation can even be recorded and analyzed later along with similar recorded explanations made by others who engaged in the same task. This method, called *stimulated recall*, minimizes the interference in the thinking act that is created by interruptions of an observer seeking to keep the respondent "thinking aloud." It also provides specific referents to the respondent to help him or her recall what was going through his or her mind in executing the skill.[8] Where the respondent is involved in the follow-up analysis of a video recording of such an activity, analysis can be facilitated by use of questions such as:

1. What were you thinking when you did this (particular procedure)?
2. Why did you do this?
3. What other ways could you have done this? Why didn't you?
4. How would you help someone else do this same procedure?
5. How do you know you were doing this correctly or adequately?

By interviewing several individuals doing the same skill and then analyzing and comparing with them the transcripts or tapes of their actions and/or running report on what they did, teachers can identify some of the key features of a skill, enough to use as guidelines in planning lessons to introduce the skill to their students.

In using the task presented in Figure 6.5 we might find that, for Problem I, respondents might list the following as unstated assumptions:

One has to have writing to have history.

Africans were inferior to Europeans.

Writing, the wheel, and the plough are signs of civilization.

Military defeat suggests mental weaknesses.

Change in Africa came from the outside—Europe.

In explaining how any of these were identified as assumptions, the respondents might indicate that they, in general: (1) scanned the passage, (2) found some statements or assertions, (3) found other sentences that seemed to be conclusions based on but lacking explicit connections to these assertions, (4) identified what was in the related assertion (premise) and not in the conclusion, (5) identified what was in the conclusion and not in the related assertion (premise), and (6) combined these two elements to form the missing link (premise) or unstated assumption.

Thus, one phrase "without writing and so without history" contains a premise—without writing (Africans had no writing)—and a conclusion "so without history" (so Africans had no history), but leaves unstated the link between them. Here, the unstated assumption of the author is that without writing there can be no history.

Premises: *Without writing there can be no history.*
Africans had no writing.

Conclusion: Therefore, Africans had no history.

The phrases "*without* the wheel, . . . *without* the plough" connect to "the African was helpless"; what is assumed but left unsaid is that *with* the wheel and the plough, and all they stand for, Africans might have been stronger, that these elements are, in fact, synonymous with civilization. Analysis of the second problem and probing can flesh out a description of the procedure used, rules followed, and prior knowledge employed. It would soon become evident that an unstated assumption is a missing premise of a syllogism and that words like *so, therefore,* and *consequently* are often clues to the existence of such assumptions. Repeated interviews or analyses using this or a similar task can help identify the major attributes of the skill of finding unstated assumptions.

Teachers can also serve as their own sources of skill attributes by engaging in what is often called *retrospective analysis.* Working with a partner or two, teachers can engage in doing the skill and video tape themselves as they engage in it. Upon completion of the task, they can together analyze the tape to help them clarify what they did as they executed the skill. Or several teachers may engage in executing the skill and then attempt, without any prompts, to recall what they did in their minds as they executed the skill. In analyzing their effort, the following questions prove useful in helping to focus on the key steps in the skill procedure, important principles or rules followed in executing the procedure, and knowledge that proved useful in the process:

1. What did we do to get the result? What did we do first, next, next, and so on?
2. What do we know that allowed or led us to do each step?

3. How did we know what to do next?
4. How did we know we were achieving, or getting closer to achieving, our goal?

By answering these or similar questions, teachers can reconstruct, albeit in tentative terms, what went on in their own minds as they executed a skill. They can then use this information to prepare a tentative description of the skill that they can use as a basis for planning a series of lessons on the skill. This process, in short, consists of three steps:

1. Define the skill.
2. Do it—execute it.
3. Discuss how it was executed.

After defining the skill to be investigated, an individual, working with one or two others, can simply execute the skill. Then, after completing the skill task, those involved in doing it can reflect on and try to outline what they did in their minds to execute the skill.

An example of how an individual or several individuals can do this will perhaps clarify this approach. Suppose a teacher wished to identify the major attributes of the skill of detecting bias in a written statement. First, the teacher can recall or identify some common synonyms for *bias*, and look up several dictionary definitions of the term. Bias is commonly taken to be synonymous with preference, slanted view, or inclination. It is a slanted, often objectively untested, opinion about, or view of, something. A useful dictionary definition may be that a bias is an inclination for or against something that inhibits an impartial judgment. Then, after finding some written statements that may contain bias, the teacher and a colleague or two may start by analyzing a given statement to see if it shows evidence of bias. A history teacher might find the following statement useful for this purpose. It was written in England in the early nineteenth century. Is it biased?

1   Some of the lords of the loom employ
2   thousands of miserable creatures (i)n the
3   cotton-spinning work. The poor creatures
4   are doomed to toil day after day fourteen
5   hours in each day in an average heat of eighty-
6   two degrees. Can any man with a heart in his
7   body refrain from cursing a system that
8   produces such slavery and such cruelty?

9   These poor creatures have no cool room

10   to retreat to, not a moment to wipe off the

11   sweat, and not a breath of air. The door

12   of the place wherein they work, *is locked*

13   *except* at tea-time. If any spinner be

14   found with his *window open,* he is to pay a

15   fine.

16   For a large part of the time the abom-

17   inable stink of gas assist(s) in the

18   murderous effects of the heat which the

19   unfortunate creatures have to inhale. Children

20   are rendered decrepit and deformed and thou-

21   sands upon thousands of them (die) before

22   the age of sixteen.[9]

In reading this statement, one does not go far before deciding that there is considerable bias in it. Seeing the word "Lords" may initially arouse this suspicion because the word may have perjorative connotations. Continued use of words such as "miserable creatures" or "poor creatures" (instead of laborers or workers) and of words like "doomed" and "toil" suggest an effort to arouse sympathy for laborers. The leading question starting on line 6 reinforces this sympathy, as does the over-generalization in lines 9–15—*no* cool room, *not* a moment, *not* a breath. Not one? The italicized words draw attention to the facts that the workers were confined and were punished if they altered the conditions of that confinement. The adjectives used in the concluding lines simply trigger additional sympathy for the workers. The general pattern of all these devices is to elicit sympathy for the workers; little if anything favorable about the mill owners can be found. This statement certainly appears to be biased!

Discussion with others of how one arrives at this conclusion or reflection on what one did to arrive at it helps articulate some aspects of the skill of detecting bias. Having reaffirmed the purpose of looking at the statement—to identify whether or not it is biased—one starts reading to look for evidence of bias. Such evidence seems to pop up almost immediately. Repeated use of emotionally charged words alert us to the possibility of bias here. The leading question tells rather directly the author's preference, while at the same time putting the reader in a "no win" position of agreeing with him or, in fact, being inhumane—heartless! The author's use of italics further makes clear his position. As one reads, noting items like these, a pattern begins to emerge—repeated use of these devices seems to evidence a sympathy for the workers. The obvious lack of balance in the statement suggest rather strongly a negative attitude toward the mill owners who are presented as creating all the horrible conditions suffered by the workers.

What does one do, then, in executing the skill of detecting bias? In retrospect, it seems as if one may:

1. State the goal—to look for evidence of bias.
2. Read the data line-by-line or phrase-by-phrase to find indications of bias.
3. Look for any pattern or common relationship among these bias indicators.
4. Match the perceived pattern to some criteria of what constitutes bias.
5. Judge the extent to which bias seems to be found, and state the bias.

To understand this operation as completely as possible, it is worth doing it again. The following statement proves useful for this purpose. It, too, was written in England at about the same time as the preceding statement. Is this statement biased?

1	I have visited many factories and I never
2	saw children in ill-humor. They seemed to
3	be always cheerful and alert, taking pleasure
4	in the light play of their muscles—enjoying
5	the mobility natural to their age. The scene
6	of industry was exhilarating. It was de-
7	lightful to observe the nimbleness with which
8	they pieced the broken ends as the mule-carriage
9	began to recede from the fixed roller-beam and
10	to see them at leisure after a few seconds ex-
11	ercise of their tiny fingers, to amuse them-
12	selves in any attitude they chose. The work
13	of those lively elves seemed to resemble a
14	sport. They envinced no trace of (exhaus-
15	tion) on emerging from the mill in the evening;
16	for they skip about any neighboring play-
17	ground.[10]

From the previous experience, one recalls that bias is often revealed by excessive use of emotionally charged words (especially adjectives), by one-sided reports, by leading questions, and by exaggeration and overgeneralization. One can then search through this statement line-by-line looking for use of such devices. They seem to be there, but this time the bias seems to be a positive one, giving an impression that labor in these mills was akin to being at summer camp, a fun, envigorating, and stimulating experience! In doing this procedure a second time, it seems that recalling the different types of clues to bias is something that actually is often done between steps 1 and 2 in the original outline of the procedure. Thus, a more complete description of the procedure for detecting bias seems to be:

1. State the goal.
2. Recall clues to bias—use of "loaded" words, "loaded" questions, rhetorical questions, overgeneralization, one-sidedness, and so on.
3. Go through the data line-by-line or piece-by-piece to find evidence of these clues.
4. Identify any pattern among these clues.
5. Match the pattern of clues to the recalled standards of what constitutes bias.
6. Judge the extent of the match.

Interestingly, what emerges from such reflective analysis is that different individuals may execute this—or virtually any—thinking operation in slightly different ways. For example, although many may agree that the process described above represents how they seem to do it, others might indicate that in trying to decide whether some written document is biased, they:

1. State the goal.
2. Start examining the data.
3. Find one or two clues to bias, such as a "loaded" word or two.
4. Guess there is a bias and what it is.
5. Search for corroborating clues.
6. Identify a consistent pattern in the clues confirming the inferred bias.
7. State the bias.

Additional procedures may also be reported. Neither of these procedure descriptions represents "the correct" procedure. Both are workable. Both are useful procedures that can be used to detect bias.

There is a knowledge component to this skill, as well. Knowing some of the devices, such as loaded words and one-sided presentations, indicative of bias provides clues to look for to detect bias as well as criteria for judging what we find or don't find. The clues noted in these example statements, of course, are not the only clues to or evidence of bias. When searching for bias in a newspaper, for example, position of an article on a page, size of headline, and use of accompanying graphics may also give evidence of bias. Bias in a film might be revealed by the use of color vis-à-vis black and white, the way background music is used, and the content of the frames that accompany the narration. The skill of detecting bias in data is used with all kinds of media, audio as well as visual and written. Knowledge of these things about bias constitutes an important component of the skill of detecting bias.

In its most sophisticated form, the skill of detecting bias is certainly much more complex than it appears in this introductory encounter. As individuals become experienced in using this skill with a variety of media, their understanding of it deepens. Of course, the procedure by which this description of a thinking skill has been generated may not lead to the identification of any principles associated with the skill or of how the procedure may operate when used in other contexts. But enough has been identified here for a teacher to prepare at least a tentative description of this important thinking operation, as shown in Figure 6.6. Using this description as a target, a teacher can then plan a sequence of lessons on this skill. Introducing this skill to a number of classes will provide additional insights into the key attributes of the skill which, in turn, will provide a useful springboard for learning this skill.

In generating a description of the key attributes of any thinking skill, the first step in this process, as illustrated here (*defining the skill*), helps to develop a mental set appropriate to executing the skill. Brainstorming synonyms first or looking them up in a dictionary or thesaurus assists in this process by making it easier to articulate a reasonably accurate definition. Checking this definition against several dictionary definitions and revising it to include the key parts of these definitions is also appropriate at this point. In some instances, identifying examples of a skill (e.g., in the case illustrated here, examples of a "bias") make it easier to generate both synonyms and an accurate definition.

After doing or executing the skill with one or two colleagues, those involved can discuss what they did in their heads as they engaged in doing the skill. As they *discuss* this, they should list what they report under "steps," "rules," and "knowledge." By collecting what is recalled under these headings, it is easier to identify the key attributes of the skill being analyzed. These headings can also serve as search cues by which individuals may probe their memories to assist in recalling what they did or thought as they executed the skill. By use of this three-step 3-D

DETECTING BIAS

DEFINITION: Finding a one-sided or slanted view for or against something
bias: preference, slanted view, partiality, untested inclination that inhibits an impartial judgment

STEPS

Procedure A
1. State your purpose.
2. Identify the clues to look for, including
   - "loaded" or emotionally charged words
   - overgeneralizations
   - "loaded" or rhetorical questions
   - imbalance in presentation
   - opinions stated as facts
3. Take the material apart piece-by-piece or line-by-line to find the clues.
4. Identify patterns among or consistency of the clues found.
5. State evidence to support patterns found.
6. Judge the extent of the bias.

Procedure B
1. State your purpose.
2. Skim data/object.
3. Predict the bias when identifying first clues.
4. Search for corroborating clues
   - "loaded" or emotionally charged words
   - overgeneralizations
   - "loaded" or rhetorical questions
   - imbalance in presentation
   - opinions stated as facts
5. Search for a pattern in the clues.
6. State the bias found.

RULES
1. When to search for bias?
   - when an account seeks to persuade
   - in judging the accuracy of a source or statement
   - in identifying an author's point of view
   - . . .
2. How to start?
   - pick one clue and look for it, then pick another and search for it, etc.
   - . . .
3. What to do if . . .
   - you find little bias? Compare it to another piece of material on the same topic.
   - the vocabulary is unfamiliar? Use a dictionary to clarify meanings.
   - . . .

KNOWLEDGE
1. Of clues to or criteria of bias
2. Of the subject of the "account" being analyzed

Figure 6.6 A Tentative Description of a Thinking Skill

process of *define, do,* and *discuss,* teachers and others can identify, at least tentatively, some of the key attributes of virtually any thinking skills and strategies.

Written descriptions of individuals engaged in thinking can also provide insights into the major attributes of a thinking skill. Thoughtful analysis and discussion of exactly what these individuals do in their minds and why they do it can reveal a rather useful, but albeit tentative, description of a strategy or skill. Some useful descriptions do exist.[11] They can be used by teachers for purposes of identifying the key attributes of thinking skills they wish to introduce, as well as instructional materials in lessons designed for helping students develop their own metacognitive skills.

Student Execution of a Skill

Student efforts to engage in a skill can also provide insights into the key attributes of a thinking skill. In fact, with some caution, teachers can use the experiences of students in their classes who are attempting to carry out a skill to identify, at least tentatively, some of the major elements of the procedure, some rules or principles, and any useful knowledge that constitute any thinking still. Continued use of this procedure and sharing of what is discovered with other teachers engaged in similar teaching can lead to at least a tentative, introductory acquaintance with the skill. Armed with this information about a skill, a teacher can then introduce this skill to students in a very direct way.

One way to do this is to give students, working in pairs or triads, a task analysis activity similar to that described earlier (in Figure 6.5) as a basis for stimulated recall or retrospective analysis. Such an activity can be used by below-average as well as above-average students. By identifying the differences between how students of differing abilities execute the skill or try to execute it, teachers can identify not only how those most skilled do it but can also spot common faults exhibited by those who fail to execute it well. What is learned about the skill can be incorporated into descriptions of the skill communicated to other teachers and test designers, as well as into lessons designed to introduce the skill to students. In doing the latter, teachers can share with those students unable to do the skill ways the better students do it. Teachers can also intervene at appropriate places with those students who do not do it well to show them what they need to do to become more skilled at this operation.

It is important to note that task analysis devices such as this one are not primarily instructional in intent. They are for gathering data. What they yield may be most iodiosyncratic; only when considerable numbers of such interviews have been administered under the most controlled conditions and carefully analyzed is one able to venture even a tentative description of the skill in question. Of course, such an activity might also *launch* instruction in a specific skill, but much more would have to be done beyond raising student consciousness about the skill to teach it to any degree of proficiency.

Another way to have students help generate some key attributes of a skill is to introduce them to a skill using the following procedure:

1. Introduce the skill in question by giving its name, synonyms, and a simple definition of it.
2. Have the students execute the skill as best they can, using material provided for them.
3. Then have the students recall how they carried out the skill, the steps in the procedure they used, and any rules, principles, or knowledge they knew or used to guide them through the task. Even though not all students will have done the same things in the same ways, a tentative outline of several procedures, some rules, and some associated knowledge may emerge.
4. Next, have the students execute the skill again, keeping in mind what has been discussed about how they executed the skill previously.
5. Finally, have them report how they did the skill the second time, seeking the same kinds of information as above about the skill and revising the tentative outline of the skill attributes to accommodate new information.

Use of this strategy with average to above-average students can help teachers develop a tentative, though sketchy, outline of the major attributes of most thinking operations. Repeated use of this strategy on the same skill in different classes can help clarify key skill attributes and elaborate them. As teacher and students continue to apply the skill and to reflect on how they do it, the teacher's knowledge of the skill will grow, as will student expertise in using it. In fact, use of this strategy enables teachers to begin actually to teach a skill while at the same time learning more about it.

CAUTIONS ABOUT DEFINING SKILLS

Of course, each of the sources of skill descriptions described here has flaws. How expert is the expert selected to interview or observe? How does one reconcile different sets of attributes for the same skill? How does one know specifically he or she is getting information about the skill that presumably is being analyzed? These questions expose the limitations of the sources of and procedures for defining thinking skills presented here. However, these procedures are productive beginnings and can yield useful information. When used judiciously and in combination with each other on each skill, they may be the only practical way open to teachers and curriculum builders for developing the detailed skill descriptions teachers need to teach thinking skills and strategies as effectively as possible.

There are also other caveats to remember. Most importantly, the skill attributes identified represent working hypotheses only. They should not be assumed to be the only descriptions of how one proceeds to execute these skills. Our knowledge of a skill changes over time as the data it is used on becomes more sophisticated, complex, and abstract, as the purposes for which the skill is used change, and as experience in using the skill accumulates. Thus, any description should be considered, at best, incomplete and tentative, to be used only as a guide in teaching, learning, and testing rather than as the only description or model.

These cautions notwithstanding, detailed descriptions of the thinking operations selected for teaching are indispensable to effective instruction and testing. When communicated in a format like those in Figures 6.3 and 6.6, these descriptions have many advantages. A description of each skill selected as a major instructional goal or object of testing can be included in a curriculum guide, textbook manual, or test manual to inform teachers of the major attributes of skills they are supposed to teach. All teachers in a system can thus share a common definition of the skills they teach, and test makers can better ensure some congruity between the skills as they test them and classroom teaching of these skills. Instructional materials designers can use such skill descriptions for generating instructional activities and learning materials, and may even find it useful to include similar descriptions in the instructional materials they produce. Test designers can use these descriptions as the basis for the test items they develop. Students can even use the building or fleshing out of such descriptions as learning targets or worksheets. In spite of the potential weaknesses inherent in the procedures and sources from which these skill or strategy descriptions may be generated, such detailed descriptions of thinking operations in the format used here can be invaluable aids to the teaching and learning of thinking.

Teachers especially can consult the sources or use the procedures identified in this chapter to articulate or clarify the nature of the thinking skills and strategies they are charged with teaching. If these operations are to be taught well, teachers can not enjoy the luxury of waiting for some experts to prepare such descriptions before they attempt to start teaching them.

ENDNOTES

1. Robert H. Ennis, "A Logical Basis for Measuring Critical Thinking Skills," *Educational Leadership 43*, 2 (October 1985): 46.

2. Linda S. Flower and John R. Hayes, "Problem Solving Strategies and the Writing Process," *College English 39*, 4 (December 1977): 449–461.

3. John R. Hayes, *The Complete Problem Solver* (Philadelphia: The Franklin Institute Press, 1981), pp. 51–69.

4. Robert J. Sternberg, "How Can We Teach Intelligence?" *Educational Leadership 42*, 1 (September 1984): 40; see also Patricia A. Alexander, "Training Analogical Reasoning Skills in the Gifted," *Roeper Review 6*, 4 (April 1984): 191–193.

5. Ann L. Brown, Joseph C. Campione, and Jeanne D. Day, "Learning to Learn: On Training Students to Learn from Texts," *Educational Researcher 10* (February 1981): 17; Walter Kintsch and Teun A. vanDijk, "Toward A Model of Text Comprehension and Production," *Psychological Review 85*, 5 (September 1978): 363–394.

6. Michael Scriven, *Reasoning* (New York: McGraw-Hill, 1976), p. 39.

7. Edward Feigenbaum and Pamela McCorduck, *The Fifth Generation: Artificial Intelligence and Japan's Computer Challenge to the World* (Reading, Mass.: Addison-Wesley, 1983), pp. 79–80, 85.

8. John Edwards and Perc Marland, "What Are Students Really Thinking?" *Educational Leadership 42*, 3 (November 1984): 63–67.

9. Adapted from William Cobbett, *Political Register LII* (November 20, 1824). Italics in the original.

10. Adapted from Andrew Ure, *The Philosophy of Manufacturers: Or An Exposition of the Scientific, Moral and Commercial Economy of the Factory System of Great Britain* (3d ed.) (London: H. G. Bohn, 1861), p. 301.

11. See, for example, Arthur L. Costa, "How Scientists Think When They Are Doing Science," in Arthur L. Costa, ed., *Developing Minds: A Resource Book for Teaching Thinking* (Alexandria, Va.: Association for Supervision and Curriculum Development, 1985), pp. 114–117; and also Carol Madigan and Ann Elwood, *Brainstorms and Thunderbolts: How Creative Genius Works* (New York: Macmillan, 1983).

7

Identifying Thinking Skill Procedures

Even though the procedures by which we execute a thinking skill only partially describe a particular thinking skill or strategy, a general understanding of these procedures is extremely helpful in planning, assessing, and carrying out instruction in a thinking operation. These procedures can serve not only as general teaching and learning targets but also as skeletal frameworks around which students can build fuller, more sophisticated understandings of these operations as they gain experience in employing them. In effect, understanding the major steps in the procedure that distinguishes any thinking skill or strategy can serve as a starter for both effective teaching and learning of any thinking operation. This chapter outlines key steps in the procedures that constitute a variety of important thinking skills and strategies. Appendix B presents more complete descriptions of these and additional thinking skills and strategies.

Few authoritative descriptions of most thinking operations now exist. However, as indicated in the preceding chapter, classroom teaching experience, study of the professional literature, reflective analysis, and interviews with experts have led a number of educators, social scientists, and cognitive psychologists to outline descriptions of what they believe to be the major procedures that constitute some thinking operations. Teachers, program developers, and test makers can use these procedures and descriptions as a basis for planning instruction, initiating student learning, and assessing these operations.

MAJOR THINKING STRATEGIES

Problem solving and decision making are two of the most important major thinking strategies that can, and should, be taught in our schools. Each of these consists of a number of major steps and each of these steps consists of a number of subordinate steps. Furthermore, each of the steps in these two strategies incorporates a number of thinking operations of various levels of complexity, as outlined in Chapter 2. Although no single model or description of either strategy has won nation-wide acceptance for educational purposes, few dispute the value of using some tested model of each strategy as a basis for teaching and training. Several alternative conceptualizations of problem solving and decision making follow for use in planning instruction in these important thinking strategies.

Problem Solving

Much has been researched and written about the nature of problem solving. Over the past thirty years, cognitive psychologists, mathematicians, engineers, philosophers, and educators have contributed a great deal to understanding this thinking strategy.[1] The many different models of this strategy they have proposed share a number of common features. For example, all models of problem solving move from identifying a problematic situation to its resolution; all involve inventing hypothetical solutions; all involve some type of active testing or judging of the proposed solutions. Gyorgy Polya, a renowned mathematician, outlined the basic elements of this process in his famous book, *How to Solve It*, when he described a general process of problem solving as consisting of four steps: understanding the problem, devising a plan to resolve it, executing the plan, and looking back on the plan to ascertain its strengths and weaknesses.[2]

As common as these features are to most models of this strategy, several different general approaches to problem solving seem to be widely used and recommended. One is a generalized model useful in virtually any problematic situation. One version of this strategy consists of these five steps:

1. Recognizing that a problem exists (problem finding)
2. Representing the problem

3. Devising or selecting a plan to solve the problem
4. Executing and monitoring the solution plan
5. Evaluating the results

A rather detailed description of this general model is suggested by John R. Hayes, a cognitive psychologist, and other specialists in problem solving.[3] The key steps in this procedure are similar to those described in Chapter 3.

In *recognizing a problem*, step 1 of this procedure, an individual identifies a condition or situation in which there are discordant elements, gaps, or inconsistencies in the data. Problematic situations may be of different types, ranging from well-defined to ill-defined in terms of available data and parameters. *Representing the problem*, the next step, involves making both internal (mental) "models" as well as external (paper and pencil) representations of the perceived problem. Four elements are considered at this point: the desired goal, the present situation, actions (sometimes called operators) that could change the present state to the desired state, and constraints or restrictions on these operators. Such representations may be in the form of sketches, mathematical formulas, diagrams, or analogies.

A variety of techniques may be chosen as one engages in step 3, *devising or selecting solution plans*. These techniques range from simple trial and error to the use of established formulas or other tested methods. Brainstorming, scanning, restating the problem in various forms, working backward, focusing, and projecting may all be used to generate potential solutions. Where a problem does not seem readily amenable to resolution, one can generate analogous problems and, by applying these same techniques to the analogous problems, gain insights into ways the real problem can be resolved. A type of means-end analysis may also be used, in which the problem solver (1) lists the differences between the present and ideal states, (2) finds a way to eliminate each difference, (3) compares the conditions needed to apply each required action to the existing conditions, and (4) eliminates any differences found between the required and present conditions.[4] After identifying techniques and actions that give promise of resolving the problem, the problem-solver sequences them into a strategy, allocates appropriate time for the execution of each part of the plan, anticipates obstacles that may crop up in executing the strategy, and devises ways of overcoming these obstacles in case they do arise.

In *executing the plan* (step 4), one monitors what is being done through the use of feedback generated by the use of the planned strategy and repeated judgments regarding the extent to which the results close the gap between the existing condition and the ideal state or goal. As this occurs, adjustments may be made to the plan, and new solution techniques may be adapted or generated. Indeed, new perceptions of the problem arising in this process may lead to dramatically different solution plans being formulated and tried until the problem is resolved.

In *evaluating the results of the solution plan* (step 5), a problem-solver seeks to determine the extent to which the solution meets the goals and conditions originally specified. But this person does even more. He or she judges not only the reasonableness and accuracy of the solution but also the efficiency of the techniques and strategy used to bring about the solution. Finally, the results of this evaluation are incorporated into one's memory. The problem-solver determines what was learned about how to solve this particular type of problem, as well as about solving this problem itself, and then stores it in memory for future use when a similar problem arises in the future. Thus, by consolidating the experience, an individual's repetoire of problem-solving strategies increases just as his or her expertise in this important thinking process increases.[5]

This brief description of a general problem-solving strategy represents one type of problem solving. It draws heavily on recalled techniques for solving classes or types of problems (step 3) and does not specify how to go about selecting these solution techniques or strategies. Because it is a generalized strategy, supposedly applicable to any so-called "real life" problems, many solution techniques must be learned and stored in memory to employ this procedure successfully. This thinking process thus relies heavily on a broad base of knowledge about problem solving and about the various contexts in which problem solving occurs or is likely to occur.

Knowing how to employ this strategy of problem solving is one important segment of the knowledge component of problem solving. Professor Alan Schoenfeld has identified a number of heuristics that can guide one in applying this strategy, especially in the area of mathematics. Figure 7.1 outlines these rules of thumb. Schoenfeld relates these heuristics to a five-step strategy for managing a problem-solving task: analysis, design, exploration, implementation, and verification. By employing these rules as appropriate, one can execute the general problem-solving strategy described above in a most productive manner.[6]

Figure 7.2 outlines a second problem-solving procedure. This description combines the major operations of a number of problem-solving procedures typical of the social and physical sciences.[7] The major steps in this procedure are enumerated down the center of the model; the boxes on either side identify the cognitive operations that constitute each key step. Employing this procedure consists of proceeding through the major steps noted here and also executing the specific operations that constitute each step.

In this procedure, *defining the problem* (step 1) consists essentially of three operations: becoming aware that a problem exists, identifying the real or fundamental problem, and making the problem manageable. The

Analysis

1. Draw a diagram if at all possible.
2. Examine special cases.
   a. Choose special values to exemplify the problem.
   b. Examine limiting cases to explore the range of possibilities.
   c. Set any integer parameters to 1, 2, 3, . . . , in sequence, and look for an inductive pattern.
3. Try to simplify the problem.
   a. Exploit symmetry
   b. Use "without loss of generality" arguments (including scaling).

Exploration

1. Consider essentially equivalent problems.
   a. Replace conditions by equivalent ones.
   b. Recombine the elements of the problem in different ways.
   c. Introduce auxiliary elements.
   d. Reformulate the problem by
      i) changing perspective or notation
      ii) considering argument by contradiction or contrapositive
      iii) assuming you have a solution, and determining its properties
2. Consider slightly modified problems.
   a. Choose subgoals (obtain partial fulfillment of the conditions).
   b. Relax a condition and then try to reimpose it.
   c. Decompose the domain of the problem and work on it case by case.
3. Consider broadly modified problems.
   a. Construct an analogous problem with fewer variables.
   b. Hold all but one variable fixed to determine that variable's impact.
   c. Try to exploit both the result and method of solution in any related problems which have similar form, "givens," and conclusions.

Verification

1. Does your solution pass these specific tests?
   a. Does it use all the pertinent data?
   b. Does it conform to reasonable estimates or predictions?
   c. Does it withstand tests of symmetry, dimension analysis, or scaling?
2. Does it pass these general tests?
   a. Can it be obtained differently?
   b. Can it be substantiated by special cases?
   c. Can it be reduced to known results?
   d. Can it be used to generate something you know?

Source: Alan H. Schoenfeld, "Can Heuristics Be Taught?" in Jack Lockhead and John Clement, eds., *Cognitive Process Instruction* (Philadelphia: Franklin Institute Press, 1979). Reprinted with permission.

Figure 7.1 Heuristics for Guiding Problem Solving

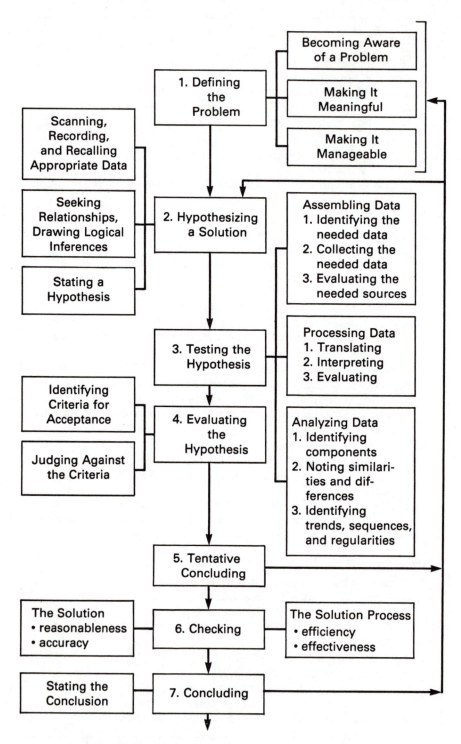

Figure 7.2 A Problem-Solving Strategy

first operation requires becoming aware of a gap between an ideal state and a present condition, or of some inconsistency or discontinuity in a situation. Individuals can use word cues (e.g., "how many?" "how long will it take?") to identify such problems in a subject context, but must match what they hear, read, or otherwise observe with their prior knowledge in order to spot problems in unfamiliar settings. Once a problem has been spotted or sensed, it can be made meaningful by representing it in some form or paraphrasing it or relating it to the individual's own experience. To make a problem manageable, an individual needs to break it into subordinate problems, the solution to each of which advances one toward the resolution of the entire problem.

Hypothesizing solutions to a problem (step 2) consists of inventing potential solutions. This requires scanning the available data and perhaps recording or recalling additional, appropriate data, seeking connections or relationships among these data, drawing inferences, and recognizing patterns and gaps in these patterns. Brainstorming proves a useful technique at this point, as does working backward from the ideal or the goal to the existing condition. A hypothesized solution, once stated, serves as a useful focus for what follows.

Hypothesis testing—or solution finding—is by far the most time consuming and intensive part of problem solving. It involves a variety of thinking operations, including analytical, creative, and critical thinking. As described in this model, hypothesis testing (step 3) includes assembling and processing appropriate data to see if a proposed hypothesis is viable. For each hypothesis one must collect data that, if the hypothesis were true, would exist to prove it true. In more sophisticated efforts, one must also seek data that controvert the hypothesis as well as data supportive of and contradicting competing hypotheses. "If . . . then" statements are used to identify these data; *if* this hypothesis is the correct solution, *then* "such and such" evidence will occur or exist (or will *not* occur or exist).[8] Collecting such evidence may involve recall, active library research, experimentation, or any of the scores of data-gathering and processing techniques commonly used by social or physical scientists, as well as serious efforts to verify the credibility, accuracy, and utility of the data thus gathered and of its sources.

Once data relevant to a hypothesis have been gathered—or as data are being gathered—it must be translated, interpreted, and examined critically (judged for bias, assumptions, relevance, and so on). Finally, data must be analyzed, taken apart to identify its components, its possible relationship to the hypothesis and the perceived problem, and any patterns inherent in it or between it and the hypothesis.

At this point, the hypothesis must be evaluated as to the extent to which it resolves the problem. *Evaluating hypotheses* (step 4) requires clear specification of the criteria against which they are to be judged, whether criteria of accuracy, utility, thoroughness, or whatever. Again, this requires identifying the criteria to be used and matching the hypothesis being tested against these criteria. At this point a *tentative conclusion* can be stated (step 5). Before accepting this conclusion as final, however, it needs to be checked. *Checking* (step 6) involves determining whether procedural or substantive errors were made, or if other procedures might produce the same or different results. Finally, in *Concluding* (step 7), if the hypothesis has met the stated criteria, it is then considered to be the sought-after conclusion and is so designated. Hypotheses rejected due to the absence of sufficient supporting data or because of their failure to meet other criteria for acceptance are discarded. In the latter case, attention then shifts to the invention and testing of new hypotheses—or to redefining the problem—until one can find a hypothesis that is corroborated by the evidence.

Although this procedure, like the preceding procedure, is presented in linear form, it, too, is recursive. One often moves back and forth from problem identification to hypothesizing solutions, from testing a hypothesis to problem representation and hypothesis making, and so on. As one engages in each part of the procedure, new insights develop that inform other parts of the procedure.

These two problem-solving models share a number of common features. Both include identifying a problem and clearly stating it as early steps in the process; the gathering, organizing, and evaluating of data as the next immediate following step; concluding the process and checking or evaluating the solution. What appears to differ is what happens between organizing the data for solving the problem and working out a solution. In the case of the generalized strategy, the intervening steps consist of picking a solution strategy from a number of potentially useful strategies and executing it. In the case of the second model, the intervening steps consist of hypothesis making and testing. However, this latter procedure can be conceived of as simply another type of solution plan or strategy. That is, hypothesizing-testing-evaluating solutions is in itself a solution strategy that can be employed to resolve a problem, just as can be other strategies or plans such as working backward from the solution, using matrices, recasting the problem into auxiliary problems or analogical problems, and so on. In this sense, the generalized strategy of problem solving serves as a useful way to organize any approach to problem solving. Learning a wide variety of solution plans or strategies useful in different contexts and with different classes of problems then becomes as central a goal of learning *how* to resolve problems as does learning an overall general strategy itself. *Teaching problem solving must thus consist of teaching two things: first, a generalized problem-solving framework, and second, a wide variety of specific solution plans, from which students can select to use in carrying out the general strategy as appropriate.*

Each of these models of a problem-solving procedure has special utility for different kinds of problems or contexts. Individually, they are not completely descriptive of problem solving, because, as Schoenfeld's list of heuristics indicates, various rules and procedures are employed by effective problem solvers. Educators may adopt or adapt one of these models or combine both to form a broader model, depending on their instructional goals. Certainly, neither model is the only way to describe a procedure of problem solving. However, the descriptions of this procedure provided here may serve as a useful starting point for curriculum planning, instruction, and assessment of the process of problem solving.

Problem solving and its related skills are executed in a variety of contexts. Initially, it is most effective to teach this process in terms of well-defined problems—problematic situations in which the problem itself is relatively clear and straightforward, where all the data required are readily available, and where there is convergence in terms of one "best" solution. But most real-life problems are not well-defined. The exact nature of the problem to be resolved is often quite unclear. Indeed, what is a problem often depends on one's point of view and background knowledge rather than the data inherent in the situation itself. The poverty that many Americans often consider to be a problem of underdevelopment in third world nations, these nations consider to be a problem of overconsumption on the part of Americans and the West. Moreover, the data needed to invent a solution are rarely all available. Indeed, many problems have more than one workable solution. Consequently, after developing proficiency in problem solving in controlled contexts, students must receive considerable instruction and guided practice in the strategies, techniques, and heuristics of problem finding and solution finding in different kinds of ill-defined contexts similar to those found in out-of-school life, if they are ever to be able to transfer proficiency in this process to nonacademic settings.[9]

Decision Making

Although some experts consider decision making and problem solving to be synonymous, others consider these two strategies to be quite distinct. In general, whereas problem solving seems most typical of situations in which there is a correct answer on which many people can agree, decision making seems to typify situations in which there are a number of possible or workable answers, but no single correct one. Whereas problem solving works best in nonvalue-laden situations, decision making incorporates value considerations and judgments. Whereas problem solving seems to involve identifying potential solutions and then "testing" them one after the other in serial fashion, decision making done well involves first identifying as many potential alternatives as possible and, only after that has been done, evaluating them often in relation to a common set of criteria.

Finally, the general problem-solving and decision-making processes differ significantly at the point where individuals posit what to do to remedy the problem at hand. At this point in problem solving (Step 3 in the model on page 158) an individual picks and executes a solution plan that seems likely to yield the correct solution. However, in decision making, at this point an individual picks a number of potentially desirable or possible options rather than a single solution strategy. Whereas in problem solving the search is for a way to produce a correct resolution, in decision making it is for identifying the "best" option from a range of available options, resources and so on.

A variety of descriptions of the procedures thought to be unique to decision making exist.[10] Whereas no single description is probably *the* correct description of these procedures, some descriptions are more functional and thorough than others. Two such descriptions follow.

Figure 7.3 presents a model of a decision-making procedure consisting of three components: *situation analysis, alternative analysis, and choice analysis.* Each of these three major components of this procedure, in turn, consists of a number of subordinate operations or procedures. In analyzing a situation that initiates decision making, one must identify its essential components, including the goal to be attained and its key attributes, relevant features of the present condition, and the key differences between the two. It is also important at this point to identify what apparently needs to be done to close this gap, and then to identify any obstacles or other factors that inhibit such action from being taken. A thorough situation analysis also includes efforts to identify the reasons or causes for such obstacles or inhibiting factors.

Once the situation itself has been carefully delimited, alternative ways to achieve the goal can be identified and analyzed. Such analysis consists essentially of identifying a variety of conditions or criteria which the "best" alternative ideally ought to meet, collecting information on each alternative relative to each criteria, and then judging the extent to which each alternative generated meets each of the criteria. In general, such criteria change according to the type of decision to be made; however, certain criteria may well be applied to most decision alternatives. Often, some criteria are weighted more heavily than others in terms of their importance in making the impending decision. One must identify the extent to which each alternative enables one to achieve immediate as well as long-range goals. In addition, one must examine each alternative in terms of the resources necessary to employ the alternative—including readily available resources as well as resources that can serve as effective substitutes for these resources; the costs involved, in terms of money, time, and other resources, as well as in terms of what will be given up by

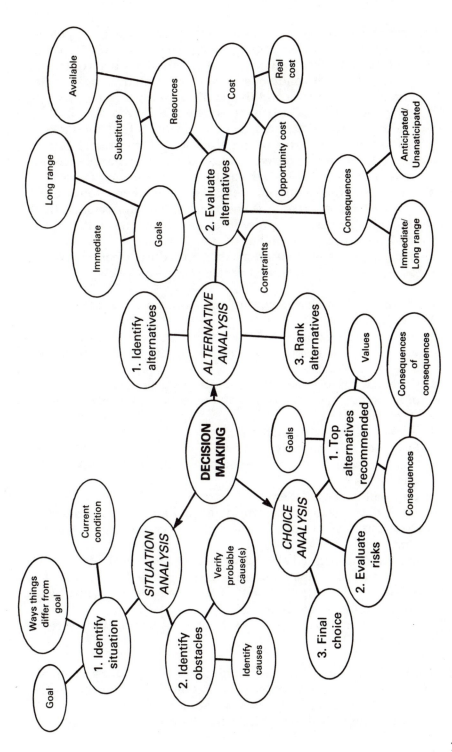

Figure 7.3 A Strategy for Decision Making

163

utilizing these resources in this manner (opportunity costs); the potential consequences, immediate as well as long range, and unanticipated as well as anticipated. Once data for each alternative have been collected for each of the criteria or conditions listed, the alternatives need to be rated in terms of each criteria and then ranked vis-à-vis each other.

Choosing the "best" alternative constitutes the third step in this decision-making strategy. This requires reevaluation of the top-ranked alternatives especially in terms of the goals sought, the values of the decision-makers, and the expected consequences. The risks inherent in each alternative also need to be identified, verified as much as possible, and evaluated. And then a final choice can be made. Thereupon, a plan of action for carrying out the decision can be made, an operation that involves a variety of planning procedures and techniques rather than decision making per se.

Other descriptions of decision-making procedures abound. Wales and Nardi, for example, conceptualize this process as follows:

1. Identify the problem requiring that a decision be made.
2. State the goal.
3. Gather information about the components of the situation— who or what is involved, where, when, and so on—and about its apparent causes.
4. Organize this information to indicate the distinguishing features of the situation—what is true and what is not true about it and what can be changed.
5. Generate alternative solutions.
6. Examine each alternative in terms of constraints on it, criteria it *must* and *should* meet, and assumptions associated with each, if it is to work.
7. Choose the "best" alternative.
8. Analyze the factors to be considered and how each can change.
9. Synthesize the information into a plan for carrying out the alternative.
10. Evaluate the planned alternative in terms of the goal, other criteria, and any anticipated positive and negative consequences to determine if the gains involved by using the alternative will outweigh the losses incurred.
11. Make a plan to evaluate the results of implementing the selected alternative.[11]

This procedure, of course, involves additional operations at each step of the way. Once it has been completed, it also calls for recommending a plan of action, implementing it, and evaluating the results.

Decision making—just as problem solving—is informed and guided by certain rules and principles of good practice. A variety of techniques may be employed to carry out each step. However, the procedures outlined in either of the models presented here offers a useful basis for teaching the thinking strategy of decision making. Each of the sets of procedures described here also constitutes a framework for using and thus learning the dozens of other, less complex, operations that constitute thinking.

MICRO-THINKING SKILLS

There is probably no better description of major information processing operations than that presented by Benjamin Bloom and his colleagues in their taxonomy of cognitive educational objectives. Figure 7.4 outlines these operations.[12] It should be noted, however, that this taxonomy does not mention many of the operations involved in some of these more general operations; for example, comparing, contrasting, and classifying are specific applications of analysis but are not mentioned in this outline. Nor does this outline include the various forms of reasoning that are also among those basic thinking operations referred to here as micro-thinking skills. What the Bloom taxonomy does do and do well is to define the operations listed in terms of their various levels of application. Exactly how one executes these operations is not included in Bloom's taxonomy.

Three micro-thinking operations used repeatedly in most major thinking processes are the skills of analysis, synthesis, and evaluation. Although these operations are not nearly as complex in their execution as are problem solving and decision making, they, too, can be described in part by the steps one goes through in executing them.

Analysis

The skill of analysis involves taking data apart and then identifying relationships among its constituent parts. This skill is an integral part of both synthesizing and evaluating. Like these two skills, analyzing is used at numerous points in the different thinking strategies. For example, one analyzes data in trying to identify a problem, in clarifying a problem, in devising hypotheses or potential solutions, and in testing the efficacy of these solutions. Analysis is one of the most widely used of all micro-thinking skills.[13]

Individuals engage in analysis on at least two different levels. At one level they analyze to find explicit features of something, attributes or components that are clearly manifested or evident. In analyzing at this level, individuals seek to make any of three different types of analy-

1. *Knowledge*—What is known. Evidence of knowledge is given by recall or recognition from memory of previous learning. The previous learning is relatively unaltered in the process.
    1.1 Knowledge of *specifics*—definitions, symbols, and specific facts (names, dates, etc.)
    1.2 Knowledge of ways of *organizing,* studying, judging ideas; of ways of treating ideas, trends and sequences, classifications, criteria by which facts are judged, methodology.
    1.3 Knowledge of *universals*—principles, generalizations, theories, concepts

2. *Comprehension*—understanding the literal message of a communication.
    2.1 *Translation*—putting communication into other form
    2.2 *Interpretation*—reordering of ideas into *new* configuration or meaning in mind of learner
    2.3 *Extrapolation*—extension of what is given, i.e., predicting on basis of given data, inferring consequences.

3. *Application*—applying an appropriate abstraction to a situation to give it meaning.

4. *Analysis*—breaking down material into its components—and detecting the way in which these parts are related.
    4.1—recognizing the parts of a communication (i.e., hypotheses, facts, opinions, assumptions, biases, value statements, conclusions, examples, evidence)
    4.2—determining relationships among elements—between hypothesis and evidence, conclusions-evidence-hypothesis, consistency part to part, relevance of parts to central idea
    4.3—recognizing organizational principles—frame of reference, point of view, patterns (form, structure)

5. *Synthesis*—putting together of elements or parts to form a new whole or a pattern not clearly there before; product is drawn from many sources and is more than what originally existed.
    5.1—producing a *unique communication*
    5.2—producing a *plan* or set of operations
    5.3—producing a set of *abstract relations*—a classification scheme

6. *Evaluation*—making judgments for some purpose, about things, using given or invented criteria.
    6.1—judging in terms of internal criteria—internal consistency, logical accuracy, citations
    6.2—judging in terms of external criteria—compared to other sources, rules of history, sources used

Source: From Benjamin Bloom et al., *Taxonomy of Educational Objectives: The Classification of Educational Goals: Handbook 1.* Copyright © 1956 by Longman Inc. Reprinted by permission of Longman Inc., New York.

Figure 7.4 Selected Micro-Thinking Skills

ses. They analyze to identify the parts of a whole (e.g., the introduction, body, or conclusion of a written text; the causes and results of a particular event; or the thesis, evidence, assumptions, and reasons that constitute an argument). Beyond this, they analyze to identify the relationship of the parts to each other and to the whole (e.g., the connections between hypothesis, evidence, and conclusion; or between causal factors and observed results). And going even further, individuals analyze to identify the organizational patterns or structures (e.g., inquiry patterns) that hold statements together.

At a second level, analysis focuses not on what is evident but on what is not readily evident, on implied rather than explicit aspects of an object, event, or communication. Thus, one can analyze a written passage for mood, or tone, or author's point of view, or frame of reference. One can analyze an object to identify the chemical elements of which it is composed. One can analyze a character to identify motive or values. In these instances, analysis seeks to uncover essentially what is not readily apparent or explicit, whether these components are elements of something or a pattern of relationships among implicit components or broad structural frameworks revealed only indirectly by what is evident. Analysis can be employed to identify what is implicit in things as well as what is explicit, and to identify parts of a whole, relationships among parts, and structural patterns at both levels.

The skill of analysis is in many ways unique among thinking skills. Like most other micro-thinking skills, this skill is distinguished by a relatively straightforward procedure. But unlike most other thinking skills, analysis also consists of task-specific knowledge and rules that shape the use of this procedure. There is a substantive knowledge component to this skill that seems to be lacking in many other thinking operations.

One does not customarily analyze something for no reason at all. Instead, analysis is goal directed. We analyze for a purpose—to find something. Thus, to engage in any analysis it is necessary first to determine what one expects, wants, or needs to find; having done this, one then identifies the specific criteria or clues that will guide us to that goal. For instance, we are guided in analyzing to find the parts of a paragraph by knowledge of what these parts are—we seek a topic sentence, a concluding sentence, supporting evidence, and so on. In analyzing the same paragraph for evidence in support of a claim, we know that we have to find an assertion or claim, pieces of evidence supportive of that claim, and perhaps reasoning and unstated assumptions that link the evidence to the claim. The skill of analysis consists, in large part, of *knowledge of many different sets of criteria*, each descriptive of a particular thing one seeks to identify by means of analysis. An individual who is good at analysis of part-whole relationships knows the components of paragraphs, theories, arguments, or other structures, and how these components hook together. An individual who knows the major parts of a particular literary form such as novel or short story, tragedy or satire, can better analyze purported examples of such a form than can one who has no such knowledge. Applying criterial knowledge to purported examples of phenomena is what analysis is all about. Knowing what clues or evidence to look for is as important as doing the looking.

Whereas the knowledge component of analysis varies according to purpose, the procedure that constitutes analysis does not. It appears that regardless of any specific purpose, the procedure of analysis generally consists of taking something apart to find pieces or parts of it and then identifying the connections or patterns perceived to exist among the identified parts. Although there are a number of variations of these essential features, analysis generally proceeds as follows:

1. Identify the purpose of the analysis.
2. Recall or otherwise identify the clues, or evidence, to look for to accomplish this purpose.
3. Search the data piece by piece or line by line to find these clues or evidence.
4. Identify any pattern of relationships among the data, clues, or evidence.
5. State the results of the analysis, providing evidence to support these results.

The keys to successful analysis are thus twofold: (1) knowing what clues or criteria or evidence to search for and (2) engaging in a systematic search through the data to find such clues, criteria, or evidence. Those most successful at employing this skill recall the kinds of clues or evidence they need to find in order to accomplish their stated objective; having a precise objective, in effect, tells them what kinds of clues or criteria they need to recall. Once these clues (step 2) have been identified or recalled, they conduct a rather pain-staking search through the data to see if they can find any evidence of these clues and of how they relate to each other. This micro-thinking skill is one of the most important of all thinking operations, serving as an essential element of creative as well as critical thinking, of problem solving as well as of decision making and conceptualizing.

Synthesis

A synthesis is a unique communication, something that did not exist in its present form until it was just generated. The products of synthesizing come in many forms and include topic sentences, hypotheses, general-

izations, concepts, paintings, plans of action, theories, musical composi-
tions, plays, short stories, and oral reports. The essential steps in synthesizing consist of:

1. Identifying a topic
2. Collecting information, ideas, and impressions about it
3. Arranging the information into categories, labeling each, and
   combining or subdividing categories as appropriate
4. Inferring relationships or connections among the categories of
   information
5. Stating the inferred relationship(s)

This procedure of collecting, classifying, combining, and constructing
can be applied to generate, for example, a single generalization about
the early English colony at Jamestown, given this information:

There was a shortage of corn

Maleria caused many deaths

Indians and Europeans fought each other

By going through the above steps, one might produce this generalization: Life was difficult in early Jamestown. Unsubstantiated by additional inquiry, this generalization may have only the status of an hypothesis; substantiated by further research and analysis, however, it
might conceivably become a conclusion.

The procedure of synthesizing also enables one to generate a more
complex synthesis, as when given the topic, *presidential primaries*, and
this information:

Exhaust the candidates

Enlighten voters

Last a long time

Cost tremendous amounts of money

Often divide a party internally

Involve people in grassroots activity

Sometimes focus on important issues

Because there are at least two different types of information included
here, a synthesis may appear at first to be difficult. But by classifying the
information into two categories and then identifying the relationships

between these two categories, it is possible to assert that "Presidential primaries produce both positive and negative results." or "Even though presidential primaries are useful, they often produce negative results." Where contradictory information seems to exist, casting a generalization in terms of "even though" or "in spite of" statements helps accommodate these data.

The skill of synthesis making is employed repeatedly in decision making and problem solving. It is used to invent thesis statements as well as concluding sentences, concepts, as well as theories. And the steps that one appears to go through in any of these tasks seem to be those described here.

Evaluation

Like synthesizing, the skill of evaluation is used repeatedly in larger thinking strategies such as decision making and problem solving. It is used in decision making, for example, in deciding which alternative is the best alternative and, prior to that, in deciding the extent to which each alternative meets the criteria used to analyze all alternatives. Any thinking operation that involves making a judgment involves evaluation. This skill consists primarily of these steps:

1. State the purpose of the evaluation—whether one is judging factual accuracy, symmetry, or whatever.
2. Identify and define the criteria to be used, whether already given or self-generated.
3. Identify the clues to or evidence of the selected criteria.
4. Search the data piece by piece to find the evidence or clues.
5. Match the evidence or clues found to the standards implied by each criterion.
6. Judge the degree of match for each criterion.
7. Combine the results of each match to determine the overall evaluation.
8. State the overall evaluation.

One can utilize this procedure to evaluate any object, idea, event, proposition, or other phenomena. When combined with knowledge of the specific criteria appropriate to the kind of evaluation sought, an individual can execute this skill with some degree of proficiency.

CRITICAL THINKING

Critical thinking involves judging the worth, accuracy, or authenticity of a source, information, thoughts, arguments, or claims.[14] Individuals engage in critical thinking when they assess the truth of statements, the validity of arguments, or the soundness of proposals.[15] Critical thinking presupposes neither unfavorable nor favorable judgments. It is rarely engaged in as an end in itself, but rather is part of a larger effort that seeks clarification or understanding of some subject. It is used as repeatedly in the processes of making decisions or resolving problems as it is in argument analysis or development. Importantly, the judgments arrived at through critical thinking are themselves also subject to further critical thinking.[16]

Critical thinking is less a process or strategy through which one proceeds in sequential fashion than it is a collection of thinking operations from which one may choose to determine the weaknesses or merits of something.[17] The most commonly used of these operations include, but are not limited to, the following:

1. Distinguishing between statements of verifiable facts and value claims
2. Distinguishing relevant from irrelevant information, claims, or reasons
3. Determining the factual accuracy of a statement
4. Determining the credibility of a written source
5. Identifying ambiguous claims or arguments
6. Identifying unstated assumptions
7. Detecting bias
8. Identifying logical fallacies
9. Recognizing logical inconsistencies in a line of reasoning
10. Determining the strength of an argument or claim

One does not need to employ all these operations in order to engage in critical thinking, nor does one necessarily use any of these in a given order. Rather, one can engage, for example, in identifying relevant information—distinguishing it from irrelevant information, identifying unstated assumptions, and identifying inconsistent reasoning, and have engaged in critical thinking. In the course of determining the strength of a claim, however, one may engage in virtually all these operations en route to making a final appraisal of how strong or believable the claim is.[18]

Each critical thinking operation listed above consists of both a procedure and a set of criteria or standards as well as certain operating rules. In executing any critical thinking operation one identifies the set of criteria to be used, searches through the argument, source, or information being examined to find evidence related to these criteria, and then judges and justifies the extent to which the evidence fits the criteria. The final assessment expresses the judgment, provides reasons for the judgment, and identifies the rules or criteria used as standards for making the judgment.[19]

Thus, for example, in judging the credibility of a written source, one first identifies the indicators or criteria of credibility to be employed. These might be a reputable author with: a reasonable degree of expertise; the absence of a conflict of interest; the existence of a known risk to his or her reputation; the use of accepted methods to develop the information communicated; the quality of his or her research; and agreement of the source with other sources on the subject.[20] Then, the relevant information is examined piece by piece to find evidence related to these criteria. Finally, any evidence found is matched to the standards implied by these criteria to produce a judgment about the degree of credibility to be given the source.

All critical thinking operations consist of essentially the same generic procedure. To engage effectively in any of the critical thinking operations listed above, one usually proceeds to:

1. State the purpose (goal) of the analysis.
2. Identify the criteria or rules to be used.
3. Search the data piece by piece (line by line or component by component) to locate evidence of these criteria/rules.
4. Identify any pattern (regularities, repetitions, common associations) among this evidence.
5. Match the evidence and perceived patterns in the evidence against the previously identified criteria or rules.
6. Determine (judge) the extent to which the ideal set of standards or criteria have been met.

This six-step procedure involves two distinct types of thinking. It first requires analysis of some data—taking it apart to find specific evidence of the criteria relevant to a particular critical thinking operation (as when one searches to identify evidence related to credibility, for example) and to identify whatever pattern may exist among the evidence found. Second, evaluation is required—a judgment about the extent to which the evidence found matches the criteria considered to be indicative of what is being sought (credibility, in the above example). Virtually all critical thinking operations employ this two-part, six-step procedure, or some process very close to it.

What is unique to each critical thinking operation is the criteria or rules that serve as the standards that typify that aspect of critical thinking. In attempting to identify biased data, for example, one looks for evidence of such criteria as emotionally charged words or exaggerated claims, and for a pattern in which this evidence seems to accumulate. In trying to identify statements of verifiable fact, one seeks evidence that a statement is objectively demonstrable as true or false, or that it has already been proven to be true. The criteria used to judge the existence of bias differ from the criteria one looks for to identify statements of verifiable fact or unstated assumptions, but the procedure one goes through to apply these criteria is essentially the same. Each critical thinking operation requires reference to a specific set of critieria that enables one to judge the extent to which something meets a specific condition or is a particular type of product or behavior.

Figure 7.5 outlines both the general steps through which one can proceed in executing any of these particular critical thinking operations, and the clues or criteria used in each of eight critical thinking operations: distinguising the relevant from irrelevant, distinguishing statements of verifiable facts from value judgments, identifying bias, identifying unstated assumptions, judging the credibility of an observation or of a written source, determining the quality of a generalization, and determining the strength of a conclusion. Other critical thinking operations have their own criteria. Knowing these criteria and the standards they imply enables individuals to use the procedure outlined here to objectively examine statements, sources, or ideas in order to judge their authenticity, worth, or accuracy.

One very important critical thinking operation is that of determining the strength or quality of an argument—a claim or position supported by a line of reasoning and evidence. Commonly, an argument consists of an assertion (or conclusion), an explanation of the assertion, reasons for it, and alternative conclusions with reasons and evidence that challenge them. In its simplest form, determining the quality of an argument involves identifying an assertion (conclusion) and then examining its supporting reasoning and assumptions to determine if they are accurate, relevant, logical, and free of inconsistencies and fallacies. However, Scriven's description, referred to earlier, lists a more complicated, seven-step procedure for carrying out this operation:

1. Clarify the meaning of the argument.
2. Identify the stated and unstated conclusions.
3. Determine which premises support which conclusions.
4. Identify and state any unstated assumptions.
5. Determine the reliability/reasonableness of the inferences and premises.
6. Consider other relevant arguments.
7. Make a final judgment about the overall argument.[21]

In its more complex form, determining the quality of an argument involves even more operations. Figure 7.6 outlines one description of the major components of this complex operation. Not surprisingly, one engages in most other critical thinking operations enroute to making a final determination about the quality of any argument.

Relevancy
definition
example
attribute
detail/fact
explanation/reason
evidence for/against
a relationship

Fact   or   *Value Judgment*
precise   opinion
certain   subjective
objectively   personal
demonstrable/   (adjectives)
testable
(no adjectives)

Bias
a pattern of:
exaggeration/over-generalization
"loaded" words
opinions asserted as facts
imbalance (one-sidedness)
loaded images
loaded questions

Unstated Assumptions
gap between conclusion or
assertion and a premise
two claims without a linking
statement
clues: so, thus, therefore, without . . .

1. Identify your goal or purpose.
2. Identify the criteria/clues to use.
3. Search the data piece-by-piece to find evidence of the criteria or clues.
4. Identify any pattern among the evidence—how they are connected to one another.
5. Match the evidence/clues and pattern found to the ideal/standard.
6. Judge the extent/degree of fit/match between evidence found and the criteria/standards.

Credibility of an Observation
short time between report
and observation
report by observer him/herself
minimal inferring
reporter believed observation
to be accurate
corroboration by other sources

Strength of a Conclusion
reasonable assumptions
conclusion does explain
the evidence
conclusion is consistent
with known facts
competing conclusions are
inconsistent with known
facts
conclusion seems reasonable

Quality of a Generalization
typicality of the data used
width of coverage
nature of sample

Credibility of a Written Source
author reputation for accuracy
expertise of author
absence of conflict of interest
known risk to author's reputation
use of accepted methods by author
agreement with other sources

Figure 7.5 Key Critical Thinking Skills

1. Decide if the statement to be evaluated is an argument (rather than an excuse, disagreement, or explanation)
   1.1 Search for components of an argument
   1.2 Identify a line of reasoning in support of a statement
2. Identify the main claim (thesis, assertion, conclusion)
   2.1 Clarify meaning of the statement
   2.2 Pick the main claim made
3. Analyze the argument
   3.1 Arrange subclaims/premises in order
   3.2 Remove irrelevant information
     • repetitious statements
     • examples
     • dramatic pieces
   3.3 Distinguish statements of fact from value judgments
   3.4 Identify unstated assumptions (missing premises)
   3.5 Identify bias
4. Evaluate the argument, for:
   4.1 Substantive accuracy of evidence/facts
     • determine sufficiency of evidence given
        significance
        relevance
        accuracy (truth/probability/acceptability)
     • determine sources, identify their
        accuracy
        reliability
        appropriateness
   4.2 Logic of line of reasoning given
     • determine adequacy of line of reasoning
     • determine applicability to the case
   4.3 Ambiguities/equivocation, seeking
     • inconsistencies
     • loopholes
     • fallacies
5. Evaluate inferences for validity
   5.1 Determine soundness
     • degree of support given
     • degree of support known to exist
   5.2 Determine applicability
6. Consider other arguments
   6.1 In support of claim
   6.2 Contrary to claim
   6.3 In support of alternative claims

continued

Figure 7.6 Determining the Quality of an Argument

---

7. Judge the quality of the argument
   7.1 Is it logically valid?
   7.2 Is it truthful (accurate)?
      • probably true?
      • acceptable?
   7.3 Is is strong?
      • modestly strong?
      • weak?
      • unacceptable?

Figure 7.6 (*Continued*)

As noted in Chapter 2, critical thinking consists of more than a set of cognitive operations. It also consists of very specific dispositions—inclinations to act in a certain way.[22] These dispositions motivate, reinforce, and guide critical thinking. Effective critical thinkers accept the general need for and, indeed demand, evidence and logical reasoning to support whatever is asserted to be true.[23] Elliot Eisner identifies these dispositions as including those to justify anything by providing reasons, to value skepticism, and to consider alternative views.[24] The dispositions that drive critical thinking are almost certainly as much a part of this kind of thinking as are the operations of which it consists.

CAUTIONS TO KEEP IN MIND

The descriptions of the thinking skills presented here should be used with caution. First of all, these descriptions constitute working hypotheses only. They should not be presumed to be the only descriptions of how one proceeds through these skills and strategies. Rather, they represent one conceptualization of how such operations are executed.

Moreover, thinking operations, as noted in Chapter 5, consist of more than procedures. As indicated in that chapter, they also consist of rules and other types of knowledge in addition to the set of procedures by which they are executed. Furthermore, they are informed by the subject matter with or in which they are applied. In addition, thinking in general consists of attitudes or dispositions supportive of these skills. Although knowledge of a specific procedure helps define the skill of which it is part, this procedure is only part of the complete skill.

The procedures presented here should not be taught without scrutiny or without regard for adaptations made according to the content in which they are applied. Nor should they be taught literally as procedures to be remembered precisely as stated. Rather, they should be taught and used as guidelines only; students should continually revise, amend, and elaborate these procedures as they engage in them. These procedures may thus serve as starting points for guiding practice in these skills, but not as absolute ends in themselves.

Finally, these descriptions of skill procedures are tied closely to subject areas in which they are developed and to a level of expertise in executing them. They change over time as one matures and as the data with which they are used become more sophisticated, complex, and abstract, as the purposes for which these skills are used change, and as one's experience in using them increases. Any description we contrive of these procedures should be considered, at best, imperfect and tentative, to be used as a guide in teaching and learning rather than as a prescriptive model.

The preceding cautions notwithstanding, descriptions of skill procedures as presented here and elsewhere in the literature are extremely useful. In a very practical sense, such descriptions enable teachers and materials developers to prepare clear lessons designed to demonstrate and to provide guided practice in how to execute the thinking skills being learned. These descriptions can also serve as the basis of simple mnemonic devices to assist students in remembering how to execute newly developing thinking skills. For example, the main steps in the procedure of analysis can be arranged as follows to aid students in recalling how to do this skill:

Agree on your purpose

Pick needed criteria and clues

Analyze to find needed clues

Relate clues to each other and to criteria

Tell what you find

The first letters of the first word in each step spell APART, which is the essential feature of analysis. A similar device can be created to help students remember and organize one way of engaging in the skill of synthesis:

Get your data

Arrange it in groups

Tell the label of each group

Hook groups into new groups

Establish connections among groups

Report these connections

Each of these devices can be shared with students as they are learning these skills. Students can use them to recall how to do the skill and to serve as frameworks on which to build increasingly more complete understandings of and improved competencies in using these skills. Such devices can be produced by creative students and teachers for any thinking skills taught.

Not only do descriptions of skill procedures serve as a springboard for initiating teaching of skills, but they can serve as a framework for identifying and interrelating the rules, criteria, and operational procedures that emerge in applying these procedures in the classroom. The format used in describing the skill of detecting bias (Figure 6.6 in the preceding chapter) serves this purpose well. Appendix B consists of tentative descriptions of other thinking skills and strategies presented in this format. By providing similar drafts of such descriptions for each skill selected as a major teaching goal in a curriculum guide, teachers can be informed of some of the components of the skills they are supposed to teach but about which they may be uninformed. Availability of such descriptions can thus encourage and assist teachers to launch instruction in thinking skills and can also provide some degree of consistency across all teaching. Although descriptions of the procedures that may constitute a skill may be somewhat tenuous at the moment and even only partially descriptive of the skills of which they are deemed to be a part, they offer an excellent springboard for initiating teaching and learning of thinking skills.

ENDNOTES

• 1. Norman Frederiksen, "Implications of Cognitive Theory for Instruction in Problem Solving," *Review of Educational Research 54*, 3 (Fall 1984): 363–407; John Dewey, *How We Think* (Boston: D. C. Heath, 1910); John R. Hayes, *Cognitive Psychology: Thinking and Creating* (Homewood, Ill.: Dorsey Press, 1978); Gyorgy Polya, *How to Solve It* (Princeton: Princeton University Press, 1945/1973).

2. Polya, *How to Solve It*.

3. John R. Hayes, *The Complete Problem Solver* (Philadelphia: The Franklin Institute Press, 1981).

4. Ibid., pp. 1–49.

5. Polya, *How to Solve It*; Hayes, *The Complete Problem Solver*.

6. Alan H. Schoenfeld, "Can Heuristics Be Taught?" in Jack Lockhead and John Clement, eds., *Cognitive Process Instruction* (Philadelphia: The Franklin Institute Press, 1979), pp. 315–338.

7. Barry K. Beyer, *Teaching Thinking in Social Studies* (Columbus, Ohio: Charles E. Merrill, 1979), pp. 42–65.

8. Maurice P. Hunt and Lawrence E. Metcalf, *Teaching High School Social Studies* (2d ed.) (New York: Harper & Row, 1968), pp. 68, 108–109; Beyer, *Teaching Thinking*, pp. 49–50.

9. Frederiksen, "Implications of Cognitive Theory,"; Robert J. Sternberg, "Teaching Critical Thinking, Part I: Are We Making Critical Mistakes?" *Phi Delta Kappan 67*, 3 (November 1985): 194–198.

10. Joe B. Hurst, Mark Kinney, and Steven J. Weiss, "The Decision-Making Process," *Theory and Research in Social Education 11*, 3 (Fall 1983): 17–43; Hayes, *The Complete Problem Solver*, pp. 145–196; Charles H. Kepner and Benjamin B. Trego, *The New Rational Manager* (Princeton, N.J.: Princeton Research Press, 1981).

11. Charles E. Wales and Anne Nardi, *Successful Decision Making* (Morgantown, W. Va.: Center for Guided Design, West Virginia University, 1984).

12. Benjamin Bloom et al, *Taxonomy of Educational Objectives—Handbook I: Cognitive Domain* (New York: Longmans, 1956).

13. Ibid., pp. 144–150.

14. Robert Ennis, "A Concept of Critical Thinking," *Harvard Educational Review 32*, 1 (Winter 1962): 81–83.

15. Kenneth B. Henderson, "The Teaching of Critical Thinking," *Educational Forum 37*, 1 (November 1972): 45–52.

16. Ennis, "A Concept of Critical Thinking"; Robert Ennis, *Critical Thinking and Education* (New York: St. Martin's Press, 1981); Ted Feeley, Jr., "Critical Thinking: Toward a Definition, Paradigm and Research Agenda," *Theory and Research in Social Education 4*, 1 (August 1976): 1–19.

17. David H. Russell, *Children's Thinking* (Boston: Ginn and Co., 1956), p. 302; Feeley, "Critical Thinking," p. 5; Edward N. Glaser, *An Experiment in the Development of Critical Thinking* (New York: Bureau of Publications, Teachers College, Columbia University, 1941).

18. Barry K. Beyer, "Critical Thinking: What Is It?" *Social Education 49*, 4 (April 1985): 270–276.

19. Ennis, "A Concept of Critical Thinking."

20. Robert H. Ennis, "A Logical Basis for Measuring Critical Thinking Skills," *Educational Leadership 43*, 2 (October 1985): 46.

21. Michael Scriven, *Reasoning* (New York: McGraw-Hill, 1976), p. 39.

22. John McPeck, *Critical Thinking and Education* (New York: St. Martin's Press, 1981), p. 162; Ennis, "A Logical," p. 46.

23. Godwin Watson and Edwin Glaser, *Manual for the Watson-Glaser Critical Thinking Appraisal* (New York: Harcourt Brace Jovanovich, 1980), p. 1.

24. Elliot Eisner, "The Kind of Schools We Need," *Educational Leadership 41*, 2 (October 1983): 54.

8

Organizing
Thinking Skills
for Teaching

Selecting thinking skills and strategies for instruction and describing the major attributes of these operations are important first steps in developing a thinking skills program. Organizing these skills for instruction is another equally important and perhaps even more challenging task. This consists essentially of three related tasks: (1) developing a hierarchy of thinking skills and strategies to be taught, (2) sequencing these thinking operations across a curriculum, and (3) keying them to specific subject areas and grade levels. Once these tasks have been accomplished, attention can be directed to devising an instructional system appropriate to the effective teaching of these skills and to deciding where in each course these skills can be taught. This chapter presents examples of various types of thinking skill sequences and guidelines for producing them. The chapter concludes with a model K–12 thinking skills scope and sequence.

HIERARCHIES OF THINKING SKILLS AND STRATEGIES

Thinking skills are rarely used in isolation from each other. For example, individuals do not classify data without comparing and contrasting their perceived attributes. Moreover, individuals rarely classify data simply to classify it. Once they have classified data, people infer generalizations or relationships that were not so readily apparent up to that time. Classifying and inferring meaning go together, just as comparing and contrasting relate closely to classifying. Like the skills of classifying and inferring, all thinking operations are used in varying combinations with each other.

Thinking skills and strategies are very much related to each other in another way, also. Some operations, while part of larger, more complex strategies, also consist of numerous subordinate skills. Defining a problem, part of a strategy of problem solving, consists of a number of subordinate skills, including separating relevant from irrelevant data. An individual's ability to use any thinking operation often depends on mastery of prerequisite or subordinate thinking operations. Specific thinking skills take on special utility and meaning according to the context or framework in which they are employed. Any effective thinking skills program should be built upon some clearly defined explication of how the thinking operations that constitute the program relate to each other.

The Uses of a Skills Hierarchy

Thinking skills hierarchies have several important uses. Such hierarchical arrangements of thinking operations clarify interrelationships among the operations in the hierarchy. These hierarchies indicate which operations may be prerequisite to effective or efficient use of other operations and which are superordinate or subordinate to others. Having such hierarchical arrangements of these skills assists curriculum developers immensely in building a scope and sequence for teaching.

Most educators today are familiar with the taxonomy of cognitive educational objectives developed by Benjamin Bloom and his colleagues in the 1950s.[1] This classification of objectives relates one level of cognitive operations to another, with each level including all those beneath it. Figure 7.4 in the preceding chapter outlined this hierarchy. The implications of this taxonomy seem abundantly clear: If, in order to evaluate data one must also recall, understand, apply, analyze, and synthesize these data, then in order to teach and learn the skill of evaluation, one needs also to teach and learn how to engage in these preliminary operations. Any skill hierarchy carries with it a similar implication for instruction.

One should not misinterpret this implication, however. Simply because an individual uses some very specific skills in engaging in broader strategies or more complex skills does *not* mean that these subordinate skills must be formally taught before introducing or teaching more inclusive skills or strategies. Indeed, one can begin instruction by teaching the major steps in a larger process as a framework in which other, more precise, operations are performed. Thus, for example, one can introduce a general strategy for problem solving or decision making in early grades and teach, in general terms, four or five main steps in this strategy. Then, on a "need-to-use" basis, the specific skills that are prerequisite to a part of each step can be introduced and taught. Such an approach to instruction provides a functional context for skill learning as well as skill using, and enhances motivation to learn the particular skills being taught.[2] Adopting this approach to teaching thinking skills means students do not have to delay engaging in major thinking processes because they have not yet learned all prerequisite skills. Moreover, students do not have to aimlessly learn every prerequisite skill before they can understand how these skills can be functionally combined.

Finally, a hierarchy of thinking skills assists in diagnosing learning as well as planning for teaching. Students experiencing difficulty in executing a particular thinking operation or strategy may be deficient in executing subordinate or prerequisite skills rather than in the general operation they are learning. Reference to a thinking skill hierarchy may thus be useful in identifying the prerequisite skills in which instruction is needed before the overall process or skill can be executed as well as desired.

Some Thinking Skill Hierarchies

A survey of five different thinking skills hierarchies suggests the range of thinking hierarchies that have been developed over the past several years. These by no means exhaust the number of such hierarchies that have or could be developed. Educators may adopt any one of these hierarchies, combine two or more to fit their own understandings of thinking skills, or use existing hierarchies simply as referents in building or evaluating their own thinking skills hierarchies or models.

Figure 8.1 repeats the hierarchy of functional thinking skills presented in Chapter 3. By way of brief review, these thinking operations are directly related to the concept of functional thinking also presented in that chapter. The operations listed in this figure do not include data-gathering methods such as listening, reading, or observing, but rather focus entirely on information processing and higher level thinking operations that have a practical, functional utility in everyday thinking and in academic study.

The operations described in this figure fall into three levels, ranging from information processing skills at the simplest level (Level III), to critical thinking operations at the next highest level (Level II), to major thinking strategies such as decision making at the highest level (Level I) of complexity and inclusivity. The operations listed as micro-thinking and reasoning skills undergird the critical thinking operations listed as Level II skills. They are also used at various places and in various combi-

I. THINKING STRATEGIES

Problem Solving

1. Recognize a problem
2. Represent the problem
3. Devise/choose solution plan
4. Execute the plan
5. Evaluate the solution

Decision Making

1. Define the goal
2. Identify alternatives
3. Analyze alternatives
4. Rank alternatives
5. Judge highest-ranked alternatives
6. Choose "best" alternative

Conceptualizing

1. Identify examples
2. Identify common attributes
3. Classify attributes
4. Interrelate categories of attributes
5. Identify additional examples/nonexamples
6. Modify concept attributes/ structure

II. CRITICAL THINKING SKILLS

1. Distinguishing between verifiable facts and value claims
2. Distinguishing relevant from irrelevant information, claims, or reasons
3. Determining the factual accuracy of a statement
4. Determining the credibility of a source
5. Identifying ambiguous claims or arguments
6. Identifying unstated assumptions
7. Detecting bias
8. Identifying logical fallacies
9. Recognizing logical inconsistencies in a line of reasoning
10. Determining the strength of an argument or claim

III. MICRO-THINKING SKILLS

1. Recall
2. Translation
3. Interpretation
4. Extrapolation
5. Application
6. Analysis (compare, contrast, classify, seriate, etc.)
7. Synthesis
8. Evaluation

Reasoning

inductive
deductive
analogical

Figure 8.1 Major Thinking Operations

nations in the strategies listed under Level I. Each of the critical thinking skills listed in Level II essentially combines analyzing and evaluating, and is more complex than any of the micro-thinking skills. However, like the micro-thinking skills, these critical thinking skills are also used at various places and in various combinations in the Level I strategies. Problem solving, decision making, and conceptualizing—and other strategies of similar complexity such as comprehending—are complicated, umbrella-like processes. They consist of many of the other skills listed here, and arrange these skills in various combinations and steps to carry out the overall process. A more detailed analysis of this hierarchy can be found in Chapter 3.

Figure 8.2 presents a skills hierarchy developed by *Project IMPACT*, a thinking skills program developed initially for junior high schools but

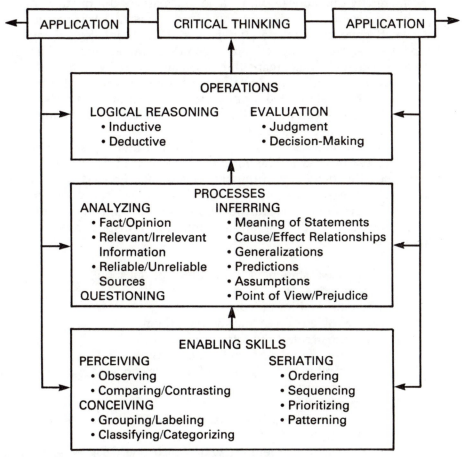

Source: Reprinted with permission from IMPACT.

Figure 8.2 Project IMPACT Universe of Critical Thinking Skills

with obvious applicability throughout any K–12 curriculum.[3] This hierarchy conceptualizes thinking as consisting of, first, enabling skills, moving upward in degree of complexity to processes such as questioning and analyzing, and then on to what it conceives as the major operations of reasoning and evaluation. Each level of skills includes a number of subordinate operations. Each operation supports and leads to those above it in the hierarchy.

A hierarchy of thinking operations developed for the California State Department of Education social studies curriculum is shown in Figure 8.3. This hierarchy, conceptualized as a process model, includes a number of critical thinking and other skills placed in a problem-solving framework. Prerequisite to these operations are four more basic skills. Students who demonstrate proficiency in all these skills, according to the hierarchy guidelines, will be able to (1) assess information, define problems, weigh evidence, and draw conclusions; (2) participate in society as effective citizens; and (3) defend and justify intellectual and personal values, present and critique arguments, and appreciate the viewpoints of others.[4] Unlike many thinking skills hierarchies, this one is set in a specific content area—social studies—and reportedly differs from skill hierarchies established for other subject areas in this state's overall curriculum. However, the skills listed in this hierarchy seem quite applicable to most other subject areas as well.

Figure 8.4 consists of a sequence of critical thinking and reasoning skills devised by critical thinking specialist Robert Ennis. At the time he developed this hierarchy of thinking operations, Ennis defined critical thinking as "reasonable reflective thinking that is focused on deciding what to believe or do."[5] He further defined critical thinking as consisting of two components: dispositions and abilities. As dispositions, he listed the following:

1. Seek a clear statement of the thesis or question.
2. Seek reasons.
3. Try to be well-informed.
4. Use credible sources and mention them.
5. Take into account the total situation.
6. Try to remain relevant to the main point.
7. Keep in mind the original and/or basic concern.
8. Look for alternatives.
9. Be openminded.
   a. Consider seriously points of view other than one's own ("dialogical thinking").
   b. Reason from premises with which one disagrees—without letting the disagreement interfere with one's reasoning ("suppositional thinking").

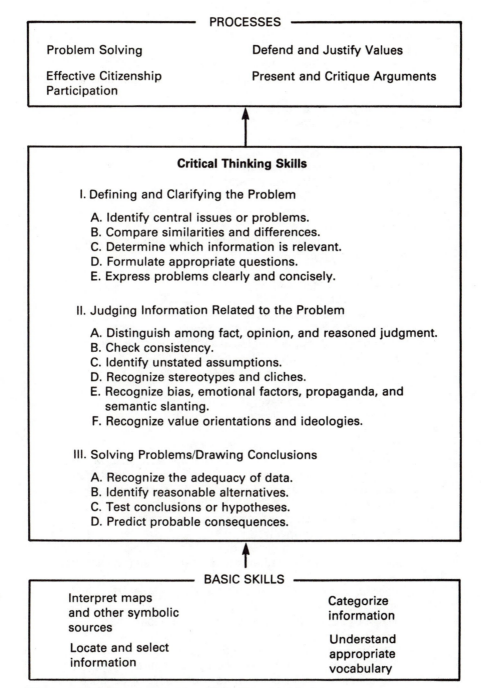

PROCESSES

Problem Solving

Effective Citizenship Participation

Defend and Justify Values

Present and Critique Arguments

Critical Thinking Skills

I. Defining and Clarifying the Problem

   A. Identify central issues or problems.
   B. Compare similarities and differences.
   C. Determine which information is relevant.
   D. Formulate appropriate questions.
   E. Express problems clearly and concisely.

II. Judging Information Related to the Problem

   A. Distinguish among fact, opinion, and reasoned judgment.
   B. Check consistency.
   C. Identify unstated assumptions.
   D. Recognize stereotypes and cliches.
   E. Recognize bias, emotional factors, propaganda, and semantic slanting.
   F. Recognize value orientations and ideologies.

III. Solving Problems/Drawing Conclusions

   A. Recognize the adequacy of data.
   B. Identify reasonable alternatives.
   C. Test conclusions or hypotheses.
   D. Predict probable consequences.

BASIC SKILLS

Interpret maps and other symbolic sources

Locate and select information

Categorize information

Understand appropriate vocabulary

Figure 8.3 California Thinking Skills Process Model

Elementary Clarification
1. Focusing on a question
   a. Identifying or formulating a question
   b. Identifying or formulating criteria for judging possible answers
   c. Keeping the situation in mind
2. Analyzing arguments
   a. Identifying conclusions
   b. Identifying stated reasons
   c. Identifying unstated reasons
   d. Seeing similarities and differences
   e. Identifying and handling irrelevance
   f. Seeing the structure of an argument
   g. Summarizing
3. Asking and answering questions of clarification and/or challenge, for example:
   a. Why?
   b. What is your main point?
   c. What do you mean by "_____"?
   d. What would be an example?
   e. What would not be an example (though close to being one)?
   f. How does that apply to this case (describe case, which might well appear to be a counterexample)?
   g. What difference does it make?
   h. What are the facts?
   i. Is this what you are saying: _____?
   j. Would you say some more about that?
Basic Support
4. Judging the credibility of a source; criteria:
   a. Expertise   e. Use of established procedures
   b. Lack of conflict of interest   f. Known risk to reputation
   c. Agreement among sources   g. Ability to give reasons
   d. Reputation   h. Careful habits
5. Observing and judging observation reports; criteria:
   a. Minimal inferring involved
   b. Short time interval between observation and report
   c. Report by observer, rather than someone else (i.e., not hearsay)
   d. Records are generally desirable. If report is based on a record, it is generally best that:
      1) The record was close in time to the observation
      2) The record was made by the observer
      3) The record was made by the reporter
      4) The statement was believed by the reporter, either because of a prior belief in its correctness or because of a belief that the observer was habitually correct

Figure 8.4 Ennis's Hierarchy of Critical Thinking and Reasoning Skills

    e. Corroboration
    f. Possibility of corroboration
    g. Conditions of good access
    h. Competent employment of technology, if technology is useful
    i. Satisfaction by observer (and reporter, if a different person) of credibility criteria (#4 above)

Inference

6. Deducing, and judging deductions
    a. Class logic—Euler circles
    b. Conditions logic
    c. Interpretation of statements
        1) Double negation
        2) Necessary and sufficient conditions
        3) Other logical words: "only," "if and only if," "or," "some," "unless," "not," "not both," etc.
7. Inducing, and judging inductions
    a. Generalizing
        1) Typicality of data: limitation of coverage
        2) Sampling
        3) Tables and graphs
    b. Inferring explanatory conclusions and hypotheses
        1) Types of explanatory conclusions and hypotheses
            a) Causal claims
            b) Claims about the beliefs and attitudes of people
            c) Interpretations of authors' intended meanings
            d) Historical claims that certain things happened
            e) Reported definitions
            f) Claims that something is an unstated reason or unstated conclusion
        2) Investigating
            a) Designing experiments, including planning to control variables
            b) Seeking evidence and counterevidence
            c) Seeking other possible assumptions
        3) Criteria: Given reasonable assumptions
            a) The proposed conclusion would explain the evidence (essential)
            b) The proposed conclusion is consistent with known facts (essential)
            c) Competitive alternative conclusions are inconsistent with known facts (essential)
            d) The proposed conclusion seems plausible (desirable)
8. Making and judging value judgments
    a. Background facts
    b. Consequences
    c. *Prima facie* application of acceptable principles

Figure 8.4 (*Continued*)

    d. Considering alternatives
    e. Balancing, weighing, and deciding
Advanced Clarification
  9. Defining terms, and judging definitions: three dimensions
    a. Form
      1) Synonym
      2) Classification
      3) Range
      4) Equivalent expression
      5) Operational
      6) Example—nonexample
    b. Definitional strategy
      1) Acts
        a) Report a meaning ("reported" definition)
        b) Stipulate a meaning ("stipulative" definition)
        c) Express a position on an issue ("positional," including
          programmatic and "persuasive" definition)
      2) Identifying and handling equivocation
        a) Attention to the context
        b) Possible types of response:
          i) "The definition is just wrong" (the simplest response)
          ii) Reduction to absurdity: "According to that definition, there is an outlandish result"
          iii) Considering alternative interpretations: "On this interpretation, there is this problem; on that interpretation, there is that problem
          iv) Establishing that there are two meanings of key term, and a shift in meaning from one to the other
    c. Content
10. Identifying assumptions
    a. Unstated reasons
    b. Needed assumptions: argument reconstruction
Strategy and Tactics
11. Deciding on an action
    a. Define problem
    b. Select criteria to judge possible solutions
    c. Formulate alternative solutions
    d. Tentatively decide what to do
    e. Review, taking into account the total situation, and decide
    f. Monitor the implementation
12. Interacting with others
    a. Employing and reacting to "fallacy" labels (including)
      1) Circularity   4) Glittering term
      2) Appeal to authority   5) Namecalling
      3) Bandwagon   6) Slippery slope

Figure 8.4 *(Continued)*

7) Post hoc	15) Vagueness
8) Non sequitur	16) Equivocation
9) Ad hominem	17) Straw person
10) Affirming the consequent	18) Appeal to tradition
11) Denying the antecedent	19) Argument from analogy
12) Conversion	20) Hypothetical question
13) Begging the question	21) Oversimplification
14) Either-or	22) Irrelevance

b. Logical strategies
c. Rhetorical strategies
d. Presenting a position, oral or written (argumentation)
   1) Aiming at a particular audience and keeping it in mind
   2) Organizing (common type: main point, clarification, reasons, alternatives, attempt to rebut prospective challenges, summary—including repeat of main point)

Figure 8.4 (*Continued*)

    c. Withhold judgment when the evidence and reasons are insufficient.
10. Take a position (and change a position) when the evidence and reason are sufficient to do so.
11. Seek as much precision as the subject permits.
12. Deal in an orderly manner with the parts of a complex whole.[6]

Ennis divided the cognitive abilities that, in his judgment, constitute critical thinking into five levels, beginning at the most basic level with what he labeled "elementary clarification." Above this level, he added, in ascending order, four other categories: basic support, inference, advanced clarification, and strategy and tactics. This way of organizing thinking skills arranges skills in terms of complexity as well as inclusivity. According to Ennis, strategies and tactics provide a context and umbrella for all the other skills listed.

The McREL thinking skills hierarchy (now known as *Tactics*) shown in Figure 8.5 also includes dispositions as well as cognitive components.[7] Robert Marzano, its principal developer, argues that in many cases students lack confidence in their own abilities to engage successfully in thinking of almost any kind. Consequently, this program attends to developing techniques of attention control and goal setting, as well as what is called "power thinking"—such as the value of continued effort, a trust in life, and the usefulness of experience. These disposi-

Restructuring
Elaboration
Solving Everyday Problems
Academic Problems
Invention

Matching
Analogical Reasoning
Extrapolation
Evaluation of Evidence
Formal Logic
Evaluation of Value
Decision Making

Storage and Retrieval

Content Thinking
Concept Attainment
Concepts/Attributes
Pattern Recognition
Macro-Patterns
Nonlinguistic Patterns
Synthesizing
Proceduralizing

Learning to Learn
Attention Control
Deep Processing
Power Thinking
Goal Setting
Activity Framework

Source: R. Marzano and C. L. Hutchins, *Thinking Skills: A Conceptual Framework* (Aurora, Col.: Mid-Continent Regional Educational Laboratory), 1985.

Figure 8.5 McREL (*Tactics*) Hierarchy of Thinking Skills

tions McREL seeks to develop antecendent to as well as simultaneous with development of the cognitive skills themselves. The remaining levels of the McREL skills hierarchy arrange thinking operations in terms of function and complexity, moving from content-related thinking operations to reasoning skills.

Although there is obviously no commonly accepted hierarchical structure for all thinking operations, the various thinking skill hierarchies presented here, and others that have been developed thus far,

BORDERS BOOK SHOP #16
5612 CASTLETON CNR LN
INDIANAPOLIS IN 46250
(317) 849-8660

CLERK ID_____   REGISTER ID____

SUN, AUG 01, 1993 04-07 PM

VS 4262111703635   0394

SALE TERM# 0001 RF# 055

AMOUNT $ 78.65

AP 015474

I AGREE TO COMPLY WITH
THE CARDHOLDER AGREEMENT
SIGNATURE

X_____

WHITE - MERCHANT YELLOW - CUSTOMER

share two major features. First, most arrange their skills from the simplest data-gathering and processing operations at the lowest level to more complex all-inclusive, umbrella-type processes at the highest levels. Some thinking skills lists even imply a hierarchy but are not necessarily presented as such. For example, the thinking operations that constitute the Strategic Reasoning program seem to represent this latter type. They consist of thing-making (conceptualizing), qualification (identifying attributes), classification, structure analysis (identifying the parts of a whole), operation analysis (identifying steps in a process), and analogy-making.[8] The sequence seems to be one of increasing degrees of abstraction and inclusivity; analogy making seems to combine or require use of all of the operations that precede it in this list. Most thinking skills programs imply, if they don't present them explicitly, some type of hierarchy of skills, based on principles of skill complexity and inclusivity.

Most hierarchies of thinking skills, or, for that matter, even lists of skills selected for instruction, also share a second common feature. They include only a limited number of skills. By doing so, they follow sage advice. A limited number of thinking skills taught in depth over an extended period give promise of more effective learning of thinking than does rapid fire coverage of huge array of skills. The verb *to cover*, it should be noted, means "to take in or hide from view," and that is precisely what happens when curricula call for the teaching of dozens upon dozens of thinking skills. Effective learning of thinking skills requires "uncovering"—and this means *more attention to fewer thinking skills* throughout a curriculum.

Although there may be no generally accepted hierarchy of thinking skills, it should be noted that some are clearly more accurate and useful than others. Any old hierarchy is not satisfactory. Acceptable hierarchies reflect well thought-out theories and models of intelligence and/or cognition. Some may combine both affective and cognitive elements; some, such as Robert Sternberg's triarchic model of intelligence, may combine metacognitive as well as cognitive elements;[9] some may combine all three elements. Whatever hierarchy is proposed ought be supported by a rationale based on appropriate theory and research.

With this caution in mind, program developers can adopt or adapt an existing hierarchy of a limited number of thinking skills and strategies to be taught across a curriculum. Or, they can devise a hierarchy of their own locally chosen skills. Regardless of the format such an arrangement takes, a skills hierarchy proves most useful in determining which skills should be taught when in a sequence and in combination with which other skills. Such a hierarchy also helps define a context in which meaningful instruction in thinking can occur.

SEQUENCING THINKING SKILLS

Once the thinking skills selected for teaching have been identified and put into some hierarchy or other pattern that clarifies and reveals their interrelationships, these skills should be sequenced for instruction. Putting skills into a sequence enables teachers, materials developers, and test makers to deal with the very practical and pressing decisions that must be made about which skills to introduce and teach at what grade level, in what subject areas, and in what form. Without the resulting scope and sequence of thinking skills, no purposeful thinking skills program can be successfully implemented.

Developing a sequence of thinking skills selected for instruction is necessary to accommodate three important features of thinking skills. First, such a sequence acknowledges the often complicated relationship between and among these operations. Some relatively simple thinking operations are basic or prerequisite to other more complex operations; for example, being able to analyze is crucial to being able to engage in most critical thinking operations. In other instances, some skills constitute important parts of other skills; for instance, comparing, contrasting, and classifying constitute part of the process of conceptualizing. By sequencing skills in order of their complexity and inclusivity, one can ensure proper student proficiency in the various segments that make the whole operational.

Second, as pointed out earlier, thinking operations of any type are not learned at a particular point and remain unchanged thereafter. Thinking and thinking operations change and develop, becoming more complex and sophisticated over time as individuals mature, add to their experiences, and consciously apply these operations to tasks of increasing complexity and diversity. The skill of classifying, for example, changes over time and experience to become increasingly complex; simple classification at one level, becomes rather sophisticated multivariant classification at another. Any effective thinking skills sequence acknowledges the changing nature of its components as students mature and learn.

Finally, skills work differently in different subject areas and life contexts. To put it another way, the subject matter or contexts in which skills are applied to some extent inform and shape how these skills are employed.[10] Skills need to be transferred into and elaborated in a variety of subject matter areas once they have been introduced. An effective thinking skills sequence calls attention to this need and provides repeated opportunities in a variety of contexts to elaborate, refine, and transfer the skills that constitute the core of a thinking skills program.

Psychologist Jermome Bruner once noted that any concept could be taught in an intellectually honest fashion to any youngster at any grade level.[11] Many educators seem to believe this of thinking operations, also. Although this may be true, however, the important question is, just because a skill may be taught at any grade level, should it be? Most experts suggest that the most effective skill learning and teaching build on a readiness to learn that may mean withholding instruction in some skills until later grades, even though students might on their own engage in some simple version of these skills earlier. This does not mean waiting for readiness to develop naturally; indeed, one function of schooling is to accelerate readiness. What it does mean, however, is that decisions as to what to teach when should be based as much on the time and effort it may take to achieve a high degree of proficiency in a particular skill at a particular grade level as on where the skill fits in a sequence of thinking skills. The opportunities lost to teach other things by spending inordinate amounts of time in providing formal thinking skill instruction to young learners may not justify teaching a large number or certain kinds of thinking operations before students are ready to benefit from such instruction.

Time can be saved and learning can be accelerated perhaps if serious thinking skill instruction is saved for intermediate grades and beyond. Such a plan does not mean students cannot or will not engage in thinking during preceding years. It simply means that they will do so in an environment that encourages thinking by rewarding it, stimulating it, providing many opportunities for it, and in effect creating a classroom atmosphere that clearly says, "It's fun to think—it's okay to think—come on, let's think!" Too much instruction or drill in specific skills at an early age may well inhibit or discourage their use, especially if high risk is involved. Thus, the early elementary grades may well be a time best devoted to creating a classroom climate conducive to independent thinking, engaging students in repeated use of very generalized thinking strategies, developing habits or dispositions supportive of effective thinking, and thus developing readiness for later instruction in specific thinking skills. At best, where some skill instruction is deemed advisable, informal teaching of simple heuristics useful in sparking thinking (heuristics like the PMI, CAF, and C&S taught in deBono's *CoRT* program) might well be the focus of instruction rather than detailed instruction in specific cognitive operations.

To be most useful for teaching and learning, a thinking skills sequence should differ from skills sequences typically found in most school curricula guides. Conventional thinking skills sequences usually consist of different thinking skills listed for different subjects at different grade levels. Rarely are the same skills repeated in a number of grades or subjects; rarer still is there any recognizable rationale for the sequence.

More useful thinking skills sequences, however, trace a skill across a number of grade levels and subjects and build one skill upon another but always in a context that gives functionality to the skills being taught.

Several different types of such thinking sequences exist. Examples of two of these follow. Table 8.1 outlines a sequence of thinking skills developed by the Illinois Renewal Institute.[12] Examination of this sequence reveals a pattern of progressive development of different dimensions or applications of each skill included in the sequence. Predicting in grades K–6 becomes hypothesizing at the next level and predicting

Table 8-1 A Sequence of Thinking Skills

	Level I (K–4)	Level II (5–8)	Level III (9–12)
Creative Synthesis	Brainstorming (Idea Collecting)	Brainstorming	
	Imagining (Visualizing)	Making Analogies	Goal Setting
	Predicting (Guessing)	Hypothesizing	Predicting Trend Analysis
	Seeing Relationships (Analogies) (Association)	Reasoning by Analogy	Discovering Possibilities and Finding Solutions
Critical Analysis	Discovering Patterns	Discerning Descrepancies	Identifying A Problem
	Attributing	Analyzing Bias/ Relevancy	Analyzing Bias/ Relevancy/Assumptions
	Comparing/Contrasting	Analyzing Ambiguity/Paradox	Proving with Data
	Classifying (Sorting)	Classifying with Matrix	Proving Data Reliability
Logic	Sequencing	Sequencing	Setting Priorities
	Finding Cause/ Effect Relationships	Processing Cause/ Effect	Cause/Effect Analysis
Evaluative Problem Solving	Recognizing Fact/ Opinion/Fantasy	Making Inferences	Weighing Costs and Benefits
	Justifying	Justifying Decisions	Justifying a Point of View (Advocate Argument)
	Finding Problems Finding Solutions	Creative Problem Solving	Analytic Problem Solving

trend analysis at the highest level. Justifying at Level I becomes justifying decisions in grades 5–8 and justifying a point of view in grades 9–12. Although precise definitions of each skill are not included in the sequence, it may be assumed that the intent is to teach each skill in more elaborate form at each level.

Table 8.2 outlines the sequence of thinking skills developed in 1986 for social studies courses throughout California. Each column describes the skill as it is to be performed by the end of a specific grade level. Basic concepts underlying these skills are, according to this sequence, to be introduced in the elementary grades. By the third grade, students are supposed to be able to execute all of the skills listed in the column for third grade. By the end of the sixth grade, students are expected to have mastered all the skills listed under that grade level, and so on, continuing through all the grades listed in this table.[13]

These skills become increasingly complex and subtle as the sequence advances. As Table 8.2 indicates, the skill of distinguishing clear from unclear formulations of simple issues and problems (grade 6, I, a) builds on the previously introduced skill of observing and identifying the main idea and is elaborated by adding to it the dimension of identifying central issues or problems (grade 8, I, a), and at subsequent levels delineating "controversy components" and distinguishing "real and stated issues." Predicting consequences (grade 6, III, d) apparently builds on the skill of putting simple hypotheses into "if . . . then" statements introduced by the third grade, and moves through predicting possible consequences (grade 8, III, d) to anticipating and assessing desirable and undesirable consequences (grade 12, III, e). Thus, each version of the skill builds on prerequisite skills or elaborates additional, often more subtle, dimensions of the same skill. In effect, the sequence, moves from concepts underlying each skill through a simple version of it to a more elaborate, complex version of the skill.

Although unstated in the skill sequence itself, this particular sequence also envisions an increasing sophistication in student application of these skills. According to the documentation accompanying the sequence, third-grade students are supposed to demonstrate understanding of the ideas and concepts basic to each skill. By the next levels, they are expected to be able to apply them (with guidance if necessary) in simple form (sixth grade) and later without guidance in rather "straightforward" contexts (eighth grade). At succeeding levels of performance, students are expected to use these skills, with prompting, in more complicated, indirect, and subtle contexts (tenth grade), and finally, by the twelfth grade, applying them without any prompting in their reading, oral, and wirtten work.[14]

This thinking skill sequence, much more so than other sequences, casts the skills to be taught in a functional structure—in this instance,

Table 8.2 Critical Thinking Skill Continuum for History–Social Science

Third Grade	Sixth Grade	Eighth Grade
I. Defining and Clarifying the Problem a. Makes careful observations b. Identifies and expresses main idea, problem or central issues c. Identifies similarities and differences d. Organizes items into defined categories e. Defines categories for unclassified information f. Identifies information relevant to a problem g. Formulates questions h. Recognizes different points of view **II. Judging and Utilizing Information** a. Identifies obvious stereotypes b. Distinguishes between fact and opinion c. Identifies and explains sequence and prioritizing d. Identifies evidence that supports (or is related to) a main idea e. Identifies obvious assumptions f. Identifies obvious inconsistency and contradiction g. Identifies cause and effect relationships **III. Drawing Conclusions** a. Recognizes the adequacy of data b. Identifies cause and effect relationships c. Draws conclusions from evidence d. Puts simple hypotheses into "if," "then" sentences	**I. Defining and Clarifying the Problem** a. Identifies central issues or problems b. Identifies similarities and differences c. Understands the concept of relevance and irrelevance d. Formulates appropriate questions e. Expresses problems and issues f. Recognizes obvious individual and group value orientations and ideologies **II. Judging and Utilizing Information** a. Identifies stereotypes and cliches b. Identifies obvious bias, propaganda, and semantic slanting c. Identifies facts, opinions, and reasoned judgments d. Identifies inconsistency and contradictions e. Identifies assumption f. Identifies evidence **III. Drawing Conclusions** a. Recognizes the adequacy of data b. Identifies cause and effect relationships c. Draws conclusions from evidence d. Predicts consequences e. Hypothesizes f. Reasons with analogies and generalizations	**I. Defining and Clarifying the Problem** a. Identifies central issues or problems b. Compares similarities and differences c. Determines which information is relevant d. Formulates appropriate questions e. Expresses problems clearly and concisely **II. Judging and Utilizing Information** a. Distinguishes among fact, opinion, and reasoned judgment b. Checks consistency c. Identifies unstated assumptions d. Recognizes stereotypes and cliches e. Recognizes bias, emotional factors, propaganda, and semantic slanting f. Recognizes value orientations and ideologies **III. Drawing Conclusions** a. Recognizes the adequacy of data b. Identifies reasonable alternatives c. Tests conclusions or hypotheses d. Predicts probable consequences

Tenth Grade	Twelfth Grade

Tenth Grade

I. Defining and Clarifying the Problem
  a. Delineates controversy components
  b. Identifies criteria that serve to organize data
  c. Identifies fallacies of relevance
  d. Formulates appropriate questions
  e. Paraphrases accurately
  f. Distinguishes among diverse viewpoints

II. Judging and Utilizing Information
  a. Recognizes subtle manifestations of stereotypes and cliches
  b. Recognizes subtle manifestations of emotional factors, propaganda, and semantic slanting
  c. Distinguishes among fact, opinion, and reasoned judgment
  d. Recognizes subtle or indirect inconsistencies
  e. Demonstrates a sensitivity to questionable assumptions
  f. Recognizes subtle differences in judging the sufficiency of data

III. Drawing Conclusions
  a. Justifies the selection of an alternative
  b. Distinguishes between possible and probable consequences
  c. Concludes only what is justified by the evidence
  d. Understands opposing points of view and reasons with them
  e. Recognizes fundamental problems in causal reasoning, generalizing, and arguing by analogy
  f. Recognizes indirect or extended implications

Twelfth Grade

I. Defining and Clarifying the Problem
  a. Identifies central issues or problems
    1. Distinguishes real and stated issues
  b. Compares similarities and differences
    1. Analyzes system similarities and differences
  c. Determines which information is relevant
    1. Evaluates degrees of relevance
    2. Assesses different interpretations of data
    3. Summarizes positions and their supporting evidence
  d. Formulates appropriate questions
  e. Expresses problems clearly and concisely

II. Judging Information Related to the Problem
  a. Distinguishes among fact, opinion, and reasoned judgment
  b. Checks consistency
    1. Recognizes subtle consistencies and inconsistencies
  c. Identifies unstated assumptions
    1. Recognizes unstated fundamental assumptions
  d. Recognizes bias
    1. Identifies emotional factors, propaganda, semantic slanting, stereotypes, and cliches
    2. Converts biased materials into unbiased form
  e. Recognizes value orientations and ideologies
  f. Distinguishes between false and accurate images

III. Solving Problems/Drawing Conclusions
  a. Recognizes and assesses cause and effect and mutliple causation
  b. Draws warranted conclusions
  c. Identifies reasonable alternatives
  d. Tests conclusions or hypotheses
  e. Predicts probable consequences
    1. Assesses desirable and undesirable consequences
  f. Demonstrates the ability to come to a reasoned judgment in reading, writing, and speech

Source: California Assessment Program, 721 Capitol Mall, Sacramento, California 95814 *or* P.O. Box 944272, Sacramento, California 94244-2720.

one that resembles problem solving (see Figure 8.3). By relating them to each other in terms of a thinking strategy rather than in terms of a simple skill hierarchy, the functional utility of each of the specific skills in the sequence is more readily apparent and the framework in which it can be taught more obvious. Like most sequences, however, such a sequence still seems to require teaching some form of each specific skill at each level, in effect requiring (in this instance) the introduction or reintroduction of some eighteen thinking skills every two years.

Other kinds of skill sequences may be devised. As they are, special efforts are required to eliminate weaknesses common to many of them. Like many other skill sequences or lists, the skill sequence reproduced in Table 8.2 also suffers from several of these weaknesses. Some skills are so vague or undefined (such as "delineates controversy components"—grade 10, I, a) that it is almost impossible to understand what they are supposed to mean. The use of ill-defined technical terms, without straightforward skill definitions, communicates little to program developers or teachers, and thus mitigates against their successful teaching and learning. Moreover, failure to key the sequential development of a particular skill to the same sequence of numbers in the skill sequence— such as mixing the skill of distinguishing between fact and opinion (II, b and c) with the skill of detecting bias (II, a and d)—unnecessarily obscures the connections between the different levels of the same skill. As a result, producing an effective skill teaching program is likely to become more difficult than it need be. To be most useful to program developers or teachers, any skill sequence ought to use nontechnical language or provide clear definitions and examples as well as present the skills in a pattern that makes crystal clear their interrelationships.

Thinking strategies can be elaborated in developmental sequence in somewhat the same way as the critical thinking skills just described. Figure 8.6 illustrates one such developmental sequence for the strategy of problem solving. At the introductory level (I) this strategy might be presented in terms of a basic five-step process with a few subordinate steps included under each major step. At a later level (II) a new step may be added, as can be additional subordinate steps under many of the other major steps. Later elaborations (III and IV) can add additional subordinate steps or procedures and especially additional types of general solution plans or strategies. Thus, over a number of years, the basic steps in the strategy can essentially remain the same, but what can be done to execute each step can be elaborated. In this way, students' knowledge of the strategy can grow and develop as they gain experience and expertise in applying it in a variety of increasingly complex situations and contexts.

Figure 8.7 provides a similar developmental elaboration of a decision-making strategy. Again, the essential steps in the strategy can remain the same with additional subordinate steps being added in each successive elaboration of the strategy. The additions under the step of analyzing alternatives are especially crucial, for students need to use and learn a wide range of criteria for analyzing alternatives and, eventually, how to weigh each in terms of making choices. As students gain proficiency in using the initial model of this strategy (I), they can then elaborate it as in model II. After several years of developing proficiency, students can move on to learn a more detailed model (as in III) that may even have broader application than the previous ones. Because each model builds out of the preceding one, the students' learning of this strategy, as with the problem-solving strategy described previously, can expand and become more sophisticated as they become experienced in using it.

Skill sequences like these, by themselves, rarely make clear the real complexity of the skills listed. Obviously, not all thinking skills and strategies are of equal complexity or utility. Certainly, recognizing the adequacy of data and formulating questions are much more complex operations—even in their simplest forms—than the skill of identifying relevant information. It is important to recognize these differing degrees of complexity in planning instruction, for more time will be required to teach the more complex skills than will be required to teach the less complex skills to the same degree of proficiency.

Thinking skills sequences cannot clearly delineate the essential attributes or components of each skill identified. Only detailed skill descriptions prepared as outlined in Chapter 5 can do this. However, what sequences such as these (especially the California sequence) do and do well is to indicate how specific skills grow and evolve with experience and progress from simple to increasingly complex operations. Showing this growth or increasing skill complexity is an essential attribute of any useful thinking skills sequence. While skill sequences are necessary to effective skills teaching, they are not sufficient in and of themselves to ensure such teaching.

KEYING SKILLS TO SUBJECT AREAS AND GRADE LEVELS

To ensure effective teaching of thinking skills and strategies, responsibility for introducing and teaching them must be allocated to specific subjects and grade levels. Yet, at the moment, there is no widely accepted or research-based grade level sequence for introducing instruction in thinking skills or strategies. Piagetians often assert that more complex thinking operations should be introduced only after a solid foundation of simpler, prerequisite skills has been established. Based on their research, they argue that certain skills such as classification, seria-

I

Identifying the Problem
Locating problem statement
Putting in own words:
  Goal
  Present condition
  Gap/obstacle
Defining terms

Representing the Problem
Pictures

Choosing a Solution Plan
Stating goal to be achieved
Deciding how to get there
  Trial and error
  Selected procedures
  Breaking into subproblems

Carrying Out the Plan

Checking

II

Identifying the Problem
Picking out problem statement
Defining terms

III

Recognizing the Problem
Picking out problem statement (given)
Distinguishing problematic condition and
  its elements
  Goal
  Present state
  Nature of gap/obstacles
Identifying controversy-producing
  elements
Identifying primary/secondary problems
Stating the problem

Organizing Data
Picking out key terms
Clarifying terms, data
Distinguishing relevant from irrelevant
Identifying and securing needed data

Representing the Problem
Pictures
Diagrams
Numbers
Words

Choosing a Solution Strategy
Stating goal to be achieved
Deciding how to get there
  Trial and error

IV

Recognizing the Problem
Picking out problem statement (if given)
Identifying problem components in data
  Inconsistencies
  Present state/ideal state
  Nature of gap/obstacles
  Probable cause of gap/obstacles
  Operators
Identifying controversy-producing
  elements
Identifying primary/secondary problem
Identifying category of problem

Organizing Data
Picking out key terms
Clarifying terms, data
Distinguishing relevant from irrelevant
Identifying and securing needed data
Stating the problem

Representing the Problem
Pictures
Diagrams
Numbers
Words
Formulas

Putting in own words:
Goal
Present state
Nature of the gap

Organizing Data
Picking out key terms
Clarifying terms, data
Distinguishing relevant from irrelevant
Identifying needed data

Representing the Problem
Pictures
Diagrams

Choosing a Solution Plan
Stating goal to be achieved
Deciding how to get there
Trial and error
Selected procedures, formulas
Using matricies
Turning into auxiliary problems
Breaking into subproblems

Carrying out the Plan and Monitoring

Checking

Using matrices or graphs
Turning it into auxiliary problems
Breaking into subproblems
Making and testing hypotheses

Carrying Out the Planned Strategy
Monitoring
Removing obstacles

Evaluating
Solution—in terms of goals, reasonableness
Solution process—in terms of effectiveness

Choosing a Solution Strategy
Stating goal to be achieved
Deciding how to get there
Trial and error
Selected formulas
Using matrices and graphs
Turning it into auxiliary problems
Breaking into subproblems
Making and testing hypotheses
Working backward
Using analogous problems
Using models

Carrying Out the Planned Strategy
Monitoring
Using alternative strategies
Identifying, removing obstacles

Evaluating/Checking
Solution—in terms of goals,
reasonableness, alternative solutions
Solution strategy—in terms of efficiency,
effectiveness

**Anticipating Future Problems Related to
the Solution**

Figure 8.6 Sequential Development of a Problem-Solving Strategy

I	**II**	**III**
Identify Goal	*Identify Goal*	*Identify Goal*
Goal	Goal	Goal
Current Condition	Immediate	immediate/long range
Obstacles/gaps	Long range	Current conditions
Alternatives	Current condition	Obstacles/gaps
Brainstorming	Obstacles/gaps	Causes of obstacles
Analyze Alternatives in	Cause of obstacles	Verification of Causes
Terms of:	*Alternatives*	*Alternatives*
Goal	Brainstorming	Brainstorming
Consequences	Synectics	Synectics
Costs	*Analyze Alternatives in*	*Analyze Alternatives in*
Resources Available	*Terms of:*	*Terms of:*
Rank Alternatives	Goals	Goals
in terms of above	Consequences	Consequences
criteria	long range/short	long range/short
Choose	range	range
	Costs	anticipated/
	real costs	unanticipated
	opportunity costs	consequences of
	Resources	consequences
	Constraints	Costs
	Rank Alternatives	real costs
	In terms of above	opportunity costs
	criteria	Resources
	Choose	available
	Determine risks	substitute
	Choice	Constraints
		Rank Alternatives
		in terms of above
		criteria
		Choose
		Choose from top
		alternatives
		Determine risks
		Final choice
		Plan (optional)

Figure 8.7 Sequential Development of a Decision Making Strategy

tion, and conservation seem to be basic to all other forms of thinking and should be introduced as early as possible in the primary grades.[15] However, philosophers such as Matthew Lipman and Richard Paul assert and believe they can demonstrate just the contrary, that primary grade children can learn reasoning and other critical thinking skills often considered to be "higher order" or more complex skills.[16] Because reasoning skills are, in their judgments, so important to skillful thinking, they favor introduction of these thinking skills in the earliest grades. Consensus is simply lacking over which thinking operations ought to be introduced at which grade levels.

Nevertheless, decisions about grade or subject placement must be made in building any effective thinking skills scope and sequence. And these decisions must be based on criteria of some sort. One place to start, of course, is by placing skills to be taught where they currently are already introduced or "executed" in existing courses, texts, or subject areas. By doing so, program developers can at least capitalize on what teachers may be used to doing or on materials that they already employ to "teach" certain skills. But making skill placement on the basis of what is now done may also simply perpetuate a less-than-desirable skill teaching sequence. Criteria other than "readiness to teach" need to be taken into account in deciding where to introduce instruction in any particular thinking skills or strategies.

Experience suggests that considerations implied by the following questions should be taken into account in determining where in a thinking skills sequence to introduce any specific thinking skills and strategies:

1. If introduced at a given grade level, will the skill build on skills already introduced?
2. If introduced at a given grade level, will the skill lead to or support or be part of another skill or strategy to be introduced later?
3. Does the subject matter to be used at this level provide numerous examples and opportunities for use of and instruction in the skill?
4. Can an understandable form of the skill or strategy be learned relatively easily by students at this grade level given their previous learning and experience?

Answers to these questions, of course, do not tell program developers specifically what grade level or subject may be best suited for introducing a particular skill. Such decisions may always remain rather arbitrary. But developers can apply these questions to all skills and strategies already selected for inclusion in a multi-grade sequence. When combined with consideration of time constraints, a desire to minimize skill overload at any one grade level or subject, and reference to the hierarchy of thinking skills to be taught, consideration of these factors can enable program developers to produce a viable sequence.

A MODEL K–12 THINKING SKILLS SEQUENCE

A practical scope and sequence for teaching thinking can be devised by applying the preceding criteria. In its most complex form, this sequence consists of metacognitive operations and selected dispositions as well as cognitive skills and strategies. Figures 8.8 and 8.9 present the key components of this scope and sequence keyed to grade levels and major subject areas of a K–12 curriculum.

Thinking Skills and Strategies

Figure 8.8 indicates those points in a K–12 thinking skills curriculum where selected thinking operations can be formally *introduced*, the subject areas to which these introductions can be assigned, and the general nature of each thinking skill or strategy included in the sequence. In addition, it indicates how the substance of major thinking strategies can be elaborated upward through the grades. In essence, this scope and sequence calls for the introduction of a few new skills or strategies in selected subjects over a number of years with continued guided practice, elaboration, and transfer of previously introduced skills and strategies in spiral fashion over subsequent years. Transfer and elaboration across subject areas at appropriate grade levels can also be an integral part of this thinking skills sequence.

The specific thinking skills and strategies incorporated in the sequence described in Figure 8.8 are drawn from the skills hierarchy described in Figure 8.1 that appears earlier in this chapter. This thinking skills curriculum calls for the following sequence:

1. The skills of comprehending, comparing/contrasting, classifying, and seriating are explicitly introduced in the primary grades in reading instruction, and thereafter elaborated in terms of more sophisticated attributes and applications to a variety of subjects and contexts in succeeding grades. By the late intermediate grades, these operations can be incorporated into a strategy of conceptualizing, which can be elaborated through application to increasingly abstract tasks in a variety of subject areas in later grades.

2. Problem solving can be introduced in mathematics and science starting in the third grade or so in the form of a simple problem-solving strategy and several simple solution strategies. The number of steps in the general strategy and the complexity of operations that constitute each step can then be increased periodically as students move upward through the grades. Problem-solving strategies and techniques can be transferred into other subject areas on a "need-to-use" basis after they

have been introduced and taught to some degree of proficiency in these two initial subjects. Figure 8.6 outlines a problem-solving strategy that might constitute this sequence. This strategy is an elaborated version of the problem-solving strategy explained in Chapter 7 and elaborated earlier in this chapter.

3. Simplified versions of analysis (analysis of part-whole relationships, of the components of various phenomena such as paragraphs, short stories, newspapers, regions, and so on), synthesis, and evaluation can be introduced in subjects where they are most appropriate beginning in the fourth or fifth grade and refined, added to, and transferred to other subjects in succeeding grades. Figure 8.8 illustrates how these specific skills can be elaborated as students move upward through the grades.

4. Social studies and language arts provide useful contexts for introducing a simplified model of decision making in the first year of middle or junior high school and then for elaborating this process in subsequent years. Students are increasingly pressed to make important personal, academic, and even preliminary career choices in these years and realize the value of proficiency in this strategy at these grade levels; the content of language arts and social studies courses are repleat with opportunities for and examples useful in teaching this strategy at this level. Figure 8.8 outlines the attributes of a decision-making strategy that might constitute such a sequence.

5. Critical thinking skills like those listed in Figure 8.1 can be introduced starting in the third or fourth grade through a number of subject areas including science, language arts, and/or social studies, as appropriate. Several of these skills can be introduced in each subject in succeeding years with previously introduced skills being practiced, elaborated, and transferred to other subjects over subsequent grades. Selecting appropriate critical thinking skills for introduction at specific grade levels can be facilitated by understanding the nature of various critical thinking operations.

These operations are of three general types. One type includes relatively straightforward skills that require little special knowledge, use simple rules, and consist of rather simple procedures. Skills such as distinguishing relevant from irrelevant data are of this type. Other skills, relatively simple in their procedures but requiring more knowledge in terms of criteria, and being able to "read between the lines" constitute a second type, which includes skills of detecting unstated assumptions and recognizing logical fallacies. More complex skills, such as determining the strength of a claim, consist of a number of subordinate skills and constitute the most complex of all critical thinking operations. Based on

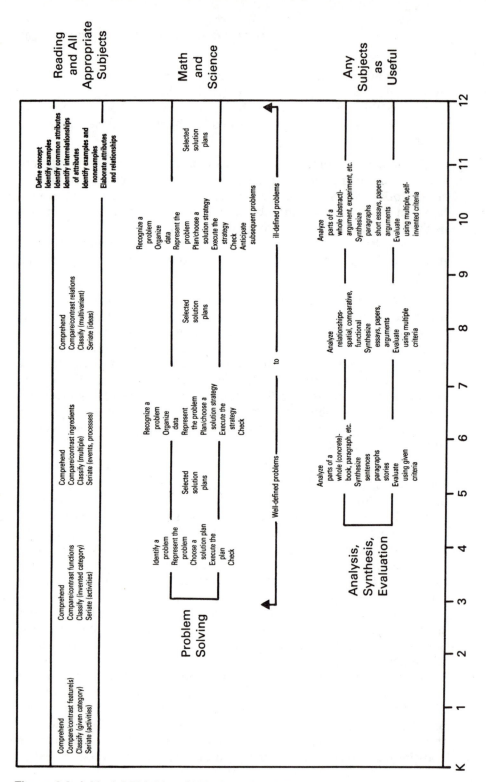

Figure 8.8 A Model Thinking Skills Scope and Sequence

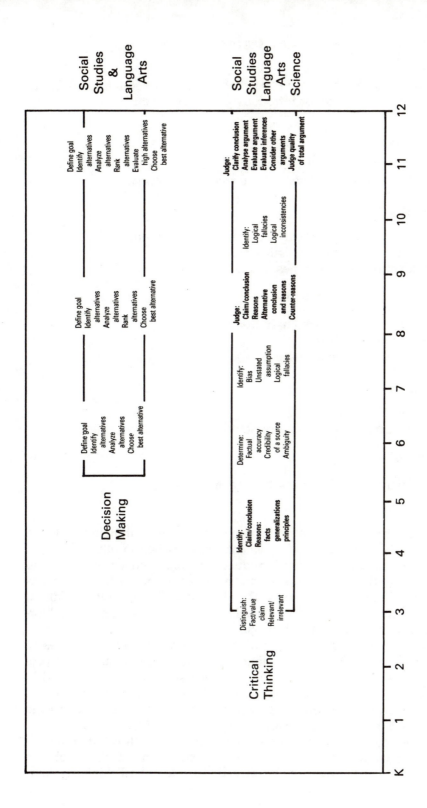

Critical
Thinking

Decision
Making

Social
Studies
&
Language
Arts

Social
Studies
Language
Arts
Science

K   1   2   3   4   5   6   7   8   9   10   11   12

Distinguish:
Fact/value
claim
Relevant/
irrelevant

Identify:
Claim/conclusion
Reasons:
facts
generalizations
principles

Determine:
Factual
accuracy
Credibility
of a source
Ambiguity

Identify:
Bias
Unstated
assumption
Logical
fallacies

Define goal
Identify
alternatives
Analyze
alternatives
Choose
best alternative

Define goal
Identify
alternatives
Analyze
alternatives
Rank
alternatives
Choose
best alternative

Define goal
Identify
alternatives
Analyze
alternatives
Rank
alternatives
Evaluate
high alternatives
Choose
best alternative

Judge:
Claim/conclusion
Reasons
Alternative
conclusion
and reasons
Counter-reasons

Identify:
Logical
fallacies
Logical
inconsistencies

Judge:
Clarify conclusion
Analyse argument
Evaluate argument
Evaluate inferences
Consider other
arguments
Judge quality
of total argument

209

the different levels of complexity of these critical thinking skills, an appropriate sequence for introducing them may be as follows:

Grades 3–4

- distinguishing between verifiable facts and value claims
- distinguishing relevant from irrelevant information

Grades 5–6

- determining the factual accuracy of a statement
- determining the credibility of a source
- identifying ambiguities in language

Grades 7–8

- identifying unstated assumptions
- determining bias
- identifying logical fallacies

Grades 9–10

- identifying logical fallacies
- recognizing logical inconsistencies in a line of reasoning

Grades 11–12

- determining the strength of an argument

Implementing instruction in this sequence of critical thinking skills can be done the same way as implementing instruction in other skills and processes listed above. Once introduced and practiced to some degree of proficiency, each of these skills can be refined, elaborated, and transferred into different subject areas. The elaborated content of these skills at subsequent grade levels can be similar to that of the skills of the California sequence described in Table 8.2.

Of course, it is not necessary to wait until the higher grades to introduce the skills of determining the strength of an argument or producing a strong, reasoned argument. Such skills can be introduced in simplified form prior to or in conjunction with the introduction of any of the other critical thinking skills listed here and, by so doing, can provide a context for using and teaching many of these skills.

Teaching specific critical thinking skills in the context of an overall skill of argument analysis provides students with a set of hooks on which to "hang" their newly learned discrete critical thinking skills.

Initially, argument analysis might take the form of simply identifying the components of an argument; this skill can be introduced around the third, fourth, or fifth grade. A year or two following its introduction, the skill could be elaborated to include identifying chains of arguments as well as simple argument structures. By late junior-high school, students could be learning the skill of judging the strength of an argument, which might consist of (1) identifying the main conclusion or claim of the argument and then (2) examining the reasons given for relevance, accuracy and sufficiency. Later work with this skill could add analysis of the structure of the reasoning presented as well as analysis to determine logical consistency and to identify logical fallacies. At still later grades this skill may be elaborated as the seven-step procedure outlined by Scriven and described in the preceding chapter. By the eleventh or twelfth grade, if the above sequence is followed, the detailed procedures of determining the strength of an argument outlined in Figure 7.6 in the preceding chapter could serve as a goal for instruction and learning.

Figure 8.8 illustrates the developmental nature of this practical thinking skills scope and sequence by showing how various thinking operations can be elaborated at succeeding grade levels. This particular thinking skill scope and sequence, with perhaps some modifications, is appropriate for use in any school system.

Dispositions and Metacognitive Operations

Teaching thinking, to be most effective, must provide explicit instruction in more than the skills and strategies that constitute the meaning-making component of thinking. Such teaching must also attend directly to the metacognitive operations and dispositions that guide and support skillful thinking. As in the case of cognitive skills and strategies, instructional attention to these metacognitive operations and dispositions may be spread across a number of grade levels. Selected attributes of each can be emphasized at different grade levels and continuously reinforced thereafter. However, due to the nature of these operations and dispositions and the way in which they seem normally to develop, grade placement and distribution as well as instruction should differ from that used to teach thinking skills and strategies. The desirability of preventing skill overload at any one grade level also suggests where and how these metacognitive operations and dispositions might best receive instructional attention.

Special emphasis on developing dispositions supportive of thinking should commence in and characterize instruction in the elementary grades, while direct instruction in metacognition should be introduced and emphasized in the secondary grades. Most attitudes and values seem to be fairly fixed in most individuals by the middle or junior high-school years.[17] Consequently, it appears that sustained attention to developing the attitudes and values that underlie the dispositions supportive of skillful thinking begin as early as possible, in the primary grades. Individuals' metacognitive abilities, on the other hand, seem to blossom around the age of eleven or so, at the beginning of the middle or junior high-school years.[18] Thus, emphasis on metacognition might best characterize these grade levels with direct instruction in metacognitive operations following in the high-school years. Not only would this distribution of teaching emphasis capitalize on students' apparently natural development, but it would also capitalize on their readiness to learn and reduce demands on teachers who would simultaneously be engaged in teaching specific thinking skills as well.

Figure 8.9 presents one possible scope and sequence for developing key thinking dispositions and metacognitive skills. It indicates, first, where explicit attention to these dispositions might be *introduced*. As this figure indicates, a limited number of dispositions can be introduced and emphasized each year over a four- to six-year period. As new ones receive attention each succeeding year, those previously introduced should be reinforced and demonstrated until by the end of junior high or middle school these dispositions and the behaviors to which they give rise can be expected to be a demonstrated part of students' normal behavior, *out* of class as well as *in*.

As Figure 8.9 also indicates, teachers following this approach can begin by emphasizing the dispositions of seeking more information, seeking and giving reasons and evidence in support of a claim, and so on. Teachers can then add deliberate, continuing attention to dispositions supportive of open-mindedness, seeking a number of alternatives and being objective, and so on. By staggering introductory emphasis on a few new dispositions each year and by reinforcing those introduced earlier, teachers can perhaps assure better development of these dispositions because they will have more time to attend to fewer new dispositions each year and will not be overwhelmed at the start. Such an approach minimizes skill overload for both teacher and students. While students are thus receiving direct instruction in some selected thinking skills and strategies in the elementary grades, they can also develop a commitment to the attitudes and values that support and guide the use of these operations. Teachers can then continue to reinforce these dispositions throughout succeeding grades, but in more indirect fashion.

Explicit, continuing instruction in metacognitive skills and strategies can commence in the middle or junior high grades as attention to thinking dispositions declines in frequence and directness. This is not to say there should be no attention to metacognition in prior grades. It simply means that while students may be asked in elementary grades to engage in or execute metacognitive-type operations or tasks there need be no

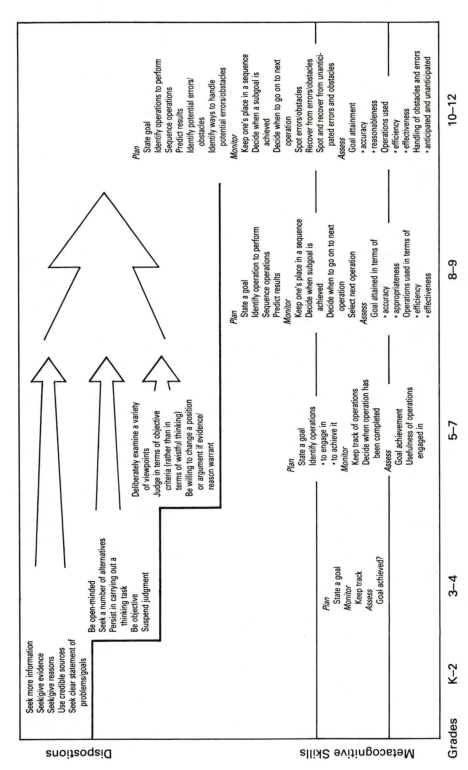

Figure 8.9 A Scope and Sequence for Introducing and Elaborating Metacognitive Skills and Dispositions

Dispositions

Seek more information
Seek/give evidence
Seek/give reasons
Use credible sources
Seek clear statement of problems/goals

Be open-minded
Seek a number of alternatives
Persist in carrying out a thinking task
Be objective
Suspend judgment

Deliberately examine a variety of viewpoints
Judge in terms of objective criteria (rather than in terms of wistful thinking)
Be willing to change a position or argument if evidence/reason warrant

Metacognitive Skills

Plan
State a goal
Monitor
Keep track
Assess
Goal achieved?

Plan
State a goal
Identify operations
• to engage in
• to achieve it
Monitor
Keep track of operations
Decide when operation has been completed
Assess
Goal achievement
Usefulness of operations engaged in

Plan
State a goal
Identify operation to perform
Sequence operations
Predict results
Monitor
Keep one's place in a sequence
Decide when subgoal is achieved
Decide when to go on to next operation
Select next operation
Assess
Goal attained in terms of
• accuracy
• appropriateness
Operations used in terms of
• efficiency
• effectiveness

Plan
State goal
Identify operations to perform
Sequence operations
Predict results
Identify potential errors/obstacles
Identify ways to handle potential errors/obstacles
Monitor
Keep one's place in a sequence
Decide when a subgoal is achieved
Decide when to go on to next operation
Spot errors/obstacles
Recover from errors/obstacles
Spot and recover from unanticipated errors and obstacles
Assess
Goal attainment
• accuracy
• reasonableness
Operations used
• efficiency
• effectiveness
Handling of obstacles and errors
• anticipated and unanticipated

Grades   K–2   3–4   5–7   8–9   10–12

213

direct instruction in how to so do in these grades. Instead, teachers can have students plan or help plan, monitor, and assess classroom activities, gradually engaging them in doing the same for academic and, in the later intermediate grades, simple thinking tasks as well.

More direct instruction in metacognitive operations can begin in the middle or junior high-school grades. However, steps must be taken to minimize skill teaching overload as well as to avoid having learning metacognitive operations interfere with learning of cognitive skills at these grade levels. Thus, instruction in metacognitive operations may be indirect rather than direct even into the early high-school grades. But as students demonstrate desired levels of proficiency in the cognitive skills and strategies they are learning, teachers can provide increasingly direct and sustained instruction in metacognitive skills and strategies. Figure 8.9 outlines a sequence of metacognitive operations as they might be introduced and elaborated at selected grade levels. Whereas skills early in the sequence would best be developed by teacher modeling and continued class application, those in the later years could be the subjects of more direct instruction.

Providing effective instruction in thinking is a big order. Specific thinking skills and strategies must be explicitly introduced and repeated, and guided practice must be provided over a period of time. And these operations must be elaborated or taught to transfer beyond the setting or context in which they were introduced. Beyond this, attention must be given to metacognitive strategies and skills as well as to major dispositions that support thinking. Such instruction, however, cannot be provided all at once. For best results, attention to each of these aspects of thinking must be distributed throughout a curriculum, with explicit introduction and instruction in each, staggered across grades and across selected subject areas. Special care must also be taken to minimize interference with cognitive skill learning and at the same time to capitalize on student readiness to benefit most from instruction. The sequences of instruction presented in Figures 8.8 and 8.9 suggest ways of arranging such instruction.

GUIDELINES FOR SEQUENCING THINKING SKILLS

The thinking sequences described here illustrate and clarify important principles that can serve as guidelines for developing an appropriate scope and sequence for thinking in any school curriculum. These principles apply especially to the sequence of thinking skills and strategies selected for instruction as presented in Figure 8.8, but are applicable in general to the sequential development of metacognitive operations and dispositions, as well. In brief, these guidelines are as follows:

1. Think small. Select only a limited number of significant thinking operations to include in any thinking skills curriculum. Effective instruction to a high degree of proficiency in any complex thinking operation requires repeated attention and considerable time. Any K–12 thinking skills program that consists of more than two dozen or so thinking skills and strategies runs the risk of the same kind of superficial teaching and learning that typifies conventional skill teaching.

2. Build complex skills on less complex skills. Instruction in skills that are deemed to be prerequisites to other skills should precede those other skills in the sequence. Thus, instruction in comparing, contrasting, and classifying should precede more complex forms of analyzing or conceptualizing.

3. Avoid skill overload at each grade level. Introduce only a few—perhaps two or three—*new* skills in each course or cluster of courses at a single grade level, or even at every other grade level. It takes considerable time to learn a new skill to a high degree of proficiency and to transfer it beyond its original context. While new skills are being taught, previously introduced skills must be elaborated and/or reinforced through repeated application with instructive feedback, as necessary. All this instruction takes time. Avoid skill overload or overkill by limiting the number of new skills added each year or two to the students' growing skill repetoire.

4. Stagger the *introduction* of specific skills across grade levels and subjects, reducing the number of new operations to be learned each year in each subject, thus making it possible to overlearn these skills at this point. Perhaps only two or three major new skills should be newly introduced in a course or cluster of courses while continuing to reinforce and transfer other skills introduced in preceding grades.

It is neither necessary nor practical to teach every thinking skill in a curriculum in some form at every grade level. Such a practice leads inevitably to skill overload, sloppy skill instruction, and superficial skill learning at best. Instead, the number of thinking skills and strategies to be taught can be distributed over a number of subjects, courses, and grade levels, and their introduction can be staggered over a period of years. Such procedures reduce the number of thinking operations to be introduced in each grade or course and permit more thorough teaching and learning of these skills and strategies.

5. Assign responsibility for introducing each thinking skill or strategy to several subjects at the same grade level rather than to just a single subject. This reduces skill learning overload on students, helps ensure skill learning even if such instruction in one subject area is, for whatever reason, less than successful, and creates numerous opportunities for

systematic teaching for transfer. Assigning the same two critical thinking skills to social studies and science at a given grade level, or assigning the introduction of problem solving to both math and science at another grade level, illustrate this principle. In either case, allow one subject area to introduce the skill formally and teach it to some initial proficiency in the context or media in which it was originally introduced. Then transfer the skill into a second subject and while instruction continues in the first subject, teach students also how to execute the skill in the second subject as well.

6. Provide instruction in any single skill across several grade levels. The most important thinking skills grow and develop over time and are useful in a variety of subjects or contexts, academic as well as out of school. Instruction and independent application should continue over a number of years until students can independently use, on their own initiative and without guidance, a variety of thinking skills to solve problems, make decisions, conceptualize, and analyze, assess, or produce arguments.

7. Go slowly. Add new thinking skills and strategies to the sequence gradually, only as teachers demonstrate confidence and proficiency in their teaching of those introduced earlier. This same principle also applies to attention given to metacognitive operations and to the dispositions that serve as goals of instruction. First, implement a basic thinking operations sequence and, when this has been in operation several years, then introduce formal and sequenced instruction in metacognition and dispositions. Avoid overwhelming teachers and students with dozens of new skills and strategies right from the start.

8. Introduce and teach thinking skills in the context of major strategies that give these skills utility and function. When introducing a new skill, hook it to other operations with which it is often used. Thus, specific skills such as distinguishing relevant from irrelevant data, when introduced as part of the major step of identifying a problem in the context of a problem-solving process, become much more meaningful and take on more value than if introduced simply as one of a long list of isolated skills. For example, never teach only generating alternatives without engaging students in analyzing the alternatives they generate and making choices, even if these latter operations have to be done initially in rather simple fashion because students have not received instruction in how best to engage in them.

Set instruction in a new skill in the context of other skills, even if students may not yet have received as much instruction in some of the other skills pertinent to the new skill. That instruction can be provided in due course. It is most useful to plan to teach the steps in a thinking strategy as a holistic operation and then in the context of the overall strategy to elaborate, teach, and reteach the detailed operations, knowledge, and rules that constitute each step.

9. Reinforce, elaborate, and transfer thinking skills and processes into new contexts in spiral fashion to refine them in terms of complexity, degree of sophistication, and subtlety. For instance, the simple skill of classifying data into given categories should be later elaborated in terms of classifying into self-invented categories, then of classifying the same data into a variety of category systems, and, finally, of multivariate classification at its most sophisticated level as students apply it upward through the grades.

Organizing thinking skills for effective instruction and learning requires considerable attention beyond listing and describing the operations to be taught. Most of this planning must be done *before* effective classroom instruction can occur. When, however, this task is approached as outlined here, and appropriate attention is given to each part of this task, the classroom teaching and learning of these skills will be sharply enhanced.

ENDNOTES

1. Benjamin Bloom et al., *Taxonomy of Educational Objectives—Handbook I: Cognitive Domain* (New York: Longmans, Inc., 1956).

2. Carl Bereiter, "Elementary School: Necessity or Convenience?" *Elementary School Journal* 73 (May 1973): 435–446.

3. *Project IMPACT* (Costa Mesa, Calif.: Orange County Department of Education, 1984).

4. *Assessment of the Critical Thinking Skills in History-Social Science* (Sacramento: California State Department of Education, 1985), p. 6, 29–31.

5. Robert Ennis, "A Logical Basis for Measuring Critical Thinking Skills," *Educational Leadership* 43, 2 (October 1985): 46.

6. Ibid.

7. Robert J. Marzano and C. L. Hutchins, *Thinking Skills: A Conceptual Framework* (Aurora, Col.: Mid-Continent Regional Educational Laboratory, 1985).

8. John J. Glade and Howard Citron, "Strategic Reasoning," in Arthur L. Costa, ed., *Developing Minds* (Alexandria, Va.: Association for Supervisors and Curriculum Development, 1985), pp. 196–202.

9. Robert J. Sternberg, *Beyond Intelligence: A Triarchic Theory of Human Intelligence* (New York: Cambridge University Press, 1985).

10. John McPeck, *Critical Thinking and Education* (New York: St. Martin's Press, 1981); David H. Russell, *Children's Thinking* (Boston: Ginn and Company, 1956), p. 283.

11. Jerome S. Bruner, *The Process of Education* (Cambridge, Mass.: Harvard University Press, 1963), p. 12.

12. Illinois Renewal Institute, Inc., 200 East Wood St., Suite 250, Palatine, IL 60067.

13. Peter Kneedler, California State Department of Education, 1986.

14. *Assessment of the Critical Thinking Skills in History-Social Science*, pp. 29–31.

15. Irving E. Sigel, "A Constructivist Approach for Teaching Thinking," *Educational Leadership 42*, 3 (November 1984): 8–22.

16. Richard W. Paul, "Critical Thinking: Fundamental to Education for a 'Free Society'," *Educational Leadership 42*, 1 (September 1984): 4–15; Matthew Lipman, "The Cultivation of Reasoning Through Philosophy," *Educational Leadership 42*, 1 (September 1984): 51–56.

17. Bruce R. Joyce, "Social Action for Primary Schools," *Childhood Education 46*, 5 (February 1970): 135.

18. E. L. Chiappetta, "A Review of Piagetian Studies Relevant to Science Instruction at the Secondary and College Level," *Science Education 60*, 2 (April–June 1976): 253–261; Arthur L. Costa, "Mediating the Metacognitive," *Educational Leadership 42*, 3 (November 1984): 57–62.

9

Selecting Appropriate Teaching Strategies

Identifying, defining, and organizing the thinking operations and behaviors to be included in a thinking skills program are certainly important parts of any effort to develop a viable thinking skills program. Important as they are, however, these efforts represent only a starting point rather than an end point in such an effort. For no matter how well organized, how thoroughly researched, or how attractively displayed are the components and structure of a thinking skills program, it is what happens in individual classrooms to translate these elements into learning that determines the ultimate effectiveness of such a program. Providing instruction appropriate to improving student proficiency in thinking is as much a part of developing a thinking skills program as is planning the structure of that program. This chapter explains the ingredients of classroom instruction that are essential to the development of high degrees of student proficiency in thinking skills and strategies. It also explains how teachers can integrate skills teaching lessons into their existing courses and subjects.

A FRAMEWORK FOR TEACHING

There are many strategies and techniques from which to choose to teach thinking. Question asking, by teachers, texts, or worksheets, is one of the most popular, especially where these questions are sequenced at levels of increasing difficulty. Engaging students in discussions or debates, assigning frequent student writing, and even exhorting students to "Think" and then to "Think again!" and finally to "Think harder!" are also widely used techniques to teach thinking. As popular as these methods may be, however, they share one common failing. Either singly or in combination with each other, they do *not* teach thinking.

None of these techniques show students *how to execute* the thinking operations they need to execute the tasks assigned. What these techniques actually do and often do well is to provide opportunities to think, to stimulate, and to encourage thinking. They are quite useful as devices for exercising or practicing thinking. But by itself, practice is not enough. For students to develop some degree of proficiency in the skills and strategies—both cognitive and metacognitive—that constitute thinking, actual instruction in how to execute these skills and strategies is required.

Specialists in teaching thinking often classify the various methods used to accomplish this task into three broad categories: approaches that provide for the teaching *of* thinking, those that provide teaching *for* thinking, and those that involve teaching *about* thinking. The teaching *of* thinking, as described initially by Dr. Ronald Brandt and later elaborated by educators Jay McTighe and Arthur Costa, consists essentially of providing systematic, direct instruction in explicitly detailed attributes of specific thinking skills and strategies.[1] In such teaching, the thinking operations themselves are what is to be learned. On the other hand, teaching *for* thinking, as McTighe notes, consists essentially of providing students "opportunities to practice and 'exercise' thinking skills."[2] Such teaching seeks to stimulate and encourage thinking customarily by using methods like those described above, but usually focuses on the subject matter products of such thinking rather than on how these products are generated. Teaching *about* thinking consists of helping students become aware of their own and others' thinking processes.[3] It involves helping students articulate and consciously monitor their own thinking as well as analyze how others, usually experts, engage in specific thinking operations. Any approach to teaching thinking can be classified as one or more of these types of teaching.

Whereas these three labels aptly describe the various approaches to teaching thinking, this tripartite distinction sometimes gives the impression that use of these approaches may be an "either-or" proposition. This is not the case at all. Teaching thinking involves deciding not which of these approaches to employ but rather deciding *how* best to weave all three approaches together to produce significant skill learning. Any worthwhile thinking skills program should employ the teaching *of*, *for*, and *about* thinking in appropriate combinations to achieve its skill learning goals and objectives.

1. The skill is *introduced.*
2. The skill is *practiced* frequently, *with* instructive *guidance.*
3. Students *practice* the skill at the teacher's command but *without any teacher guidance.*
4. The skill is *transferred* to a new setting or context, or *elaborated.*
5. Students receive *guided practice* applying the skill frequently in the new context or as newly elaborated.
6. Students *use the skill on their own* in combination with other skills to accomplish thinking tasks.

Figure 9.1 A Framework for Teaching Thinking

Probably the most effective combination of these teaching approaches involves, first, the teaching *of* thinking—providing direct instruction in how to execute specific thinking skills and strategies. This can then be followed by teaching *for* thinking—providing frequent opportunities for students to practice, with decreasing instructive guidance, these skills. And throughout both kinds of teaching, students need to learn *about* thinking by repeatedly reflecting on and discussing what they and others do in their heads as they execute various thinking operations. When combined in this sequence, these approaches constitute a useful framework for organizing instruction in any thinking skill or strategy. Figure 9.1 outlines this framework.

In this thinking skill teaching framework, teachers provide a series of lessons on *each* skill or strategy that moves students from focused introduction to the skill or strategy through various types of practice and elaboration, to autonomous use of the skill. Each of the six types of lessons represents teaching approaches that can be categorized as either teaching *of,* teaching *for,* or teaching *about* thinking. Of these, those providing for the teaching *of* and *about* thinking are most crucial.*

STRATEGIES FOR TEACHING THINKING

A variety of strategies may be used to conduct lessons in each stage of the framework described above. Those strategies differ for each of the types of lessons in this framework. Understanding these strategies in detail and being familiar with the research grounding of each enables teachers to use them as needed with the precision that reaps their full

---

* For a detailed explanation of these and similar strategies, with examples, sample lesson plans, and model tests, see Barry K. Beyer, *Practical Strategies for the Teaching of Thinking* (Boston: Allyn and Bacon, 1987).

potential in teaching thinking. This section describes how each of these strategies may be used to carry out lessons at each of the six stages in the thinking skill teaching framework presented here.

Introducing a New Thinking Skill

Whenever students are expected to learn a new thinking skill, it should be introduced to them as explicitly as possible. This means that a teacher should provide instruction in how to execute the skill, with a minimum of interference from subject matter or other skills. Research on skill learning and teaching suggests that in this stage of thinking skill learning, students need to overlearn the skill.[4] This requires, first, a focus directly on the specific operations, criteria or knowledge, and rules that constitute the overall skill.[5] Explicit focus on and discussion of the components of a skill in its introductory stage appears essential for helping students develop the conscious awareness of how the skill works that is preliminary to becoming proficient in applying it.[6]

Research also suggests three techniques useful in introducing any thinking skill.[7] Modeling appears to be extremely useful for this purpose. This involves demonstrating the procedures and principles involved in executing the skill and providing students with cues that highlight these components of the skill as they are demonstrated.[8] Student articulation and discussion of a skill's attributes are also helpful at this point, especially in helping students to mentally walk through what constitutes a skilled operation.[9] Finally, student discussion of what they do in their heads as they execute the thinking skill helps raise to a level of consciousness how their thinking occurs; this is important in helping students take informed control of their own thinking.[10] Researchers Walter Doyle and Barak Rosenshine identify these techniques as the core of "direct instruction."[11] Use of these techniques and strategies constitute the teaching *of* thinking—teaching where the focus is explicitly and consistently on the skill being taught.

Teachers can implement these techniques in several different ways to introduce any thinking skill. One way employs the principles of inductive learning, an approach similar to those favored by developmentalists.[12] The second employs the more didactic, directive teaching described by Doyle and Rosenshine.[13] These two approaches are best conceived of as prototype strategies on either end of a range of strategies useful in introducing thinking skills. Many variants of these approaches may be found between them.

An *inductive* strategy for introducing a new thinking skill or strategy might proceed as follows: (1) First, the teacher introduces the skill by writing its label on the board, getting synonyms and a definition for it from the class (or providing them himself or herself) and seeking examples of where students may have engaged in this operation before (in classwork or outside of school). If, for example, the skill involved is that of distinguishing relevant from irrelevant information, the teacher and students find or devise a working definition of relevance/irrelevance, identify appropriate synonyms for these terms, and give an example or two of something relevant and irrelevant to a topic in the course or in their out-of-class daily lives. (2) Students then execute the skill as best they can without any further instruction. They simply decide whether given information samples are relevant or irrelevant to teacher-specified topics.

(3) In the next step, students reflect on, verbalize, and discuss what they did in their heads to distinguish relevant from irrelevant information in the activity just completed. (4) Then the students execute the skill again, applying it to a new data set. They do so by incorporating whatever they wish from what they did or heard in the preceding discussion about the procedure they attempted to use originally. (5) To conclude, the students review how they engaged in the skill, articulating the basic steps in the procedure and important rules to follow in executing this thinking operation.

Where a skill is judged too difficult for students and where a teacher understands fairly well how to execute it, a quite different strategy can be used to introduce it. In launching this *directive* strategy, the following steps are implemented: (1) The teacher introduces the skill in the same manner as in the previously described strategy—writing the label on the board, developing synonyms and a definition for it, and helping the students recall examples of where they may have earlier performed something like it or seen someone do it. (2) However, instead of then asking the students to do it, the teacher describes exactly how an expert executes the skill. The teacher would now explain step-by-step how the skill is executed and would note any important principles, criteria, or rules that guide its use. (3) Next, the teacher demonstrates the skill with whatever contributions students can volunteer, highlighting important operational cues as the demonstration proceeds. (4) The teacher reviews with the students reasons for executing the skill procedures and any knowledge related to the skill. (5) Then the teacher has the students apply what they have seen, heard, and discussed to execute the skill themselves using the same kind of data and the same media as used in the demonstration. (6) To conclude this introductory lesson, the teacher guides the students in reflecting on and discussing the extent to which they followed the steps modeled for them, what they did in their heads to execute the skill, any modifications they thought they were making in the modeled procedure, and what they had learned about the skill.

These two introductory strategies share a number of common features. Both require anywhere from thirty to forty-five minutes, depending on the complexity of the skill, the abilities of the students and their previous experience with the skill, and the type of subject matter that serves as the vehicle for applying the skill. Both strategies provide for modeling the skill, in the inductive strategy by students who do it reasonably well in the initial application of the skill, and in the directive strategy by the teacher or other model. In both strategies teacher and students explicate the steps in the procedure by which the skill is executed. Both strategies also involve students in reflecting and discussing what they do in their heads as they execute the skill.

Most importantly, the focus throughout each strategy is on the skill. The introduction to each lesson clearly establishes learning the skill as the lesson objective. It also helps students develop the mental set needed to call up previous experience related to the new skill. Thereafter, each strategy focuses exclusively on the components of the skill. In spite of temptations to engage in discussion of subject matter, especially where students offer inferences of questionable validity, the teacher must, in such an introductory lesson, put discussion of subject matter aside until the next lesson and keep student attention on the attributes of the skill. Concluding the lesson by reflecting on or reviewing how the skill works and the rules that guide its execution completes both strategies. This ensures continuing, explicit attention to the skill throughout its introduction.

Each of these skill-introducing strategies has disadvantages as well as advantages. It is clear, as researcher Walter Doyle has pointed out, that students do often develop thinking strategies as a result of their own experimentation and that such invention leads to a deeper understanding both of subject matter and process. However, such an approach is also as likely as not to lead to the invention of dysfunctional thinking strategies.[14] Helping students unlearn these flawed inventions greatly complicates the subsequent learning of more effective strategies that were the target in the first place. Although this kind of lesson is generally valuable with better students and with relatively easy skills, teachers employ the inductive approach to introducing a thinking skill at some risk.

The directive skill-introducing strategy has its advantages and disadvantages as well. Use of this strategy obviously requires that a teacher know in some detail how to execute the skill being introduced. Where such is not the case, this strategy is extremely difficult to use well. Even where a teacher does know something about the skill, this strategy may not work well if the teacher is unable to communicate clearly the key operations that comprise the new skill.[15] However, where such instruction is understood, students usually "pick up" quickly the key steps in executing a new skill. Although some educators fear such "telling" about a skill may produce simply mindless imitation rather than real learning, educators like Paul Chance and others indicate that exactly the opposite occurs. In actuality students freely adapt and personalize the model even as they use it for the first time.[16] Some researchers believe that such an introductory strategy is especially valuable even when not well understood because it may initiate a chain of thinking that may help some students invent a strategy or skill or their own anyway.[17] And such invention may produce a much more effective strategy than could have been invented by the student without the more directive instructional approach.

Both kinds of skill-introducing strategies, as well as their variants, can be used to launch learning of any thinking skill or strategy at any grade level in any subject. But they must be used with awareness of their limitations as well as of their strengths. Either can be used to introduce a thinking skill or strategy—either spontaneously, as when a teacher senses that students cannot execute a thinking operation they need to complete a subject-matter task at hand, or at a specific point where a teacher has planned to introduce a new skill or strategy to the students. Regardless of which particular strategy is used, or whether it is used spontaneously or is planned in advance, for best results it should exhibit the features of a skill introduction described here. Use of such a lesson contributes immeasurably to increased student understanding of and to their own increased proficiency in executing any thinking skill or strategy.

Guiding Practice in a New Skill

Of course, no student should be expected to demonstrate proficiency in a particular thinking skill simply on the basis of one introductory lesson in it. Unlike the teaching of information, which can normally be presented in a single lesson, teaching a thinking skill requires continued attention to the skill over an extended period of time. Research suggests these follow-up skill lessons should be frequent, require relatively small amounts of time (twenty minutes or so), and be spaced out intermittently over a period of time.[18] Moreover, as Benjamin Bloom and other experts have noted, these lessons should provide immediate instructive feedback and correction for the students.[19]

In fact, the key to such "practice" lessons is continued teacher and peer guidance and instruction in how to execute the skill. Such instructive input can precede, follow, or be simultaneous with application of the skill. In one strategy useful in providing such guided practice:

1. The teacher *introduces* the skill to be used, exactly as in the introductory lesson strategies.
2. The teacher, with student help, *previews* how to execute the skill by reviewing with the students what they already know about

the steps to go through and what rules or principles need to be followed.

3. The students *apply* the skill to the same type of data as used in the introductory lesson, periodically checking what they are doing against what they articulated earlier as they previewed the skill, taking corrective steps as needed.

4. The students *reflect* on how they executed the skill, considering especially any obstacles they encountered and how they dealt with them and any modifications they made in how they carried out the skill.

Executing this strategy customarily takes twenty minutes or so. Once completed, students can move into a discussion of the subject-matter products generated by their application of the skill.

A number of guided practice lessons (using strategies like this one) should follow any lesson introducing a thinking skill. Although there have been no specific guidelines derived from research as to how many, a teacher will know when to move into conventional, student self-directed practice or use of the skill by observing when his or her students reach a level of proficiency where a detailed introduction, previewing, and reviewing are no longer necessary.[20] It would not be uncommon, however, for students to require anywhere from four to ten guided practice lessons in a newly introduced thinking skills or strategy. Use of these lessons continues the teaching *of* thinking initiated by the introductory lessons described here.

Applying a Skill Independently

Once a thinking skill or strategy has been explicitly introduced and students have received sufficient guided practice to be able to apply it on command without any teacher assistance at all, self-directed application or practice of the skill is most appropriate. It is at this point that most techniques conventionally used to teach *for* thinking become useful. These include using teacher-asked questions, especially those that appear to require the use of the skills being learned, completing worksheets that require use of these same skills, engaging in debates or discussions, using data bases to solve problems, writing essays or paragraphs, writing out answers to end-of-chapter "Questions for Critical Thinking" or similar exercises, and engaging in inquiry or discovery activities.

It is important to remember, however, that these techniques do not, by themselves or in any combination with each other, provide instruction in a skill. What they do, instead, is to put students into situations where, if they choose to engage, they are forced to use what thinking skills they already have. Such situations are essentially practice activities. They call on students to execute a particular skill or skills as best they can without instructive help. And such practice is precisely what is needed at this point in learning a new thinking skill. Although amounts and frequency of practice required vary with the skill being learned as well as with student backgrounds and abilities, it may take three or more such lessons spaced increasingly apart to get students to the point where they can demonstrate proficiency in using the skill on their own.[21]

It is important to note that such practice is but a part of what is needed to develop proficiency in any thinking skill or strategy. Although it is a necessary ingredient in skill learning, unguided practice, by itself, is not sufficient to develop mastery. Teachers who rely only on these practice techniques to "teach" a thinking skill or strategy are providing only a minor part of what is needed by students or novices to learn a new thinking operation. Research suggests that self-directed practice becomes useful only after explicit introduction to a specific skill and guided practice in applying that skill have been provided.[22] By providing opportunities to practice a skill in which direct instruction has *already* been provided, as in the framework described here, teachers can maximize the effects of both practice and instruction in skill learning. Thus, teaching *for* thinking is a useful part of a framework for teaching thinking skills, but remains no substitute for actually instructing students in how to execute a skill or strategy *before* such practice is provided.

Transferring or Elaborating a Thinking Skill

Contrary to common assumptions, thinking skills and strategies do not transfer automatically to contexts or settings that differ from those in which they were initially developed. Thinking operations are very much tied to the contexts or media in which they are first executed. Thus, in order to help students generalize a thinking skill—to be able to apply it or transfer it to a variety of subjects, settings, or contexts—teachers must explicitly show them how. In a word, lessons must provide instruction in a thinking skill or strategy in a variety of settings after it has been mastered in the initial context. Too often teaching thinking skills ignores this important step.[23]

Teachers can do several things to help students learn how to transfer, generalize, or elaborate a newly learned thinking skill. After explicitly introducing a new skill and providing guided practice to the point where students can apply it effectively on their own, a teacher can conduct a lesson showing students how to apply the skill in a new context. Teachers who wish students to apply a skill in their subject area that was introduced in another subject can do the same thing. This requires use of virtually the same kinds of strategies used to introduce a skill and provide guided practice in it. Here, the teaching *of* thinking comes into play once again.

Using a previously learned skill in a new context usually appears to students as if they are learning a new skill. To help them make this transfer, a teacher can, in effect, reintroduce the skill in a single thirty-minute lesson as follows:

1. Introduce the skill, as in the preceding strategies.
2. *Review* what students already know about the skill.
3. Explain and demonstrate how the skill is executed in the context to which it is now to be transferred.
4. Have the students review the key attributes of the skill as illustrated in the demonstration.
5. Have the students apply the skill in this new context, providing instructive feedback as needed.
6. Have the students reflect on what they did in their heads as they executed the skill in this new context.

This strategy differs from the directive introductory strategy described earlier only in its second step. Here, students *review* what they already know about executing the skill before they try to apply it in the new context. Thus, they then have to concentrate on essentially only one new thing—the context—when they apply the skill. In such a lesson, students do all those things considered to be essential to introducing a new skill—they see it modeled, focus on its attributes, and discuss and hear what goes on in their and others' minds as they execute the skill. The focus is kept on the skill rather than on the subject matter used as a vehicle for executing it.

Guiding Practice in the Skill in the New Context

Once a previously learned skill has been reintroduced in a new context or media as described here, students must receive guided practice in applying the skill in this new setting until they achieve the level of proficiency desired. This guided practice must be mixed between applications of the skill in the original context as well as in the newer context to which it is being transferred. As students apply the skill (with appropriate corrective feedback) to a variety of contexts, they move toward generalizing the skill.[24] The same teaching strategy used in guiding the initial practice in a new skill (as used in Stage 2 of the framework presented here) proves useful at this point. From two to five or more lessons using this strategy may be required before students are able to engage in completely autonomous application of the skill or strategy in the various contexts in which it has been taught up to this point. Again, these guided practice lessons involve essentially the teaching *of* thinking.

Using the Skill Autonomously

The final stage in this framework for teaching thinking skills and strategies is similar to the third or practice stage in all but two major respects. Like that earlier stage, this type of lesson is a time when students are expected to apply the skill without any further instruction or teacher guidance. Thus, the techniques typical of the teaching *for* thinking approach are most appropriate once again, including use of teacher questioning, discussions, debates, discovery learning, responding to worksheet questions, and so on. Ideally, such practice should include opportunities to apply the skill in the context or media in which it was originally presented as well as in the other context(s) to which it is being transferred. Students need frequent but intermittent opportunities to practice the thinking skills and strategies on their own in a variety of contexts.

Two features of such practice differentiate it from practice in Stage 3 of the framework described above, however. First, opportunities must be provided at this point to apply the skill or strategy being practiced in combination with other thinking skills and strategies previously learned and without specific teacher direction as to precisely which skills these should be. Students should have numerous opportunities to decide, in effect, which operations are appropriate to a particular task and to execute them on their own.[25] And this is precisely what distinguishes most teaching *for* thinking approaches.

Second, by this point in teaching thinking, teacher-asked questions should have given way to student-asked questions. For as long as student thinking waits on teacher questions to trigger it, students remain dependent on others to launch their own thinking. If independent learning is a goal of teaching thinking, students should be taught how to invent and ask their own questions. Although question asking is not a thinking skill per se, it does involve the use of many thinking operations. Helping students learn how to ask their own questions, providing them guided practice in so doing, and giving them opportunities to do so should be important aspects of teaching. Certainly by this stage in teaching thinking, student learning should be characterized by considerable student-generated questioning. Teaching students how to develop effective questions of their own can be accomplished by providing instruction using the six-stage skill teaching framework explained here.

Teaching a thinking skill or strategy to transfer thus duplicates the process of introducing a new skill as it moves from introduction through guided practice to autonomous application or self-directed practice. As a teacher provides lessons to move students toward independent use of the skill, it involves the teaching *of* thinking as well as teaching *for* thinking. By combining and sequencing techniques useful in both of these teaching approaches, teachers can provide the kind of instruction research suggests will lead to the highest degrees of skill proficiency maintained over the longest period of time.

DEVELOPING METACOGNITION

Teaching thinking involves more than teaching the specific skills and strategies by which we manipulate data to produce meaning. It also involves teaching those metacognitive operations and dispositions by which we direct, control, and drive these skills and strategies. This involves teaching *about* thinking, for it consists primarily of teaching students to deal explicitly with their own or others' thinking. As shown in Figure 9.1, attention to this aspect of teaching thinking occurs throughout most of the thinking skill teaching framework described here. It can also be the focus of special lessons that focus on how experts execute thinking tasks.

Engaging students in thinking about their own thinking is one of the key features of each of the introductory, guided practice and transfer lesson strategies for teaching thinking skills described earlier. Each of these strategies devotes explicit attention at specific points in a lesson to helping students reflect on, talk about, and hear others talk about what they do in their minds as they execute the thinking skill or strategy they are learning. By repeated attention to the key operations in which one could engage when thinking about his or her own thinking, teachers can help students develop the inclination and skills necessary to engage in metacognition whenever they have thinking tasks to perform.

Such teaching, initially, should be indirect. That is, students can be encouraged and assisted in articulating what they did in their own minds as they executed specific cognitive operations, but they should not be directly taught the skills involved in executing such control. Such teaching at this stage should be more a part of learning a specific thinking skill than learning how to employ the key operations that constitute metacognition. This approach minimizes interference created by having one kind of skill learning compete with another. Moreover, it acknowledges what research suggests about student readiness to engage purposefully in metacognition—that most average youngsters do not seem to be able to do so with relative success until they begin to move into the stage of formal abstract reasoning around age eleven.[26] Efforts to develop metacognition up to this point may be most productive when devoted to developing readiness for metacognition rather than attempting to provide explicit, direct instruction in its operations.

Teachers can employ a number of techniques to provide such indirect instruction about metacognition. They can model for students the key operations of planning a task (whether a thinking task or a physical activity), monitoring it as it is executed, and assessing how well it is carried out. Teachers can also have students help them plan, monitor, and assess class learning activities, and can reinforce student efforts to do the same with homework assignments and problem-solving and decision-making tasks. They can label what students are doing in executing a thinking task with terms that designate the various major steps in metacognition. Teachers can also encourage students to paraphrase, restate, or elaborate each other's thinking plans or processes. Finally, teachers can use various types of questions to move students through the various aspects of metacognitive thinking without any formal instruction in how to develop answers for such questions.[27] Such techniques fall short of formal instruction in "how to do it," and focus instead simply on providing opportunities to "do it" as best one can. They constitute more a teaching *for* metacognition rather than a teaching *of* it. But by engaging students in metacognitive tasks, teachers set the stage for subsequent direct instruction in this level of thinking.

More direct instruction in metacognitive operations can be provided as students begin to demonstrate mastery of the major cognitive skills and strategies being taught, starting perhaps in the intermediate or secondary grades. Teachers can model and explain in detail how they execute thinking tasks and invite students to help them carry out these tasks, always taking care to explain why as well as how they perform the operations they do.[28] Teachers can pair students to engage in thinking tasks, assigning one student to execute the task while describing aloud what and why he or she is doing as the second student in the pair records what the first is doing or guides him or her through the task by questioning the moves being made. Educator Arthur Whimbey's Thinking Aloud Paired Problem Solving (TAPPS) procedure provides a useful model for such an approach.[29] Finally, teachers can teach directly a strategy of metacognition and its component operations, perhaps by providing lessons in these operations built around the six stages of the skill teaching framework outlined here.

Teachers can also foster metacognition by providing lessons in which students analyze how experts have executed specific kinds of thinking operations. Students can examine the accounts of political leaders who describe how they made a decision, or of scientists who describe how they resolved a scientific problem, or of artists who explain how they invented or created a symphony, sculpture, poem, or painting. A number of such case studies exist.[30] By making them the subjects of lessons, teachers can help students identify and analyze the operations performed by experienced thinkers and thus encourage them to incorporate what they discover into their own thinking processes.

As part of such teaching, attention must also be given to those dispositions that support and drive skillful thinking. These dispositions, such as a willingness to persist in a thinking task, a desire to provide and receive evidence and sound reasoning in support of any claim, and other similar attitudes, are outlined in Chapter 3. Since such attitudes or thinking habits develop early in life (by the middle school years at the latest), they should be a focus of teaching starting in the primary grades.[31] However, these dispositions cannot be taught in exactly the same way as the cognitive and metacognitive operations are best taught. Teaching dispositions, like the teaching of other attitudes and values, takes longer than teaching specific skills and strategies and requires use of those techniques commonly associated with affective education.

Teachers can use at least three techniques to foster development of those dispositions that support and drive thinking. They can model those behaviors that demonstrate these dispositions; that is they can consistently give evidence and reasons to justify their assertions, cite credible sources as bases for their statements, seek additional information in making decisions, and so on. They can also insist that students exhibit behavior that reflects these dispositions and engage students repeatedly in activities that require use of these behaviors and dispositions. And teachers can reinforce such thinking behaviors whenever they see them exhibited. Consistent use of these techniques can contribute significantly to developing the kinds of dispositions that underlie skillful thinking.

The essence of teaching *about* thinking, then, is that thinking—one's own or someone else's—is the subject of study. Students think about thinking, study it, talk about it, and enact it consistently. By doing so, they raise to a level of consciousness their own thinking so they can take deliberate control of it—so they can consciously plan, monitor, and direct it. And they develop those attitudes that dispose them to behave in ways supportive of such thinking. As they demonstrate such affective and metacognitive behaviors, the effectiveness of their own thinking improves and they become more skillful at engaging in those executive functions of the mind that guide and support effective thinking.

Teaching thinking skills, then, as organized in the framework presented here, involves the teaching *of*, teaching *for*, and teaching *about* each specific thinking skill or strategy selected for instruction. Providing lessons that incorporate these three different approaches to teaching thinking can help students develop the high degree of proficiency in thinking that most educators and program developers envision as an outcome of teaching thinking. Failure to provide any or even one of these kinds of lessons in a thinking skill may drastically limit the chances of achieving this goal.

SEQUENCING SKILLS TEACHING LESSONS

Sequencing instruction to provide the lessons required to carry out the skill teaching framework just described involves preplanning on the part of both program developers and classroom teachers. This planning is often the link missing between a curriculum-wide thinking skills scope and sequence and effective classroom teaching of these operations. It consists of deciding specifically where, in a course, the thinking operations selected for instruction are to be "taught." Essentially this task consists of two steps.

First, teachers or program developers must identify the different skills and strategies assigned to a specific course or grade level in terms of whether they are thinking operations (1) to be newly introduced and practiced, (2) to be reinforced, having been introduced and practiced in previous grades or subjects, (3) to be elaborated or transferred beyond what they were in previous grades or subjects where they were introduced and practiced, or (4) to receive minimal attention and be treated in the more conventional manner. Figure 9.2 presents a chart that can be used for this purpose. Grade levels on the chart may be adjusted to reflect the scope of the school's or department's skill program. Columns may include single skills or clusters. Or, the chart may list subjects rather than grade levels, and a series of such charts may be produced for all subjects at *each* grade level. Identifying these skills by grade levels and subjects should precede decisions about how and where in a specific course to provide the kind of instruction each kind of thinking skill requires.

The next step involves keying instruction in each skill to the appropriate stage(s) of the skill teaching framework. This framework, it will be recalled, consists of six stages: introduction, guided practice, independent application, transfer or elaboration, guided practice, and autonomous use. To do this, one must decide specifically where in a course each skill to be emphasized is to (1) be formally introduced and/or receive guided practice to some degree of independent application, or (2) be elaborated or transferred to new contexts and receive additional guided practice and autonomous use, and/or (3) be used repeatedly by students without further instruction.

For a thinking skill that is to be newly introduced in a specific course or grade, such planning consists of identifying those places in a course where the skill can be taught at each stage of this framework. Figure 9.3 diagrams one such plan in terms of weeks (or what even could be chap-

234

Grade Levels and/or Subjects

	K–2	3–5	6–8	9–12
Skills to Be Introduced and Practiced				
Skills Previously Introduced, to Be Transferred and Elaborated				
Skills Previously Taught in a Number of Contexts, to Be Reinforced				
Other Skills to Be Taught as Presently Taught				

Figure 9.2 A Chart for Identifying Thinking Skills and Strategies According to the Types of Teaching Required

Week: I II III IV V VI

I — INTRODUCE
II — GUIDED PRACTICE
III — GUIDED PRACTICE
IV — GUIDED PRACTICE
V — APPLICATION INDEPENDENT
VI — APPLICATION INDEPENDENT

VII — TRANSFER
VIII — GUIDED PRACTICE
IX — GUIDED PRACTICE
XII — GUIDED PRACTICE
XIV — APPLICATION INDEPENDENT

X — GUIDED PRACTICE
XI — APPLICATION INDEPENDENT
XIII — APPLICATION INDEPENDENT

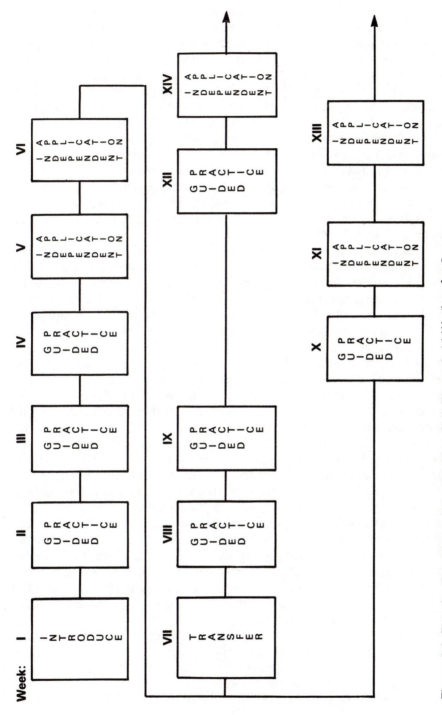

Figure 9.3 Plan for Teaching a New Thinking Skill Through 14 Weeks of a Course

235

ters in a text). After the skill is formally introduced during week I, for instance, using teaching strategies appropriate to this task, this sequence provides three guided practice lessons (weeks II, III, and IV) and at least two lessons (one each week V and VI) in which the students apply the skill on teacher command but without instruction. During week VII, skill transfer can be initiated, using an appropiate teaching strategy. Thereafter, students will have guided practice in this skill during weeks VIII, IX, and XII, with at least one self-directed application of the skill during week XIV, the last week of the semester. During the next semester, students can have additional guided practice lessons in this version of the skill, followed by application opportunities. Simultaneous with the practice of the skill in the new context, students will practice the skill as originally introduced (week X) with appropriate teacher guidance and will have at least two opportunites to apply it on their own (weeks XI and XIII).

This skill teaching plan thus requires two full class lessons (to introduce it and to transfer it to a new setting or context); at least seven guided practice lessons, distributed among both versions of the skill, each requiring about half a regular class period of attention to the skill; and at least five opportunities to apply it, in its two forms. Devoting this much time and explicit instruction to the skill over these fourteen weeks will, this plan presumes, enable students to develop a high level of proficiency in executing the skill. Of course, additional instruction can be provided if it turns out students need it, or the number of guided practice lessons can be reduced if students reach the desired levels of independent use sooner than anticipated.[32] And there is no reason why such instruction need be compressed into fourteen weeks; this sequence of lessons can be expanded over two semesters to accommodate instruction in other skills as well as to leave intervening weeks where there is no formal skill instruction, especially toward the end of the sequence.

In planning a sequence of lessons for a single, new skill, a number of factors must be considered. First, each lesson has to be keyed to a place in the subject matter being studied that naturally calls for use of the skill. If the skill being considered is classifying, each of these lessons must be in places in the course where classifying data is called for or useful. By providing instruction at such points—whether it be in the form of rather detailed introduction, or guided practice, or teaching for transfer—the skill has greater utility for students and, consequently, the students are better motivated to attend to learning it.[33]

Second, the subject matter to be used at each point in the sequence must readily fit the skill. If the skill is classifying, for example, there must be data that can be classified without stretching it or turning to nonsubject matter to execute the skill. Third, the kind of data (lists of words or phrases, for example) used to execute the skill must remain the same up to the transfer lesson. Perhaps then the skill can be newly applied to pictures or paintings and practiced with this new media while simultaneously receiving continued practice and application with words and phrases, as originally introduced. Fourth, the data used in the introductory and guided practice lessons must be data clearly understood by the students. A new skill cannot be practiced initially with new content or this content will so interfere with the skill that the skill will not be learned.

Finally, enough opportunities have to be found for guided practice and application of the skill. In the case of the example in Figure 9.3, twelve such opportunities have been identified. Whether these opportunities, with use of an appropriate teaching strategy in each lesson, will prove sufficient can be determined only by actually carrying out the planned sequence of lessons. If a teacher has been accurate in judging the fit between skill and opportunities presented to use it with the course content as well as with student learning abilities, the desired skill learning should occur. However, when such sequencing becomes difficult or impossible, or when learning does not occur, it may well be that the skill to be taught is inappropriate for the assigned subject matter or grade level.

It is important to note that the lesson sequence just outlined applies to only one newly introduced thinking operation. However, teaching thinking skills or strategies in any single course or grade involves teaching more than one thinking skill or strategy. In planning, one has to sequence *all* the thinking operations slated to receive instruction. Not only does one have to sequence lessons through the skill teaching framework for *each newly introduced thinking skill,* but lessons must be planned for at least two other types of thinking skills as well. These include: (1) thinking skills that have already been introduced and taught to transfer in a variety of contexts in preceding courses or grades, and (2) thinking skills that may have been introduced and practiced to some degree of proficiency but not yet taught to transfer in the preceding subjects or grades. Teachers need to sequence all lessons for *all* three kinds of thinkings skills in any course or grade level. Different types of lessons in the skill teaching framework need to be provided for each of these types of skills.

Figure 9.4 outlines a skill teaching sequence for four thinking skills over a fourteen-week period. Two of these skills are to be newly introduced in this course or grade (Skills B and C). Since a third skill (Skill A) has been introduced, practiced, and taught to transfer in the preceding course or grade, it requires only one guided practice lesson early in the course (week I) and then a series of opportunities to apply the skill independently (weeks III, V, IX, XII). A fourth thinking skill (Skill D), however, introduced and practiced in the preceding course, must re-

Week:	I	II	III	IV	V	VI	VII	VIII	IX	X	XI	XII	XIII	XIV
Skill A	Practice Guided		Application Independent		Application Independent				Application Independent			Application Independent		
Skill B		Introduce	Practice Guided	Practice Guided		Practice Guided	Application Independent	Application Independent			Transfer	Practice Guided	Guided Practice	Guided Practice
Skill C					Introduce	Practice Guided	Practice Guided		Practice Guided	Application Independent		Application Independent	Guided Practice	Guided Practice
Skill D			Practice Guided	Application Independent	Application Independent		Application Independent	Transfer	Practice Guided	Guided Practice	Guided Practice		Application Independent	

Figure 9.4 Plan for Teaching Four Thinking Skills Through 14 Weeks of a Course

238

ceive additional guided practice and use, followed by lessons transferring this skill to a new context and guided practice and autonomous application of the skill in both the original and newly introduced contexts. Note that in such a sequence the introduction of new skills and the transfer of other skills is staggered to minimize their interfering with each other and to reduce the instructional as well as the learning demands.

In sum, planning a sequence of thinking skills lessons *within* a course or across several courses is an extremely important part of teaching thinking skills. It is time-consuming, for it requires that classroom teachers or materials designers sit down with the skill sequence and skill descriptions, instructional objectives, course text, and text materials to decide where in their courses the thinking skills selected for instruction can be taught in the instructional framework suggested here. Such planning should not be done by teachers in isolation from each other, either. A teacher of one subject or grade level ought to be aware of the kind of instruction provided in other courses or grade levels in any particular skill, and how far through the instructional framework teaching of each major skill has progressed up to the point where his or her course or grade begins. Each teacher also needs to know what is expected in terms of thinking skill proficiency by those teachers who will have their students next semester or next year.

Too often, this planning task is left to teachers to accomplish as part of their regular daily or weekly lesson planning. At times (especially for those experienced in the direct teaching of thinking skills), such spontaneous planning or teaching proves quite possible, of course. However, it is important to plan in advance where thinking skills might be taught in a specific course in order to identify appropriate opportunities for such teaching. Identifying such opportunities in advance of actual classroom teaching reveals the extent to which the subject is appropriate for teaching the skill or the skill is appropriate for the particular subject matter or materials to be used. Such planning also provides for smoother teaching. Keying skill instruction to places in a course where it can be used serves to validate the earlier choice of skills, the skill scope and sequence, and the assignment of skills to subject and grade levels. And such planning makes possible the most effective teaching of thinking skills and strategies.

TESTING THINKING SKILLS AND STRATEGIES

No instruction in thinking would be complete without appropriate assessment of the quality of student learning resulting from such instruction. Classroom teachers should assess the thinking skills they teach (metacognitive as well as cognitive) as a continuing part of their own regular classroom assessment procedures. They should do so for three reasons. Such assessment, especially in the form of tests, motivates student learning. Research clearly indicates students attend to what they are held accountable for. And classroom tests and grades, for most students, represent one important type of accountability.[34] Such assessment also provides diagnostic evidence about the quality of teaching as well as learning. Also, when properly interpreted, the results can lead to changes in instruction designed to improve thinking skill teaching and learning. Finally, classroom assessment of student thinking provides a measure of student growth and development which is, if only indirectly, indicative of the degreee of success of the instructional program provided.

Teachers can use a variety of written tests to assess student proficiency in executing specific thinking skills and strategies. A number of such tests are commercially available for this purpose. (See Chapter 11.) However, their use on a classroom basis is probably neither advisable nor possible for most teachers. Cost and the mechanics of scoring put these tests beyond their use. In addition, although these tests measure selected thinking skills, most teachers find it impossible to locate a single commercial instrument that assesses the specific skills they might wish to teach. Finally, since most of these instruments are not tied to any specific subject matter, they are likely to assess student ability to transfer a skill rather than to use it as instructed. Such measures are thus probably inappropriate for assessment of skill learning, especially at the introductory level.

Teachers can produce their own written tests for this purpose, however. Questions designed to elicit information about or exercise specific thinking skills or strategies can be attached to regular unit and semester tests in any subjects where these thinking skills are being taught. Although such instruments may be flawed initially by teacher inexperience in developing appropriate test items, teachers can, with a little training and some practice, develop them well enough to provide useful assessment information.

Unit thinking skills tests can be short, consisting of as few as six or seven questions for each skill to be assessed. They may consist of multiple choice or other appropriate objective test items as well as open-ended problem statements or tasks wherein students are asked to produce an answer and tell how they devised that answer. For any single specific thinking operation to be assessed, these tests can ask for definitions of a skill, call for students to pick out examples of it in use, have students execute the skill (showing their work), and finally, explain to other students, presumably less familiar with the skill than they, how to execute it.* Students can also be asked to identify which skill(s) or strategies might be most appropriate to a given thinking task and be given tasks which require use of several skills in sequence.[35] Such test items can use data from the subjects students are studying as well as experiential data and data from novel contexts, if the skills being tested have been taught to some degree of transfer.[36]

Just as teaching specific thinking skills requires different kinds of lessons depending on where students are in learning these skills (whether they are learning a new skill for the first time, or transferring a skill introduced sometime earlier, or practicing skills already taught to transfer) so, too, must classroom tests of these skills differ. Tests that directly assess in-depth proficiency in specific skills appear to be most useful in assessing learning of newly introduced skills. Tests modeled on the better reading tests or the Scholastic Aptitude Test—where a paragraph is followed by a series of questions, each cued to a separate skill—may best test proficiency in a number of skills that have been taught to some degree of transfer. Tests like the *Cornell Test of Critical Thinking*, where specific skill are assessed in the context of a continuing narrative or problem, may best assess proficiency a range of thinking skills that have been taught for some time. Regardless of the type of thinking operation being tested, however, classroom tests should provide students with the data or information to be used in executing the skill in order to minimize the extent to which recall of information inhibits or interferes with effective use of a thinking skill. Tests that embed skilled operations in questions that also require recall of previously learned information do not appear to provide satisfactory measures of thinking skills or strategies, at least at the introductory level of learning these operations.

It should be noted that objective tests rather than essay tests prove most useful in assessing student proficiency in specific thinking skills. Regardless of the task specified in any essay question, task, or directions, rarely can an essay response be keyed directly to any specific thinking operation (though some essays clearly give evidence of higher order thinking as well as of recall). Furthermore, few teachers evaluate essays for the kinds of thinking they are believed to elicit anyway. Rather, essays are usually evaluated in terms of the amount of relevant and correct information and examples provided, kinds and number of sources cited, grammar, construction, and even style. Essays may offer some measure of general thinking ability or level of thinking, but they

---

* Detailed explanations with examples of how to produce such classroom tests may be found in Barry K. Beyer, *Practical Strategies for the Teaching of Thinking* (Boston: Allyn and Bacon, 1987).

do not provide very accurate information about specific thinking skills or strategies.

One significant effort has been made, however, to make essay tests more precise for this purpose. Robert Ennis and Eric Weir have devised a critical thinking essay test that may offer a way to do just this.[37] But much testing and refining of this approach to assessing student thinking remain to be done. At the moment, using essays to measure thinking skills is a dubious art, at best. Objective tests, as described here, seem to be the most useful way for classroom teachers to assess student proficiency in the thinking skills and strategies they are teaching.*

Producing classroom tests of thinking does not take much time, but it may require some training because few teachers are experienced in developing such measures. But these instruments can be made and do prove very useful, both in motivating skill learning and in assessing student proficiency in specific thinking skills. When structured in specific ways, thinking assessments can also provide information useful in diagnosing and improving instruction. Consequently, using instruments such as these and other appropriate assessment procedures is an important part of teaching thinking. An effective thinking skill program should provide for such classroom testing on a continuing basis.

SUMMARY

There is more to teaching thinking than the kinds of strategies and techniques that teachers conventionally use to direct or assess classroom learning. Certainly the learning climate of classrooms and of the entire school directly affects the success of these strategies—so, too, does the way in which teaching is tied to student study of subject matter and the thoroughness of such study. Both the learning environments and subject matter content in which thinking is taught and practiced affect considerably what is learned as thinking, as well as the extent to which it is learned. Yet, of all the variables affecting the development of student thinking in schools, the strategies and techniques by which teachers seek to direct and promote such development (both via instruction and testing) are perhaps the most significant. Without use of those strategies most appropriate to the task, the other variables contribute little to improvement of student thinking.

In the final analysis, a thinking skills program or curriculum—whether district-wide, department-wide, or in a single classroom—will be only as effective as the classroom teaching and testing employed to

---

* For procedures and instruments for assessing program effectiveness, see Chapter 11.

carry it out. The teaching strategies used must do more than simply make students think. They must do more than encourage, challenge, foster, and/or provide opportunities for practicing thinking. To be most effective in improving student thinking, teachers must employ strategies that provide explicit instruction in how to execute the thinking operations that are to be learned. This means using strategies that provide for the teaching *of* and *about* thinking as well as those that provide for the practice of thinking. For practice to really pay off in improved student thinking, research and experience clearly suggest that it should be combined with explicit introductions to the major operations that constitute thinking, repeated guided practice in executing these operations, the teaching of these operations to transfer, and appropriate assessment of student skill learning. And such teaching must attend also to developing student habits and dispositions of thinking as well as the metacognitive operations by which we guide thinking. Only by using these teaching approaches can any thinking skills curriculum or program be expected to produce the kind of student proficiency in thinking that constitutes the goal of a worthwhile thinking skills program.

ENDNOTES

1. Ronald Brandt, "Teaching of Thinking, Teaching for Thinking, Teaching about Thinking," *Educational Leadership 42*, 1 (September 1984): 3; Jay McTighe, "Teaching for Thinking, of Thinking, and about Thinking," *School 33*, 2 (June 1985): 1–6; Arthur L. Costa, "Teaching For, Of, and About Thinking," in Arthur L. Costa, ed., *Developing Minds: A Resource Book for Teaching Thinking* (Alexandria, Va.: Association for Supervision and Curriculum Development, 1985), pp. 20–23.

2. McTighe, "Teaching for Thinking," pp. 3–4.

3. Costa, "Teaching For, Of, and About Thinking"; McTighe, "Teaching for Thinking," pp. 4–5.

• 4. Michael I. Posner and Steven W. Keele, "Skill Learning," in Robert M. W. Travers, ed., *Second Handbook of Research on Teaching* (Chicago: Rand McNally College Publishing, 1973), pp. 805–831; Barak V. Rosenshine, "Teaching Functions in Instructional Programs," *Elementary School Journal 83*, 4 (March 1983): 335–353; Jack Lochhead and John Clement, eds., *Cognitive Process Instruction: Research on Teaching Thinking Skills* (Philadelphia: Franklin Institute Press, 1979).

• 5. Norman Frederiksen, "Implications of Cognitive Theory for Instruction in Problem Solving," *Review of Educational Research 54*, 3 (Fall 1984): 382; see also John E. McPeck, *Critical Thinking and Education*, (New York: St Martin's Press, 1981), p. 18, and Robert J. Sternberg, "How Can We Teach Intelligence?" *Educational Leadership 42*, 1 (September 1984): 47.

6. Catherine Cornbleth and Willard Korth, "If Remembering, Understanding, and Reasoning Are Important . . ." *Social Education 45*, 3 (April 1981): 278; McPeck, *Critical Thinking and Education*, p. 18; Rosenshine, "Teaching Functions."

7. Jane Stallings, "Effective Strategies for Teaching Basic Skills," in Daisy G. Wallace, ed., *Developing Basic Skills Programs in Secondary Schools* (Alexandria, Va.: Association for Supervision and Curriculum Development, 1983), pp. 1–9; Ann Brown, Joseph C. Campione, and Jeanne D. Day, "Learning to Learn: On Training Students to Learn from Texts," *Educational Researcher 10* (February 1981): 14–21; Robert Sternberg, "How Can We Teach Intelligence?" pp. 38–50; Benjamin Bloom, *Human Characteristics and School Learning* (New York: McGraw-Hill, 1976).

8. David W. Pratt, *Curriculum Design and Development* (New York: Harcourt Brace Jovanovich, 1980), p. 313; Posner and Keele, "Skill Learning"; Rosenshine, "Teaching Functions."

9. Rosenshine, "Teaching Functions."

10. Brown, Campione, and Day, "Learning to Learn"; Sternberg, "How Can We Teach Intelligence?"; Elizabeth Bondy, "Thinking About Thinking," *Childhood Education 17*, 2 (March/April 1984): 234–238; Arthur L. Costa, "Mediating the Metacognitive," *Educational Leadership 42*, 3 (November 1984): 57–62.

11. Walter Doyle, "Academic Work," *Review of Educational Research 53*, 2 (Summer 1983): 159–199; Barak V. Rosenshine, "Content, Time and Direct Instruction," in Penelope L. Peterson and Herbert J. Walberg, eds., *Research on Teaching*, (Berkeley: McCutchan, 1979), pp. 28–56.

12. Irving Sigel, "A Constructivist Perspective for Teaching Thinking," *Educational Leadership 42*, 3 (November 1984): 18–22.

13. Doyle, "Academic Work," pp. 169–170; Rosenshine, "Content, Time and Direct Instruction."

14. Doyle, "Academic Work," pp 169–170.

15. Ibid., p. 174.

16. Paul Chance, *Thinking In the Classroom: A Survey of Programs* (New York: Teachers' College Press, 1986), p. 122; Russell Gersten and Douglas Carnine, "Direct Instruction in Reading Comprehension," *Educational Leadership 43*, 7 (April 1986): 77.

17. Doyle, "Academic Work," p. 174.

18. Posner and Keele, "Skill Learning."

19. Bloom, *Human Characteristics*; Rosenshine, "Teaching Functions," pp. 340–341; Posner and Keele, "Skill Learning," pp. 807, 813–814.

20. Posner and Keele, "Skill Learning."

21. Ibid.

22. Bryce B. Hudgins, *Learning and Thinking* (Itasca, Ill.: F. E. Peacock, 1977), pp. 142–172; Posner and Keele, "Skill Learning."

23. Brown, Campione, and Day, "Learning to Learn," p. 15; Hudgins, *Learning and Thinking*, pp. 142–172; Herbert J. Klausmeier and J. Kent Davis, "Transfer of Learning," *Encyclopedia of Educational Research* (New York: Macmillan, 1969), pp. 1483–1493; Herbert Simon, "Evidence on Transfer," in D. T. Tuma and F. Reif, eds., *Problem Solving and Education: Issues In Teaching and Research* (Hillsdale, N.J.: Erlbaum Associates, 1980), pp. 882–884; David N. Perkins, "Thinking Frames," *Educational Leadership 43*, 8 (May 1986): 4–10.

24. Hudgins, *Learning and Thinking*, pp. 142–172; Posner and Keele, "Skill Learning."

25. Carl Bereiter, "How to Keep Thinking Skills from Going the Way of All Frills," *Educational Leadership 42*, 1 (September 1984): 75–78.

26. H. T. Epstein, "Growth Spurts During Brain Development: Implications for Educational Policy and Practice," in J. F. Chall, ed., *Education and The Brain* (Chicago: University of Chicago Press, 1978); Martin Brooks, Esther Fusco, and Jacqueline Grennon, "Cognitive Levels Matching," *Educational Leadership 41*, 8 (May 1983): 4–5; Eugene Chiappetta, "A Review of Piagettian Studies Relevant to Science Instruction at the Secondary and College Level," *Science Education 60*, 2 (April–June 1976): 253–261.

27. Costa, "Mediating the Metacognitive," pp. 57–62; Bondy, "Thinking about Thinking," pp. 234–238.

28. Pratt, *Curriculum Design*, p. 313; Posner and Keele, "Skill Learning," pp. 820–823; Ann Marie Palincsar and Ann L. Brown, "Reciprocal Teaching of Comprehension-Fostering and Comprehension-Monitoring Activities," *Cognition and Instruction 1*, 2 (Spring 1984): 117–175.

29. Arthur Whimbey, "Teaching Sequential Thought: The Cognitive Skills Approach," *Phi Delta Kappan 59*, 4 (December 1977): 255–259; Arthur Whimbey, "Students Can Learn to be Better Problem Solvers," *Educational Leadership 37*, 7 (April 1980): 560–565; Superintendent of Public Instruction, *Development of Problem Solving Skills for Vocational and Educational Achievement: Student Workbook*, (Olympia: Washington State Department of Public Instruction, 1976).

30. See, for example, Arthur L. Costa, "How Scientists Think When They Are Doing Science," in Arthur L. Costa, ed., *Developing Minds*, pp. 114–117; Carol Madigan and Ann Elwood, *Brainstorms and Thunderbolts: How Creative Genius Works* (New York: Macmillan, 1983).

31. Bruce R. Joyce, "Social Action for Primary Schools," *Childhood Education 46*, 5 (February 1970): 135.

32. Posner and Keele, "Skill Learning," pp. 813–818, 820–824.

33. Carl Bereiter, "Elementary School: Necessity or Convenience?" *Elementary School Journal 73* (May 1973): 435–446.

34. Doyle, "Academic Work," pp. 178–181.

35. Harold Berlak, "New Curricula and Measurement of Thinking," *Educational Forum 30*, 3 (March 1966): 303–311.

36. Edys S. Quellmalz, "Needed: Better Methods for Testing Higher Order Thinking Skills," *Educational Leadership 43*, 2 (October 1985): 29–36.

37. Robert H. Ennis and Eric Weir, *The Ennis-Weir Critical Thinking Essay Test* (Pacific Grove, Calif.: Midwest Publications, 1985).

10

Implementing
a Thinking Skills
Program

In initiating a district, subject, or building-wide program for the teaching of thinking, there is more to be attended to than the structure and content of the program and the strategies to be employed in delivering that content. Attention must also be given to how the teaching of thinking is introduced into the classroom. Among the many variables that need to be attended to in this regard, three stand out: classroom and school climate, the instructional materials to be used, and the abilities of the teachers to carry out the program as designed. To be successfully implemented, any newly developed thinking skills program requires attention to all three. This attention must be ongoing, from the very beginning of the development process, even though specific action about each may not be taken until it is time actually to install the program. This chapter outlines the most important aspects of these three variables insofar as they may affect the successful implementation of a thinking skills program.

DEVELOPING CLASSROOM AND SCHOOL CLIMATES SUPPORTIVE OF THINKING

To be most effective, the learning of thinking requires school and classroom climates conducive to this task. The methods and substance of classroom instruction should be reinforced rather than contradicted by the environment in which it is carried out. Developing and maintaining classroom and school climates supportive of thinking are essential if a school-wide thinking skills program is to be effective.

In many instances classroom and school environments do not contribute as much as they could to the teaching and learning of higher order thinking. In fact, Professor Larry Cuban, an experienced classroom teacher and school administrator, claims that historically most schools have presented and continue to present "an organized inhospitality" to thinking.[1] Teaching and learning thinking skills, he claims, have been inhibited over the years by crowded classrooms and the row-upon-row arrangement of students in them, as well as by the recitation-lecture methods employed by most teachers. In Cuban's judgment, excessive reliance on single texts, and the tendency to see teaching as transmitting and learning as doing as one is told, have also limited the effectiveness of the teaching of thinking. Minimum competency testing and uncritical acceptance of textbook content by students and teachers alike merely contribute to this situation. For the teaching of thinking to be most productive, these conditions must be replaced by conditions that encourage and support thinking in all classrooms and throughout a school, Cuban argues. Many other educators would endorse his view.

Environments most conducive to the teaching and learning of thinking are characterized by conditions and an atmosphere where *thinking can occur*, where *thinking is valued*, where *thinking is supported* by teacher, administration, parents, and students, and where *thinking itself is frequently a subject of reflection, analysis, and discussion*. The seating and teaching arrangements in such classrooms encourage student interaction rather than limit it. Such arrangements allow students to face each other rather than line up looking at the backs of heads. These arrangements also put a teacher's desk at the *back* or side of a room as a work station rather than in the front as a command post. Teacher and student behavior in thinking classrooms involve guessing, challenging, and questioning, as well as inventing, justifying, and a healthy intellectual risk-taking. A thinking environment is electric with intellectual activity and with processing information to make it meaningful rather than with storing or reciting information or meanings invented by others. Learning climates such as these make possible purposeful instruction in and development of thinking.

School-wide environments that support thinking are characterized by actions and arrangements that clearly give value to this important aspect of learning and teaching. Such environments honor thinking. As trophies and other forms of recognition are provided for outstanding athletic skills, so, too, are appropriate types of recognition provided for outstanding academic and thinking activities and performance. As school time and resources are provided for the former, so, too, are time and resources provided for teaching and learning thinking. Although skillful thinking may not have the stadium or crowd appeal of an athletic event or dramatic production, its value for the individuals involved and society as a whole clearly outstrips that of most other skills or skilled performances. School administrations and faculties cognizant of this provide school climates that support and honor skillful thinking.

SELECTING APPROPRIATE INSTRUCTIONAL MATERIALS

As with most other instructional programs, a thinking skills program requires the use of a variety of instructional materials. These materials may include virtually any media from textbooks and workbooks to filmstrips, video tapes, audio recordings, computer programs, recorded television programs, newspapers, and worksheets. They may be commercially prepared or teacher developed. But whatever form they take or media they employ, materials selected for teaching thinking skills in any subject must meet certain criteria if they are to be helpful in teaching thinking. Two of these criteria are especially important.

First, the materials used in thinking skills instruction—especially textbooks, computer programs, and activity books—should clearly distinguish among three kinds of thinking skills and strategies: (1) those being introduced for the first time to be learned to some degree of proficiency through the use of these materials, (2) those introduced in earlier grade levels or in other subjects and to be elaborated or transferred further in these materials, and (3) those introduced and generalized in earlier courses or other subjects that are simply to be reinforced in these materials. Different kinds of learning activities and instructional guidance are needed to accomplish these different tasks. Instructional materials should provide the kinds of instruction and practice appropriate to each.

Second, materials provided for teaching thinking must help *teach* thinking. That is, they must do more than provide activities, problems, or tasks that simply require students to execute or practice certain skills. To be most useful, these materials should also provide instruction to students in precisely *what* the thinking skills are that they are to learn, in *how* to go about executing these skills, and in *any rules* or *criteria* they need to know to execute these skills most efficiently and effectively. And this instruction should include repeated lessons on *each* skill selected for instruction. Single "exposures" to each of a large number of skills do not provide such instruction.

Of course, not every single piece of instructional material used in a specific course must provide the whole range of instruction required to learn selected thinking skills. Different materials may emphasize different stages in skill learning. One piece of material, for instance, may provide only skill exercise activities. Another may provide guided practice. But where a number of different materials are combined for skill instruction, at least one should provide the actual teaching required to make practice and exercise productive. Instructional materials that provide only practice are not enough.

Where a textbook or computer program serves as the core or major instructional material in a course that includes teaching thinking skills, these materials and their associated materials must provide the complete range of instruction necessary to learn the skills being taught. Texts can provide such instruction in a variety of ways. Previously introduced and learned thinking skills can be practiced through end-of-chapter activities or workbooks, as is commonly done now, although brief review instruction in how to execute such skills can be incorporated in the text itself or in the teacher's manual or on blackline masters. However, skills to be newly introduced require a series of instructional lessons. A lesson providing clear instructions or suggestions on how to execute each new skill should be followed by a number of lessons in the text, workbook, and other supplemental material providing guided practice in each skill. Thereafter, end-of-chapter or workbook exercises can provide the independent practice required to develop a higher degree of proficiency in these skills. Skills requiring transfer or elaboration in the content of the text require specific instruction in the text or from the teacher in how to make the transfer or elaboration. And repeated practice—with instructive guidance—must also be provided for each important skill being thus transferred or elaborated. To be useful in a thinking skills program, textbook and computer programs that purport to teach selected thinking skills or strategies must provide a number of lessons on each skill or strategy that move students through the various stages of skill learning toward mastery.

What might such a textbook program that actually *teaches* thinking skills look like? A single thinking skill or strategy to be newly introduced in the program may be introduced within a textbook chapter in a one- or two-page spread, employing an appropriate skill-introducing strategy. To be effective, this introduction should exhibit the features essential to a skill introduction, as outlined in Chapter 9. And to be most useful to teachers and students, this introduction should use materials or data in a form familiar to the students and clearly related to the content of the chapter in which it appears.

Thereafter, a number of guided practice lessons on this same skill should appear, scattered appropriately through the text, activity book, and/or blackline masters. These one-page lessons can use a guided practice strategy similar to that outlined in Chapter 9. Other useful formats can also be devised as long as they incorporate with applying the skill the three essential features of effective practice strategies: (1) introductions that develop mental set, (2) a review or preview of essential attributes of the skill, and (3) follow-up reflection on how the skill was executed. These guided practice lessons should be a part of the student materials so students have ready access to the instructional guidance they usually need at this stage of learning a skill. The initial few practice lessons should also be spaced close enough to each other to be mutually reinforcing. These lessons should use the same kinds of data as used in the introduction of the skill, and they should support or grow out of the subject matter in the text where these lessons appear.

Only after a number of such lessons have appeared should students be put in a position where they are expected to execute the skill without any further instructional guidance at all as in most end-of-chapter activities. Even at such points minimum guidance can still be provided by *naming* the skill that students are to employ (e.g., "*Analyze* the following document to see what *clues to bias* you can find" rather than "Read the following account.") and/or by referring to the page numbers where the skill was introduced or practiced previously. Independent practice of a skill is most productive only *after* students clearly understand, as a result of a detailed introduction and appropriate guided practice, how they can execute it.

To transfer a thinking skill to a new data set or media, the sequence of lessons described above can be repeated for each new context to which the skill is to be applied. To simply reinforce a previously taught skill, however, requires fewer applications of the skill preceded only by one or two lessons that provide instructive review in how to execute the skill. Different combinations of skill lessons will be appropriate for skills at different stages of learning. All these lessons take space, of course, but not all this space need be in a textbook or computer program itself. While some of these lessons can and should be included in the text, others can be included in accompanying materials, including teachers' manuals, filmstrips, or other documentation. But to be complete, it all must be a part of the total materials that comprise the core of instruction in a particular course.

Computer programs can provide similar skill instruction. Programs designed to teach thinking skills—rather than simply to exercise skills presumed to have been learned earlier—can provide instruction within the program or in special paper and pencil teacher-directed lessons described in the program documentation. If included in the program itself, such instruction can be provided as an integral part of the program or as a "help" segment of the program to which students can turn on a "need to know" basis. But the same principles apply to these computer programs as to textbook programs—instruction in how to execute a particular skill must be followed by repeated guided practice and only then by independent practice in executing a skill.

Teachers and administrators selecting instructional materials for use in thinking skills courses or programs should select only those materials that provide actual instruction in thinking skills. Such instruction must be readily accessible to the students. In this instruction, focus should initially be on the skill rather than on subject matter. The skill should be modeled or demonstrated and the key attributes of the skill should be clearly articulated. Materials for use in intermediate grades and beyond should also involve students in reflecting on and discussing how they execute the skill, and these materials should provide students repeated opportunities to execute the skill with instructive guidance available as needed.

In sum, instructional materials most useful in teaching thinking skills and strategies should:

1. Focus on a few thinking operations rather than on a large number of them.
2. Provide repeated opportunities for instruction in and practice of the same skill or strategy.
3. Provide instruction that moves from introducing each skill or strategy through guided practice, to independent use, using strategies appropriate to each type of instruction.
4. Provide instruction and guided practice in how to elaborate or transfer a skill to data sets, media, or contexts other than those in which it was introduced, but only after proficiency in the skill has been demonstrated in the context in which it was originally developed.
5. Relate the thinking operations emphasized in one text or program to those emphasized in preceding and subsequent texts or programs in the same subject, and to thinking operations studied in other texts, programs, and subjects studied at the same grade level.
6. Use terminology to describe the thinking skills and strategies taught that is the same used to describe these operations in other subjects, programs, and texts at the same and preceding grade

levels, and/or provide a glossary or other aids designed to minimize confusion over such terminology.

7. Test directly the thinking skills and strategies in which instruction is provided.

Testing the thinking skills and strategies taught is especially important. Instructional materials should be accompanied by instruments designed to assess levels of student proficiency in and knowledge of the skills and strategies they purport to teach. These instruments can be objective tests. They should provide continued assessment of the same skills and strategies throughout the duration of a course, and thus may be of increasing length as the course progresses. Like all useful thinking skills tests, these tests should not embed the skills being assessed in content that students are asked to recall. Nor should they use strange or unfamiliar content until students have received instruction in how to transfer or "bridge" the skill being assessed to a variety of contexts and data sets. Rather, these instruments should provide the content or data to which the students are to apply the skill. Most importantly, such tests should require students "to show their work" or explain how they executed the skills being assessed. Testing is as important a part of skill instruction as is the teaching that precedes it. Textbook and computer programs used in teaching thinking skills in any subject should include both. In selecting instructional materials, schools should insist that their treatment of thinking skills meet the criteria outlined above (or similar criteria) if they are to be considered for adoption.

PROVIDING APPROPRIATE STAFF DEVELOPMENT

No newly developed thinking skills program has much chance of being implemented as designed without some attention to staff development. A number of reasons make such training necessary. In most instances, classroom teachers and administrators have not had training in the teaching of thinking skills or strategies. Nor have many of them studied in any formal way the thinking skills or strategies they are asked to teach or supervise. Whereas teachers usually recognize the uniqueness of many curriculum innovations and their own lack of knowledge about the subject area with which it deals and so can perceive some value in accommodating to it, such is often not the case in regard to thinking skills programs. Rather, many teachers are honestly convinced they already know how best to teach these skills. Few are really aware of how great is the gap between what they know now about this area of teaching and what has been recently uncovered by researchers and developers that would be of immediate help to them. Coupled with an often intense commitment to and interest in "teaching children" or teaching a specific subject, this lack of awareness about what they (administrators as well as teachers) *don't know* about teaching thinking skills makes staff development for thinking skills programs somewhat difficult. But considerable staff development may have to be undertaken in order to carry a thinking skills program from curriculum guide into effective student learning.

Guidelines for Effective Staff Development

To be most effective, staff development for new thinking skills programs, especially locally-developed programs, must:

1. Be continuous over an extended period of time.
2. Involve administrators as well as teachers.
3. Involve *all* teachers—including those who will teach the students after they receive initial instruction in the program as well as those who will do the instruction in the program itself.
4. Address the needs and concerns of educators involved in implementing the program as well as their concerns about the program.
5. Provide extended education as well as training and coaching in the program to be implemented.[2]

Provide Continuous Development

Staff development at its best involves more than training teachers and administrators how to execute—or supervise the execution of—a program developed or adopted by others. It also consists of involving these same teachers and administrators in developing or adopting the program. Furthermore, staff development is not something to be attended to only *after* a program has been developed; it must be attended to from the very beginning of the program development or adoption process. Involvement of those who will eventually be responsible for implementing a new program serves more than a commitment-generating function. It is itself educational and an indispensable form of training in the program being devised.

Surely, teacher and administrator commitment to any thinking skills program being implemented is a *sine qua non* of its success. But more than peripheral involvement in generating or approving the program is often required to achieve and maintain such commitment. Teacher and administrator representatives (and even perhaps board of education members and representatives of parent groups) must directly and actively engage in the study and decision-making process that makes the initial determination of what needs to be done in a school or system to improve student proficiencies in thinking and in developing or adopting the program designed to bring about this improvement. Their work must be done on school time—not as an after-school, on-top-of-every-thing-else, add-on assignment. Developing an effective thinking skills program can be a time-consuming task. Certainly it is a serious one with far-reaching implications. As such, it deserves the full attention and support of all involved.

This is not to say that a sense of involvement on the part of all teachers is unnecessary. It most certainly is necessary. Teachers, administrators, and parents need to be continuously informed of what is occurring in the development or adoption process. There should be no surprises down the line when decisions are eventually made or announced. Teachers must have opportunities to see and discuss options under consideration, to experiment in the most risk-free context possible with these options, to share their own thoughts and volunteer suggestions regarding what can and should be done, and to participate as much as possible in the entire effort. These can be accomplished through a variety of means—including placing items about the program being developed in faculty or parent newsletters, offering "awareness" workshops on thinking skills, providing opportunities for attendance at thinking skills presentations at professional conferences, conducting presentations and discussions at regular department and building level faculty meetings, providing demonstrations of various approaches to teaching thinking skills during district-wide staff development days, conducting informal reading and discussion groups, circulating and discussing relevant journal articles in faculty meetings, and offering small grants for thinking skills materials with which teachers can experiment in their own classrooms. Endeavors in all of these areas must begin with the initiation of any effort to address the issue of thinking skills and continue throughout this effort.

Involve Administrators as Well as Teachers

As educational leaders, administrators at all levels ought to be involved in any staff development effort regarding a thinking skills program. Many share the same impressions and have the same gaps in their knowledge about the effective teaching of thinking as do teachers. Moreover, administrators need to understand thoroughly what is involved in executing any new thinking skills program. This understanding is best developed by engaging in the intellectual effort of designing the program as well as in the effort of executing it once it is in place. As supervisors and potential evaluators of teaching performance in the program, administrators need to experience repeatedly what is required to make the program work at the classroom and individual student levels. They need training and supervised experience, just as do teachers, in how to engage in the teaching required to implement any newly adopted thinking skills program as well as in the procedures to be used for faculty development, supervision, and evaluation.

Involve All Teachers

Thinking skills and strategies cannot be learned to any degree of proficiency in a single lesson, unit, grade level, or subject alone. As indicated in Chapter 9, to be effective the teaching of these operations must be a continuous enterprise. This means that all teachers in a system must receive some training in the specific thinking skills to be taught in a school or school system. The teachers who will be directly involved in teaching the program must receive the kinds of training that will enable them to carry forward the program as designed. In addition, teachers who will be teaching the students before they enter the program, if it is not a complete K–12 program, must understand what the program requires by way of prerequisite skills, dispositions, and/or learning conditions. Equally important, teachers who will teach students after they leave the program or a particular part of it or who will be teaching these students in other subjects need to understand the program so they can provide repeated, explicit opportunities for students to practice the skills they learned in these other subjects, so they can reinforce these skills, and so they can help students transfer these skills to and elaborate them in the subject matter they teach or use. All teachers in a school system require training in a new thinking skills program if it is to be effective.

Address Teacher Needs and Concerns

It is only natural that developers or supervisors of a thinking skills program care about the quality and integrity of the program being implemented. But teachers and administrators not actively involved in the development or adoption process often—at least initially—do not share this same concern. Rather, research indicates that in the early stages of implementing an innovation many teachers express needs that relate more to their own classroom survival, performance, or planning than to faithfully implementing the program.[3] In order to ensure that a new thinking skills program is carried out as designed, program developers must first address these very real and pressing teacher needs.

Table 10.1 describes the stages of concern typically voiced by teachers about an educational innovation or change in which they may be

Table 10.1 Stages of Concern: Typical Expressions of Teacher Concern About an Innovation

	Stages of Concern	Expressions of Concern
I M P A C T	6 Refocusing	I have some ideas about something that would work even better.
	5 Collaboration	I am concerned about relating what I am doing with what other instructors are doing.
T A S K	4 Consequence	How is my use affecting kids?
	3 Management	I seem to be spending all my time in getting material ready.
S E L F	2 Personal	How will using it affect me?
	1 Information	I would like to know more about it.
	0 Awareness	I am not concerned about it (the innovation).

involved.[4] Staff developers need to be aware of these stages and what they imply about teacher interests and perceived needs during the implementation process. If some teachers are at the awareness level of concern only—and some assuredly will be no matter what has been done during the development or decision-making process—developers must speak to the needs implied by this stage. For teachers needing information only (stage 2), such information must be provided before they can even be expected to consider becoming involved—or, if required to be involved, before they give the kind of effort required to maintain the program's integrity. Because not all teachers express the same types of concerns about a new program, staff development cannot be the same for all at any given time. Any worthwhile staff development program must build on this awareness, anticipate what kinds of needs teachers will express, and have appropriate responses and assistance already developed when implementation commences.

One way to anticipate teacher concerns is to identify the kinds of changes implied in a new program. If the program is to employ the strategies and teach the operations described in the preceding pages, the types of new teacher behaviors to be developed will include those that demonstrate continuous teacher use of the new teaching strategies described in Chapter 9, knowledge of the skills they are teaching, and systematic testing of student thinking skill proficiency. Students will be expected to apply the skills they are being taught at increasing levels of sophistication on their own initiative, in appropriate places, and in conjunction with the use of other relevant skills. They will be expected to focus on procedures as well as products of thinking, and, especially those in secondary grades will be expected to think about and discuss their own thinking. These behaviors imply changing teacher and student awareness of *what* is being taught and is to be learned—skills instead of content; of turning attention to *how* answers are derived as well as to the correctness of the answers; of giving *repeated attention* to the same subject (a skill) rather than one-shot exposures to an endless train of subjects; and of *focusing on skill attributes,* as well as on subject matter. Effective staff development will assist teachers and administrators in accommodating to these changes.

Teachers customarily express many personal concerns about newly instituted thinking skills programs. One of the most common concerns involves time. Where, teachers wonder—frequently loudly—will they find the time to plan for teaching these skills and find the time to fit such teaching into their already overcrowded courses? This is a real concern for most teachers. To introduce and teach each new thinking skill to a high degree of proficiency may require the equivalent of three or four hours of classroom instructional time. For three skills, this means up to a dozen or so hours, something many teachers may feel they simply don't have. Anticipating this concern, staff developers need to help teachers find the required time, time that is not taken out of subject matter deemed to be crucial.

There are several ways to help teachers deal with this concern. Program developers can anticipate it by limiting the number of thinking skills to be introduced and taught in-depth at each grade level, and by assigning only a few such skills to each subject area or cluster of subjects at any one grade level. They can even provide teachers with descriptions of the attributes of the skills to be taught as well as outlines of where in their subjects these assigned skills can be most easily taught (similar to those presented in Figures 9.3 and 9.4). Providing teachers with model lesson plans keyed to their texts and course outlines—or with time and help in preparing such plans—can also be most helpful in dealing with this concern.

Another way to deal with teacher concerns about time is to help teachers use better the classroom time they have for instruction. Familiarizing or training them with principles of instruction such as those espoused by Madeline Hunter can help immensely in this regard. Tasks normally done by teachers (such as collecting money, monitoring study halls, etc.) can be eliminated, and the time that becomes available can be used to plan and train for teaching thinking. Where possible, class periods can be lengthened, to allow more time to attend to thinking. In preparing to launch a thinking skills program, teachers need to be engaged in tasks such as preparing items for unit thinking skills tests, or making lesson plans or lesson plan models to introduce, transfer, or provide guided practice in specific skills. Teams of teachers can be given common planning periods in which to plan, observe, and share lessons and materials. Administrators and other nonteaching personnel can cover classes to free teachers for training, observing, and planning. Teachers can even be released from teaching periodically to attend to these tasks.

Another way to get time for in-class instruction in thinking skills is to eliminate some of the subject matter included in the courses. Many teachers feel bound to "cover," as they say, immense amounts of subject matter, usually racing through it at a pace few students can match. The compulsion to cover subject matter is a major inhibitor of the adequate teaching of thinking skills.

Supervisors must do more than simply encourage or tell teachers to give up some coverage of subject matter, however. They must actually sanction ways to do so. For example, department or grade level committees can identify, with supervisor approval, chapters or topics to be omitted or given only the briefest attention. Units normally given a week's attention can be cut to one day, with essential information given to the students on handouts. Duplication across courses can be eliminated or reduced, especially where some courses seem to repeat year after year the same subject matter. Special efforts must be made to see to it that tests, however, do *not* attempt to assess learning of the subject matter thus eliminated. Time for teaching thinking skills *can* be found. It is up to program developers and supervisors to help teachers find this time and to do this before expecting a new thinking skills program to be fully implemented.

Provide Education, Training, and Coaching

The role of pre-service and in-service education and training in ensuring the proper execution of educational programs of all types has long been acknowledged. Indeed, training programs are often an integral part of newly proposed educational programs, including those dealing with the teaching of thinking. However, the ingredients of such training often vary. It is only recently that the research of educators such as Bruce Joyce and Beverly Showers has made clear the crucial elements in the most effective teacher training programs.[5] The staff development component of any thinking skills program must contain these important elements if the program is to be implemented as designed.

Benjamin Bloom has noted that individuals achieve high degrees of expertise in something only as a result of considerable "encouragement, nurturance, education and training."[6] According to Joyce and Showers, these are precisely the ingredients essential to any program that hopes to equip teachers or others with new skills. In order to develop proficiency in the strategies and skills most useful in the teaching of thinking, especially those teaching skills described in Chapter 9, a training program must include four major elements. It should:

1. Provide education—through lectures, reading, and discussion—in the theories and research upon which the teaching strategies, skills, and other components of the program to be implemented are based.
2. Demonstrate repeatedly how these strategies work via films, lesson transcripts, and simulated lessons, with the teachers themselves serving as students, and then with small groups of typical students, with accompanying analysis and discussion of each demonstration.
3. Include repeated practice and observation in the use of these strategies and skills with small groups, first of one's peers and then of students, and then in regular classroom settings, with feedback provided by those expert in the strategies being applied.
4. Provide coaching—repeated application and analysis of the new strategies with peer group support and the feedback of someone trained in the strategies or skills being learned.

The specific kinds of training necessary to implement a thinking skills program should vary according to teacher needs. Thus, a school system may provide different levels or kinds of training designed to fit the expectations or needs of teachers at various stages of familiarity with what is required of them to carry out the program. For some, perhaps, courses in specific types of thinking such as problem solving or critical thinking should be available, courses in which instruction models the kinds of strategies teachers will be expected to use in their own classrooms. Such courses may well seek to make teachers more aware of and informed about their own thinking. For others, especially those unfamiliar with the teaching of thinking, a series of workshops designed to provide information about the importance of teaching thinking might be appropriate. These sessions could also present information about and demonstrate various approaches to teaching, thinking, and provide opportunities to discuss and explore teaching options appropriate to improving the teaching of thinking. Such training may well aim at raising teacher awareness of thinking as a process in their own classrooms and subjects.

For other teachers, training in using the teaching strategies they are to use in their classrooms may be quite appropriate. Such training can be build around repeated designing, teaching, and critiquing of lessons using these teaching strategies. Not surprisingly, the skill-teaching framework and teaching strategies contained in Chapter 9 of this book and its companion volume are exactly those most appropriate for teaching teachers how to use these same skills in their own classrooms.* Teachers should be introduced to each new teaching strategy they are expected to use by introducing, elaborating, and providing guided practice in that strategy. They also need to be introduced to strategies for identifying the components of a thinking skill, and to procedures for assessing student proficiency in thinking skills. Then, teachers must be provided guided practice in applying them to the point where they demonstrate a high degree of proficiency in executing these strategies before they are expected to use them regularly on their own initiative in their own preparation or teaching. Some teachers will require relatively few demonstrations, observation, and application tries to become proficient in these aspects of skill teaching. Others, however, may require anywhere from ten to twenty relevant experiences and considerable coaching before they will feel comfortable enough to use the teaching strategies effectively or able to identify the attributes of a thinking skill or produce a good thinking skills test. Education in the theory and research underlying these elements of skill teaching is also essential for successful, independent use of these strategies and their transfer into regular classroom teaching. Such learning may be hard work and frustrating. This frustration needs to be forecast to the teachers in training so they realize it is inherent in the task at hand and not any fault of their own.

---

* Barry K. Beyer, *Practical Strategies for the Teaching of Thinking* (Boston: Allyn and Bacon, 1987).

Staff developers can facilitate such training in many ways. Teachers can be encouraged to share their frustrations and concerns in small group discussions; demonstrations of how to deal with these can be conducted; teacher success stories can be shared; teachers receiving training can develop their own agendas of what they need in order to succeed with the new program; and the training program can be kept flexible enough to allow a change in timetables as new concerns crop up or additional time is required to deal with specific issues. Most importantly, however, some skills and strategies (or additional tasks such as test making) can be introduced after the teaching gets underway. Any type of evaluation of skill teaching for summative purposes during such training should be suspended. The less complex and threatening the training is, the greater will be its chances of success.

A number of materials may prove useful in a program designed to teach teachers how to teach thinking skills. They are listed in Figure 10.1. When used in various combinations, these materials may provide the kind of in-service as well as pre-service education and training needed by teachers to help them develop the expertise and confidence to teach thinking skills effectively and efficiently. It is important to note here that materials related to various thinking operations themselves should be included in such training; focus should be as much on what it is teachers are to teach by way of thinking as on how they are to teach and test it. Discussion and application of the various thinking skills to be taught, as well as demonstration, analysis, repeated application, and discussion of the teaching strategies to be used, must be a part of any training program.

The staff development required to enable teachers to implement a thinking skills program that aims at the teaching of thinking cannot be done in one three-hour workshop. An extended and continuous training program is required. Such a program may begin while the thinking skill program is being developed or as the adoption process is underway. During this period, teachers can informally try out approaches being considered and experiment with them as they test them and learn more about them. The multisession demonstrating, practicing, and coaching that follows will be more productive as a result of this preliminary experience with elements of the program.

Such training can be provided in a number of ways. It could be provided by scheduling teachers so those teaching the same skills and same courses have time to observe each other and to plan or share experiences together. One school system established a staff development program built around teams of four to five teachers, all scheduled for the same preparation period; after receiving special training, one member of the team then met daily with the rest of the team to train them. Another school proposed to employ five permanent substitutes

MULTIMEDIA

Teaching Skillful Thinking (Alexandria, Va.: Association for Supervision and Curriculum Development, 1986).

Four video tapes in which leaders in the field of teaching thinking explore issues and approaches in teaching thinking and classroom scenes demonstrate various techniques, programs, and approaches useful in teaching thinking. An in-service leadership manual provides transparency masters, readings, and activities for four staff development workshops.

Available from: A.S.C.D.
125 North West Street
Alexandria, VA 22314

Building Students' Thinking Skills (Washington: National Education Association, 1987).

A multimedia training program consisting of a booklet of twenty articles on teaching thinking in general and in different subjects, four filmstrips on applying and evaluating student thinking, video tapes providing an overview of thinking skills, and a training manual outlining nine workshops for teaching thinking skills.

Available from: National Education Association
1201 16th St., N. W.
Washington, DC 20036

A.F.T. Critical Thinking Project

A 35-hour training-of-trainers program in the teaching of critical thinking, using the analysis of video tape classroom vignettes, a text, and manual. Conducted by A.F.T. trainers.

Available from: American Federation of Teachers
555 New Jersey Av. NW
Washington, DC 20001

BOOKS AND MANUALS

Barry K. Beyer, *Practical Strategies for the Teaching of Thinking* (Boston: Allyn and Bacon, 1987).

Designed for teachers and supervisors, this book explains, with lesson plans and sample lessons, strategies to use in teaching thinking skills

Figure 10.1 Selected Training Materials on the Teaching of Thinking

from introduction through guided practice to transfer. Describes selected thinking skills and explains, with examples, how to make classroom assessments of thinking and thinking skills.

Arthur L. Costa, ed., *Developing Minds: A Resource Book for Teaching Thinking* (Alexandria, Va.: Association for Supervision and Curriculum Development, 1985).

A resource book of articles, short essays, checklists, and commentaries dealing with various aspects of teaching thinking, including a rationale, creating school conditions for thinking, defining thinking, thinking curricula and teaching strategies, and brief descriptions of selected thinking skills programs.

Paul Chance, *Thinking In the Classroom: A Survey of Programs* (New York: Teachers' College Press, 1986).

An in-depth review of six instructional programs for teaching thinking, accompanied by a survey of the current interest in teaching thinking and a suggested approach to incorporating the teaching of thinking into various school subjects.

John Bransford and B. S. Stein, *The IDEAL Problem Solver: A Guide for Improving Thinking, Learning and Creativity* (San Francisco: W. H. Freeman, 1984).

An introduction to a process of problem solving, this book presents a model for analyzing processes underlying effective problem solving and then discusses ways to improve learning new information, comprehension, generating alternatives, criticizing ideas, creativity, and effective communication. Numerous examples are provided.

Robert A. Sternberg, *Intelligence Applied* (New York: Harcourt Brace Jovanovich, 1986).

A book designed to help one increase and understand intelligence, this is based on the author's triarchic theory of intelligence. Chapters focus on the components of intelligence, coping with novelty, automatizing information processing, and practical intelligence. Includes strategies and exercises.

Steven Toulmin, Richard Rieke, and Allan Janik, *An Introduction to Reasoning,* 2nd ed. (New York: Macmillan, 1984).

A step-by-step introduction to logical reasoning and argument analysis, with sections on determining the soundness and strength of argu-

Figure 10.1 *(Continued)*

ments, detecting common fallacies, and critical analysis. Concludes with sections on selected fields of reasoning including legal, scientific, management, and ethical reasoning, and reasoning about the arts.

Arthur Whimbey and Jack Lochhead, *Problem Solving and Comprehension* (Philadelphia: Franklin Institute Press, 1982).

Designed to help increase one's powers to analyze problems and comprehend. This book outlines methods useful in attacking complex ideas and then gives guided practice in applying these methods to a variety of comprehension and reasoning questions. Numerous application exercises.

Figure 10.1 *(Continued)*

for a three-year period—one in each of the major subject areas. Each six-week marking period these teachers were to replace five teachers freed to receive intensive training every day, all day, for those six weeks and then return to their classrooms while the substitutes replaced another five teachers to engage in similar training. Over a three-year period, this procedure would enable a school system to train ninety teachers on district time. Still another school provided thinking skills resource teachers to demonstrate thinking skills teaching strategies, help teachers understand the skills to be taught, assist teachers in preparing skill tests or test items, and observe their teaching in order to help them improve it. Provisions for personal consultation and assistance with regard to teaching and testing are as important to a training system as are sample materials and written guidelines.

Staff development programs vary widely in format and scheduling. To be most effective in helping teachers translate a thinking skills scope and sequence into appropriate classroom learning, these programs should be continuous, over a long period of time, offer different kinds of assistance to faculty having different needs, and be conducted on school time or with appropriate support during summer training workshops. The quality of staff development shapes considerably the success of any new educational program and thinking skills programs are no exception.

SUMMARY

The way in which a newly developed existing curriculum is implemented, whether in a single building or subject or on a district-wide basis, has a great deal to do with its eventual success or failure. Considerable effort is required to translate a program from its written documentation in the form of a scope and sequence and curriculum guides to actual classroom instruction and improved student thinking. Among the factors that contribute to the successful implementation of such a program, the most significant seem to be attention to the instructional climate of a school and its classrooms, selection and use of appropriate instructional material, and appropriate staff development. Proper attention to these elements of program development will go far toward ensuring that any thinking skills program, whether developed locally or selected from existing programs, is likely to achieve the goals it was designed to accomplish.

ENDNOTES

1. Larry Cuban, "Policy and Research Dilemmas in the Teaching of Reasoning: Unplanned Designs," *Review of Educational Research 54*, 4 (Winter 1984): 655–681.

2. Bruce Joyce and Beverly Showers, *Power in Staff Development Through Research on Training* (Alexandria, Va.: Association for Supervision and Curriculum Development, 1983).

3. Gene E. Hall and Archie A. George, *Stages of Concern About the Innovation: The Concept, Initial Verification and Some Implications* (Austin: University of Texas Research and Development Center for Teacher Education, 1978).

4. Ibid., p 10.

5. Joyce and Showers, *Power in Staff Development*.

6. Benjamin Bloom, *Developing Talent in Young Children* (New York: Ballantine Books, 1985), preface.

11

Supporting and Maintaining a Thinking Skills Program

A newly implemented thinking skills program is most likely to succeed where it receives considerable administrative and institutional support. Such attention involves providing continuing, public administrative support for the program and those involved in executing it. It also involves continuing assessment and revision of the program. The extent to which reasonable and appropriate school or district-wide efforts are devoted to these tasks often determines not only the ultimate effectiveness of the program but, indeed, whether or not it will even survive. This chapter focuses on this critical component of developing a thinking skills program and the key tasks of supporting, assessing, and revising the program.

SUPPORTING A THINKING SKILLS PROGRAM

Newly installed educational programs rarely survive or flourish without nourishment and support. Thinking skills programs especially require such attention. Administrative support—*explicit* administrative support—publicly affirms the value and import of such a program within the school curriculum, as well as helps teachers and students over the countless obstacles that may crop up during the initial years of the program. Certainly this support must include providing the financial resources for the training and learning materials needed to carry out the program. Beyond this, three other kinds of support seem most important. Ongoing training of teachers, provisions for individualizing student skill learning, and the availability of appropriate curriculum support materials and opportunities to develop them can contribute significantly to the long-run maintenance and success of a thinking skills program.

Classroom Coaching and Teacher Support

Learning a new skill, Bruce Joyce claims, is often "an invitation to incompetence." This may be especially true of teachers attempting to learn new ways to teach thinking skills because many have developed ways they believe already accomplish this goal. Unlearning old ways and trying new ways to the point of feeling comfortable in executing the new ways and being willing to use them continuously in regular classroom settings are difficult and frustrating undertakings. Coaching seems to be the key to such skill learning for it provides continued support and companionship as well as opportunities to learn from one's peers in relatively risk-free situations. Without coaching, Joyce insists, transfer from training sessions to regular classroom use is highly unlikely.[1]

One way to provide supportive coaching for teachers learning to use new classroom strategies to teach thinking skills is to form teams of teachers and administrators. By repeated cooperatively planning, observing, analyzing, and revising lessons using these strategies, coaching teams can help teachers learn how to execute these strategies with expertise and confidence, thus easing them over the rough spots that inevitably occur when learning new approaches to teaching.

Helping teachers transfer any new skill from training sessions to classroom practice requires continued and explicit attention to the ingredients of effective classroom teaching of thinking skills. This includes attention to classroom climate, the attributes of the thinking skills or strategies being taught, and the strategies used to conduct the lessons employed. Of these, classroom strategies are of major importance.

Figures 11.1 and 11.2 provide checklists for the three kinds of skill teaching lessons that form the core of effective thinking skills instruction as described in Chapter 9. These checklists can be used for four purposes: (1) They can serve as aids in evaluating textbooks and other learning materials to be used in teaching thinking skills. (2) They can be used as guidelines in planning lessons. (3) They can serve as aids in

For Introducing or Transferring a Thinking Skill or Strategy

Teacher _____ Observer _____

Subject: _____ Date _____ Time start: _____ end: _____

A. Context of the lesson	Yes	No
1. The skill is		
1.1 of sufficient import to warrant detailed attention.	___	___
1.2 based on other prerequisite skills.	___	___
1.3 appropriate to the ability level(s) of the students.	___	___
1.4 introduced at a time it is needed to accomplish a content-related objective.	___	___
1.5 appropriate to the substantive function of the lesson.	___	___

B. Conduct of the lesson

	Yes	No
2. The purpose for attending to the skill at this point is:		
2.1 clearly stated.	___	___
2.2 appropriate.	___	___
3. The skill is clearly introduced by		
3.1 giving its label.	___	___
3.2 defining it.	___	___
3.3 giving synonyms for it.	___	___
3.4 giving appropriate examples of its use	___	___
• in everyday life.	___	___
• in previous coursework.	___	___
3.5 relating it to other skills.	___	___
4. The skill is modeled/demonstrated.	___	___
5. The major components of the skill are explained, or reviewed, including:		
5.1 key procedures for using it.	___	___
5.2 its key rules/principles.	___	___
5.3 knowledge needed to use it.	___	___
6. Students engage in the skill		
6.1 prior to its explanation or demonstration.	___	___
6.2 after having it explained or discussed.	___	___
7. Students explain/discuss what goes on in their heads whlle using the skill		
7.1 as they engage in the skill.	___	___
7.2 after they engage in the skill.	___	___
8. If there are several skill applications in this lesson, the data/media to which the students apply the skill are in the same form.	___	___
9. Students		
9.1 modify given skill components.	___	___
9.2 suggest major skill components.	___	___
10. In concluding the lesson, *students*		
10.1 define the skill.	___	___
10.2 give synonyms for it.	___	___

Figure 11.1 Skill Teaching Checklist for Introducing or Transferring a Thinking Skill or Strategy

	Yes	No
10.3 tell when/where it can be used.	——	——
10.4 articulate its key components.	——	——
10.5 relate it to other skills.	——	——

C. Components of the lesson

11. The focus of the lesson was		
11.1 clearly on the skill.	——	——
11.2 consistently on the skill.	——	——

12. The teaching strategy used was		
12.1 inductive.	——	——
12.2 directive.	——	——
12.3 other_____ .	——	——

13. The teaching strategy used was appropriate to		
13.1 the complexity of the skill.		
13.2 the ability level of the students.	——	——
13.3 experience of the students.	——	——
13.4 the time available.	——	——
13.5 content goals sought.	——	——

Figure 11.1 *(Continued)*

reviewing lesson plans before they are used in classrooms to see if they contain all the essential ingredients for a particular lesson. (4) They can be used by observers to follow a strategy as it is actually executed in a classroom so appropriate feedback can be provided to the teacher. In all four instances, use of these checklists can keep the planners' or observers' attention on the critical aspects of thinking-skill teaching, which is essential if these teaching strategies are to be mastered by teachers to the point they can and will use them on their own in their own classrooms after receiving appropriate training in their use.

These checklists prove especially useful in observing classroom instruction in thinking skills. Each is relevant to a different kind of skill teaching lesson. As will be recalled from Chapter 9, teaching any thinking skill requires a series of lessons that move from introduction through guided practice to transfer, and, eventually, to autonomous use. These instruments relate to three key kinds of lessons in this sequence. In order to use them appropriately either in lesson planning or observing classroom teaching, one must know (1) the kind of lesson being taught or to be taught—whether it is intended to introduce a skill, provided guided practice, or so on—and (2) the kinds of teacher and student behaviors essential to that type of lesson. These checklists contain both kinds of information.

For Guiding Practice of a Thinking Skill or Strategy

Teacher _____ Observer _____

Subject: _____Date_____ Time start_____end____

	Yes	No	Notes

A. Context of the lesson

1. The skill lesson is
   1.1 on a skill of sufficient import to warrant this degree of attention. ____ ____
   1.2 one of a series of similar lessons on this same skill. ____ ____
   1.3 spaced appropriately after the most recent preceding lesson on this skill. ____ ____
   1.4 appropriately tied to course content. ____ ____

B. Conduct of the lesson

2. The purpose for using the skill at this point is
   2.1 clearly stated. ____ ____
   2.2 appropriate. ____ ____

3. The skill is clearly introduced, by
   3.1 giving its label. ____ ____
   3.2 defining it. ____ ____
   3.3 giving synonyms for it. ____ ____
   3.4 giving appropriate examples of its use ____ ____
      • previously in class. ____ ____
      • in everyday life. ____ ____

4. The major components of the skill are articulated *before* the skill is used including
   4.1 its key procedures. ____ ____
   4.2 its rules/principles. ____ ____
   4.3 the knowledge needed to use it. ____ ____

5. The skill is deliberately applied to relevant content. ____ ____

6. The major components of the skill are articulated and justified *after* the skill is used, including:
   6.1 its key procedures. ____ ____
   6.2 its rules/principles. ____ ____
   6.3 the knowledge needed to use it. ____ ____

7. Modifications and/or additions in the skill components are articulated, considered, made. ____ ____

8. Where and when the skill can be used is discussed. ____ ____

C. Components of the lesson

9. The focus is clearly on the skill throughout the above portion of the lesson. ____ ____

10. The media/content form in which the skill is applied is similar to that in which it was initially presented (or extended). ____ ____

11. The components of the skill are reviewed *before* students discuss the content results of using the skill. ____ ____

Figure 11.2 Skill Teaching Checklist for Guiding Practice in a Thinking Skill or Strategy

Figure 11.1 provides a general checklist for lessons introducing a thinking skill or strategy or transferring/elaborating it. It is divided into three parts: a *content* part (I) related to the skill or strategy being taught, a *conduct* part (II) relating to the actual execution of the lesson, and a *components* part (III) dealing with the lesson as a whole. Parts I and III can be completed after a lesson plan analysis or classroom observation has been conducted, preferably with reference to the course outline or curriculum guide and/or text. Completion of Part II, however, requires analysis of the lesson plan itself or close observation of the teacher and students as the lesson actually is taught. Items 2 through 10 refer to the essential features of introductory and transfer/elaboration strategies, including the introduction (item 3), modeling (4), discussion of the skill attributes (5), metacognition (7), data used (8), and student work with the skill (6, 9, and 10). To have read or observed an effective, indeed exemplary, thinking skill introductory or transfer lesson, one would want to have recorded a "yes" for virtually every one of the items on this checklist.

Figure 11.2 presents a checklist for a guided practice lesson in a thinking skill or strategy. This checklist contains the same three parts as the preceding checklist—focusing on the context, conduct, and components of the lesson. As in the preceding checklist, the items under *conduct of the lesson* relate to the key features of strategies for guiding student application of a newly introduced skill. To have read or observed a most effective lesson of this type, one would have to have recorded a "yes" for virtually all of the items in this part of the checklist as well as on the other two parts. This checklist can be used in planning and observing any skill teaching lesson focusing on guided practice.

Few, if any, conventionally accepted indicators of the teaching of thinking can be found on either of these checklists because they simply do not indicate skill *teaching* is going on. However, more conventional criteria, such as level of teacher questions, response time, degree of student interaction, and so on, would be appropriate for a checklist related to independent use of a thinking skill already introduced or elaborated and already practiced with some type of instructive guidance. Such checklists already exist in most school districts. When used appropriately, all these checklists can help teachers learn how to use teaching strategies most appropriate to the task of teaching thinking. Indeed, such checklists can be used as outlines for guiding the planning of thinking skills lessons. Supervisors or peers can provide considerable support to teachers learning to use these teaching strategies by using these or similar checklists in observing their trial or sample lessons. These checklists reinforce the kinds of techniques most useful in teaching the kinds of thinking skills lessons that constitute the effective teaching of thinking.

Administrators and supervisors can provide other kinds of instructional support, too. They can serve as brokers of teaching ideas by bringing together teachers who they believe would benefit by sharing ideas. As facilitators, administrators and supervisors can take the lead to initiate opportunities for training, or peer observation, or similar experiences, and can break down barriers to securing materials, time, and help for improving classroom instruction. Sometimes administrators and supervisors need to be cheerleaders, encouraging those who are experiencing difficulties and calling attention to successes. At times they might have to be helpers, actually covering a class so a teacher can watch a colleague try a newly learned lesson strategy or confer with another teacher to plan a skill teaching lesson. Finally, administrators and supervisors may also have to serve as protectors as they shield teachers from adverse criticism for teaching thinking skills—for, like it or not, not all segments of society believe schools should teach any thinking skills above the levels of recall and simple translation or interpretation.

Supporting Student Learning

Not all students learn at the same rate, nor do all have the prerequisite skills often required to learn a new thinking skill in a regular classroom setting. Some students may require more instruction than others to achieve an acceptable degree of proficiency in a thinking skill. Providing for such individual learning needs is an important part of supporting any thinking skills program.

Continuing classroom instruction in a skill throughout the course or year in the form of repeated lessons, providing guided practice as well as teaching for transfer, helps classroom teachers accommodate different rates of skill learning in their own classes. Yet more assistance may be required in some cases. Additional, commercially developed thinking skills programs may be useful for this purpose, but they cannot be of the skill practice-only type which seems to predominate at the moment. Computer programs also offer the potential for providing such individual remediation or instruction, although this potential has not yet been realized. Teachers could provide this individualized attention, if freed from some classroom duties, or if a resource teacher were added to the faculty precisely for this purpose, but this is a costly endeavor. What, then, can schools do to provide the additional, extra-class instruction some students need to learn thinking skills? One source of such help may well be the students themselves. The vehicle might be a "skills lab."

The success of writing and math labs in improving student proficiency in these subjects over the years suggests that similar labs devoted to thinking could produce the same results for students having difficulties in mastering the thinking skills being taught in a school. Such labs can be established in elementary, middle/junior high, and high schools. These labs can be staffed with the students who demonstrate proficiency in thinking skills and who might volunteer for such duty. These students could be offered a special course for credit which would require them to tutor students in the lab for a period each day and meet once every other week or so with their peers and a teacher to discuss and refine their tutoring skills and to refine their thinking skills as well. This experience would benefit both tutors and tutees! Students needing help could receive the individual attention useful in skill learning, especially if the tutoring sessions employed a thinking-aloud, paired approach like that developed by Arthur Whimbey and Jack Lochhead.[2] Tutors would gain new insights into thinking and refine their thinking skills even further. A school employing labs of this nature would offer students needing remediation or special assistance the opportunity to receive it without imposing significant additional demands on teacher time or incurring additional costs.

Curriculum Support Materials

Effective classroom teaching of thinking skills requires certain kinds of curriculum support materials as well as training and coaching. Detailed descriptions of the key attributes of the thinking skills and strategies to be taught should be available to all teachers. Skill descriptions like those presented in Chapter 6 (Figure 6.6) are useful for this purpose. Where appropriate, descriptions of a skill as it is to be taught and elaborated in the primary, intermediate, junior, and senior high grades will differ to show the increasing complexities and sophisticated attributes of that skill. Teachers in a district should be familiar with all models of such skills so they know what skill learning at least should have preceded theirs and toward what version of the skill their teaching should lead. Such descriptions should be elaborated and revised as teachers share with each other what they learned about these operations and as they gain experience in teaching and using them. Teachers should remember to use such skill descriptions as descriptive learning targets rather than as prescriptive goals. Appendix B presents such descriptions.

Other similar items should also be provided for teachers. Model lesson plans for using the strategies described in Chapter 9 should be available. A clear scope and sequence of thinking skills, ideally in the detail suggested in Chapter 8, should be in the hands of all teachers and discussed in depth by them. Sample skill test items must also be available to teachers, as should model skill tests. Most of these items can be incorporated in a thinking skills curriculum guide or teaching manual that should document any district, building, or subject area thinking skills program.

ASSESSING A THINKING SKILLS PROGRAM

"How well does it work?"

Developing and implementing a thinking skills program requires answers to this question, and this means some kind of continuing program assessment.

Assessing a thinking skills program serves many purposes. It can be used to ensure that the program is being delivered as designed. It can keep teachers, students, and parents aware of the importance of improving thinking skills. And frequent assessment can also serve both formative and summative purposes.

During the development of a scope and sequence of skills for the program, such assessment can provide diagnostic information that may help establish entry level thinking skill proficiency and, by inference, insights into the kinds of skills that need to be taught at specific points in the program. During the implementation and teaching of the program, proper assessment can pinpoint areas of skill learning and teaching where instructional improvements may be required or where changes in the skills being taught may be advised. When used for summative purposes, thinking skills testing can indicate the extent to which the program has made a significant difference in student learning of both skills and subject matter. Such information can identify strengths and weaknesses in the program, information useful in making decisions about adoption, continuation, funding, training, and so on. Assessment of any thinking skills program is as essential in shaping the quality of the program as it is in helping to make policy decisions about its implementation, maintenance, or expansion. Such assessment can occur at the classroom as well as at the district, building, or grade level, and it may assess teacher, administrator, and student behaviors.

Assessing Student Learning

One major measure of the quality of a thinking skills program is the quality of its product—student proficiency in thinking. A school may use any of several methods to assess this proficiency. It could, for example, use student performance on paper and pencil tests as a measure of thinking skills proficiency. At least four different kinds of tests may be used for this purpose.

A number of commercially distributed tests designed to assess proficiency in specific thinking skills are available. Figure 11.3 describes briefly some of the more popular and useful of these tests. Some of these instruments are normed, others are not. Some are timed tests, others are not. Most are group tests, but several can or must be administered on an individual basis. These instruments vary widely in construct and measure a variety of thinking skills and operations. Probably no single one

Objective Tests

Cognitive Abilities Test (1985) by Elizabeth Hagen and Robert L. Thorndike. Riverside Publishing Company, 8420 Bryn Mawr Ave., Chicago, IL 60631. For grades K–12. A research test of three twenty-five item sections, timed, on: *verbal* skills of detecting similarities, sentence sense, classification and analogies; *quantitative* skills of relating and seriating; *nonverbal* skills of figure classification, synthesis, and analogies.

Cornell Critical Thinking Test, Level X (1982) by Robert H. Ennis and Jason Millman. Midwest Publications, P.O. Box 448, Pacific Grove, CA 93950. Seventy-six items, timed, for grades 4–14; sections on induction, deduction, observation, determining credibility, meaning, and assumption identification.

Cornell Critical Thinking Test, Level Z (1982) by Robert H. Ennis and Jason Millman. Midwest Publications, P.O. Box 448, Pacific Grove, CA 93950. Fifty-two items, for advanced or gifted high school students, college students, and other adults; sections on induction, deduction, observation, credibility, defining, and assumption identification.

Kaufman Assessment Battery for Children by A. S. Kaufman and N. L. Kaufman. American Guidance Service, Publisher's Building, Circle Pines, MA 55014. An individually administered battery for grades 2–8 on three scales: *sequential processing*—hand movement, number recall, word order; *simultaneous processing*—partial visibility, face recognition, *Gestalt* closure, triangles, matrix analogies, spatial memory; and *acquired achievement*—expressive vocabulary, faces and places, arithmetic, riddles, reading-decoding, reading-understanding.

New Jersey Test of Reasoning Skills (1983) developed by Virginia Shipman. IAPC, Test Division, Montclair State College, Upper Montclair, NJ 07043. Fifty items, untimed, for grades 4–college; syllogistic reasoning, contradictions, causal relationships, assumption identification, induction, good reasons, and others.

Ross Test of Higher Cognitive Processes (1976) by John D. Ross and Catherine M. Ross. Academic Therapy Publications, 20 Commercial Blvd., Novato, CA 94947. One hundred five items, timed, for grades 4–college; sections on identifying analogies, deduction, identifying missing premises, abstract relations, sequencing, questioning, relevance in mathematics problems, and analysis of attributes.

Structure of the Intellect Learning Abilities Test by Mary and Robert Meeker. Western Psychological Services, 12031 Wilshire Blvd., Los Angeles, CA 90025. Grades K–12, assessing twenty-six cognitive abilities including recall, evaluation, convergent and divergent production; figural, symbolic, and sematic dimensions of content; and product dimensions of units, classes, relations, and systems.

Watson-Glaser Critical Thinking Appraisal (1980) (forms A and B) by Goodwin Watson and Edward Glaser. The Psychological Corporation, a subsidiary of Harcourt Brace Jovanovich, 7500 Old Oak Blvd., Cleveland, OH 44130. Eighty items; two forms, timed or untimed; for grades 9 through adult; sections on inference, assumption identification, deduction, conclusion-logically-following-beyond-a-reasonable-doubt (interpretation), and argument evaluation.

Whimbey Analytical Skills Inventory (1979) by Arthur Whimbey. Franklin Institute Press, Box 2266, Philadelphia, PA 19103. Thirty-eight items, untimed, for grades 4–12; sections include following directions, mathematical analogies, problem solving, analogical reasoning, trends and patterns, differences/similarities, sorting.

Figure 11.3 Thinking Skills Tests

Essay Test

The Ennis-Weir Critical Thinking Essay Test (1983) by Robert H. Ennis and Eric Weir. Midwest Publications, P.O. Box 448, Pacific Grove, CA 93950. For grades 7 through college. Students read a nine-paragraph "letter to the editor" and then have forty minutes to write a ten-paragraph letter in response critiquing paragraph by paragraph, with a summary paragraph, the quality of thinking in the original letter. This instrument seeks to measure the following critical thinking skills: getting the point, seeing the reasons and assumptions, stating one's point, offering good reasons, seeing other possibilities, and responding appropriately to or avoiding: equivocation, irrelevance, circularity, reversal of an if-then (or other conditional) relationship, the "strawperson" fallacy, overgeneralization, excessive skepticism, credibility questions, and the use of emotive language to persuade.

Figure 11.3 (*Continued*)

of these tests measure all the thinking skills or strategies taught by any single school system, department, or teacher. However, use of several of these instruments in combination may provide information about enough of the key operations taught in any program to make possible informed judgments about program quality and areas where improvements can be made.

Other kinds of tests may serve these purposes just as well, however. Some experts suggest that the effectiveness of a thinking skills program can be measured adequately by instruments other than tests of specific thinking skills. Researcher Arthur Whimbey, for example, suggests that measures of reading comprehension correlate well enough with measures of specific reasoning skills to recommend their use in place of special thinking skills tests.[3] Specifically, he claims that since three specific reasoning programs resulted in improved scores on reading comprehension tests, schools can determine the effectiveness of such programs by "plotting reading comprehension gains over one year (or preferably two years) of training." The reasoning skills students develop will be manifested as accelerated improvement in reading ability, so no other special test is needed.[4] Given the excessive amount of testing commonly done in most schools and the fact that most schools as a matter of course already administer reading comprehension tests on a periodic basis, such an alternative is most attractive. If Whimbey's claim is accurate, no additional special thinking skills tests need be administered to assess the quality of a thinking skills program.

Even more indirect measures of student thinking skill proficiency may also be possible. Educator Thomas Estes, in surveying the research on instruction in reading some years ago, found that instruction in specific cognitive skills resulted in higher student scores on end-of-course subject matter examinations when compared to student test scores in the same courses using the same texts but not receiving instruction in these skills.[5] If this holds true for instruction in specific thinking skills or strategies, then the need for special skills tests may be even less. Student achievement on subject matter final examinations may be a sufficient, if indirect, measure of the effectiveness of thinking skills instruction.

Teacher-made classroom tests of thinking skills may also provide useful information about both skill teaching and learning. Whereas such tests must be scrutinized carefully to determine their reliability and validity, they can—if constructed as suggested in Chapter 9—provide information about student learning useful in informal program evaluation and in formative evaluation. Those tests that are administered periodically throughout a course offer good opportunities, especially to pinpoint places in instruction where changes or improvements need to be made. Analysis of the results can also provide information about student learning useful in programmatic decision making.

An assessment using any of the preceding kinds of instruments may be as elaborate or simple as desired. One or more tests may be administered to all students involved in the thinking skills program or to a sample of students only. Results can be evaluated against program goals or local or national norms. Or, an assessment program can seek, by pre- and post-instruction testing, to measure gains made by students in the program after a period of instruction. Whatever instruments or combination of instruments are used, attention to the level of assessment, the procedures used, and the interpretations of the results is crucial for valid and reliable assessment and subsequent curricular and instructional decisions.

In selecting and using (or even devising) paper and pencil tests to assess student thinking, a number of cautions should be observed, however. If a decision has been made to employ instruments that assess specific thinking skills, decisions about which of these to use must be made with care. Too often school systems employ instruments that do not assess the skills its teachers are teaching or believe they are teaching; or to put it another way, too often teachers do not teach the skills supposedly assessed on a given instrument. Congruence between skills tested and taught is essential for accurate and valid appraisal of classroom teaching as well as of program effectiveness and student proficiency in thinking. Administrators must ensure there is a match between tests used and skills taught in a thinking skills program, if feedback and judgments are to be valid, fair, and useful. Test instruments provide some measures of the skills they assess; they provide no measure of skills not assessed, which may be even more important components of thinking than those tested. Consequently, more than one measure may have to be used if a school seeks to assess the full range of thinking skills in which it claims to be providing instruction.

Furthermore, most available thinking skills tests, themselves, leave something to be desired in their content and structure. Most of these measure discrete skills clustered in separate sections of a test rather than measure these skills as they are employed in any complete thinking act. That is, most tests have a series of items measuring, for instance, analogies, followed by another series on, perhaps, assumption identification, and so on. There appears to be only one major test—the Cornell Test of Critical Thinking—that makes any systematic effort to assess thinking skills as they are executed in the context of a complete act of thinking. This instrument tests specific skills as they are executed in the act of solving a continuing problem that runs throughout the test. Assessing catalogues of skills used in isolation from each other may not, as educator Harold Berlak pointed out some years ago, produce as accurate a measure of thinking as could or should be done.[6]

Thinking skills tests now available have other limitations, also. None seem to measure metacognitive operations or dispositions related to thinking. Few, if any, assess skills at differing levels of understanding, such as at the levels of awareness, of application in structured and unstructured situations, and of metacognitive planning and explication. Few, if any, assess specific skills at differing levels of sophistication or in a variety of transfer situations. Few, if any, seem to use models of the skills they test-defined clearly enough to generate either appropriate test items or information educators can use in improving skill learning. Many tests embed thinking skill items in content or academic subject matter, a practice that often mixes skill use with recall of content, thus seriously limiting the value of the test as a measure of skill proficiency alone. Many tests have no norms nor data reporting their correlation with other measures of thinking. With the possible exception of the Ross and Cornell tests, few tests assess a comprehensive set or the range of thinking skills and strategies that might be included in even the simplest thinking skills program. Although tests such as those listed in Figure 11.3 may be useful in evaluating a thinking skills program, their limitations must be noted and considered when choosing them or evaluating and interpreting the information they generate.

Even specific items on many tests are of questionable value in measuring thinking. Many thinking skill test items are open to multiple interpretations, depend considerably on knowledge completely unrelated to the skills supposedly being assessed, and, indeed, often employ data unfamiliar to test takers. One question on such a test, for example, shows a picture of a funeral procession and then asks test takers, among other things, to identify from a list of reasons the one that best explains why people have funerals. This question is listed as measuring the skill of intepretation. More than likely, however, it measures recall—or guessing. A question on another test asks students, as a measure of their ability to execute the skill of comparing and contrasting:

In which of the following were the Federalists and Jeffersonians most alike?
a. Their attitudes towards France.
b. The economic groups that supported them.
c. The way they interpreted the Constitution.
d. Their attitudes toward maintaining American independence.

Such a question is more a measure of recall of information than it is of any other skill. Failure to respond as desired by the question maker may result from either lack of knowledge or inability to recall data, as well as inability to execute the skill of comparing and contrasting. Reliance on test items such as these as measures of skill proficiency is hardly sufficient for effective evaluation of thinking skills programs or even individual proficiency in thinking.

Given the problems with many thinking skills tests noted here, the kind of assessment most suited to evaluating a thinking skills program may well consist of measuring student learning gains as revealed by pre- and post-instruction testing. Certainly any test administered ought to be congruent with the skills that are taught and with the levels of skill proficiency and informational background of the test takers. And these tests ought to assess student skill proficiency in the contexts in which the skill has been learned, rather than assessing ability to generalize a skill by assessing skill use in novel or unfamiliar contexts. Certainly measures of thinking and of skill use in complete thinking tasks are also necessary, as are measures of proficiency in single, isolated skills. Designing and conducting an evaluation of a thinking skills program, while essential, requires thoughtful planning, careful analysis of the data and of the tests, and caution in interpreting the results.

Program assessment may use measures other than paper and pencil tests, also. Educator Arthur Costa and other educators suggest that teacher and perhaps even parent and peer observation of student thinking behavior can provide the evidence necessary to judge the effectiveness of a thinking skills instructional program. Whereas such observations may not provide as much insight as one would like into student proficiency in specific thinking skills or strategies, it can provide a useful measure of the degree to which students are developing the dispositions, attitudes, and values supportive of skillful thinking. Observation of student thinking behavior over a period of years may thus be a useful measure of the impact of a thinking skills program.

What can program evaluators look for as indicies of skillful thinking? Costa, echoing the research of Benjamin Bloom, Lois Broder, Reuven Feuerstein, Arthur Whimbey, and others, has identified ten behaviors illustrative of skillful thinking. Good thinkers, he asserts:

1. persevere when the solution to a problem is not immediately apparent
2. are less impulsive—they do not jump to conclusions
3. exhibit flexibility in thinking
4. can articulate how they go about executing a thinking task
5. check for accuracy before submitting the results of their thinking
6. use precise terms to describe how and what they are thinking
7. demonstrate confidence in their abilities to execute a thinking task
8. initiate questions and pose problems
9. use previous knowledge and past experience
10. use thinking skills and strategies in contexts other than those used in classrooms.[7]

Using specially constructed observation instruments, a number of teachers can collect and record over a year or several years observed instances of behaviors taken to be illustrative of thinking exhibited by one or more individual students. Figure 11.4 presents one such instrument that could be used to identify the general thinking behavior of any student. Figure 11.5 illustrates a similar instrument for observing or recording student execution of a specific thinking operation, in this instance, decision making. Similar instruments could be prepared for any other thinking skill or strategy, for metacognition or for any other aspect of thinking as well.

Of course, appropriate observation of even one student over an extended period by a single teacher can be extremely time-consuming, involve considerable paperwork, and, if observers are untrained, can be of questionable reliability. Observations collected by several teachers about one student over a long period can help reduce reliability errors, but problems of time, paper work, and training remain. Moreover, trying to collect and record such data for dozens of students makes the task even more difficult. Such observation reports are also subject to serious abuse, both in interpretation and the use to which results are put.*

---

* For a detailed analysis of other observation instruments and problems inherent in using them, see Barry K. Beyer, *Practical Strategies for the Teaching of Thinking*. (Boston: Allyn and Bacon, 1987).

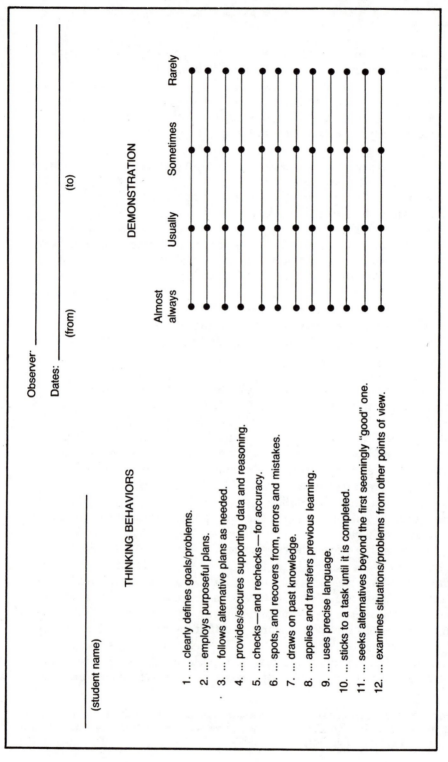

Figure 11.4 A General Thinking Behaviors Observation Report

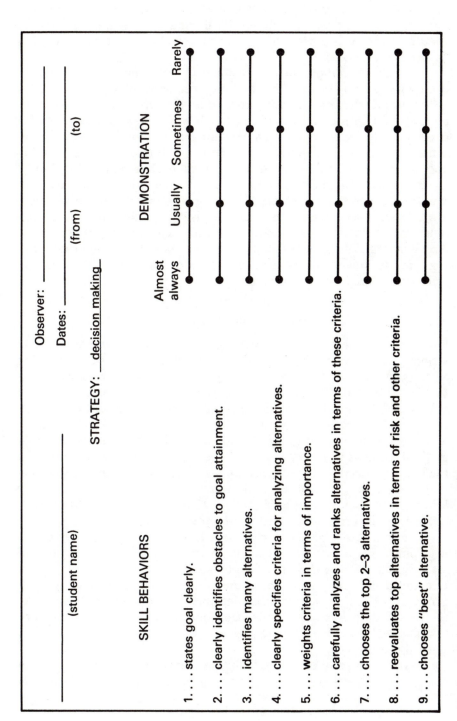

Figure 11.5 Thinking Observation Report

Educators and parents must exercise extreme caution in interpreting reported observations of student "thinking" behaviors. Such data should never be accepted as conclusive evidence regarding thinking proficiency or lack of it.

With these cautions in mind, however, systematic observation or even self-reporting of student "thinking" behaviors may provide at least informal and tentative insights into student thinking. Such insights may be useful for improving teaching as well as for making programmatic decisions. The extent to which any change in student thinking behavior can be linked to classroom instruction might then indicate something about the quality of that instruction as well as about student learning.

In spite of the limitations inherent in various kinds of assessment, classroom assessment of student thinking is essential to effective teaching as well as learning of thinking. Used with caution, the results can help improve day-to-day instruction and measure student progress. Any thinking skills program, to be effective, should provide for continuing and systematic assessment of classroom learning of the thinking skills being taught in the program.

Assessing Teaching/Learning Activities and Materials

Evaluating the learning and teaching activities and materials used in school classrooms provides a second type of assessment of a thinking skills program. Certainly, what goes on in classrooms provides important insights into the quality of any such program. Information about these activities and the materials used in carrying them out can be collected from a number of sources and in a number of ways. One important source of such information is classroom observation. Another method is analysis of the various materials used in classroom instruction (including lesson plans, texts, and other instructional materials and media), course outlines, and unit and semester tests. All of these provide information useful in assessing the effectiveness of any systematic thinking skills program as well as in improving its effectiveness.

The checklists presented in Figures 11.1 and 11.2 prove very useful in evaluating classroom instruction in thinking skills. Observers and planners should use checklists like these, if they wish to develop accurate and useful judgments about the degree to which a thinking skills program is being implemented as designed. The checklists are also useful in providing feedback to a teacher for instructional improvement or to make well-founded judgments about the quality of instruction in a thinking skills program.

In observing any class in which thinking skills are being taught, an observer needs to know the stage in a framework for instruction at which such instruction is being provided so as to know what kinds of behaviors to look for. Moreover, one observation of a class does not provide information about the extent to which such teaching typifies the classroom nor the extent to which the sequence of instruction is being carried out. Repeated observations of lessons at different points in the skill-teaching framework are required to make such judgments.

Use of these or similar checklists can be extremely helpful in assessing and improving teaching and, indirectly, of judging program quality. Because these checklists incorporate the findings of skill learning and teaching research, as well as the recommendations of experts on the teaching of thinking, they can be used with the confidence that, if the behaviors identified on them are carried out as indicated, student skill learning will be enhanced considerably.

Classroom observation can focus on student as well as teacher behaviors. Again, however, looking for behaviors conventionally assumed to indicate thinking on the part of students may not provide the kind of information most useful in assessing the teaching of thinking skills. Instead, observers need to look for the extent to which students give and seek reasons and evidence in discussing claims or assertions, the kinds of questions the students ask, and the extent to which students cite and critically evaluate sources of information in their responses or discussions. The behaviors identified above also serve as keys to student thinking. A classroom where behaviors like these are exhibited consistently and frequently is more likely to be one that teaches thinking than does a classroom characterized generally by lecture, recitation, and teacher-asked questions.

Analysis of textbooks, workbooks, writing activities, media, lesson plans, and tests can also provide information about the nature and quality of the teaching of thinking that occurs in classrooms where these are used. The features of textbooks, other written instructional materials, and microcomputer software that typify materials designed for *teaching* thinking were described in Chapter 10. Lesson plans that incorporate instruction in specific thinking skills should employ the teacher and learner activities outlined on the observation checklists presented in Figures 11.1 and 11.2 and in Chapter 9. And the unit tests that teachers give students should explicitly test the thinking skills they are supposed to be teaching, as indicated also in Chapter 9. As important as are the features of these activities and materials, the consistency and frequency of their use is also important in indicating whether skill teaching may be going on. The pattern of use of these and the way they are interrelated are also indicative of the nature of thinking skill instruction in a classroom. Examination of these elements of instruction is indispensable to a thorough assessment of a thinking skills program.

CONTINUOUS PROGRAM REVISION

Like the thinking skills and strategies they seek to teach, thinking skills programs change over time—or should be allowed to change—as they accommodate to the realities of classroom instruction and teacher and student abilities. Not uncommonly, the best scope and sequence will neglect some prerequisite skills or place some skills for instruction at levels where they are too difficult to learn given the time available for teaching. Skills assigned to one subject area for introduction may turn out to have been better assigned to another. New thinking skills and strategies can be added as instructional goals as teachers develop proficiency and confidence in their teaching of those originally assigned. Many revisions may be called for as a thinking skills program is conducted over the first years of its existence. Program developers must be prepared to make these revisions.

Assessment is important in accomplishing this task. Periodic assessment of student skill proficiency can provide the feedback necessary to make productive revisions in a scope and sequence as well as in classroom teaching strategies. Monitoring of student skill learning and of what teachers learn about the skills they are teaching can allow developers to refine descriptions of the skills that are being taught. It also enables developers to decide which additional skills should be added to or dropped from a curriculum or which should be reordered in the scope and sequence.

Program developers or supervisors should establish procedures and vehicles for using the data generated by assessment and monitoring of the skill teaching and learning to improve the original thinking skills program. In periodic meetings, teachers can review what they have been doing in order to suggest revisions, refine skill descriptions, or devise new teaching sequences and strategies. Analysis of tests or other kinds of assessments can alert developers to areas where revisions may need to be made. Student interviews may also provide such information. Regardless of the specific mechanisms employed, a well-planned revision effort ought to characterize a thinking skills program once it has been in operation for several years.

SUMMARY

A clearly articulated, well-grounded, and well-defined thinking skills program distinguishes schools that are committed to developing individuals for their roles as competent, contributing citizens in a rapidly changing and shrinking world. Developing or revising such a program is an undertaking of enormous importance. It is also one of the few program development efforts that can unite an entire faculty in a common effort. In developing such a program, those involved learn a great deal about thinking as well as about teaching. Furthermore, this effort can bring together teachers from a variety of subject areas and grade levels. The resulting thinking skills program will cut across all grade levels and subject areas and give coherence and unifying purpose to a curriculum, regardless of the levels to which it applies. The program can involve *all* teachers. It can touch *all* students, for teaching thinking is for all students. Developing a thinking skills program can be a dynamic, intellectually stimulating and personally envigorating process.

To be most useful to teachers and students, a thinking skills program should consist of, at the least, six key components:

1. A scope and sequence of clearly defined thinking operations, arranged in a developmental, integrated sequence at three levels
   * cross a number of contiguous grade levels, preferably grades K–12, indicating which skills are to be taught at which grade levels
   * in major subject areas, by grade levels, indicating where each skill included is to be (1) introduced, given guided practice and used independently, and (2) transferred, practiced, and applied by the students
   * within each subject by chapters in texts or units in a course indicating specifically where opportunities exist for providing instruction in each of the instructional stages noted above.
2. The use of an instructional framework and teaching strategies that provide explicit instruction in how to execute the operations included in the program.
3. Explicit, school-wide attention to the attitudes and dispositions that support and drive skillful thinking.
4. A support system that provides, among other necessary supports, continuing staff development appropriate to the teaching required, use of appropriate instructional materials, and use of curriculum guides that include model lesson plans and unit/semester skills tests.
5. An assessment program that provides both continued classroom testing by teachers of thinking skills and strategies being taught as well as continued assessment of program effectiveness.
6. Continuing revision of the entire program as the program is adjusted to the realities of classroom teaching, as teachers become increasingly proficient in teaching these operations, and as students develop, with this instruction, their proficiencies in thinking.

Developing such an instructional program requires careful planning and considerable effort and time. An effective thinking skills program does not spring up overnight. Producing a program as described here involves the following steps or tasks:

1. Identify program goals and develop a rationale.
2. Define thinking, thinking skills, and the major components of skillful thinking and their interrelationships.
3. Devise a structure for the overall program.
4. Select the thinking operations to comprise the core of the program.
5. Define in detail the attributes of these operations for purposes of guiding instruction and assessment.
6. Sequence and organize the operations to be taught across grade levels and subjects and within specific courses.
7. Select and sequence teaching strategies that will provide actual instruction in how to execute the thinking operations to be learned, and establish classroom testing procedures to facilitate such instruction and learning.
8. Provide the materials and training required to implement the program.
9. Provide the support and assessment necessary to ensure the successful continuation of the program.
10. Provide for continuing revision, updating, and expansion of the program once it has been implemented.

The preceding chapters have described in detail what needs to be done to carry out each of these tasks, some options open to developers, and some procedures and guidelines to follow that will expedite the development process and ensure positive results. Of these guidelines, the following baker's dozen bear repeating:

1. Think small, to start. Introduce only a few new thinking skills or strategies each year or two. Avoid overloading teachers and students in any one subject or grade level with too many new skills to learn each year.
2. Select as the core operations for the initial scope and sequence thinking skills and strategies that are of major significance in thinking, and useful to students outside of school as well as in academic learning.
3. Stagger the introduction of thinking operations across a number of grade levels. Avoid trying to "teach" every skill at every grade level.

4. Provide instruction in any skill across a number of grade levels and subjects to ensure transfer.
5. Introduce and teach specific thinking skills and strategies in subject matter courses where they are most directly applicable.
6. Use instructional strategies that minimize content interference in introducing a new skill, that provide repeated, guided practice, and that help students generalize—transfer and elaborate—the skills being taught.
7. Spread responsibility for initial instruction in and reinforcement of important skills or strategies by assigning their introduction and practice to several, related subjects at the same grade level.
8. Add skills and strategies to the core of skills and strategies that comprise the original program as teachers gain expertise in the teaching of thinking and as students become increasingly proficient in thinking.
9. Build the complex skills on the less complex and develop skills and strategies from their simplest dimensions toward their more complex, sophisticated versions.
10. Allow teachers to teach any thinking operations they wish in addition to the core skills, as long as primary attention is given to the core skills.
11. Eliminate some subject matter coverage or reduce the attention devoted to some subject matter learning in order to secure the time required to teach new skills to some degree of proficiency.
12. Remain tentative. Be willing to cut, add, or modify skills to be taught, to revise skill descriptions, and to alter teaching sequences as classroom experiences with students suggest.
13. Use test results and the results of other forms of assessment with caution. There may be much less to most existing measures of thinking than meets the eye.

Developing a thinking skills program is not strictly a linear, one-step-at-a-time process. It is, as in most program development, recursive. In completing one step, new insights develop into work completed earlier. When this occurs, developers should return to what they have done already and revise it. For example, in attempting to identify and describe the critical attributes of already selected thinking operations, the importance of other skills omitted from the selected list may suddenly become apparent. This should result in the revision of the list of skills selected as the core of the program. Each step in the development process informs and shapes what has been done earlier as well as subsequent steps along the way, and developers should acknowledge and take advantage of this. The most workable thinking skills programs evolve and develop over time as developers, then classroom teachers, and finally students grapple with the intricacies of thinking and the skills and strategies that are believed to be essential in carrying it forward.

Moreover, in developing a thinking skills program it is important to think ahead. Developers should not wait to deal with staff development or implementation or assessment until after a program has been drafted. These aspects of program building or change must receive continuing attention throughout the planning and drafting of the program. If the costs and other implications for staff development of including certain kinds of skills at certain grade levels are not considered in selecting and sequencing skills to be included in the program, for instance, such decisions may well produce a program that simply will not become a classroom reality. Developing a thinking skills program involves juggling many concerns at one time and is, itself, an exercise in higher order thinking!

CONCLUSION

"To most people," James Bryce wrote many years ago, "nothing is more troublesome than the effort of thinking."[8] For many educators developing and implementing a thinking skills program may be equally troublesome, especially where this effort involves creating a local thinking skills curriculum completely from scratch. Such an effort may also be dangerous, for improved student thinking can be unsettling to some. As Caesar said of Cassius in Shakespeare's *Julius Caesar*, "Beware that man. He thinketh too much. Such men are dangerous!"

Troublesome or dangerous or not, the improvement of student thinking has long been and is today even more so a major goal of formal schooling in the United States. As pointed out in Chapter 2, Descartes's observation several centuries ago that "I think; therefore I am" aptly captures the importance of this goal. Helping students achieve the fullest potential of their minds certainly contributes to their self-identity and self-awareness as well as to their capacities to cope, function, and contribute in the world. Achieving these goals is the ultimate justification for developing an effective thinking skills program.

ENDNOTES

1. Bruce Joyce and Beverly Showers, *Power in Staff Development Through Research on Training* (Alexandria, Va.: Association for Supervision and Curriculum Development, 1983).

2. Arthur Whimbey, "Teaching Sequential Thought: The Cognitive Skills Approach," *Phi Delta Kappan 59*, 4 (December 1977): 255–259.

3. Arthur Whimbey, "You Don't Need a Special Reasoning Test to Implement and Evaluate Reasoning Training," *Educational Leadership 43*, 2 (October 1985): 37–39; Edward A. Morante and Anita Ulesky, "Assessment of Reasoning Abilities," *Educational Leadership 42*, 1 (September 1984): 71–74.

4. Whimbey, "You Don't Need," p. 39.

5. Thomas H. Estes, "Reading in the Social Studies: A Review of Research Since 1950," in James L. Laffey, ed., *Reading in the Content Areas* (Newark, Del.: International Reading Association, 1972).

6. Harold Berlak, "New Curricula and Measurement of Thinking," *Educational Forum 30*, 3 (March 1966): 303–311.

7. Arthur L. Costa, "Thinking: How Do We Know Students Are Getting Better At It?," *Roeper Review* (April 1984): 197–198.

8. John Bartlett, *Familiar Quotations*, 15th ed. (Boston: Little Brown and Company, 1980), p. 635.

Appendix A:
Selected Thinking
Skills Programs

Educators considering adoption of an existing thinking skills program will find a large number of such programs from which they can choose. This appendix provides concise summaries of some of the more popular programs designed to teach thinking. Each of these programs is described in terms of its major goal, intended audience, assumptions, skills taught, process/materials, time requirements, and developer(s). Although these descriptions are based on the most accurate information available at the time they were prepared, some changes have undoubtedly been made in these programs since then. The addresses provided at the end of each description will be helpful for obtaining further information on these programs.

Descriptions prepared by Dr. Barbara Presseisen, Research for Better Schools, Inc., and James J. McTighe, Maryland State Department of Education. Used by permission.

BASICS

GOAL   To enable teachers to teach students the different thinking skill strategies they need to learn facts, concepts, principles, attitudes, and skills, and to apply these thinking strategies in dealing with out-of-school situations.

INTENDED AUDIENCE   Teachers of all level students.

ASSUMP-TIONS   All curriculum objectives can be classified by the type of learning (and thinking) required of students.
Teachers can be trained to build thinking strategies into their lessons.

SKILLS   Teachers are taught to build anticipating, attitude formation, classifying, comparing/contrasting, concept formation, generalizing, inferring, making choices, and observing into their lessons.

PROCESS/ MATERIALS   Developer/trainers train local leaders who, in turn, conduct staff development programs in which teachers learn how to plan and conduct lessons that use BASICS thinking and learning strategies as the means for achieving their content objectives. Focus is on how to guide students in doing the appropriate type of thinking to accomplish the task.

TIME   Minimum of fifteen to twenty days over a two-year period with a one-year periodic follow-up.

DEVELOPERS   Sydelle Seiger-Ehrenberg and Lyle M. Ehrenberg. Program is based on work by Hilda Taba.

AVAILABLE FROM   ICI Services, Ltd.
301 South Third Street
Coshocton, OH 43812
(614) 622-5344/5341

BUILDING THINKING SKILLS

GOAL	To teach students cognitive skill development and analytical reasoning.
INTENDED AUDIENCE	Middle elementary students and junior high-school students, or secondary students with limited vocabularies.
ASSUMPTIONS	Four types of thinking skills are necessary for successful academic performance: similarity and difference, sequence, classification, and analogy.
SKILLS	Figural similarities, sequences, classifications, and analogies; verbal similarities, sequence, classifications, and analogies.
PROCESS/ MATERIALS	The program presently includes four books, with two more promised. All books contain pencil-and-paper exercises on thinking skills basic to content objectives. These written exercises are followed by class discussions during which the thinking process is examined, clarified, and refined. Follow-up exercises provide practice and reinforcement.
TIME	Variable.
DEVELOPERS	Midwest Publications Company, Inc.
AVAILABLE FROM	Midwest Publications Company, Inc. P.O. Box 448 Pacific Grove, CA 93950

CoRT (COGNITIVE RESEARCH TRUST)

GOAL
: To teach students to develop original solutions to problems by learning to change their perceptions. (The lessons focus on the perceptual aspect of thinking.)

INTENDED AUDIENCE
: Developer believes that thinking is best taught to nine- to eleven-year-olds. However, it has been used with students from ages eight to twenty-two. The lessons have been taught to students ranging in I.Q. from below 80 to above 140. The lessons have also been used with groups of mixed ability.

ASSUMP-TIONS
: Intelligent people are not necessarily skillful thinkers. Perception is more important than judging other people's ideas.
Lateral thinking is what is important.
Lateral thinking is not necessarily sequential, is unpredictable, and is not constrained by convention.

SKILLS
: Perception tools that help students function better in his or her life outside of school. An example of such a "tool" is the PMI (Plus, Minus, Interesting) which is intended to help students develop the habit of considering new ideas without immediately judging them as good or bad, right or wrong. Students are taught to "do an OPV" (Other Point of View) or "do a CAF" (Consider All Factors) when making decisions.

PROCESS/ MATERIALS
: The CoRT program has six sections, each containing ten lessons. After section 1, the lessons can be used in any order. Process consists of a teacher giving an explanation of a "tool" and students practicing using it in a variety of situations.

TIME
: One lesson (thirty-five minutes or longer) each week for three years.

DEVELOPER
: Edward de Bono. Cognitive Research Trust is the name of de Buno's organization in Cambridge, England.

AVAILABLE FROM
: Pergamon Press, Inc.
Fairview Park
Elmsford, NY 10523

CREATIVE PROBLEM SOLVING (CPS)

GOAL
To develop in students the abilities and attitudes necessary for creative problem solving.

INTENDED AUDIENCE
Gifted middle level and all secondary students.

ASSUMP-TIONS
Creativity involves the application of knowledge, imagination, and judgment to problem solving.
Everyone has creativity.
Creativity can be increased through teaching and practice.

SKILLS
Sample skills include sensing problems, observing and analyzing facts, deferring judgment, discovering new relationships and ideas, evaluating consequences, developing action plans, and developing feedback systems.

PROCESS/MATERIALS
Students are provided many opportunities to practice solving problems. Materials include a student activity book and an instructor's guidebook. This guidebook offers additional exercises, readings, films and test sources.

TIME
Varies. Material is best used in instructional blocks of sixty minutes. Plans for short and long programs are suggested.

DEVELOPER
Sidney J. Parmes. Program is based on the work of Alex F. Osborn.

AVAILABLE FROM
Creative Education Foundation
437 Franklin Street
Buffalo, NY 14202

CRITICAL ANALYSIS AND THINKING SKILLS (CATS)

GOAL To teach how to apply rules of good critical thinking in analyzing issues and problems.

INTENDED AUDIENCE Students in grades 9–12.

ASSUMP- TIONS Critical thinking can be developed through systematic application of a planned process.

SKILLS Teaches a six-step procedure of specifying the issue, identifying critical areas, predicting consequences, evaluation, assessing sources, and deciding. These steps are based on four rules and applied in eleven manuals to American and world history, government, literature, careers, critical reading, essay writing, and other areas.

PROCESS/ MATERIALS Using any of eleven different teacher manuals, teachers provide instruction in the process and structure the issue analysis, class discussion, and written activities. Manuals provide detailed lesson plans.

TIME Generally applied four times, each time to a different issue, during a single twenty-week semester.

DEVELOPERS Terry Applegate and Keith Evans.

AVAILABLE FROM Terry Applegate
4988 Kalani Drive
Salt Lake City, UT 84117

CRITICAL THINKING—BOOKS I AND II

GOAL
To develop the skills of critical thinking.

INTENDED AUDIENCE
Students in grades 7–12. Book I is a prerequisite to Book II.

ASSUMPTIONS
Students learn to think most effectively through involvement in thinking activities followed by analysis and discussion of the thinking processes used.
Thinking skills can be explicitly identified and taught.

SKILLS
Contain a wide variety of thinking skills including skills of logical reasoning, "if . . . then" statements, double negatives, substitutions, probable/possible, propoganda techniques, argument analysis, advertising techniques, and more.

PROCESS/ MATERIALS
Workbook exercises serve as springboards for class analysis and discussion with teacher as discussion leader. Can be used as separate course or units or within subject matter course.

TIME
Used regularly, at least once a week.

DEVELOPER
Anita Harnadek.

AVAILABLE FROM
Midwest Publications
P.O. Box 448
Pacific Grove, CA 93950

CRITICAL THINKING IN AMERICAN HISTORY

GOALS
To teach students how to evaluate historical interpretations.
To expand students' perceptions of history—to help them to see that there are many different viewpoints in history.
To help students construct better arguments.
To make students better, more skeptical citizens.

INTENDED AUDIENCE
The materials were developed for students in high school history courses. However, they have been used successfully with junior high school and college students also. The lessons vary in difficulty. For example, there are three lessons on immigration—for low ability, average, and advanced students.

ASSUMP-TIONS
Thinking skills are learned best when taught in regular subjects.
Thinking skills should be taught directly and reinforced regularly.
Students learn thinking skills more effectively when they are confronted with problems that require the use of thinking skills.

SKILLS
Analysis and evaluation skills to assess claims and arguments, such as identifying and evaluating evidence, analyzing cause and effect arguments, identifying fallacies, and evaluating historical analogies. Students first use the skills to evaluate rival interpretations from the booklets, then use them to judge claims made in class discussions, and finally to write logical arguments on historical questions.

PROCESS/ MATERIALS
Critical Thinking in American History consists of four booklets: Exploration to Constitution, New Republic to Civil War, Reconstruction to Progressivism, and Spanish American War to Vietnam. Each unit is comprised of a student booklet (containing the historical problems), a teacher's guide (containing lesson plans), and a source materials envelope (containing worksheets for some lessons and test questions for each topic). There are approximately twenty-four lessons in each unit.

TIME
These are supplementary materials for a one- or two-year course in American History. They were designed to allow

the teacher flexibility in choosing what skills to teach and when to teach them.

DEVELOPER   Kevin O'Reilly, Social Studies teacher at Hamilton-Wenham Regional High School, South Hamilton, Massachusetts.

AVAILABLE   Critical Thinking Press
FROM   775 Bay Road
South Hamilton, MA 01982

FUTURE PROBLEM SOLVING

GOAL
To develop students' creative problem-solving skills as they consider ways to solve predicted problems of the future. Program also embraces several other objectives: (1) to increase students' written and verbal communication skills, (2) to help students become better team members, (3) to develop and improve students' research skills, (4) to enable students to integrate problem-solving process into their daily lives, and (5) to improve students' analytical and critical thinking skills.

INTENDED AUDIENCE
Grades 4–12. A noncompetitive primary version has also been designed for students in grades K–3. To date, the program has appealed primarily to gifted students.

ASSUMPTIONS
Consideration of issues related to the future helps students prepare for the future.
Problem-solving skills and creativity are necessary to function effectively.
Creativity and problem solving can be taught.

SKILLS
Skills relate to the formal problem-solving process developed by Osborn and Parnes

PROCESS/ MATERIALS
Practice problems are the heart of the program. Teams of four students receive a set of practice problems. Students employ the following steps in solving these:
Research general topic.
Brainstorm possible problem related to the given situation.
Identify one underlying problem.
Brainstorm alternative solutions.
Develop five criteria for evaluating solutions.
Identify the best solutions.
Results of this process are sent to trained volunteers who review these. State & National Bowls and Scenario Writing contests are held each year.

TIME
Varies; often one hour per week.

DEVELOPER
E. Paul Torrance. Program is based on the problem-solving model of Alex Osborn and Sidney Parnes.

AVAILABLE FROM
Future Problem Solving Program
Coe College
Cedar Rapids, IA 52402

HIGHER-ORDER THINKING SKILLS (HOTS)

GOAL   To engage students in higher-order thinking activities in order to strengthen their basic skills and social confidence.

INTENDED AUDIENCE   Chapter I students in grades 3–6. Can also be used with average students.

ASSUMP-TIONS   Basic skills is not a prerequisite for engaging in higher-order thinking skills.
Thinking activities should be organized in the same manner that the brain seems to organize information in long-term memory.

SKILLS   Developing and testing problem-solving strategies, interpreting computer feedback, integrating and synthesizing information, and generalizing across content areas.

PROCESS/MATERIALS   This is a pullout-type program with heavy reliance on computer activities. Students work in a computer lab. Work on the computer is preceded by a discussion in which teacher poses challenge questions for students to work on.

TIME   Chapter I students would have four lessons per week; average students would need less.

DEVELOPER   Stanley Pogrow. Program is based on the cognitive psychology theories of the organization of information in the brain.

AVAILABLE FROM   Stanley Pogrow
College of Education
University of Arizona
Tucson, AZ 85721

INSTRUMENTAL ENRICHMENT

GOAL   To develop thinking and problem-solving abilities in order to become an autonomous learners. (To alter the characteristically passive and dependent cognitive style of slow learners to that of active, self-motivated, independent thinkers.)

INTENDED AUDIENCE   Upper elementary, middle, and secondary students. Supplements regular curriculum. Involves teacher training.

ASSUMP-TIONS   Intelligence is modifiable.
Cognitive development requires direct intervention and mediated learning experiences which result in students learning how to learn.

SKILLS   Skills taught are mental operations such as: gathering information, problem solving, classifying/comparing, orientation in space, recognizing relationships, following directions, planning, organizing, logical reasoning, inductive and deductive reasoning, and synthesizing.

PROCESS/ MATERIALS   Students do paper-and-pencil lessons called "instruments" which are followed by teacher-led discussions. The program emphasizes this teacher mediation. The cognitive tasks are not subject-specific but parallel the subject matter being taught. Whatever the particular focus of an instrument, its larger purpose is to further develop the students' conscious thought processes and to aid in their discovering practical applications for those processes.

TIME   Two to three hours a week over a three-year period. Can be adapted to a two-year cycle. Teacher training has involved a minimum of forty-five hours each year.

DEVELOPER   Reuven Feuerstein.

AVAILABLE FROM   Curriculum Development Associates, Inc.
Suite 414, 1211 Connecticut Avenue, NW
Washington, DC 20036

JUNIOR GREAT BOOKS

GOAL
To enable students to read interpretively and to think independently and reflectively.

ASSUMP-
TIONS
To read interpretively is to think independently and reflectively.

INTENDED
AUDIENCE
Students from second grade through high school. Designed for students reading at grade level or above. There is also a two-day in-service course to prepare teachers to use the program.

SKILLS
Students develop the habit of reading critically, interpreting what they read, and supporting their interpretations with ideas and facts from the readings. They also learn new ways of looking at themselves, their fellow participants, and the world around them.

PROCESS/
MATERIALS
It is a reading and discussion program based on a method of learning called shared inquiry. Teachers act as discussion leaders and lead discussions on problems of interpretations to which they themselves are not sure of the answer. They view students as partners in a joint effort to uncover new meanings in some of the outstanding works of literature of the past and present. In addition to the reading selections, each Junior Great Books Series includes a short course on interpretive reading—statements and exercises on shared inquiry that are designed to teach and reinforce reading comprehension and discussion skills.

TIME
Students meet—usually once a week—for twelve sessions to discuss a story everyone has read in advance. Discussions last for thirty to ninety minutes, depending on grade level.

DEVELOPER
The Great Books Foundation

AVAILABLE
FROM
The Great Books Foundation
40 East Huron Street
Chicago, IL 60611
312 323-5870

MAKING CHANGES

GOAL
: To teach students a set of generalizable cognitive strategies which can be used on any open-ended problem to increase the range of possible solutions considered.

INTENDED AUDIENCE
: Students in grades 7–10.

ASSUMPTIONS
: Schools have a responsibility to teach skills for dealing with problems that have no right answer and no set method of attack.
The best way of teaching these is within the context of meaningful and provocative problem-solving ventures and simulations.
Such a course must also attempt to make pervasive changes in students' attitudes, beliefs, and dispositions.

SKILLS
: Program teaches knowledge of problem solving and group processes; skills in analyzing, weighing criteria, and judging ideas; strategies such as using the checkerboard and checklist to generate ideas; attitudes such as confidence and increased tolerance of ambiguity; and dispositions such as perserverance in problem-solving tasks.

PROCESS/ MATERIALS
: The program materials include a teacher's guide, student lesson books, transparencies, and handouts. The program is organized into four units. The first and third units address problem solving. The second unit is an introduction to futures studies. The fourth unit concentrates on two methods for specifying consequences and for exploring alternatives futures.

TIME
: Thirty-two to fifty periods of forty-five minutes.

DEVELOPERS
: John W. Thomas, Research for Better Schools.

AVAILABLE FROM
: ETC Publications
Drawer 1627-A
Palm Springs, CA 92263

MAKING JUDGMENTS

GOAL — To teach students to use logical and pragmatic standards for assessing information and solving evaluative problems.

ASSUMP-TIONS — Critical thinking is the application of learned skills. Skills for critical thinking are best taught independent of the curricula in the context of problem-solving ventures.

INTENDED AUDIENCE — Middle-school students (grades 6–9).

SKILLS — The lessons teach students to make reasoned decisions by weighing evidence, identifying persuasive appeals, evaluating empirical claims, developing counter arguments and critical interpretations, and making inferences.

PROCESS/MATERIALS — The instructional package is divided into several independent courses including: Advertising—a course in evaluating persuasive techniques and empirical claims; Causation—a course in testing hypotheses and designing research studies; Conflict—a course in evaluating evidence and testimony; and Reporting—a course in assessing factual reports and interpretations. Each course offers a variety of materials including: individual lesson books and workbooks, small and large group activities, board games, enrichment problems, and simulations. Each course introduces a distinct role model. Learners assume the duties of a consumer advocate, a public health investigator, a conflict counselor, a courtroom lawyer, or a newspaper reporter.

TIME — Each course contains five to six lessons. Each lesson takes twenty-five to forty-five minutes to complete.

DEVELOPER — John W. Thomas, The Humanizing Learning Program, Research for Better Schools, Inc.

AVAILABLE FROM — Research for Better Schools, Inc.
444 N. Third Street
Philadelphia, PA 19123

ODYSSEY

GOAL
To enhance the ability of students to perform a wide variety of thinking skills.

INTENDED AUDIENCE
Upper elementary and middle school students. The program originally developed for use in Venezuela as part of that country's Project Intelligence. It is intended for regular heterogeneously grouped classes.

ASSUMP-TIONS
Performance of intellectually demanding tasks is influenced by various types of factors.
Some of these are modifiable and can be taught.

SKILLS
Skills include careful observation and classification, deductive and inductive reasoning, the precise use of language, the inferential use of information in memory, hypothesis generation and testing, problem solving, inventiveness and creativity, and decision making.

PROCESS/ MATERIALS
Approach is deliberately eclectic. It combines knowledge from current cognitive research with the methods of direct instruction. Some lessons involve a Socratic inquiry approach, while others are based on Piagetian-like analysis of cognitive activities. Still others emphasize exploration and discovery. Materials include six teacher manuals and student books:
Foundations of Reasoning
Understanding Language
Verbal Reasoning
Problem Solving
Decision Making
Inventive Thinking
These are intended to be used in the above order.

TIME
Three to five lessons per week. Each lesson about forty-five minutes.

DEVELOPER
A team of researchers from Harvard University, Bolt Berarek and Newman Inc., and the Venezuelan Ministry of Education. D. N. Perkins helped to develop a portion of this program (creative thinking) and has popularized the *Inventive Thinking* materials.

AVAILABLE FROM
Mastery Education Corporation
85 Main Street
Watertown, MA 02172

OLYMPICS OF THE MIND

GOAL	To develop creative thinking skills through team involvement in problem-solving competitions.
INTENDED AUDIENCE	All grade and ability levels. Competition is divided into grade level groups: 　I—grades K–5 　II—grades 6–8 　III—grades 9–12
ASSUMP-TIONS	Skills of creative problem solving can be developed through practice. Team problem-solving competition provides motivation for developing creativity, cooperation, and planning skills. High achievement or high I.Q. are not prerequisites to success.
SKILLS	Emphasizes problem definition, brainstorming alternative solutions, experimentation and testing hypotheses, as well as planning, designing.
PROCESS/ MATERIALS	Students work in teams to work practice design problems and then school teams participate in local and regional competitions with teachers as "coaches."
TIME	Offered as an extra-curricular activity in most schools with voluntary student participation
DEVELOPERS	Sam Micklus and Ted Gourley.
AVAILABLE FROM	OM Association P.O. Box 27 Glassboro, NJ 08028

PHILOSOPHY FOR CHILDREN

GOALS
To improve reasoning abilities by having students think about thinking as they discuss concepts of importance to them.

INTENDED AUDIENCE
Kindergarten through high school levels, but it is generally used in the upper elementary and secondary levels.

ASSUMP-TIONS
Children are by nature interested in philosophical issues such as truth, fairness, and personal identity.
Children should learn to think for themselves.

SKILLS
Program lists thirty thinking skills that it fosters—some of these are drawing inferences, making analogies, forming hypotheses, and classification.

PROCESS/ MATERIALS
Students read special novels with inquisitive children as characters, then engage in classroom discussions and exercises. Each chapter contains a number of "leading ideas." The author's objective is for students to identify with the characters and to join in the kinds of thinking depicted in the readings. However, students from lower-class and even lower-middle-class backgrounds may have trouble relating to the characters in the stories, who come across as very middle or even upper-middle class in their values and orientations. The early elementary portion of the program provides students with a broad array of situations that challenge them to practice reasoning and inquiry skills; the middle school portion introduces them to the principles underlying such practices; and the later portion enables them to apply their cognitive skills to a variety of academic and life situations.

TIME
About two and one quarter hours weekly for the entire year.

DEVELOPER
Matthew Lipman.

AVAILABLE FROM
Institute for the Advancement of Philosophy for Children
Montclair State College
Upper Montclair, NJ 07043

PROJECT IMPACT (Improving Minimal Proficiencies by Activating Critical Thinking)

GOAL — To improve student performance in mathematics, reading, and language arts by infusing critical thinking instruction into the content areas.

INTENDED AUDIENCE — Middle and secondary levels. Although designed as an alternative approach to remedial reading and math at the junior and senior school levels, it is compatible with various other content areas and grade levels. Staff development is required for implementation.

ASSUMPTIONS — Thinking skills are basic to the learning process. Thinking skills can be successfully taught to all students. Thinking skills must be related to the curriculum.

SKILLS — Sample skills include: classifying and categorizing, ordering, identifying relevant and irrelevant information, formulating valid inductive and deductive arguments, and rendering judgments.

PROCESS/ MATERIALS — Skills are presented in a lesson plan format. The Curriculum Materials Kit provides a language arts and a mathematics handbook containing sixty teacher-developed lessons. Small-group and individualized instruction is emphasized, but large-group instruction and discussion are also used. Study sheets accompany each lesson and are written at various levels of vocabulary and task difficulty. Learning activities include oral and written reports, research projects, art work, and dramatic presentations. Four filmstrips are included in each kit. The program also has "Home Enrichment Learning Packets" which are sent home with students. These contain supplementary materials to reinforce the aspects of skills identified as the most difficult for students to grasp.

TIME — Two to three hours per week.

DEVELOPER — S. Lee Winocur.

AVAILABLE FROM — S. Lee Winocur
Center for the Teaching of Thinking
2132 Magnolia Street
Huntington Beach, CA 92646

STRATEGIC REASONING

GOAL
: To teach students the fundamental thinking skills, reasoning abilities, and problem-solving techniques for functioning effectively in and out of school. Students are made aware of these, taught to use them, verbalize them, and apply them.

INTENDED AUDIENCE
: Upper elementary, middle, secondary, and community college level. It can be used in English, reading, math, social studies, and science courses. For any given population of students, appropriate instructional levels are identified and assigned. Minimum amount of staff development required for implementation.

ASSUMPTIONS
: There are six primary, natural thinking skills that form the core of all thinking and problem solving.
The ability to use these productively depends on experience and training.
These six skills can be taught to all students within the regular classroom.

SKILLS
: Six thinking skills taught are:
Identification (thing-making)
Description (qualification)
Classification (organization)
Structure Analysis (part-whole relations)
Operation Analysis (sequencing)
Seeing Analogies

PROCESS/ MATERIALS
: Students do group activities and pencil-and-paper exercises. Teachers lead discussions of processes and rationale. Specific procedures differ for each of the four stages (see under **Goal**). Each stage has a complete set of student and teacher materials; no additional materials are needed.

TIME
: One period per week.

DEVELOPER
: John Glade. The program is based on Albert Upton's work. See A. Upton. (1961). *Design for Thinking*. Palo Alto, Calif.: Pacific Books.

AVAILABLE FROM
: Innovative Sciences, Inc.
Park Square Station
P.O. Box 15129
Stamford, CT 06901-0129
800 243-9169

STRUCTURE OF THE INTELLECT (SOI)

GOAL
: To equip students with the necessary intellectual skills to learn subject matter content and to think critically.

INTENDED AUDIENCE
: All students and adults. Can start as early as first grade. Staff training and retraining needed for implementation.

ASSUMP-TIONS
: Intelligence consists of 120 thinking abilities that are a combination of such things as comprehending, remembering, and analyzing, contents which are words, forms, or symbols, and products which are in single units, groups or relationships.
Individual differences in these factors can be assessed with SOI tests and improved with SOI materials.
(Educators are given at least a two-day seminar in which they are shown how intelligence can be taught and learned.)

SKILLS

Language Arts/Reading

Basic
- Concept formation
- Differentiating concepts
- Comprehending verbal relations
- Comprehending verbal systems

Enrichment
- Memory for implied meanings
- Judging verbal implications
- Problem solving
- Interpreting verbal meanings
- Using analogical ideas
- Creative writing
- Creative interpretation
- Creative grammatics

Arithmetic, Mathematics, Science

Basic
- Comprehending space
- Conserving abstracts in spatial perspectives
- Deduction/formal logic
- Inductive reasoning
- Decision making

Enrichment
- Discriminating notational transformations
- Producing notational transformations
- Comprehending inferences
- Judging symbolic results
- Producing symbolic implications
- Creative consequences

PROCESS/ Students use materials (some three-dimensional)
MATERIALS prescribed for them based on a diagnostic test. Computer
software gives analyses and prescriptions.

TIME Two half-hour lessons a week are recommended. Can
vary.

DEVELOPER Mary Meeker. Program is based on Guilford's theory of
intelligence.

AVAILABLE SOI Institute
FROM 343 Richmond Street
El Segundo, CA 90245

TALENTS UNLIMITED

GOAL	To help teachers recognize and nuture multiple talents of students.
INTENDED AUDIENCE	Students of all ability levels, grades 1–6.
ASSUMP-TIONS	Virtually all children have above-average talent in at least one of the six "talents" addressed by the program. Students become more confident and successful in school when teachers acknowledge and build on these talents.
SKILLS	Emphasizes decision-making skills, productive thinking skills, predicting, planning, and communication skills.
PROCESS/ MATERIALS	Teacher provides direct, systematic instruction in the various talent areas and then helps students apply these talents in the regular subject areas. Teacher manual is available but teachers are to produce their own lessons using model lessons in the manual.
TIME	To be taught within various subject areas throughout the school year.
DEVELOPERS	Mobile County (Alabama) Public Schools.
AVAILABLE FROM	Talents Unlimited 1107 Arlington Street Mobile, AL 36605

Appendix B:
Selected Thinking
Skills and Strategies

The following pages offer brief descriptions of twenty important thinking skills and strategies. These descriptions present what appear to be the essential attributes of each operation. They have been derived from expert opinion, reflective analysis, and cognitive research. They are presented here for use by teachers and instructional materials developers as guides for preparing lessons, tests, and other materials and activities designed to help novices master these operations.

Each description includes one or more definitions, a description of one procedure that can be used to execute the operation, and some rules and knowledge used in carrying out the operation. Although most of these skill descriptions present only one procedure for executing an operation, there are obviously several ways experts go about employing these skills. Indeed, several of these descriptions present more than one procedure.

The attributes outlined in these descriptions seem to be those most commonly employed. There are, of course, more expert rules and knowledge related to each operation than are included in these descriptions. However, those listed here are those that appear to be most useful to novices and beginners. Additional rules and knowledge can be added as they become evident.

These descriptions should be considered tentative and incomplete. Cognitive operations change as our understanding of and expertise in using them change over time. Thus, these descriptions are open-ended in describing the attributes of each operation (as indicated by the symbol . . .). Teachers should feel free to add to or modify all of these descriptions as they and their students become comfortable in using and teaching them and as they come to understand how they are executed with some degree of expertise.

Contents

Analysis	Fact/Value Judgment
Argument (elements)	Factual Accuracy
Argument (strength)	Logical Fallacies
Bias	Point of View
Classification	Prediction (Extrapolation)
Comparison/Contrast	Problem Solving
Credibility of a Source	Relevance/Irrelevance
Decision Making	Stereotypes
Evaluation	Synthesis
Evidence Finding	Unstated Assumptions

ANALYZING

DEFINITION   Taking apart (disassembling, deconstructing) in order to perceive or establish a pattern or relationship(s)

STEPS

Procedure A
1. Identify the purpose for analyzing.
2. Select clues/criteria to use.
3. Examine the data piece-by-piece to identify evidence of these clues or criteria.
4. Compare evidence found to establish pattern(s), link(s), or other interconnections.
5. State results of the analysis.

Procedure B
1. Identify the purpose for analyzing.
2. Scan the data to identify clue(s) or pattern(s) of significance.
3. State the clue(s) or pattern(s) inferred or found.
4. Reexamine the data to find additional supporting evidence.
5. Reexamine the data to find evidence contradicting original inference.
6. Confirm or reject clue(s) or patterns established.
7. State the results of the analysis.

RULES
1. When to analyze?
   - to clarify a problem, test a hypothesis, produce a synthesis, or evaluate something
   - to identify the particular features of something
   - to establish relationships
   - to judge the worth, accuracy, or relevance of something
   - . . .
2. How to start?
   - state clues or criteria to look for
   - scan the data to find "something" germane to the task
   - . . .
3. What to do if . . .
   - you cannot identify clues or criteria to use? Consider what ought to "be there" if a positive result is to occur or what should not be there if a negative result is to occur.

- contradictory clues are found? Consider the results ambiguous or insufficient.
- . . .

KNOWLEDGE   1. Clues related to specific analytical tasks such as logical fallacies, bias, assumptions, stereotypes, author's frame of reference, etc.
2. Subject matter related to material being analyzed
3. Specific applications of analysis, such as comparing, contrasting, classifying, etc.
4. Related skills, such as extrapolating, synthesis, evaluation

IDENTIFYING THE ELEMENTS OF AN ARGUMENT

DEFINITION   Identifying the parts of an argument
argument: a justified position, reasons in support of a
conclusion

STEPS   1. Recall the elements that constitute an argument,
including:
* conclusion
* reasons (specific facts, rules, generalizations) in
support of the conclusion
2. Search through the given explanation
sentence-by-sentence and phrase-by-phrase to identify
these elements.
* signal words for conclusions: *thus, therefore, so,
consequently, as a result*
* signal words for reasons: *because, since, as a result
of, for*
3. Identify and make explicit any unstated assumptions or
reasons.
4. Identify how each reason is connected to the others
and to the conclusion (such as deductive or inductive
patterns).

RULES   1. When to use?
* anytime someone is trying to convince or persuade
you of the truth, accuracy, or desirability of
something
* anytime you are trying to determine the validity of
any conclusion
* . . .
2. How to start?
* find the conclusion the author is trying to
prove—usually located in the first sentence or two,
sometimes at the end, and occasionally midway in
the argument and may be repeated at several places
for emphasis.
* find reasons the author gives in support of the
conclusion
* . . .
3. What to do, if . . .
* you cannot find a conclusion? Ask yourself "What
does the author want me to believe or do as a result
of reading/hearing this?"
* you cannot pinpoint reasons that justify the
conclusion? Ask yourself "What else has to be

assumed to be true, if you are to accept this conclusion as true?"
- you cannot determine whether or not it is an argument? Ask of each sentence: "Does this sentence support the conclusion?"
- . . .

KNOWLEDGE
1. Patterns of deductive and inductive reasoning
2. Different kinds of arguments
3. Elaborated structures that include chains or series of arguments
4. Additional ingredients of arguments that may enhance them but which do not constitute essential parts of the argument per se, such as
   - elaborating the conclusion
   - raising of alternative conclusions and refuting each with reasons (this is another self-contained argument)

DETERMINING THE STRENGTH OF AN ARGUMENT

DEFINITION
Deciding the quality or merit of reasons given in support of a conclusion.
strength: quality, merit, believability
argument: reasons given in support of a conclusion

STEPS
1. Clarify the conclusion being proved (and define any vague terms).
2. Identify the reasons, stated and unstated (presenting factual evidence, rules, generalizations), given to support the conclusion.
3. Distinguish the relevant from the irrelevant, statements of fact from value judgments, and bias.
4. Evaluate the reasons for
   - content: accuracy, sufficiency, significance
   - structure: connection to the conclusion and possibly to other reasons (logic, absence of fallacies, consistency)
5. State your judgment about the argument's strength.

RULES
1. When to use?
   - any time someone is trying to convince or persuade you of something
   - whenever you are trying to determine the validity of a conclusion
   - . . .
2. How to start?
   - clarify the conclusion being proved
   - identify the essential elements of the argument
   - . . .
3. What to do, if . . .
   - you cannot check the accuracy of evidence offered? Concentrate on analyzing the logic and consistency of the reasoning and make only a tentative judgment.
   - the conclusion is vague? Define clearly the key elements of the conclusion.
   - you cannot find all the reasons expected or needed? Ask yourself "What else must be assumed to be true, if I am to accept what is provided as true?"
   - . . .

KNOWLEDGE
1. Various criteria for determining accuracy of evidence, identifying logical fallacies, and determining the credibility of sources

2. Various structures relating premises, inferences, and conclusions
3. Criteria for soundness of an argument—to be sound an argument must have:
   - true reasons (or premises)
   - a conclusion that follows from the premises/reasons
     of necessity (if deductive)
     probably (if inductive)
   - content free from logical fallacies, irrelevancies, bias, unwarranted assumptions
   - use of appropriate conditioners, "hedges," or qualifiers

DETECTING BIAS

DEFINITION   Finding a one-sided or slanted view for or against
something
bias: preference, slanted view, partiality, untested
inclination that inhibits an impartial judgment

STEPS   *Procedure A*
1. State your purpose.
2. Identify the clues to look
   for, including:
   • "loaded" or
     emotionally charged
     words
   • overgeneralizations
   • "loaded" or rhetorical
     questions
   • imbalance in
     presentation
   • opinions stated as
     facts
3. Take the material apart
   piece-by-piece or
   line-by-line to find the
   clues.
4. Identify patterns among
   or consistency of the
   clues found.
5. State evidence to
   support patterns found.
6. Judge the extent of the
   bias.

Procedure B
1. State your purpose.
2. Skim data/object.
3. Predict the bias when
   identifying first clues.
4. Search for corroborating
   clues:
   • "loaded" or
     emotionally charged
     words
   • overgeneralizations
   • "loaded" or rhetorical
     questions
   • imbalance in
     presentation
   • opinions stated as
     facts
5. Search for a pattern in
   the clues.
6. State the bias found.

RULES   1. When to search for bias?
   • when an account seeks to persuade
   • in judging the accuracy of a source or statement
   • in identifying an author's point of view
   • . . .
2. How to start?
   • pick one clue and look for it, then pick another and
     search for it, etc.
   • . . .
3. What to do if . . .
   • you find little bias? Compare it to another piece of
     material on the same topic.

- the vocabulary is unfamiliar? Use a dictionary to clarify meanings.
- . . .

KNOWLEDGE   1. Clues to or criteria of bias
                      2. Subject of the "account" being analyzed

CLASSIFYING

DEFINITION   Putting things together that have the same feature(s); arranging into groups on the basis of (a) shared or common characteristic(s) or attribute(s); grouping, sorting, categorizing

STEPS   *Procedure A*
1. Identify the purpose for classifying.
2. Skim data to spot significant items/to get ideas.
3. Focus on an item.
4. Pick other item(s) just like focus item.
5. State (as a label) unifying/common attributes.
6. Find other items just like focus item and add to group.
7. Repeat steps 3–6 with ungrouped items until all items are grouped and labeled.
8. Combine or subdivide categories as necessary.

Procedure B
1. Identify/state purpose for classifying.
2. Specify or recall category labels to be used.
3. Search data item by item and place into appropriate categories.
4. Modify category labels, if necessary.
5. Combine or subdivide categories, as necessary.

RULES   1. When to classify? When data . . .
   • are unorganized
   • are too much to manage easily
   • don't make sense
   • . . .
2. How to do it?
   • state identifying label as soon as two items are matched.
   • use group or category label as search tool to identify other examples of it
   • . . .
3. What to do if . . .
   • data in a category vary? Subdivide (reclassify) the category.
   • the same item fits into more than one category (assuming it can take only one form)? Get new system of divisions or revise all categories.

- items are left over? Make a miscellaneous category (tentatively).
- begin to "run down?" Switch to working on a new category.
- . . .

KNOWLEDGE
1. Potential category systems
2. Information about the data or items to be classified
3. How to compare and contrast

COMPARING/CONTRASTING

DEFINITION   Determining how things are alike (similar) and/or different
compare: find a similarity, likeness, commonality
contrast: find a difference

STEPS   1. Examine the items or information to be compared to identify one or more attributes (features) of each.
2. Pick one attribute or feature and examine all other items or information to see if it can be found in each one.
3. State as a *similarity* any feature found to exist in all the items examined.
4. State as a *difference* any feature *not* found in every item examined.
5. Repeat the process as many times as necessary.

RULES: 1. When to use . . .
   • in classifying data
   • in generalizing and conceptualizing
   • when several possibilities/options are available
   • . . .
2. How to start?
   • skim the data looking for obvious attributes
   • pick one attribute and skim to see if it can be found in any of the items or data to be examined
   • . . .
3. What to do if . . .
   • differences are noted in specific attributes? Whereas specific examples of an attribute may differ, the general class of attribute examples may be similar.
   • no similarities or differences are immediately noted? Look beneath surface features to examine functions, components, composition, relationships to other (common) items.
   • something is partly similar and partly different? Qualify the description.
   • . . .

KNOWLEDGE   1. The items, information being compared
2. Careful observation

DETERMINING THE CREDIBILITY OF A SOURCE

DEFINITION
Deciding whether a source is believable
credibility: believability, reliability

STEPS
1. Recall the criteria of credibility, including
   * author's field of expertise
   * author's reputation for accuracy
   * the absence of author's conflict of interest
   * the known risk to the author's reputation if published
   * appropriateness of methods used to prepare the source
   * agreement with other sources
2. Identify kinds of information that would be evidence of these criteria.
3. Search the data or information sentence-by-sentence to find evidence related to these criteria.
4. Identify any pattern found, throughout the complete source and/or over time.
5. Compare the source to other known credible sources to identify points of agreement or disagreement.

RULES
1. When to use?
   * in determining the accuracy of information or claims in another source
   * in collecting information for use in a task
   * . . .
2. How to start?
   * ask yourself "To what extent does this author have a reasonable chance to use or get detailed, accurate information?"
   * ask yourself, "To what extent might this author have hidden motives in preparing this source—or motives that might conflict with being accurate and objective?"
   * . . .
3. What to do if . . .
   * you can't find anyting about the author(s) of a source? Compare the information in the source to other sources known to be credible.
   * you can't find any other sources to compare the source in question to? If a book, study the criticisms and comments made in reviews or critiques of the book.
   * . . .

KNOWLEDGE
1. Although a source may have a reputation for accuracy, it may still contain errors or bias. Authors do err and do write for specific purposes, some of them not always publicly acknowledged.
2. Accounts produced for private use (diaries, letters) are likely to be more credible than accounts produced for public consumption (newspaper articles, books).
3. Major sources on writers' and scholars' lives, training and publications may be found in many libraries.

DECISION MAKING

DEFINITION   Selecting an alternative from among a number of
alternatives to achieve a goal
deciding: choosing, picking, opting, selecting

STEPS   1. Identify and define clearly the goal(s) to be achieved.
2. Identify alternatives (options) by which the goal(s) can be achieved.
3. Analyze the alternatives in terms of criteria, such as:
   - goals(s)—long/short range
   - predicted consequences
     long range/short range
     consequences of consequences
   - costs
     real costs
     opportunity costs
   - resources
     available
     substitute
   - constraints
   - . . .
4. Weight and rank alternatives (in terms of the weights assigned to the criteria used)
5. Choose the top two or three alternatives
6. Evaluate the top alternatives in terms of selected criteria, such as:
   - risks
   - unanticipated consequences
   - strategies available to enact
   - values
   - . . .

RULES   1. When to use?
   - in any "choice" situation, such as selecting a course of action to follow, something to believe, etc.
   - in attempting to resolve any problem involving values or divergent "potential solutions"
   - . . .
2. How to start?
   - brainstorm potential alternatives and alternatives to these alternatives
   - establish criteria to be used and relative weight of each

- recall previous successful or comparable decision making cases
- . . .

3. What to do if . . .
   - you are inclined early toward a specific solution? Look for additional options or for evidence against a favored option. Don't jump at the first seemingly "good" alternative that turns up!
   - you assume most alternatives are of equal weight? Identify relevant uncertainties and probabilities regarding alternatives.
   - you deal with various opinions and data sources? Apply critical thinking skills to determine their worth, accuracy, credibility, relevance, biases, etc.

KNOWLEDGE
1. Understand sources of decision-making interference, including impulsiveness, conflict of interest/bias, "ends justifies the means" mentality, irrational persistance of key beliefs
2. Understand conditions and forces likely to affect alternatives and their consequences in their future occurences

EVALUATING

DEFINITION   Determining the worth, accuracy, or completeness of something, judging, appraising, assessing

STEPS
1. State and define clearly what is to be evaluated.
2. Recall or invent criteria to be used.
3. Identify clues/evidence/behaviors that give evidence of the stated criteria.
4. Search the data piece-by-piece to find evidence related to the criteria.
5. Match evidence found to idealized standards of each criterion.
6. Judge the degree of match for each criterion.
7. Combine the results of matching to all criteria.
8. Determine your overall judgment.

RULES
1. When to use?
   - in distinguishing the relevant from the irrelevant, and facts from value judgments
   - in identifying bias, stereotypes, factual accuracy, and credibility
   - in determining the validity of a proposed conclusion or the relative worth of alternatives or options
   - in ranking options
   - . . .
2. How to start?
   - select, define, and rank the criteria to be used
   - make a tentative judgment about the topic or data, then articulate the criteria you used in so doing
   - . . .
3. What to do if . . .
   - you cannot determine appropriate criteria? Search to see what criteria others use or recommend or make a tentative judgment and work backward to identify why you made the judgment you did
   - you cannot identify evidence/behaviors that would exemplify the stated criteria? Ask yourself "What would one have to do or say or believe to give evidence of or demonstrate this criteria?"
   - . . .

KNOWLEDGE 1. Criteria associated with various critical thinking
operations (e.g., detecting bias, recognizing unstated
assumptions, determining the worth of a conclusion or
accuracy of a factual claim, etc.)
2. Criteria used in judging worth, merit, truth, accuracy,
etc., in many areas

Copyright © 1988, Barry K. Beyer

IDENTIFYING EVIDENCE RELATED TO A CLAIM

DEFINITION: Finding data that demonstrate whether or not a claim, assertion, or conclusion is true
evidence: objectively verifiable data related to a claim or judgment, consisting usually of material objects, events, documents, and verbal statements

STEPS   1. Identify and define clearly the claim (assertion, statement, conclusion) to be checked.
2. Identify the kinds of evidence that would exist if the claim is true and that should exist if the claim is untrue.
3. Search the available data or information line-by-line or piece-by-piece to locate such evidence, both that supporting as well as refuting the claim.
4. Distinguish between statements of fact and value judgments.

RULES   1. When to use?
   • in trying to decide whether or not to accept as true a claim, assertion or conclusion
   • in analyzing an argument or piece of persuasive writing
   • . . .
2. How to start?
   • identify the claim
   • ask yourself "If this claim is true, what would exist (or not exist) to prove it true (or false)"?
   • . . .
3. What to do if . . .
   • a claim is backed up primarily with examples? Examples are *not* evidence.
   • much evidence offered consists of numbers? Be sure absolute numbers as well as percentages are given.
   • . . .

KNOWLEDGE   1. Deliberately search for evidence contrary to claims as well as for them
2. Evidence that is verifiable is more valid and reliable than is that based primarily on personal experience, biased observations, and appeals to authorities
3. Not all evidence is equal in weight
4. Do not accept generalizations based on only a few cases—require representative data, randomly selected, and precise communication

Copyright © 1988, Barry K. Beyer

DISTINGUISHING STATEMENTS OF FACT FROM VALUE JUDGMENTS

DEFINITION   Separating statements about things that have been proven or could be objectively proven from statements that cannot be objectively proven to everyone's satisfaction
fact: objectively proven or capable of being objectively proven
value judgment: a subjective determination about the worth of something

STEPS   1. Recall the definition of *fact* and of *value judgment.*
2. Identify criteria and clues of *fact* and *value judgment*
   - *fact:* has been or could be objectively proven
   - *value judgment:* subjective, cannot be objectively proven, indicated sometimes by use of adjectives, adverbs or ill-defined terms, words like *I think, I believe, in my judgment,* etc.
3. Examine the given data sentence-by-sentence or phrase-by-phrase applying the above clues/criteria of *fact* and *value judgment* to each piece.
4. Determine and state the extent to which each phrase or sentence meets the criteria of *fact* or *value judgment.*

RULES   1. When to use?
   - in determining the accuracy of a report or other account
   - in determining the strength of an argument
   - . . .
2. How to start?
   - look for superlatives or other adjectives as part of a statement (for a value judgment)
   - look for specific data (for a factual statement)
   - . . .
3. What to do if . . .
   - you have difficulty distinguishing the two? Ask yourself "Has this been proven or could it be proven to everyone without a shadow of a doubt?"
   - . . .

KNOWLEDGE   1. Statements may be other than facts or value judgments
2. Value judgments often tell more about the author(s) of a statement than about the subject of the statement

DETERMINING THE ACCURACY OF A FACTUAL CLAIM

DEFINITION: Determining whether or not a factual statement is true and consistent with other known facts
accuracy: correctness, exactness, consistency with other known facts

STEPS   1. Identify and define clearly the factual claim to be judged.
2. Identify the extent to which the claim is generally agreed upon as part of general knowledge.
              and/or
3. Consult credible sources to determine the extent to which they support or agree with the claim.
              and/or
4. Conduct research to replicate that which initially generated the claim.

RULES: 1. When to use?
   • when using data or sources to solve problems or make decisions
   • when factual statements are to be used to build generalizations or similar kinds of knowledge claims
   • whenever someone is trying to persuade or convince you of something
   • . . .
2. How to start?
   • restate the factual claim in your own words
   • define the key facts
   • look in credible authoritative sources for corroboration
   • identify the kind of evidence that should and should not exist, if the claim were accurate
   • . . .
3. What to do if . . .
   • the facts are presented in ambiguous or vague terms? Clarify as precisely as possible the key terms in the factual statement, referring to context and connotations if necessary.
   • the facts may be of a controversial nature? Check the statement for author's point of view, bias, stereotyping, and other forms of distortion.
   • you cannot find sources against which to check the claim? Consider it to be only possibly accurate and do not base any decision solely on it.
   • . . .

KNOWLEDGE

1. A variety of credible sources
2. Comparing/contrasting.
3. Common types of factual errors
4. Importance of representativeness, randomness, and adequacy of cases from which factual claims may be derived

IDENTIFYING LOGICAL FALLACIES

DEFINITION   Spotting ideas or assertions founded on erroneous logic or perception
fallacious: a false notion, a deceptive idea
logic: reasoned, according to rational principles

STEPS   *Procedure A*
1. Clearly state the purpose—searching for fallacies in logic.
2. Identify the claim or conclusion being asserted.
3. Identify the warrant or backing for the reasons.
4. Determine the logic of the connections between the backing/warrant and claim.
5. State your finding and support it.

Procedure B
1. Clearly state the kind of fallacy for which you are searching.
2. Identify the clues to or criteria of this type of fallacy.
3. Search through the given argument sentence-by-sentence to find evidence of these clues or criteria.
4. Determine what kinds of grounds would be more logical.
5. State your finding and support it.

RULES: 1. When to use?
   • in analyzing any (supposed) argument or effort designed to persuade or convince
   • in producing any argument
   • when an argument appeals to authority for support
   • . . .
2. How to start?
   • depending on strategy, recall characteristics of or clues to the most common logical fallacies
   • recall examples of common fallacies
   • . . .
3. What to do if . . .
   • you cannot determine the logic in a line of reasoning? Ask yourself "Does *this* follow from *that, of necessity?*"
   • find the grounds (warrant or backing) for a claim? Ask yourself "What general principle must be considered true, if I am to accept what is given here as true?"
   • . . .

KNOWLEDGE   1. Common propoganda techniques, such as bandwagon effect, strawperson, red herring, name calling, and so on
2. Common logical fallacies, such as *ad hominem,* begging the question (circular reasoning), guilt by association, appeal to compassion, and so on
3. Deductive reasoning

RECOGNIZING POINT OF VIEW

DEFINITION | Identifying the position or set of concerns from which something is observed, presented or considered.
point of view: perspective, angle, standpoint

STEPS
1. Identify the subject or topic being presented and those aspects of it emphasized by the author.
2. Identify words or phrases that suggest how the author personally feels about the subject.
3. Identify any unstated assumptions that the author seems to make.
4. Identify aspects of the subject the author does *not* talk about (but probably could have).
5. Identify the author's position (for or against, like or dislike, etc.).
6. State what the author must believe, be interested in or be concerned about as indicated by his or her position.

RULES
1. When to use?
   - when examining an argument or description that seeks to persuade or convince
   - when trying to determine the objectivity or impartiality of an argument or description
   - . . .
2. How to start?
   - identify the subjects or topics the author includes and excludes
   - look for emotionally charged words that may reveal biases or preferences
   - . . .
3. What to do if . . .
   - it is difficult to identify a point of view? Compare the material to material on the same subject by another author representing a different background.
   - . . .

KNOWLEDGE
1. Each author writes from a particular point of view
2. Some indicators of a point of view include the topics included and excluded; the emotive connotation of words used; the use of overgeneralization or hyperbole; the kinds of analogies or metaphors used and their general connotations; the assumptions which, if true, would support the position taken; and the extent all sides are presented

3. A point of view (like a telescope) limits what one can perceive as well as provides focus on selected aspects of the subject
4. A point of view (like a telescope) often distorts the objective accuracy and/or completeness of an author's report on a subject

PREDICTING

DEFINITION Stating, in advance, what will probably happen or be true next; forecasting, extrapolating, foretelling, prophesizing, projecting

STEPS 1. State and clearly define the goal or purpose of predicting.
2. Collect/skim relevant, appropriate data to identify initial patterns or trends.
3. Compare and contrast the given data to identify what stays the same and what changes.
4. Identify a pattern or trend or repetition in the data.
5. Map the preceived pattern on the data to imagine the next possible instances of the perceived patterns.
6. Determine the probability of each imagined outcome actually occuring.
7. Select the outcome most likely to occur.

RULES 1. When to use?
   • in hypothesizing, inferring about any topic or subject
   • in forming new categories or groups in any data
   • . . .
2. How to start?
   • ask yourself "What *could* happen (or be true) next?"
   • arrange the data on paper or in a diagram
   • . . .
3. What to do if . . .
   • little relevant information exists? Think of similar situations or of problems in the past or of analogies.
   • it is difficult to generate possible outcomes? Brainstorm as many as possible without regard to probabilities.
   • . . .

KNOWLEDGE 1. Comparing, contrasting
2. Various types of patterns (such as temporal, spatial, numerical progressions, functional, etc.)
3. Probabilities
4. Potential intervening conditions, variations, and influences related to the subject
5. Historical, analogical situations/problems/conditions

PROBLEM SOLVING

DEFINITION Working out a correct solution to an uncertain or
perplexing situation or to a perceived difficulty
problem: an obstacle or difficulty

STEPS 1. Identify a problem
- recognize a problem
- clarify key elements
- define terms

2. Represent the problem
- clarify the goal
- identify obstacles to a solution
- identify causes of the obstacles

3. Select or invent a solution strategy or plan
- recall appropriate plan (problem-specific or general)
- devise a new strategy (by combining elements of others)

4. Carry out the plan or strategy
- collect appropriate data
- execute the selected plan or strategy

5. Conclude
- state the results
- provide supporting evidence and reasoning

6. Check your results
- evaluate the solution
- evaluate the plan

RULES 1. When to use?
- when a desired answer is not known or when there is a cognitive dissonance
- when there is a recognized gap between the way something ought to be and the way it actually is
- . . .

2. How to start?
- identify the key elements in the problematic situation including "givens," "wants," and possible causes
- represent the elements in the situation via a diagram
- restate the problem in your own words
- recall similar problems from the past
- . . .

3. What to do if . . .
- the problem seems too complex to resolve? Break it into subordinate problems, or solve a similar or equivalent problem or one analogous to it.

- your selected solution plan does not seem to be getting results? Restate and/or redefine the problem.
- you cannot think of a specific appropriate solution strategy? Use a general strategy such as "educated guessing" or work backward from a predicted solution.
- you are unsure of the accuracy of your initial solution? Check to see if you used all relevant data, if it conforms to your predicted outcome, or if it can be derived by use of a second strategy.
- . . .

KNOWLEDGE
1. A large number of specific and general solution plans and strategies, including hypothesis-making and testing, working backward, and specific formulas, etc.
2. The possibility or nature of future problems resulting from the resolution of the current problem
3. Various critical thinking operations to use at appropriate steps of the process to determine the worth and accuracy of data collected, hypotheses generated, and assumptions employed

DETERMINING RELEVANCE

DEFINITION   Deciding whether something relates or pertains to the
matter at hand
relevance: pertaining or related to, germane

STEPS   1. State the nature of the topic or matter at hand.
2. Recall or identify criteria to look for (that would make
things relevant to the topic), such as: examples,
explanations, details of (attributes), reasons for or
against, evidence for or against, something connected.
3. Take the material apart piece-by-piece to find evidence
of these criteria.
4. Match each item found to the identified criteria.
5. Judge the extent of the match—determine the degree
of relevancy.

RULES   1. When to use?
   • a specific topic is the matter at hand
   • identifying the elements of a problem
   • there is considerable amount of information
   • collecting information for writing on a topic
   • . . .
2. How to start?
   • restate the topic or matter at hand
   • recall criteria or clues of relevance
   • pick one piece of data and decide if its relevant,
   • telling why
3. What to do if . . .
   • little appears relevant? Recall what you know about
     the topic or consult another source.
   • material "contradicts" the topic? Negative evidence
     can be relevant, too!
   • . . .

KNOWLEDGE   1. Comparing, contrasting
2. Subject being analyzed

DETECTING STEREOTYPES

DEFINITION   Determining whether a description depicts the members of a group as all having the same characteristics or attributes; identifying the extent to which overly simplified and overly generalized characteristics have been attributed to a group or individual in a way that blurs or ignores characteristics or individual members of the group
stereotype: unvarying, overgeneralized opinion or conception of some thing or group or individual

STEPS   1. Skim the given description to identify characteristics attributed to the subject.
2. Recall or identify indicators of (clues to) stereotyping
   • use of overgeneralization, exaggeration
   • linking features together that logically do not relate to each other (e.g., All football *players* are *dumb*.)
   • use of vague words, like *tricky* or *dumb*
   • use of extremes or absolutes, like *never, none, every*
   • absence of individual attributes or variations
3. Search the data piece-by-piece to find these indicators.
4. Recall what you already know about individual examples or members of the group or find other data to see if there are exceptions in individual cases to the stated characteristics.
5. State the extent to which the given characteristics thoroughly describe all members of the given group.

RULES   1. When to search for stereotypes?
   • in examining any description of any group or individual
   • in using a source suspected of being for or against the individual or group described
   • . . .
2. How to start?
   • skim the given data to identify characteristics attributed to the group
   • recall examples of other stereotyped groups and what kinds of overgeneralized traits were attributed to them
   • . . .
3. What to do if . . .
   • you can't readily identify any gross exaggerations in the description but suspect stereotyping? Ask several members of the subject group to describe

themselves or examine individual examples of the group.
- you don't know any specific examples of members of the target group? Consult an encyclopedia or dictionary or other source.
- . . .

KNOWLEDGE
1. Most people stereotype different groups in one way or another
2. Stereotypes may have positive, negative, or neutral connotations to the individual holding the stereotype
3. A particular stereotype does not imply how one *feels* about the stereotyped group unless it is particularly negative
4. Stereotyping ignores the individual traits of the various individual members of a group or class
5. Stereotypes influence one's conception of any individual members of the stereotyped group and shape behaviors toward them
6. Members of groups have their own stereotyped images of their group which often differ from the images of the group held by nongroup members
7. Knowledge of the group or individual alledgedly stereotyped can help identify overgeneralized or erroneous images

SYNTHESIZING

DEFINITION   Combining of separate elements to produce a coherent whole; pulling together, unifying, combining, creating

STEPS
1. Identify the topic or subject.
2. Collect/skim relevant information or data.
3. Classify the information into categories related to the topic/subject.
4. Identify relationships among the categories and between the categories and topic/subject.
5. State or label way(s) the categories of information are related to the topic/subject (without repeating any of the category labels).

RULES
1. When to use?
   - in making topic sentences, conclusions, hypotheses, generalizations, etc.
   - in producing a paragraph, a drawing, a map, a poem, a report, or any other unique communication
   - . . .
2. How to start?
   - identify and clearly define your topic/subject
   - brainstorm some information or data
   - find a word or phrase that includes all your categories without mentioning any
   - . . .
3. What to do if . . .
   - you cannot identify any relationships? Consider possibility of cause/effect, spatial, temporal, functional relationships.
   - you cannot combine categories into a single statement? Think of analogies or opposites.
   - your categories or data are contradictory? Produce a two-part sentence using phrases such as: "Even though . . . , this is . . ." or "In spite of the fact that . . . , this is so . . ." or "While . . . , this also is . . . ," etc.
   - if you have trouble articulating a relationship? Write a sentence that connects or relates the category labels to the topic without mentioning any of the labels.
   - . . .

KNOWLEDGE
1. A wide variety of analytical and synthetic concepts
2. Brainstorming and other idea-generating techniques

FINDING UNSTATED ASSUMPTIONS

DEFINITION   Identifying an unstated premise or assertion that must be presumed or accepted as true if that which is stated is to be considered true
assumption: presumption, supposition, something taken for granted

STEPS   1. Skim the given information to get a general idea of what it is about.
2. Look for a conclusion, as indicated by
   • signal words, such as *thus, therefore, so, consequently, as a result,* etc. (are given or implied)
   • an "if . . . then" statement (the conclusion follows the "then")
   • an implied tying up or summarizing of a series of reasons (especially where a signal word could be inserted as a preface)
3. Look for a single-reason explanation or assertion.
4. Search the given information immediately before or following a conclusion or claim to find a stated reason given to support it.
5. Identify what else should exist (be true) to link the stated reason(s) to the conclusion, if the conclusion itself is to be accepted as true.
6. State the unstated assumption.

RULES   1. When to use:
   • in determining the strength of an argument
   • someone is trying to prove that something is true
   • in trying to determine the accuracy or validity of a claim or conclusion
   • in trying to learn about an author's point of view
   • . . .
2. How to start?
   • look for missing links between a reason and a conclusion or claim
   • look for "if . . . then" statements
   • . . .
3. What to do if . . .
   • you cannot find an unstated assumption between a conclusion and a reason? Ask yourself "What else must be true, if I am to believe this conclusion because of the given reason(s)?"
   • you cannot spot a missing link? Whenever you see a *so, therefore, thus,* you may have just passed an unstated assumption
   • . . .

KNOWLEDGE
1. Conclusions or claims can only be as true or acceptable as are the assumptions (premises) upon which they are based
2. Not all lines of reasoning include unstated assumptions; in many instances assumptions are made quite explicit
3. An assumption of any kind is usually an unproven or untested claim or assertion that needs to be checked for accuracy before being accepted as true or acted upon

Copyright © 1988, Barry K. Beyer

Selected References

BOOKS AND MONOGRAPHS

R. R. Allen and Robert K. Pratt. *The Nature of Critical Thinking*. Madison: Research and Development Center for Cognitive Learning, University of Wisconsin, 1969.

John Anderson. *The Architecture of Cognition*. Cambridge, Mass.: Harvard University Press, 1983.

John Anderson. *Cognitive Skills and Their Acquisition*. Hillsdale, N.J.: Lawrence Erlbaum Associates, Inc., 1981.

Assessment of the Critical Thinking Skills in History-Social Science. Sacramento: California State Department of Education, 1985.

Joan B. Baron and Robert J. Sternberg, eds. *Teaching Thinking Skills: Theory and Practice*. New York: W. H. Freeman, 1987.

Barry K. Beyer. *Practical Strategies for the Teaching of Thinking*. Boston: Allyn and Bacon, 1987.

Benjamin Bloom and Lois Broder. *Problem Solving Processes of College Students*. Chicago: University of Chicago Press, 1950.

Benjamin S. Bloom et al. *Taxonomy of Educational Objectives—Handbook I: Cognitive Domain*. New York: Longman, Inc., 1956.

John D. Bransford and B. S. Stein. *The IDEAL Problem Solver: A Guide for Improving Thinking, Learning and Creativity*. San Francisco: W. H. Freeman, 1984.

Stephen I. Brown and Marion I. Walter. *The Art of Problem Posing*. Hillsdale, N.J.: Lawrence Erlbaum Associates, Inc., 1983.

Edward de Bono. *Lateral Thinking: Creativity Step-by-Step.* New York: Harper and Row, 1970.

T. Edward Damer. *Attacking Faulty Reasoning.* Belmont, Calif.: Wadsworth Publishing Company, 1980.

John Dewey. *How We Think.* Boston: D. C. Heath and Company, 1933.

Paul L. Dressel and Lewis B. Mayhew. *Critical Thinking In Social Science.* Dubuque, Iowa: Wm. C. Brown Company, Publishers, 1954.

Reuven Feuerstein. *Instrumental Enrichment: An Intervention Program for Cognitive Modifiability.* Baltimore: University Park Press, 1980.

Michael Friedman and Steven Rowls. *Teaching Reading and Critical Thinking Skills.* New York: Longman, Inc., 1980 (esp. pp. 169–211).

John R. Hayes. *The Complete Problem Solver.* Philadelphia: Franklin Institute Press, 1981.

David Hitchcock. *Critical Thinking: A Guide to Evaluating Information.* Ontario, Canada: Methuan Publications, 1983.

Bryce B. Hudgins. *Learning and Thinking.* Itasca, Ill.: F. E. Peacock, Publisher, 1977.

Charles H. Kepner and Benjamin B. Trego. *The New Rational Manager.* Princeton, N.J.: Princeton Research Press, 1981.

P. H. Lindsay and D. A. Norman. *Human Information Processing.* New York: Academic Press, 1977.

Michael LeBoeuf. *Imagineering: How to Profit from Your Creative Powers.* New York: McGraw-Hill, 1982.

Frances R. Link. *Essays on the Intellect.* Alexandria, Va.: Association for Supervision and Curriculum Development, 1985.

Carol Madigan and Ann Elwood. *Brainstorms and Thunderbolts: How Creative Genius Works.* New York: The Macmillan Company, 1983.

R. S. Mansfield and T. V. Busse. *The Psychology of Creativity and Discovery.* Chicago: Nelson-Hall, 1981.

Robert J. Marzano and C. L. Hutchins. *Thinking Skills: A Conceptual Framework.* Kansas City, Mo.: Mid-continent Regional Educational Laboratory, 1985.

Richard Mayer. *Thinking, Problem Solving, Cognition.* San Francisco: W. H. Freeman, 1983.

John McPeck. *Critical Thinking and Education.* New York: St. Martin's Press, 1981.

Raymond S. Nickerson. *Reflections on Reasoning.* Hillsdale, N.J.: Lawrence Erlbaum Associates, Inc., 1986.

A. F. Osborne. *Applied Imagination.* New York: Scribner's, 1963.

Sidney Parnes, R. B. Noller, and A. M. Biondi. *Guide to Creative Action.* New York: Charles Scribner's Sons, 1977.

David Perkins. *The Mind's Best Work.* Cambridge, Mass.: Harvard University Press, 1981.

Gyorgy Polya. *How To Solve It.* Princeton, N.J.: Doubleday, 1957.

Barbara Z. Presseisen. *Thinking Skills Throughout the Curriculum: A Conceptual Design.* Philadelphia: Research for Better Schools, Inc., 1985.

Project Impact. Costa Mesa, Calif.: Orange County Department of Education, 1984.

Louis Raths et al. *Teaching for Thinking: Theory and Application.* Columbus, Ohio: Charles E. Merrill Publishing Company, 1967.

Lauren B. Resnick, ed. *The Nature of Intelligence.* Hillsdale, N.J.: Lawrence Erlbaum Associates, Inc., 1976.

M. F. Rubenstein. *Patterns of Problem Solving.* Englewood Cliffs, N.J.: Prentice-Hall, Inc., 1975.

David H. Russell. *Children's Thinking.* Boston: Ginn and Company, 1956.

Michael Scriven. *Reasoning.* New York: McGraw-Hill Publishing Co., 1977.

Robert J. Sternberg. *Beyond IQ: A Triarchic Theory of Human Intelligence.* New York: Cambridge University Press, 1985.

Arthur Whimbey and Jack Lochhead. *Problem Solving and Comprehension.* 3rd ed. Philadelphia: Franklin Institute Press, 1982.

Arthur Whimbey and Linda Shaw Whimbey. *Intelligence Can Be Taught.* New York: E. F. Dutton and Co., 1975.

ARTICLES

Harold Berlack. "The Teaching of Thinking." *The School Review* 73, 1 (Spring 1965): 1–13.

Barry K. Beyer. "Critical Thinking: What Is It?" *Social Education* 49, 4 (April 1985): 270–276.

Barry K. Beyer. "What's In A Skill? Defining the Skills We Teach." *Social Science Record* 21, 2 (Fall 1984): 19–23.

Ann L. Brown, Joseph C. Campione, and Jeanne D. Day. "Learning to Learn: On Training Students to Learn from Texts." *Educational Researcher* 10 (February 1981): 14–21.

Catherine Cornbleth. "Critical Thinking and Cognitive Process." In William B. Stanley, ed., *Review of Research in Social Studies Education.* Washington: National Council for the Social Studies, 1985, pp. 11–63.

Robert H. Ennis. "A Concept of Critical Thinking: A Proposed Basis for Research In the Teaching and Evaluation of Critical Thinking Ability." *Harvard Educational Review* 32, 1 (Winter 1962): 81–111.

Robert H. Ennis. "A Logical Basis for Measuring Critical Thinking Skills." *Educational Leadership* 43, 2 (October 1985): 44–49.

Robert H. Ennis. "Critical Thinking and the Curriculum." *National Forum* 65, 1 (Winter 1985): 28–31.

Robert H. Ennis. "Logic in Thinking and Teaching." *High School Journal* 55, 6 (March 1972): 278–296.

Ted Feeley, Jr. "Critical Thinking: Toward a Definition, Paradigm and Research Agenda." *Theory and Research in Social Education* 4, 1 (August 1976): 1–19.

Norman Frederiksen. "Implications of Cognitive Theory for Instruction in Problem Solving." *Review of Educational Research* 54, 3 (Fall 1984): 363–407.

Joe B. Hurst, Mark Kinney, and Steven J. Weiss. "The Decision-Making Process." *Theory and Research in Social Education* 11, 3 (Fall 1983): 17–43.

George Munro and Allen Slater. "The Know-How of Teaching Critical Thinking." *Social Educational* 49, 4 (April 1985): 284–292.

Richard W. Paul. "Critical Thinking: Fundamental Education for a Free Society." *Educational Leadership 42*, 1 (September 1984): 4–14.

David N. Perkins. "Creativity by Design." *Educational Leadership 42*, 1 (September 1984): 18–25.

David N. Perkins. "Thinking Frames: An Integrative Perspective on Teaching Cognitive Skills." Unpublished Paper, delivered at ASCD Conference on Aproaches to Teaching Thinking, Alexandria, Va., August 6, 1985.

Neil Postman. "Critical Thinking In the Electronic Era." *National Forum 65*, 1 (Winter 1985): 4–8, 17.

Michael Scriven. "Critical for Survival." *National Forum 65*, 1 (Winter 1985): 9–12.

R. K. Wagner and Robert J. Sternberg. "Alternative Conceptions of Intelligence and Their Implications for Education." *Review of Educational Research 54*, 2 (Summer 1984): 179–223.

Index